INTERIOR DESIGN

INTERIOR DESIGN

AN INTRODUCTION TO ARCHITECTURAL INTERIORS

THIRD EDITION

ARNOLD FRIEDMANN
University of Massachusetts

JOHN F. PILE
Pratt Institute

FORREST WILSON
The Catholic University

ELSEVIER
New York • Amsterdam • Oxford

Elsevier Science Publishing Co., Inc.
52 Vanderbilt Avenue, New York, New York 10017

Sole distributors outside the United States and Canada:

Elsevier Science Publishers B.V.
P.O. Box 211, 1000 AE Amsterdam, The Netherlands

Library of Congress Cataloging in Publication Data

Friedmann, Arnold.
    Interior design.

    Bibliography: p.
    Includes index.
    I. Interior decoration. I. Pile, John F.
    II. Wilson, Forrest, 1918– . III. Title.
NK2110.F678 1982   729   82-2436
ISBN 0-444-00670-2   AACR2

Current printing (last digit)
10   9   8   7   6

Manufactured in the United States of America

CONTENTS

PREFACE TO
THE THIRD EDITION

Passage of nearly ten years since the appearance of the second revision of this book has brought to the world of architecture and interior design new topics, new concerns, and new accomplishments that call for new text and new illustrations. Most of the previous text remains as appropriate as when it was first written. It is now desirable to add new material that will make this book more timely.

Interior designers and architects are increasingly turning to new ways to make older structures remain useful into the future. The high cost of new building construction and a concern for the preservation of older structures have created new interest in a field now often labeled "adaptive reuse," the subject of a new chapter in Part IV. The other addition to Part IV deals with new, possibly more superficial developments that may be called "trends and fashions."

A new responsibility for safety, positive impact on the environment, and accommodation for the handicapped are dealt with in an addition to Part V. The new material added to Part VI deals with recent developments in lighting and acoustical technology.

The much discussed impact of the computer as a tool in every aspect of modern life is now strongly applicable to architecture and interior design. Its influence can be expected to increase. This field is dealt with in Part VII. There are also notes on concerns about professional licensing and the professional qualifying examinations now offered in the interior design field. The bibliography has been expanded to include many excellent books published in recent years.

The most visible change to this edition is the addition of many new illustrations.

The field of interior design is constantly expanding in scope and vision. Today, more is expected of the designer in regard to general knowledge and specific skills. This new addition brings the reader up-to-date with the growing character of an exciting profession.

New York, April 1982

PREFACE TO
THE REVISED EDITION

Since this book appeared in 1970, it seems to have found a place for itself as a basic exposition of a particular point of view about interior design. Along with gratifying acceptance, the authors are aware of some criticism centered around the idea that this book is "too architectural" in its approach. As it was a belief that interior design is, in fact, an integral aspect of architecture that led to the writing of the book in the first place, this criticism, when it surfaces, seems to us to be a recognition that our book has made its point. We believe now, as we did in 1970, that the habit of viewing interior space as no more than a field for "decoration" in styles generated to forward commercial ends in the manner of the fashion industry is to disavow a human need to work and live in places that derive from more serious intentions.

Young people interested in entering the design fields seem to be increasingly sympathetic to this point of view. Training to become an expert facilitator of pointless and wasteful projects has become increasingly unpopular. The vulgarity of "sales-oriented" commercial design seems more and more obvious and its commercial success is rapidly becoming less certain. The ostentation of corporate and institutional design seems less attractive as society is forced to face more serious problems. A change in attitude is surfacing that makes "decoration" distasteful as a career while so many basic human needs call for more basic concerns.

Some of these new directions are reflected in the popularity of terms that are at times used rather thoughtlessly in the service of superficial "trends," but that still represent basic new concerns. The term "environmental design" is probably only half understood by most people who hear it, but it expresses a new recognition that human environment is increasingly artificial and almost exclusively within the control of those who design and build it; there is also the realization that it is the setting for human life that influences its quality in a powerful way. The term is inclusive to whatever extent the user wishes and so can easily refer to city planning, landscape design or regional planning. If this is a source of confusion, it is also realistic in indicating that the older, more sharply defined fields of design (industrial, interior, architectural, advertising or landscape) are no longer so easily separated. All share the responsibility for generating a physical setting in which human life can be healthy and rewarding.

Increasing acceptance of these ideas confirms, we believe, the assumptions upon which this book is based. In assembling a new edition we have, then, made few revisions to the original text: most of the changes have been additions of new material. Research in behavorial science and what has come to be called "architectural psychology" have formed a new branch of interest in architecture and interior design. "Environmentalism", "super-graphics", and "office landscape" have moved from being new and experimental fields toward more central roles in professional work. The publisher's willingness to include some color illustrations has led us to expand our discussion of this important aspect of interior design work. New illustrations have been added to improve the range of visual material and to represent the work of the last five years, which is often innovative and exciting.

We recognize that no one book can include coverage of every aspect of a field that is so broad, complex, and in a constant process of development and change. We urge the reader to follow directions suggested by the enlarged bibliography, and to view this book as a starting point for further reading, study, and studio work. It is our hope that this introduction will prove a sound basis for the development of skills and a philosophy in this changing, complex, and lively field of modern life.

New York, April 1975

PREFACE

Interior design is a visual field, and it is not surprising that many beautifully illustrated books, filled with handsome photographs, have been published about it. Since it is also a serious profession, it *is* surprising that little written material devoted exclusively to interior design has ever appeared in print. The field is in fact so large and complex that any one book can only attempt to cover limited phases of the total.

This book is concerned with the basic facets of interior design and its relation to environment in general. It is written for the design student and for all those readers who have a serious interest in design and a concern for the subject which goes beyond their desire to pick up some decorating hints. It is not a "how to do it" book, but rather a text containing meaningful information, a definite point of view on design and hopefully the stimulation to read further in the field of design literature and to build upon the foundation contained in these pages towards a better understanding of manmade environment.

Many people are interested in the subject of interior design— just as many people are interested in literature, art, and music. While none of the creative fields can be mastered after reading one book on the subject, at least there is an ample selection of works pertaining to most of the other creative professions. However, as a serious profession, the field of interior design, as distinguished from "decoration," is relatively new, and this is the main reason for the shortage of serious discussion about it. Educators and leading professionals have resisted the writing of textbooks so far, because of the inherent danger that lies in the presentation of so vast a subject condensed into a single volume. It is our intention, therefore, to present our thoughts in the form and scope in which they would be presented to design students, art students, or students of interior design in a professional design curriculum. Some of the material contained herein is in fact based on lectures given during the past several years to students majoring in interior design, or students in related fields whose curriculum called for an introduction to this field.

The fact that three authors collaborated in this presentation is a further reflection of the teaching process in design schools. Traditionally, an architectural or design presentation done by students is reviewed by a jury; and in recent years much spirited classroom teaching has been handled by teams of professors rather than one individual teacher. Through this method the student benefits from other diverging points of view, yet finds out soon that in spite of differences of opinion, the basic criteria of evaluation are neither subjective nor emotional, but are criteria firmly rooted in principles of design and in trained reactions shared by all teachers and professionals.

For several years the authors have been fellow critics in various classes in the Department of Interior Design at Pratt Institute. But in spite of joint courses and discussions, each writer brings a personal area of specialization and a strongly personal point of view on design. By collaborating on this book, it has been possible to present positive ideas and theories without becoming subjective. All presentation of thought and facts was subject to discussion and revision, so that what follows is in fact a summary of three distinctly personal and divergent, yet basically cohesive points of view.

The authors would like to express a particular obligation to Harold Eliot Leeds, Interior Design Department Chairman at Pratt Institute, under whose leadership the authors have been able to work together in a lively and stimulating atmosphere. Appreciation is also expressed to the many individual designers and firms who have supplied illustrative material for this book. Every effort has been made to give full and correct credit information identifying projects, architects, designers, and photographers. A few illustrations have come from files of clippings, slide collections and other indirect sources which make tracing of origins difficult. A general apology is offered for any errors or omissions that may have occurred for this or any other reason.

INTRODUCTION

Man's desire to create a pleasant environment is probably as old as our civilization, but interior design as a profession is a relatively new field, especially in the United States. Until not too many years ago, interior design was primarily concerned with the home, and every furniture salesman or drapery hanger was a "decorator". Terminology in itself is not really important. The decorative arts are a meaningful part of interior design. It is the implication that society attaches to certain terms which makes it necessary to find clearer ones from time to time. During the past two decades the new profession emerged and the term "decorator" fell into disrepute. Today a clearer identification of the designer's activity leads many people to refer to the field as interior architecture. And more recently all those concerned with the shaping of manmade environment refer to the total field as environmental design; thus it is quite possible that ten years hence the accepted term for one practicing interior design will be "environmental designer".

Like structural engineering and landscape architecture, interior design is a specialized branch of architecture, and it is wrong to practice any specialized work out of context. The most successful buildings are those in which the interior designer and the architect work hand in hand in their planning and design, or in which the architect follows through to the last detail and material, acting as his/her own interior designer. Often the architect is concerned with the overall structure and design only, while the interior designer is devoted to the more specific aesthetic, functional, and psychological questions of the interior, and to the individual character of spaces. In a larger sense this is true also about the relation of the city planner to the architect. A planned community with thoroughly considered allocation of spaces for play, recreation, and work would not be a success with ugly buildings. A beautiful structure with poorly designed interiors would not be good architecture. In general, those projects planned jointly by all the various design professions are the best ones, and more and more large offices come into being in which design is the result of cohesive teamwork. The best interiors occur within good buildings, and it is obvious that good architecture generates good interiors.

The interrelation of several specialized activities places the obligation on the interior designer to be conversant with the language and basic knowledge in all these fields. Planning interior spaces within a completed building shell, or minor alterations in an existing building, makes it essential for the designer to understand the basic structural system, as well as the function and the materials of such a structure. Many architectural offices have established interior design departments in which the interiors are developed from the working drawings, and the interior designer must obviously be able to read and understand such drawings and express his own work in related form. The fact that many architectural offices have established interior-design departments simultaneously strengthens the union between the two disciplines and creates new career opportunities for the well-trained designer.

Because interior design is a developing profession, its boundaries are not clearly defined. Many of the professional opportunities that exist today were unheard of just a few years ago. Basically at the present time, there tend to be two major categories of interior design: "residential" and "contract".

Residential design, as the term implies, is concerned with the design of residential spaces—the design of the home. Although the needs of homeowners have not changed essentially in many years, residential designers have begun to approach these stable needs in a variety of different ways and on a more professional level. In the past, good decorators earned their livelihoods through commissions that they received from the sale of furniture or antiques. Some decorators became, by necessity, shopkeepers. Today's designers, instead of depending on commissions, charge a professional fee for their services. Residential design is still an important part of the field of interiors, but most designers specializing in this area work as individuals or maintain minimal offices.

Contract design,* the second major area, concerns itself with the design of public spaces: offices, stores, institutions, showrooms, hotels, or in fact any interior space at all. Within this area there is further specialization, and some large firms design only offices, or only hotels, or only retail stores. But considering the magnitude of the type of job a design firm may be engaged in—the design of twenty or more floors for a corporation in a high-rise office building, for example—this specialization is not surprising.

Architectural firms, with or without their own interior-design departments, often become known for specific building types as well; and there are those who work mostly on schools and college buildings, others on hospitals, and still others on apartment houses.

Within the general classification of contract design a very active and important segment of the profession is engaged in space planning for large industrial corporations, businesses, and governmental agencies. Many design firms offer services which precede the architectural or interior planning and design, by analyzing space requirements and work procedures. Their services are closely related to the management consultant's work, and are in effect advisory services, not necessarily leading to actual design performance.

That the boundaries of the interior-design profession are not clearly defined is certain. Moreover, when one begins to understand the interrelationship of all environment, one can see that this lack of definition is necessary, and is perhaps a desirable state of affairs portending hope for better-coordinated design concerning everything in our lives. The products we use at home and at work, the clothing we wear, the automobiles we ride in, and the papers we read form a strong visual influence in our daily life. Just as architects and interior designers must concentrate in certain areas of competence, other design professions specialize in certain fields. The generic name encompassing most of these other specialties whose work matters greatly to the interior designer is "industrial design".

Very much like interior design, industrial design has many

*The term "contract design" derives from the contractual arrangement between the interior designer and his clients. Such a contract usually lists the precise services to be performed by the designer, and the customary agreement includes the specification and purchase of all furnishings for the job, to be supplied by the interior designer at the professional wholesale price available to the designer. The designer's fee covers that part of his services as part of the overall contract.

specialties, ranging from automotive design, design of machinery and appliances, to the one most closely related to interiors—the design of furniture and home furnishings. No one profession can claim exclusive control of any of these activities. Furniture has been designed by architects, interior designers, industrial designers, and furniture designers. Some of the best furniture of this century has been designed by architects; and indeed some architecturally trained designers specialize in interiors; just as some trained interior designers have turned to furniture design. As a rule, however, the interior designer is concerned primarily with built-in furniture, architectural woodwork, and special furniture in sizes or designs to fit the specific requirements of a job, when not available in stock pieces. The industrial and furniture designers are mostly concerned with mass-produced pieces, and they design for manufacturers rather than for an individual client or job. This division holds true by and large, in lighting fixtures, accessories, and other interior home furnishings products. This is also the case in the field of textile, floor covering, and wall covering design—all related activities that overlap with the work of the interior designer. The training for these various specialties is somewhat different from the schooling given to interior designers and architects, but since sound principles of design know no arbitrary boundaries, it becomes apparent that a really talented and well-trained designer can move from one specialized area to another without too much difficulty.

This introduction to the field of interior design would not be complete without mentioning briefly two other major design professions, whose members are often drawn from the ranks of the interior-design professionals: stage and exhibition designers. Theatrical-set designers and those working for the film and television industry create interior spaces for highly specific purposes. Their specialty requires much technical knowledge about lighting and other specific skills, but many designers trained for the field of interiors have found challenge and satisfaction in stage design.

Exhibition and display design is perhaps more closely related to the interests and training of the industrial designer; but it also requires much knowledge of graphic design and visual communications, and is therefore a field which, at its best, is practiced in teamwork, very much like environmental design.

With the exception of architecture and engineering, none of the design specialties described here requires licensing at present. This is partially the reason for the loosely defined and flexible spheres of activity of these various professions. Designers are divided in their opinions on the need and desirability of stricter professional definitions and, eventually licensing. There are those who believe it is unwise to license any creative field and who equate the design professions with painting, sculpture, and music. But the majority of designers believe that it is in the public's and the profession's interest to establish some more rigid criteria for those who wish to be considered true professionals in any of the design areas.

The profession of interior architecture is a fairly well-established one in several European countries, with strict professional criteria prescribed by professional societies and governmental agencies. Until 1974 there were two major professional societies and several smaller groups of interior design professionals in the United States. Admissions criteria and educational requirements were not clearly enough defined and enforced to give the profession the status and public confidence enjoyed by such licensed professions as medicine, law, and architecture.

With the merger of the two societies into the national American Society of Interior Designers (ASID) qualifications for membership are more demanding and are constantly being scrutinized. Various design groups have jointly formed a national body charged with the administration of a qualifications examination that has now become a prerequisite for admission to the ASID. Another organization has been formed by the professional societies together with the educational society of interior designers to review and accredit educational programs in schools and universities. The effect of these developments might bring about licensing by state or other governmental agencies, or possibly make such formal action superfluous.

In summary, it must be emphasized that neither clarification of spheres of professional activity, nor naming the profession by a new name, will create better design. It is impossible to legislate good design into existence, and it would be wrong to forbid by law or social pressure interiors created by non-interior designers, or to limit the scope of interior design to an arbitrarily enclosed and finite space.

It is after all the final result that counts. Whether the interior was designed by an interior architect, a decorator, an architect, or another design specialist, what matters is that it has been done well. What good interior design is all about, and how to approach it, is the topic of this book.

I

WHAT IS THE PURPOSE
OF DESIGN?

The question that heads this section is one that is, oddly enough, seldom asked and almost never answered–even partially. Most of us tend to suppose that the answer must be obvious and are content to leave the matter to the people who call themselves "designers". We may like or dislike the things that they do, but asking why they are doing them does not lead to quick clear answers. Most people will offer as the the most natural answer, "the purpose of design is to make things beautiful". While this answer may satisfy some people, it turns out to be rather meaningless as a guide for someone who wants to design and to design well. Different ways of designing and widely different results meet the desire for "beauty" in different times and different places. The most elaborate of Victorian interiors seemed beautiful to the people who designed them and lived in them,

A typically overstuffed Victorian interior.

but they seem stuffy and overdecorated to us. Some sternly mechanical furniture designs of the present day seem beautiful to some of us, while others think them cold and distasteful. Does this mean that design is all a matter of taste, as people so often say? We think that it does not–if it were, such a book as this would have very little purpose –however, a careful look at the serious and basic purposes of design requires some careful thought.

In facing this question, we do not need to limit ourselves to interior design; the same purposes and guidelines that influence the interior designer apply to the architect, the industrial designer, the naval architect, the civil engineer, and any number of other professions. Our examples will sometimes come from these other fields because a point can often be made more clearly by using some self-contained simple object (a chair, a spoon, a boat, or an automo-

bile), rather than an interior which is put together of many parts and which exists inside a building, which is a design in itself.

It would also be best to be sure that the meaning of the word "design" as it is used here is clear. It is a word that is used in many different senses in English—a designer may be a person who lays out plumbing systems, makes patterns for printed fabrics, plans stage sets, chooses the right steel beams for various uses, or does any one of a great many other things. All of these meanings have in common the idea that the designer is the person who chooses the form for something that is to be made. By "form" we mean shape, color, pattern, texture, and all the aspects of the thing to be made that our senses will be aware of. To decide to build a house, construct a bridge, make a chair, or weave a fabric is not the same thing as designing it, for between deciding to do any one of those things and actually doing the job there are a great many decisions about how the thing is to be done. These are design decisions and they determine what the result will be like.

Designers, we sometimes say, "invent" the way in which things will be done, but usually we save the word "invention" for a different use. An invention is something new, a new way to do an old job or a new way of doing a job that could not be done before. When the Wright brothers invented the airplane, they gave us a way of flying—doing something that had not been possible before. They also designed the airplanes that they built. The other airplanes—built since the Wrights demonstrated their invention—were not inventions, but they were successive new designs since each type was different in form from the others which preceded it. These changes in design have gradually changed and vastly improved the airplane since its origin, but they have only been changes in the way of doing something that the Wright brothers showed us how to do. To make something in a way which exactly repeats the way such a thing has been done before involves no design at all, but deciding to make changes (usually hoped to be improvements, although they may also turn out to be detrimental) is the act of a designer. A man who makes a chair which exactly duplicates some famous historic design (perhaps a fine Chippendale original) is not a designer. Deciding to make a different kind of chair and deciding exactly how it is to be different is designing, even if the man who does this is an engineer, a factory owner, or a salesman.

Design decisions about how something is to be made of two kinds, sometimes made separately and sometimes mixed together. Some people choose to use the word "design" for only one of the two kinds of decision and so confuse discussion of the subject further. One kind of design decision is concerned with making things work better —making them more comfortable, more efficient, safer, and more economical. The other kind of decision is concerned with how

Tubular armchair designed by Marcel Breuer. (Photograph by G. Barrows)

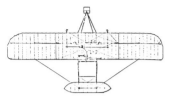

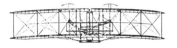

The Wright brothers' airplane.

things will look (and sometimes also with how they will feel and sound). The first category is often called "functional design"; the second, "visual" or "aesthetic design". Many designers try to limit their design work to one or the other of these aspects of the total job, but in practice the two kinds of design are so intermixed that it is almost impossible to sort them out completely.

Engineers and other people in technical occupations often like to say that they are only concerned with functional design and care nothing about aesthetics–an area that they would prefer to leave to others. However, the engineering design of, for example, a ship or airplane clearly sets the way it will look, and its designer finds himself turning out a product which is or is not a success in visual terms, no matter how much he may want to avoid the area of aesthetics. It is actually very interesting to notice that the best "technical designs" of this sort are usually admired for their appearance as well as their functionality, while peculiar and grotesque-looking pieces of engineering often turn out to work badly also.

Some designers whose training and interest is in the arts also try to make their separation of functional and aesthetic design. They would like to have nothing to do with practical matters and to think only about appearance. Some very bad buildings have resulted from this idea having swept the profession of architecture during the first half of the twentieth century. Architects tried to make their buildings look like palaces or temples and gave very little concern to how they would be planned and constructed. We all can think of examples of inconvenient and impractical schools, libraries, or railroad stations that resulted from this attitude. Fortunately, most architects now believe that the only way to design a good building is to think about practical and functional matters at the same time that the looks of the building are being considered.

Some design decisions seem at first to have little to do with "functional design". A well-engineered and technically successful airplane, for example, can be painted in any color scheme, and it would not occur to an aeronautical engineer to worry about paint colors. The designer (or owner, or whoever it is who chooses the color scheme) will, however, quickly discover that his decision concerning color has practical implications. Safety considerations, problems of heat absorption and reflection, and easy recognition and identification will therefore influence his decision. He will still have a wide range of choice, but it is not fair to say that he is purely an "artistic" designer, uninfluenced by practical matters.

To choose an example from our own field of interest, we all know that there can be a very comfortable and practical chair which is very unattractive. The designer (or manufacturer, or whoever designed such a chair) succeeded in the practical side of his work, but failed in (or never even thought about) the visual result of what he was doing. If we give such a chair to an excellent designer and ask him to "fix up" the appearance without changing anything else, he will probably find the task almost impossible (in fact he will probably refuse even to attempt the job) because of the difficulty of making improvements in appearance without making basic changes in form and construction. To design a chair that is successful both functionally and aesthetically requires that the job be done from the beginning with the understanding that the two things are inseparable.

In discussing this matter so far, we have been assuming that a successful design in either the functional or the aesthetic sense is an easy thing to recognize. Actually, matters are not quite this simple. There is usually fairly wide agreement about what constitutes a good design decision in practical terms—a more comfortable chair, a faster and safer airplane, a more convenient house plan—but success in the visual aspect of design is not nearly so easy to evaluate in a clear and decisive way. We come face to face again with the difference in attitudes in different places and at different times, and are tempted to retreat to the view that the aesthetic side of design, at least, is "all a matter of taste". Some designers whose background is in technical areas (engineers, inventors, and scientists) tend to take this position. They work with the functional aspects of design and then dissociate themselves from the visual results, leaving that side of things to anyone who would like to deal with it according to a particular kind of taste. Most designers, however, are not satisfied with the notion that their work, when it moves beyond the technical and utilitarian, is merely a matter of taste and whim. There is more to it than this, but the nature of the "more" often remains obscure and confusing.

1

THE HUMAN ENVIRONMENT

Fortunately, there are areas where agreement about what is aesthetically good is very widespread. Perhaps it will help us to look at these areas, make sure that we can agree about them, and then ask what it is that makes them so satisfying to such a wide range of people, quite irrespective of their place in geography, history, or society.

The first and most important such area of human experience is, of course, the natural environment. We all live in a common context of sky, ocean, and land surface, amid a surround made up of geological features of the earth's surface plus plant and animal life. Almost no one regards this natural surround as ugly or unaesthetic. It is almost a sacrilege to suggest that one could see a tree as untidy, the night sky as disorderly, or cloud formations as messy. We plant gardens and grow house plants; we keep a bird, cat, or dog; and we travel to country, seaside, or mountains largely because of our visual, sensual appreciation of the realities of our planet's geology, plant, and animal life.

It is interesting to examine the occasional exceptions to this almost universal fondness for the natural environment. Some people will tell us that they regard snakes, or, perhaps, spiders, or some other insect as "ugly". It invariably turns out that the real meaning of this point of view is that the "ugly" object is feared. Once the fear of spiders, or snakes, or the open sea, or any other natural reality is brought under control, that reality can be seen as strikingly beautiful. Such positive reactions to our natural habitat do not seem to be a matter of taste, they do not need to be learned, they are something that we all feel quite automatically.

The visible products of human activity, on the other hand, do not please us with anything like the consistency that we

The night sky as it appears through a telescope.

notice when we look at the natural world. We can admire a beaver dam, a bird's nest, or a wasp's nest (if we do not fear the inhabitants) very easily, but houses and towns and cities leave us less certain of our own reactions. In some way we all sense the directness and "rightness" of natural situations. The manmade elements in our surroundings only occasionally share this quality of "rightness". We are, in fact, quite justified in saying that too many human products are "ugly" or badly designed. When we say this we are recognizing that the "ugly" object or situation is not "right" and direct in the way that natural objects always are. A truly well-designed city, building, automobile, or fence post turns out to have some things in common with the natural world and will usually fit into the natural world without spoiling it. It is all too obvious that most human products do not meet this standard.

In order to be more specific about the qualities of "rightness" that natural objects and the best of manmade things share, it is worthwhile to spend some time examining the characteristics of the forms that natural things take. We find at once that they are infinitely varied. Simple rules that try to tell us that good design requires that things be simple or complex, geometric or curvilinear, symmetrical or asymmetrical simply do not apply to the natural world because the natural world includes examples of all these things. Most animals are bilaterally symmetrical, but plants often are not, and geological and landscape forms almost never are. Plants and animals

are full of curvilinear forms, but crystalline forms are geo-
metrical (think of snowflakes, for example). Sand dunes are
simple in shape, but trees are very complex. We can find
examples of subdued colors or of bright colors, varied forms
or repetitious ones, exposed structural skeletons and hidden
ones. The things that are broadly characteristic of natural
forms are more subtle and more general than any of these.

The forms of natural things are, for one thing, always a direct
result of some process which has taken place in the past and
which is continuing. The visual result is not something that has
been arranged for us to look at. We rather have developed the
ability to see in order to help ourselves understand the environment in which we live. In common with the other sighted animals, we can learn about things by looking at them. As we
look, we collect information from which we can discover what
things are, where they came from, how they work, and what
we can expect of them. Our learning is by no means complete;
we certainly do not understand the universe completely, but
our main method of learning more is by looking (aided by
whatever instruments we may invent to help us) and then trying to understand what we have seen. As we look, we can find
the traces of past events that made the universe as it is and
can find also the processes of continuing change that are tak-

ing place in it. Our landscape, its geology and geography, is a
product of events that have taken place over an almost un-
thinkably long period of time. We understand climate, the
seasons, and weather by watching events which are much
more rapid. Animate nature is, in a long-term sense, a result of
the staggeringly slow processes of biological evolution and, in
a short-term sense, is a record of the rapid processes of growth
and change in the individual organism. When we look at any
natural situation we are seeing the visual result at that given
moment of processes that have their beginnings in the infinite
past and that are continuing into a similarly endless future.

All of the natural processes that we are discussing here take
place without thought or intention, in the sense that we normally use those words; rather, they take place according to
"natural laws", which have gradually been discovered and
described by scientists who have watched and tried to understand what can be seen. The shape, size, and color of a tree, an
insect, a bird, or a man is the result, in part, of the evolutionary
process that developed the species and, in part, of the heredity
and growth history of the particular individual. There is nothing accidental or inexplicable about the product that results.
In this sense we can say that the "designs" of nature are never
arbitrary; they are always reasonable and packed with mean-

Natural camouflage. There is a large copperhead snake clearly visible in this illustration.

Typical African round hut.

ing. We may not understand the reasons behind every aspect of nature (although we are coming to understand more all the time) but any lack of understanding is the result of our limited knowledge, not the product of whimsical and pointless forms in nature.

It is interesting to look at the occasional situations in nature which seem to be exceptions to the general rule which says that natural forms are always meaningful and "honest" products of the realities which they embody. There are, of course, examples of camouflage in living things, marking patterns and colors which seem, at first, to be senseless and meaningless (even when they may be highly decorative). With fuller knowledge, it always becomes clear that such patterns and colors have very real purposes. When they are not simply camouflage colors, they turn out to have some other highly functional role such as attraction of a mate, identification of the particular species, or some similar purpose. The process of natural selection has led to the survival of succeeding generations of individuals with colors or markings which are most favorable to the life of the species. This is, in a sense, a kind of design process, even though it involves no thought or intention of a conscious sort. In some cases it is still not known what the reasons for some spectacular colors and markings may be (as in the case of some brightly colored mollusk shells); but we can feel certain that there *are* reasons and that study will eventually bring the reasons to light.

Human beings are, of course, part of nature. We are animals, however anxious we may be to pretend to something different, and the things that we make are, in one sense, natural products in the same sense that birds' nests or anthills are. Before we look at the large and often depressing differences that exist between so much of human production and the visual aspects of the rest of the natural world, we should look at some areas where the similarities are still quite clear. The simplest man-made objects and structures often seem very close to natural things. Grass huts, igloos, wigwams, and other primitive houses are often quite like nests or anthills, and usually have the same kind of logic, directness, and beauty. Simple tools and utensils have these qualities also. As man has gradually discovered more complex materials and ways of working, the appropriate equipment has almost always been handsome. We admire stone axes, bronze shields, primitive pottery, and household implements as well as more complex constructions such as sleds, rafts, and canoes. Primitive designs of this kind have, in fact, become an object for collectors and museums to seek out and display.

In such simple designing, man seems to continue to work in the same ways that natural processes work, and the results are almost always of a comparable beauty. However, as man has become more sophisticated and more self-conscious, his designs seem to have moved away from such directness. Even educated, modern man, though, continues to design in this easy and natural way when he is free of self-consciousness. There are two main kinds of design that are common in modern life in which we can still see this direct process working well. Although these two areas overlap somewhat, it is still convenient to talk about them separately, giving them the rather clumsy names of "vernacular design" and "technological design". We will consider vernacular design first.

The word "vernacular" originally was used to describe the speech and language of common people as distinguished from the formal and "learned" speech of schoolrooms and printed books. The different kinds of English spoken by a cockney Londoner, a Brooklyn workingman, and an American Southerner are each vernacular variations on standard English. The word has been taken over in design and architecture to describe the kind of design done by people without formal training and done, usually, without any special thought or planning. The work of an average carpenter or plumber when he does a job without plans or formal instructions turns out to be "anonymous" or "vernacular" design. Objects such as traditional tools (axe, hammer, saw, or wrench) or implements (egg beater, broom) or items of hardware (hinges, locks, and keys) are examples of vernacular design. Cities

Pygmy implements include hammer, adz, pail, quiver, bow and arrows.

American Indian
"serpent ware"
pottery.

A typical manhole
cover visible in any
city street.

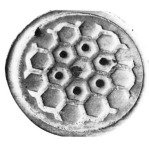

Various hammers as illustrated in a tool catalog.

are full of things that we hardly notice–such as manhole covers, fire plugs, lamp posts, and fire escapes–generally the product of some anonymous workman or draftsman who produced the designs without any special skill or effort. Many barns and other farm buildings, sheds for factories and warehouses, buildings around docks and railroads, can be called "vernacular architecture" because they are not the work of trained architects, but the doings of the workman who actually did the work of construction or, perhaps, the work of the draftsman who made drawings without any formal effort at "design".

Not all vernacular design is successful, but when we consider that it is the work of people who have no claim to special design skill, it is remarkable how often it turns out to be attractive and, in some cases, astonishingly beautiful. In many cases the best vernacular designs are not the work of one man, but are rather the products of a long tradition of craftsmanship, which also includes a tradition about how things should look. This is certainly the way the forms of ordinary hand tools came to be so highly refined and so subtly beautiful. When trained designers are asked to produce new and better designs for such products, they often find the task difficult or impossible because the vernacular tradition has already done their job so well that real improvement becomes very hard to achieve.

The vernacular designer is almost always very aware of the materials and techniques of manufacture that go into his product since he is often also the craftsman doing the actual work of manufacture or is, at least, very close to that work in point of view (and, usually, in physical location also). This makes him sensitive to this aspect of design in a way that the trained designer working on drawings in an office sometimes is not. The products of vernacular design are also usually sternly

"Vernacular" architecture
at the Ephrata "Cloister"
Ephrata, Pennsylvania.

practical in nature so that the designer is forced to think about functional matters as the most important of all considerations. Both these pressures—the pressure toward functional design and the pressure toward sound use of materials and manufacturing techniques—tend to lead the vernacular designer along lines that parallel the development of natural forms very closely. The vernacular traditions are similar to the processes of natural selection in the development of living things although they work much more rapidly and are, in comparison, shallow and superficial in their achievements. The comparison is still valid, however, and may help to explain why we respond so favorably to many vernacular products.

The vernacular way of designing has been on the decline for a long time. Perhaps this should be a matter for some regret, but it is an inevitable result of the great changes in human life that we think of as being characteristic of the modern world. The scientific discoveries that began to develop in the Renaissance led to the sequence of inventions which, taken together, are usually called the "industrial revolution" of the second half of the nineteenth century. We take these inventions and their results in our own lives so much for granted that we have to remind ourselves that it has only been during the last hundred years (or a little more) that there have been such things as steam engines, power looms, steel and concrete, sewing machines, and typewriters. Even newer is electricity with its resultants in power, lighting, telephone and radio, the automobile, airplane, and all the complex combinations of these things that are built into modern life so firmly that it is almost inconceivable to think of existing without them. All of these modern developments have tended to decrease the role of the hand craftsman and vernacular designer, to transfer the making of things to the more impersonal factory, and to bring into the foreground the kind of designer whose skill and training are of primarily scientific origins. Modern engineering is based on the realizations of modern science and mathematics that things can be planned and predicted. Trial and error is basic to the laboratory experiment, but the results of experiment can lead to predictability about new designs for new things. A modern ship or airplane is designed on paper with the aid of theoretical systems expressed through mathematics. The test tank and the wind tunnel provide the trial and error needed to perfect the designs on paper. The resultant design is then built with full confidence that it will work, and the tests of the finished product only serve to check out what had been planned in advance. It has become almost unthinkable that a new ship might sink or capsize on launching. New aircraft invariably fly although there is sometimes a period of "shaking out" before the new design is fully perfected. New buildings almost never collapse, even when their designs are highly unconventional, because the theoretical work done in advance by engineers has made it quite certain that they will stand up.

This new way of working, which is characteristic of science and engineering, and its products are usually together given the name of "modern technology". The designs resulting from modern technology, like vernacular designs, seem to have an affinity with the products of nature in their simple directness.

**The "France", now
"Norway".** (above left)
**A particularly handsome
modern ocean liner.**

The Salginatobel Bridge
(above right) **of
reinforced concrete.
Designed by
Robert Maillart in 1929.**

**A military jet aircraft,
the F-16.**

The engineer is, of course, in one sense a trained and self-aware designer who thinks very carefully and deeply about the things he plans. He is usually, however, not much concerned with how things will look and, in many cases, will absolutely deny that he cares at all about the visual results of his work. It is an interesting paradox that this line of thought in engineering so often leads to results that are visually excellent. It is, perhaps, less surprising when we note that engineering designs are usually developed to serve real practical needs in a very exacting way, and that they use materials and constructional techniques with the greatest efficiency that the state of knowledge at the time permits. This turns out to be a way of doing things that almost exactly duplicates natural processes and is closely analogous to the best work of the vernacular designer also.

If we think of an example of highly advanced technological design—such as a modern airplane, ship, or bridge—it is perfectly clear that every aspect of its planning and form are the result of solving a practical problem in the most economical and best way that available materials and techniques make possible. It is easy to assume that this means that the design is purely mathematical and scientific. Actually, if we look into the matter more closely, we discover that although such designs are heavily dependent on scientific and mathematical techniques, the actual forms are still invented forms in the same way that an artist's work is invented. Science will help the aeronautical engineer, for example, to check out how well a given shape of aircraft will perform, and will help him to make its parts adequately strong while remaining optimally light and economical. The "given shape" is, nevertheless, something that must either be invented or inherited from an earlier design. Many different aircraft shapes have been invented that have some degree of success and it has been a process rather like that of natural selection in biology that has led to the gradual elimination of all but a few typical forms that serve well for their respective purposes (transport, fighter, helicopter, etc.). It remains a very real possibility that some new form may be invented that will be quite different and better than any of the types that we now know. Such an invention would be a genuinely creative idea, which scientific and math-

Between the inner and outer walls of a Medieval town; Carcassone, France. (Photograph by John Pile)

A complex microscope of the nineteenth century.

Highway intersection seen from above.

Typical steel tower to carry high-tension electric lines.

Spherical tank.

American automobile design at its worst.

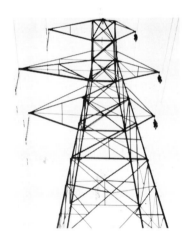

ematical techniques could check, verify, and help to develop; but the actual invention would remain a rather mystifying thing, similar to the act of artistic creation—the kind of thing that people usually call a "stroke of genius" for lack of any better way to explain it.

In the Middle Ages and especially in the Renaissance, it was thought quite natural that one man could be both a great artist and a great technical genius. In our own time, probably because of the extremely rapid development of modern science, a most unfortunate mistrust has grown up between these areas, so that an engineer will usually deny any knowledge of or interest in the arts, while most artists choose to remain both ignorant of and indifferent to technical and scientific matters. This is probably the general explanation of the clear fact that our complex and highly developed modern civilization is so ugly in its products and surroundings as compared to the simpler but more coherent worlds of the Middle Ages or the Renaissance. If there is any doubt about the validity of this comparison, it is only necessary to compare a medieval town or city (such as Carcassonne) or an eighteenth-century town (such as the restored Williamsburg, Virginia, or Sturbridge, Massachusetts) with any average modern suburb to see how inescapable the conclusion is.

Modern technology produces clear and beautiful results where it confronts a clear problem and solves it without needing to give thought to any extraneous values. A great suspension or arch bridge will surely be beautiful, unless there has been some pressure on the engineers to think about beauty. When such pressures arise, there are sometimes halfhearted attempts to "apply some beautification" through quaint or fussy details that have nothing to do with the structural or functional realities of the bridge. In such cases the engineer is turning out something that we are justified in calling "bad design". When this does not happen, however, we find technology producing such handsome things as radio and high-tension towers, water tanks, highway interchanges, ships, and aircraft. Many smaller objects—such as pieces of machinery and electronic gear, scientific apparatus and technical instruments—have these same qualities in a form no less beautiful because the objects themselves are less spectacular in size.

2

THE NATURE OF GOOD DESIGN

Now that we have recognized that so much excellent work has been done by the vernacular craftsman-designer and by the modern engineer, it comes as a disturbing shock to confront the total visual reality of our modern world and find that we must admit that only a tiny part of it can make any claim to being well designed. If we search for a well-designed house or apartment, a well-designed automobile or bus, good furniture, lamps, appliances, or any number of similar everyday things that we all must have and use, we find that anything that approaches the excellence of technological and vernacular design (not to speak of the products of nature) is very rare and only discoverable in a few situations where there has been an extraordinary effort to find and cultivate what is rather self-consciously called "good design".

This situation seems to result from the fact that our society no longer makes it possible for the craftsman or artisan to make design decisions in a way that would make him truly a "vernacular designer", and at the same time, in most cases, it does not employ a trained or skilled designer for most projects. The average house has no designer or architect, nor is it the design of the carpenter or mason; it is rather the unthinking production of the operative builder (who is primarily a businessman) influenced in some cases by the desires and tastes of the owner. Most products are designed by a manufacturer or distributor who has no contact with the physical work of production and has no training or skill in design either. Towns and cities simply "happen" under the influence of business and political pressures without any plan or design of any kind.

It is no wonder that this way of doing things produces such bad results. It is only fair, however, to point out that the work of skilled and trained designers is often fully as bad as the undesigned production we have just discussed. It has become a cliché to mention that the American automobile, the most important single item of our modern technological production, is wasteful, inconvenient, and shockingly dangerous. It is so, we need to remember, largely because of its design. Modern engineering can make cars that are convenient, economical, and safe (as is partially demonstrated by some European examples), but American cars take forms that are set in "styling studios" by trained men who claim to have some special artistic skill. While there are some architects who design excellent buildings, the majority of architect-designed buildings are just as bad as (and sometimes worse than) those built without benefit of expert design help. Interior designers and decorators produce some of the worst interior spaces ever assembled throughout the history of design.

We must make it clear that in this book we are not discussing any and all work of trained designers when we discuss "good design". We are instead talking about the quite small amount of truly excellent work done by some designers and also the good work done by some engineers, craftsmen, and talented laymen who, in one way or another, have come to understand what design really should be. To condemn so much that is the norm of modern life, and praise only a very limited range of work, may seem to the reader to reflect a narrow, arbitrary, and arrogant point of view. In order to make it clear that this point of view is in no way arbitrary or illogical, we must go back to the questions that we faced at the beginning of this chapter.

If the reader is prepared to agree with us that the products of nature, vernacular crafts, and technology are almost always excellent in design while a much larger miscellany of human products are generally not, we can again face the question of what "good" means in relation to design, armed with examples that will help to clarify our thinking.

We must make it clear once again that we are not talking about taste and are not simply expressing a particular kind of taste when we speak of a certain kind of design as "good". Taste is a very real thing which every designer must be aware of without confusing it with design quality. Taste is a system of likings or preferences that are common to a particular social group, nation, region, or period in time. It is a thing that people learn from their families, friends, and general milieu, and it has as its main purpose the distinguishing of those who have similar taste, in order that an "in group" can form which is easily identifiable as different from an "out group". To speak of "good taste" invariably turns out to mean either one's own taste or, perhaps, the taste of those that one admires most and would like to imitate. At various places and times in history very different things have been considered to be in good taste; some have been examples of excellence in design and others have not. Most of us would like to think that we have a more private and individual taste, one that is not based on a system that has such a snobbish and negative purpose. This is also a dangerous assumption, however. Anyone who is sufficiently honest with himself will be able to remember how his taste has changed over the years along with the taste of his friends, relatives, and peers. Our likes and dislikes are less unique, personal, and unchanging than we tend to think; and we can very easily find ourselves adopting likes and dislikes that make no sense in response to the taste that is current in our society.

The people who buy badly designed cars in most cases probably like the designs very well. On meditation they would agree that such cars are wasteful and dangerous, but they still find that they like them. The liking changes within a few years to dislike, which is equally irrational since the car itself has not changed; nevertheless there is nothing more generally recognized as ugly than a car five to ten years out of date. After twenty-five or thirty years the same car may again seem attractive to us. Throughout this process the actual car design remains no better and no worse than it was to start with. The change in taste merely reflects a response to the general American desire for something new (exaggerated and played on by skillful advertising), followed by the matching distaste for something no longer new which emerges after a few years have wiped out all memory of newness. The final taste swing is the equally illogical fondness for the rare and the antique that appears when the object in question has become scarce. To say that one likes or dislikes a certain design is likely to be a result of similar pressures, however much one tries to maintain an independent judgement.

"Good design" means something more permanent and more fundamental than being tasteful. It refers to qualities that can be recognized in an object whether it is in style or out, whether it is popular or unpopular. It is possible to recognize something that is well designed while not particularly liking it personally if one can come to understand that one's own personal likes and dislikes are not usually altogether rational. They are the result of one's own background and experience and include the influences of a person's own family and friends, teachers, and surroundings for better or for worse. Such personal and whimsical tastes may not be a bad thing when they are applied to the circumstances of one's own personal life, but they are not a trustworthy basis for evaluating design work, which is not personal but which is intended to be useful to people everywhere, in the present, and in the future extending even beyond one's own life-span. A personal and intuitive understanding of design can, of course, serve a designer well if, by some fortunate chance, his own tastes and intuitions lead him in directions that are meaningful for many other people; but it is not possible to count on this happening. A more reasonable approach requires setting aside one's own taste and asking the more difficult and basic questions having to do with what is really sound and wise in a more serious way than the concerns of personal taste can possibly reach.

To make one's goal as a designer the creating of things that will be "pretty", attractive, or even beautiful, although it may sound less personal and more serious than the mere application of "good taste", turns out, in fact, to be not very different. All the efforts of philosophers concerned with aesthetics and the psychologists concerned with what is usually called "experimental aesthetics" have, at least up until now, not produced any clear and logical code for making things beautiful, or even for defining with much clarity what "beauty" is. Various rules and codes dealing with proportion and balance have been helpful to one designer or another at differing times and places, but it can always be shown that other highly successful designs have no relation to any of these codes. It is not hard to accept some very general philosophical statements ("truth is beauty", for example), but the intricate problems of designing a building, a room, or a piece of furniture pose problems that such general statements cannot solve. A designer who sets out to design so as to make things beautiful will turn out, in the end, to be using taste as a guide—his own taste, that of his teachers, that of the group that he admires, or that of the critics who are fashionable. If he is successful at any level deeper than that of taste and fashion, it will be as a result of chance rather than any particular plan or point of view.

Many designers are, of course, quite content to work at this superficial level. They try to learn what is considered to be tasteful, what is coming into fashion, and what is spoken well of by critics, and they develop technical skills that make them able to work well in currently fashionable ways. There is no question that a person with a high level of visual and artistic sensitivity can have a successful career on this basis. It seems doubtful that such a superficial approach has ever led to anything very great, and it is almost impossible for it to lead to anything new since it is almost entirely imitative in nature. It is the level of design work that is usually called "styling"— that is, giving a stylish appearance to something that, in most cases, existed before and will continue to exist in the future in slightly changed forms. The unfortunate designs of many automobiles that we discussed above are the work of "stylists". The basic invention of the car and the detailed engineering of the present model are taken in hand by the "stylist" and are clothed in a collection of forms intended to make the car look very new and impressive. The stylist almost never makes any change in the things that would make the car more convenient, useful, better working, or safer and, indeed, often adds elements that hurt these qualities (think of useless tailfins, inaccessible motors, dangerous interiors, and inconveniently huge size). Styling need not be this bad, of course, but it always remains a superficial thing.

It is interesting to notice that the separation of appearance design (or styling) from invention, construction, and technical design is a very recent development. We cannot imagine that the pyramids of Egypt or the temples of ancient Greece could

The "Red House" designed for William Morris by Philip Webb in 1859. (Photograph by John Pile)

An early British locomotive. Note the "Roman" architectural design of the steam dome.

have been "engineered" first and then "styled" afterward by a specialist who had no interest in their construction. The planning, the construction, and the visual design are all of one piece. This is even more clearly true of a medieval cathedral, in which the purpose of the building, its construction, and its design are so clearly a unity that we still admire such buildings fully as much (or even more) than the best examples of modern architecture. It was the Industrial Revolution with its new ways of doing things that brought about the separation of technical design and visual design. An inventor or engineer would work out a way to make a machine (a steam engine, for example), but would then turn to an artist or architect and ask help with appearance. The "help" would then usually consist of added-on decorations that had nothing to do with the machine, but which were fashionable. The technical man, knowing that he was not an artist, did not trust himself to deal with visual design, while the designer, not understanding scientific technology, was unable to involve himself in the technical problems, and so resorted to familiar formulae from his own artistic background. It is this split between the practical side of design and its visual product which was survived into our own day and which leads to so many unfortunate results.

Several cures have been proposed for this unhappy state of things, some proposed in the nineteenth century almost as soon as the problems became apparent. One such cure, urged by William Morris in England in the second half of the nineteenth century, is usually called the "arts and crafts movement". It proposed solving the problems by giving up modern

The American clipper ship _Eclipse_, shown in a painting.

technology and replacing it with a return to the craft traditions of the Middle Ages. Although this movement produced some handsome things, it obviously remained a minor artistic movement which could do nothing to counter the spread of modern technology. "Functionalism" is another proposed solution to this problem which cannot be so easily attributed to any one man. An American sculptor named Horatio Greenough in a work published in 1852 _(The Travels, Observations, and Experiences of a Yankee Stonecutter)_ suggested that such functional objects as the clipper ships of the day were among the most beautiful products of their times. He explained their beauty by saying that their "form followed function"—that every rope and sail had a clear purpose and use and that the result, planned only to work well, was inevitably beautiful. The American architect Louis Sullivan is often identified with the phrase "form follows function", but he was, in fact, only quoting Greenough when he used it.

The idea that a building's form should be influenced by its function seems so obvious to us now that it is hard to understand that this belief made Sullivan a great pioneer, but we must remember that he was working at a time when most architects "applied" stylistic decoration to the outside of buildings without any thought for their internal workings. Actually Sullivan did not believe that function was the only determinant for a building's form and did not hesitate to use rich ornamentation of his own invention that was in no way strictly functional. The idea of "pure functionalism" did not appear until the 1920's, when European architects took up

**Decorative detail
in terra cotta, typical
of the work of
Louis Sullivan. The
Bayard Building
in New York City.**
(Photograph by John Pile)

and advanced the idea that design should concern itself with
nothing but the best possible solutions to practical problems.
Le Corbusier, for example, used pictures of automobiles, ships,
and airplanes in his book *Vers une Architecture* (1923) to illustrate the idea that the strictly functional design of these things
led to truly beautiful results. He and a number of other architects proceeded to design their buildings in the same way.

In actuality, examples of "pure functionalism" are hard to
find. Even machinery, ships, and airplanes, although their
forms are heavily influenced by practical matters, also include
any number of design decisions that are not totally determined by calculation and test. Function is a powerful determinant, but not an absolute control—otherwise there would
be only one answer to a particular design problem at a particular time in history. The architects who tried to be "pure
functionalists" soon found this out. There may be practical

pressures that determine where a door should go, but its *exact* shape and size can vary through quite a range. Function will never be able to determine its exact best color. Obviously, even the most doctrinaire functionalists must include some consideration of the materials and constructive techniques to be used. A brick house and a frame house require different designs even if they are to house the same family. Even if considerations of safety and economy are considered to be functional pressures, they do not lead certainly to the inevitable choice of one material over the other. Different forms and colors can serve a particular function equally well and the designer finds that he must use other criteria than pure function in such areas of concern. Realization that function cannot be the sole determinant in every decision has led to a decline in interest in a "pure functionalist" doctrine, but functionalist ideas survive in the view now almost universally held by competent designers that a good design must at least be a success in functional terms. This means, at base, that being functional will not guarantee that a design will be good, but that being nonfunctional will certainly make it bad. A chair can be comfortable and still be a bad design, but if it is not comfortable it cannot possibly be a good design, no matter how tasteful or attractive its looks may be. Solving functional problems well thus becomes the first requirement, the most basic precondition in the evaluation of any design.

In a similar way it has come to be generally clear that a good choice of materials and constructive techniques is basic to good design work. Each part should be of a material suitable to its job. Each material has its own visual qualities which must become part of the design. A house of wood-frame construction will have certain characteristics of appearance quite different from a house of brick or stone. Even when it may be possible without altering functional characteristics, it is never wise to make one material look like another or to use an unsuitable material for purely visual reasons. We have all seen houses with imitation brick or stone siding, and it is at once clear that these imitations never ring true and leave us wth a sense of something shoddy and false. In much the same way, each method of working materials has its own qualities which can become part of a finished object. Hand working of wood gives rise to characteristics of form and texture that are different from those that result when power tools (or "machines") do the job. Imitation of handwork with its irregularities, individual and personal details, and other distinctive characteristics is possible, through machine production, but gives rise to the same sense of falseness and

dishonesty. Sound use of materials and construction techniques will not guarantee good design, but no design can be
truly excellent unless materials and ways of working materials
are well chosen. This becomes a second precondition of excellence in any design work.

Engineers and other designers from the technological fields
usually accept these two preconditions without giving the
matter much thought, at least when they work without being
concerned over what is often called "public acceptance". An
airplane, a factory building, or a highway interchange is quite
sure to be highly functional and to use materials and constructive techniques well. It is a mistaken desire to please some
real or imagined popular taste that occasionally leads the
engineer to accept such absurdities as automobiles with tail-
fins, concrete bridges with imitation stone facings, or television
sets housed in imitation Georgian cabinetry. These senseless
extras are, in most cases, added to the basic engineering by
other people, with or without the engineering designer's con-
sent. The fact that the designer's additions to the engineer's
work are so often unfortunate should not, however, confuse
us into thinking that design is nothing but competent engineering. This would be the view of the "pure functionalist"
once again with its refusal to admit that there are innumerable decisions that cannot be made on a technical basis alone.
An airplane requires external colors and markings and designed interior spaces that involve decisions having no
important engineering implications. An automobile requires
an exterior shell and interior fittings that are quite independent of its mechanical working. A television set must be
housed in some way and its controls can be placed and shaped
in any way that its designer chooses. The design of a building
is obviously not simply a technical problem; while its very
reason for existing is the complex of useful interior spaces
that it will contain, its visible exterior can be of almost any
sort that its architect may choose.

Our point is that although function and structure are the
most basic and important determinants of design, they do
not make a complete design in any certain and reliable way.
Adding fashionable or "tasteful" visible parts to sound engineering cannot be the route to successful design either. It is
a route that may occasionally succeed, but it is far too easy to
point out the examples in which this method has led to pointless absurdity. If, then, we can agree that function and construction must underlie good design, but that success involves
something further, we must try again to identify what the
"something" is.

We need to remind ourselves that the designer is concerned with how things look, while the engineer, technician, or craftsman is not—at least in any formal way. In fact, if the engineer, technician, or craftsman *is* concerned with how his work looks, he is to that extent thinking as a designer. Obviously many engineers and craftsmen are, in fact, excellent designers. This is not, however, their main concern—it is an extra skill that is not required for their principal work. If an engineer plans a high-voltage power line to cut across country, it will be a very visible thing with its wires and huge towers. The engineer, however, will be quite satisfied if the line can be built economically and will do its job well. It may be a handsome addition to the landscape or it may be an eyesore, but this is no concern of the engineering designer. If the towers turn out to be beautiful, it may be a matter of luck, or, as we suspect, it may be because the engineer is in fact a talented visual designer—but that would also be a matter of luck, of course. Being a good engineer simply does not require skill in visual design. Similarly a good craftsman might build a very ugly piece of furniture as a result of following a poor design or no design at all; this does not mean that his craftsmanship might not still be excellent. A craftsman may build excellently designed furniture as a result of following good plans or good traditions, or as a result of being himself a good designer. Good craftsmanship, however, offers no guarantee of good design.

It is only the designer who accepts as his foremost professional responsibility a concern with how things will look (and also, in the appropriate cases, with how they will feel, sound, or even smell). Since we have already dismissed the idea that this means trying to make things tasteful or pretty, we must face the question of what it really does mean. Why is it necessary to be concerned at all with how things look? It is surprising how few people are able to offer any sort of reasonable answer to this question.

A meaningful answer must be based on some understanding of what vision is for (and the other senses, too, where they apply). No one wants to be blind, and a man who is blind must use his other senses to the utmost to partly make up the deficiency if he is to live an approximation of normal life. It is almost impossible to imagine a life in which all five senses were inoperative—plants lead such a life, but we find it very hard to think of such "living" as having anything in common with human life as we normally think of it. Living, to us, means thought processes constantly going on, and thought is so closely tied to our senses that we cannot imagine it continuing if the senses did not exist to supply the information which is the material of thought.

Everyone has tried the experiment of trying to stop thinking for a moment—it turns out to be impossible, of course. The thought "I am not thinking" begins to go through the mind and we realize that it, too, is a thought. One can, however, stop using words in thought quite easily and substitute images (or sounds). When one remembers a familiar face, or room, or tune, that is, of course, a kind of thought. It is claimed that something in the vicinity of 80 percent of the data which stock the mind of an average person have been acquired through vision. The other senses have supplied the remaining 20 percent. As we study the world around us, vision is our main tool. Even language has been made available to vision through the invention of writing. The senses, and vision particularly, are then the collectors of information on which thought is based. Thought is meaningless (or even impossible) without the data with which it deals. We cannot think about something until we have learned enough about it to support thought, and vision is our most basic tool in this learning.

In a biological sense, the senses and the brain together are the most important tools contributing to survival of the individual and the species. In its most primitive and basic uses, vision makes it possible to identify dangers, recognize food, and locate a mate. This fact applies to man just as much as to other animals; vision exists because it aids biological survival. It is this fundamental use for the visual sense that brought it into being through the process of natural selection, and the whole eye-and-brain system that we call "perception" exists solely as a means to make information about the world we live in available to our thought processes. A similar system exists in most "higher" animals and existed in primitive man for long ages before man began to invent and use the artifacts of civilization that we call "designs". Vision served first to explore the natural environment, to aid in recognizing friends and enemies among other animals and men, to discover what to eat and where to find it, and generally to make possible the kind of life that we think of as typically "human". Perhaps the satisfaction that we feel in looking at the natural world is a reflection of the fact that this is really the task for which vision developed and the only task it had until the comparatively recent development of manmade things.

As long as man uses his eyes only to study unaltered nature, the process is a matter of a strictly one-way flow of information. The visual aspect of the things looked at exists. By looking, information is collected ready to be thought about, remembered, and understood. The same process continues unchanged when we look at an object or a situation that is manmade. Our eyes collect data and our thoughts and understanding process goes to work exactly as it does with natural products. Indeed, if we recognize that man is himself a natural being, we can argue that this is still a matter of looking at the natural world. We feel, intuitively, however, that there is a difference. This difference arises out of the fact that the viewing process is no longer a strictly one-way tcehnique for taking in data. It has become a system in which the sending of the data is a process under human control just as much as is the receiving.

When a man makes something, even though he may have only the most practical purposes in mind, he has created something visible. The viewer who sees the thing that has been made, applies the same skills of sight and perception that he would apply to the natural world, but he cannot escape knowing that the form that he sees has been shaped by the thinking of the man who made it. The thought of the maker is thus communicated to the onlooker. When we look at the sky, or a rock, a worm, a lion, or a wasp's nest, we see and understand what we see, but we do not receive any communication of thought. Of our examples, only the wasp's nest is a thing made by a living creature, although we cannot really regard the design of the nest as a product of thought. The fact that it is repeated by endless generations of wasps is in itself proof that it is not the product of thoughtful planning on the part of any one wasp or group of wasp architects. Human products are the result of human design, and the process of design involves thought that becomes built into the resulting product. Natural objects have a kind of distilled history of their origins built into them also, but it is the role of the maker's thought built into the human product that makes it so subtle and complex.

Design, then, turns out to be a process for human communication. The forms that the designer (who may also be the maker) has built into his product can have meaning to the viewer, just as the words of a message have meaning to the reader. Good communication makes demands of both sender and receiver. If a message is to make sense to the recipient, the sender must take some trouble with it. He must find or invent some code or language, and put together his message with skill and care. The recipient will have to go to the trouble of learning the code or language and deciphering

The Swiss castle of Aigle.
(Photograph by John Pile)

the message before its meaning will come through. A message is not meaningless even if the recipient cannot decipher it: although its meaning will not be accessible unless the code can be discovered, the message still contains locked-in meaning—provided that the sender put meaning there. The meaning that can be locked into a design in this way can be very powerful and lasting and often turns out to be far more successful than verbal communication. Consider, for example, our understanding of the thinking of the Middle Ages. While there are works of philosophy, stories, and poems that survive from that era, most of us who are not historical scholars find this material difficult and obscure. On the other hand, it is necessary only to walk into a medieval cathedral (or even to study plans and pictures) in order to feel some very strong knowledge and understanding of the ideas of the people who built it. This communication comes through quickly and easily at the casual level of interest of the passing tourist, but it can become deeper and stronger if one will take the time to study the system of construction, the nature of the plan, the details of sculpture and decoration. We are put in touch with the builders in a way that is very direct and powerful. No verbal account of such a building or the ideas behind it can possibly equal the impact of the direct experience of the building itself.

We can say, then, that the cathedral is a "work of art". Every successful design is in some measure a work of art, because it opens a line of communication between its maker and the viewer that is more direct, more subtle, and more effective than the levels of communication achieved by the use of words. Words always stand for some reality which the reader or hearer must conjure up for himself. A work of art is a "thing" that presents itself directly to our vision (and often to the senses of touch, hearing, and even smell). If all written records of the Middle Ages were lost, the surviving buildings and artifacts would put us in very full communication with the people of those days. This is, indeed, the way in which we come to understand the civilizations that did not leave us written records and those that are not producing written records even now. Our tremendous dependence on written and spoken words in practical life and the enormous emphasis given to everything verbal in our educational system tend to blind us to the fact that words are only symbols. We do not live our lives as words or in contact with words—all reality has a substance that goes beyond anything verbal. This is the reality with which the designer and the artist are concerned.

Since every piece of human work involving building or making produces a visual result, every piece of work is automatically a kind of visual communication. This does not mean, however, that every such piece of work is equally good. There are orders of merit in every kind of communication and it is the special job of the designer to make sure that this aspect of any piece of work that he is concerned with turns out as well as possible. A comparison with verbal communication might help to make this point clear. We all know that verbal messages can vary in quality and that only the best writers and speakers are able to do really superlative jobs of conveying meaning. There can even be communications that are false and misleading. We could in fact arrange both verbal communications and designs in three rather arbitrary classes of merit something like this:

I. The most unfortunate level of communication—the level of the outright falsehood. In verbal communication this might be a misleading or distorted news report, or a piece of propaganda that has no basis in fact. The design equivalent might be a falsification of material (a frame building with imitation brick exterior), a distortion of historical place (a fake antique), or the introduction of meaningless elements for some imaginary appearance value (useless tail-fins on an automobile or a false funnel on a ship).

II. Well-meaning but inept communication is, unfortunately, the most common type of verbal and design production. The intention is not to mislead, but the results are more or less unclear and confusing. This is the level of everyday conversation, the typical news report, or the dull political speech. Facts are present, but their expression and emphasis is blurred. In a similar way, this is the character of most unthinking design and all too much self-conscious design also. The effort to make forms meaningful is present, but the skill of the designer does not lead to anything beyond the average or mediocre. Any number of designs for everyday objects, furniture, lamps, appliances, and machines would fall into this class although there is clearly quite a range from worst to best.

III. Skillful communication can, at its best, produce great works of art. In verbal communication, this means the finest of novels, plays, essays, and speeches. In design, it means those things in which the designer has made an exactly right decision about every detail of form so that the clarity of his ideas stands out in an impressive way. Every truly great building, every beautiful object is in some degree an example of this kind of strikingly successful communication. This is the kind of work that every good designer is constantly trying to do and which only the best designers actually manage with any frequency.

Continuing our analogy with writing (as verbal communication) might help to clarify one more point. It is generally understood that design is an art, but it is also clear that it is a somewhat different art from painting, sculpture, or musical composition in that most designed objects (and certainly most buildings) have a purpose beyond artistic communication in itself. Chairs are to sit on, airplanes to be flown, and houses to live in. In the "fine arts" no such practical demands exist and the painter or sculptor has no obligations except to express whatever ideas or emotions occur to him. This makes of architecture and design a somewhat special kind of art since buildings and things cannot be so freely invented if they are to serve their purposes. It is tempting to suggest that these more practical arts should not be called "arts" at all, but should be moved into some other classification of crafts or trades. Our comparison with writing helps to make it clear that this is not altogether right, however. Poetry and the creative writing of stories and novels are free to deal with any material the writer may invent for his own expressive purposes, but most writing deals with some body of factual information in the same way that design must deal with practical utility. A brilliantly written account of some event, or an explanation of some principle, is an impressive piece of artistry in the same way that the best of utilitarian designs are. Poetry, fiction, painting, sculpture, and music are comparable in being freer and more personal arts, but there is no reason to feel that they alone deserve designation as "art". Surely a medieval cathedral is fully as great a work as a medieval poem, painting, or musical chant.

Man's most important tool for survival and progress is his ability to think and understand. It is particularly important that he understand the thoughts and actions of other human beings—both his contemporaries and those who made up earlier generations. This is the reason why every human product needs, to the maximum extent possible, to embody in its physical form the richest and most meaningful body of communication possible. The designer's job is to translate his understanding of what an object is and how it is made, into form which will be accessible to anyone who encounters the object afterwards. Historic objects are meaningful to us when this job was done well and contemporary objects can be similarly meaningful. When the job of the designer is done badly or not at all, the object may serve its purpose in a narrow sense, but it offers no help to understanding and may even rise to confusion. The modern man who is content with a wasteful and dangerous automobile because its design conceals these faults from him may suffer through his mistaken contentment. The whole society suffers from the waste and damage that designs shelter. A well-designed house or chair (or, if we can find one, automobile) not only serves its user well, but puts him in direct communication with the intelligence, skill, and thought of the designer. This is a helpful thing for the individual user or owner and for the whole society.

Although we have declined to put any trust in taste or aesthetic preferences based on individual liking as a route toward good design, it is probably now time to make it clear that things that are well designed can and do give pleasure. Living in a well-designed house, sitting in a well-designed chair, sailing a beautiful boat, or playing a fine musical instrument gives us pleasure of a very direct and well-recognized kind. The pleasure comes in part from the fact that such well-designed things work well and hold up well in use, but it also comes from our sense of being in touch with the skill, intelligence, and sensitivity of the designer through his product. We admire a beautiful boat or a Stradivarius violin even if we have no opportunity to take advantage of its fine qualities for our own use, and our admiration is a very real and satisfying thing. It is, in fact, the same sense of satisfaction that comes to us when we look at those natural creations—the sky, a tree, a flower, or a bird—which almost everyone admires.

The mistrust of our taste when we confront manmade things arises because we have all been misled into accepting things that are not worthy of us (badly planned houses, clumsy furniture, shoddy appliances, faked materials) and have even been persuaded, through custom or pleasant associations that have nothing to do with the objects, to imagine that we like some of them. We can learn to love a bad house if it is our home and the scene of a pleasant life. Gradually we begin to think that it is a good house because we enjoy the life we lead in it and forget its faults. Actually we would lead an even better life in a good house and would have reason to love it both for the life it shelters and for itself. One of the most difficult and important first steps that every beginning designer must take is to sort out in his mind the pointless prejudices and taste habits that must be discarded so that a genuine sensitivity to the reality of manmade things can take the place of the discarded notions. This step would be easier, or might not even be needed, if we lived in a world where most things were well designed, so that our stock of past associations would not mislead us so often. As it is, we must search hard for the things that we can admire so that we can use them as standards of excellence by which to measure our own work.

For the designer, the satisfactions of doing a good piece of work are very real. He knows that he has solved some practical problem well; he has chosen good materials and ways of making his design; but he has also done the extra thing that makes him an artist: he has done his job in a way that will put him in direct touch with everyone who comes across his design, at any place and any future time (at least for as long as the product survives). He can feel confident that he has made good decisions and has made these decisions intelligible and meaningful as well. Making what one designs expressive in this way is one of the most basic sources of human satisfaction, and it has its direct counterpart in the matching satisfaction that comes to the viewer or user of the thing in question.

A person can go through life, as long as the minimum requirements for food and shelter are met, without having any particular sensitivity or alertness toward the surroundings in which he exists. We have all deliberately put ourselves into this kind of trancelike state of not noticing in order to get through some unpleasant experience (a ride on an overcrowded and noisy subway train, for example), but afterward we have no particular memory of the event—it might just as well never have happened as far as we are concerned. If we spend much of life in this way we are clearly missing major portions of what the experience of life can be. In comparable fashion, it is possible to make and build things so that they serve some purpose in a minimal way, but with such indifference to the visual results that they offer nothing to the user or viewer beyond their minimal practical value. Such things represent a lost opportunity to establish new lines of visual communication through which the viewer or user could come to enjoy and understand the thing that he uses. Possibly this was a matter of minor importance when human beings still spent most of their lives in contact with a natural environment that is always worthy of attention and full of meaning and sources of pleasure. As we all find ourselves spending more and more of our time in situations that are largely or totally manmade, the need to make these situations worthy of our attention becomes increasingly strong. Anyone who understands this need and tries to do the job is a designer. Doing a superlatively good design job in relation to even the smallest of problems can be an enormously satisfying task, and one that is a genuine service to everyone who comes in contact with the results.

II

THE VOCABULARY
OF DESIGN

The following section will explain in some detail, and with specific references to existing spaces, the terms that are the vocabulary of the designer. The section does not offer a simple semantic interpretation of words. The concepts described by such words as "form" or scale" have a very specific meaning to the designer, and must be clearly understood in relation to the total design process. The different ways in which we can look at objects and surroundings, react to them, and analyze them varies greatly with our background and our intent. Let us use as an example a simple object with which we are all familiar—a chair—for the purpose of discussion, any chair.

If an older person who has worked hard or walked a lot sees the chair, it will become an object most desirable for the rest and relief from physical tiredness it promises to provide. A man who is physically exhausted will not care much what the chair looks like, nor indeed whether it is comfortable in the conventional sense of the word. Just about any chair will do the trick and promise the sought-for physical relief.

If a homeowner is shopping for a chair, however, the question arises immediately what the purpose of the chair is. Is it for working, for writing, for dining, or is it for relaxing or reading? Comfort has become a more critical criterion and will be thought of differently depending on the function for which the chair is intended. Comfort may even be a disadvantage if the chair is to be used for a difficult task such as drafting or sewing, and the soft and inviting chair may be rejected if the planned function is work or study.

The businessman or furniture salesman who sees the chair will have other thoughts. Will the chair sell, and how many chairs can be sold at what profit? Is the chair of sufficient attractiveness, design quality, or novelty to attract customers, and is it an item that business competitors will be able to sell at a cheaper price?

The furniure manufacturer will examine the same chair in terms of ease of production or complexity of manufacturing, and in terms of facilities needed for production and cost. Will there be any difficulty in obtaining the required materials, will there be any problems in shipping and assembly, how many pieces can be produced in a week or a month?

The historian might look at the same chair in terms of its stylistic influences and, if it should be an antique chair, may enjoy it as a fine example of a particular period.

And finally, the aesthetician will look at the chair in terms of pure formal considerations. He will react to the chair in terms of its proportions: its line, scale, and detail, and may analyze it as if it were a piece of sculpture. He will consider the beauty of the chair's materials and he will draw mental comparisons with other chairs. He might conceivably rate it very highly, even if it should turn out to be an uncomfortable and inappropriate chair for the purpose for which it was designed.

The person who should examine the chair and understand all its implications, from all the above points of view, plus others, is, of course, the designer. Let us take the first term in the vocabulary of design and call it "form" and continue to examine the same imagined chair with which we started.

FORM

The form of the chair is its definite shape for a definite purpose. In order to understand whether it is a good form or "good design" one could simply restate some of the criteria of observation in several simple questions:

What is it?
What does it do?
Who is it for?
What is it made of?
How is it made?
Why is it made that way?
What are the structural principles?
Will it stand up?
Could it be made more simply?
How much does it cost?
Are the materials well chosen?
Is it beautiful?
Could it be improved?

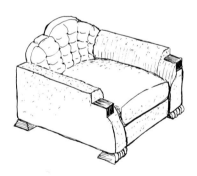

Armchair.

Logical answers to these questions can begin to give us some valid criteria in our examination of the form of the chair. Note that the question relating to beauty is just one of a series. If sensible answers can be provided to all the other questions, the chances are very good indeed that the chair is beautiful in form, and follows some of the basic principles of good design explained in Part One. The statement that "form follows function", made famous by the American architect Louis Sullivan, should also be recalled here. The examination of the chair, or indeed of any interior or structure in such terms, will be more revealing to the understanding of form than a mere evaluation in terms of aesthetics. Form, even in an abstract or sculptural sense, is guided by underlying principles of design. But it is of great importance to keep in mind that an interior space, or even our favorite chair, is not an abstract object at all; rather it is an object or a space created for a specific purpose. To express it in terms used by the aesthetic philosophers, it is a teleological object—meaning something that is created for the sake of a particular end and cause. If the chair would look like the one illustrated here, it might be called "interesting"; to some people it might even be beautiful; but it certainly would not meet many of the design criteria and basic design principles we established and would not stand up under the series of questions we listed above.

Tubular chair.

A question relating to form that is almost as basic as the question of function, is the pertinence of form to the material used. We can again use the chair as an example. When Marcel Breuer first used tubular steel in designing furniture such as the chair shown here, it was an intelligent and highly appropriate use of a flexible material and created a form that had hitherto not been possible in any other material. Undoubtedly a good craftsman could duplicate the identical form in wood, but experience tells us that wood does not have the tensile strength of steel, and would therefore break if used in this way. Today we could duplicate the chair in plastic, and again we could be sure that within no time at all the plastic material would crack and break. But one can also point to the countless examples of ugly chairs that were manufactured out of the same material Breuer used, but exaggerated in a senseless way. Many chairs were produced in tubular steel that doubled and even tripled the strands of steel for the sake of novelty only. These chairs created forms that ignored the strength and grace inherent in tubular steel by adding arbitrary non-structural members and thus violated the expressive and direct form stated so clearly in the original design.

From the simple and single object within an interior we can learn to understand the principles that are valid for a complex interior or indeed for any structure. The two illustrations here show the interior of the Four Seasons Restaurant in New York's Seagram Building, designed by Mies van der Rohe in collaboration with Philip Johnson. Philip Johnson collaborated on the design of the restaurant with an interior designer, William Pahlmann, and just for the record, although it cannot be seen in the photograph, there was further collaboration with an industrial designer, Garth Huxtable, on the flatware,

Four Seasons Restaurant, New York. Philip Johnson, architect.

china, etc. The basic form of the spaces was determined by the architecture of the building, as is the case in most interiors. The function of the space is clearly expressed in the forms of the furnishings, which leave no doubt about their appropriateness for dining.

The large space is used for dining, the smaller space as a bar; a smaller space yet acts as a link between the two and establishes a visual link connecting the two large forms, while at the same time defining the separate functions of the spaces.

In abstract terms we tend to look for a dominant form when several masses or elements combine into one composition. In the large dining space the planting creates this dominance of form and is at the same time the focal point for the diners within the space. It also happens to be the motif or "theme" of the restaurant, since the planting is changed four times a year to reflect the four seasons: hence the name of the restaurant. The very nature of a restaurant demands many small objects and forms within its total environment; and we could go down our list of questions to examine each and every chair and table in the space and would hopefully agree on appropriateness of materials and, similarly, on the form and function of all the many surface materials used. This particular restaurant was designed as a luxury establishment, which is clearly, but not ostentatiously, reflected in form and materials.

Perhaps a term borrowed from psychology can point up the need to perceive a total interior rather than its isolated parts. Psychologists use the German word *Gestalt* to name an organized configuration or pattern of experiences. Our perception is conditioned, psychologists tell us, to recognize forms grouped in familiar patterns *(Gestalts)*, and even the trained designer's first impression of an interior space is the total configuration rather than individual objects and surfaces within the space. But since the sum of many isolated parts forms this total impression, it is essential that the individual forms relate to each other in order to create a cohesive and organized form as a whole. And not only must the parts relate to each other, but they must above all relate to the dominant architectural envelope which contains them.

The illustration of the original Pan American Terminal* at New York's Kennedy Airport shows the dangers of the visual confusion that occurs when no attention is paid to the relation

---

*New York's Pan American Terminal has since been expanded and completely remodeled.

Pan American Terminal.

of the interior form to the exterior, and no attention is given
to interrelationships of the interior forms. The Pan American
building is, by the way, an exciting engineering design concept,
and potentially functions well as an international air terminal.
However, nowhere within the interior is there any reflection
of the eliptical plan of the building. Even the glazing and
mullions ignore the strong structural form of the building.
Once inside, the traveler must cope with a profusion of conflicting forms of stairs, balconies, furniture groupings, and
counters that while lacking the continuity one expects from
the strong exterior design, would also seem essential in relating various forms within a large space to each other.

Pan American Terminal.

TWA Kennedy Airport Terminal, New York. Eero Saarinen, architect.
(Photographs courtesy of TWA by Ezra Stoller (Esto))

In the literature of aesthetic philosophy there is probably no clear definition of beauty and form shared by all philosophers. There are, however, recurring criteria in references to beauty, and some of these are universal in their application to sculpture, architecture, and interior architecture. The terms *order, organization, clarity, truth,* and *expressiveness* as used by aestheticians do not always mean precisely the same thing, but will by and large help define a form as a successful entity—or if none of these terms applies—as a failure. It follows that a good form is not necessarily the most direct or simple one, although simplicity is indeed a frequent device for successful design.

For instance, the TWA terminal design by the late Eero Saarinen is certainly as complex an architectural and interior form as any recent building. Yet, upon examination it becomes obvious that an overriding order and clarity of form has been established by the designer. The building has been much criticized and praised by different critics. A valid criticism might be that the form of the building is not solely the result of an interior need and function, but a somewhat arbitrary form reminiscent of flight, forced into the function of an airlines terminal. For our purposes we must accept the initial decision concerning form and not get involved in the philosophical consideration that led to it. The form is most certainly one that reflects the material used, strongly and beautifully, and no material but concrete would have made the construc-

**TWA Kennedy Airport
Terminal, New York.**

tion of such a building possible. Each detail within the interior is logical and complementary to the exterior form. The concern for a total *Gestalt* has been carried to the point of compromising with utilitarian considerations at times, but these were compromises made essentially by the initial decision to create as powerful and cohesive a form as the finished building represents.

Form in architecture is limited only by man's imagination. Technologically we can create just about any form. Interior form is usually limited by the architectural envelope, except in those buildings in which the architect works together with the interior designer from the beginning. The important conclusion to be reached here is that criteria for understanding and judging form vary little from a single small object to a large building complex. The one warning we must voice before we conclude our discussion of form is to mention the fact that the existing environment almost always matters. We can create new interior forms—forms of make-believe and theatrical settings—but unless they are clearly intended for the stage and expressed in theatrical character, we would most likely violate the existing building and create conflict in an attempt to overpower existing form with a new, dominant, false expression.

2

SCALE

"Scale" is one of those words that has a number of dictionary definitions, depending upon the connection in which the word is used. For the designer, scale has two meanings. First, scale means the use of a small dimension to represent a larger one. In the drawing of plans, for instance, a small dimension is used to indicate a full-sized object such as a building. In the drawing of maps, even smaller scale is used to indicate even larger objects, such as mountains. A second meaning of the word (and the meaning used in this chapter) concerns the relation of objects to each other and to people. A building like New York's Empire State Building would obviously seem out of scale in a small New England village, and a king-size double bed would obviously be out of scale for use as an infant's crib.

In our discussion on form. we were able to conclude that "good" form has almost universal meaning in all aspects of our visual environments. However, when we consider scale, there is a decided difference between architecture and interior design. No building is ever out of scale by itself. Scale or appropriate scale implies the relationship of one object to other objects: be they buildings to buildings, or buildings to landscape. However, no interior ever exists in isolation: its scale relationship to the building which encloses the space and its scale relationship to other interiors is always present.

Our relation to scale is determined and conditioned by many things, but the most important factor in discussing the scale of our environment is the human body. Man is the measure of all scales, mathematical and geometric theories notwithstanding. Throughout the ages designers of buildings have attempted to establish ideal proportions, a kind of alphabet of scale if you

Nave of Laon Cathedral.

**Pennsylvania Railroad
Station, New York
(now demolished).**

wish. The rules that have been established and used are indeed helpful as guidelines to proportions, but it seems doubtful whether even the all-powerful computer of today will ever be able to substitute for the critical reaction possible through the human eye, in determining scale and proportion. The most famous of all axioms about proportion was established by the Greeks, and has been used throughout the ages by designers and mathematicians. As a guide to proper scale, the "golden section" axiom suggests that a line should be divided into two unequal parts, of which the first is to the second as the second is to the whole. No less a designer than Le Corbusier did much work on studies of scale and proportion, and developed his famous theory of proportion called the "Modulor". But at best these rules are merely guidelines. They can never substitute for the eye and judgment of the sensitive designer.

The quality and atmosphere of an interior is most strongly determined by its scale relationship to man. One of the most exciting aesthetic experiences one can undergo is to be inside a great Gothic cathedral. Regardless of one's religious beliefs, it is impossible not to be moved by the majestic and monumental proportion of a cathedral. Whatever the motives of the builders, their handling of space and light, the sheer monumentality of the space in relation to man reduces man to a scale that has profound impact on the senses. It is not important that we isolate terms and concepts of design, however we must mention light as an important aspect of the spiritual feeling created in a church or cathedral. The high placement of windows in a cathedral creates powerful and moving plays of sunlight against the subdued quality of light created by lower stained glass windows. There are structures today (such as space-craft installations) that indeed have a scale exceeding that of even the largest cathedral, but these spaces lack the quality that has been consciously incorporated in medieval religious structures. But secular structures, too, can convey this sense of exhilaration and beauty created by generous handling of scale and proportion. Economics and crowding of our cities give us fewer and fewer of these beautiful spaces. Even the few that exist are giving way to newer and more "efficient" structures. It was a sad occurrence for New York to lose the beautiful interior of the Pennsylvania Railroad Station which, replaced in a new building, looks as if a giant crushed it.

Precisely because the pressures of society and economics so seldom permit the generously-scaled interiors of past eras, the interior designer must be very aware of this changing environment. Contents and components of buildings, no matter how

Kennedy Space Center, Florida. (Photograph courtesy of NASA)

largely scaled, have always been designed to the measure of man. The furniture we use, the door opening through which we pass, the height of risers and width of treads on stairs have been more or less constant parts. While the difference of half an inch in the height of a building cannot be discerned by the eye, the difference between a one-inch table top and one measuring one and one-half inches in thickness is a very significant one. A breakfront that is 8 feet tall might have looked just right in an English eighteenth-century country house, but would look absurdly out of place in a city apartment with an 8 feet 2 inch ceiling height. Minute changes of scale in objects designed according to physiological needs are felt with forceful impact. Normal stairs, for instance, are designed in a constant ratio of tread to riser that is approximately 10 inches to 7¼ inches. Stairs which are designed for ceremonial purposes may have 12 inch treads and 6 inch risers; and the builders of eighteenth-century country homes and other fashionable residences were aware of this, deliberately designing the servants' stairs in a different scale—with 8 inch or 8¼ inch risers—which made their use uncomfortable for the servants (although perhaps it had the desired effect of keeping them in their place).

The manipulation of scale in the hand of the interior designer can ruin spaces if not carefully handled, or can overcome dull or monotonous architecture if properly handled. A lofty, high-ceiling space, or a majestically proportioned interior is not the only kind of space we ever wish to be in. In fact, a very high ceiling in a small space would throw the room quite out of proportion and would feel about as comfortable as being in an upended tunnel. For small gatherings or for individual use, a space of intimate scale is usually preferable to a monumental space. Much of home life is associated with intimacy. Even kings and nobles who occupied palatial mansions had private quarters of "normal" scale and proportions. A recent master of handling scale in residential interiors was Frank Lloyd Wright. Wright designed many houses scaled specifically to the occupant (or maybe to his own stature) and small spaces with ceiling heights below eight feet were not unusual. Above all, Wright created an excitement of flowing spaces through his manipulations of changing scale.

The need for changing scale in our environment is a psychological and physiological one. The occurrence of foyers and vestibules in buildings throughout history was more than a functional development. The functional advantage of a small entry space leading into a larger interior is the control of the elements. Two sets of doors in a foyer effectively prevent cold blasts of air into a heated interior space and by the same token provide insulation in hot climates. But passing through a smaller transitional space first, rather than suddenly entering a totally differing space and temperature level from outdoors, is also a far more pleasant way of entering a large interior space from the outside.

The earliest forms of punishment devised by society included small rooms—jail cells. And even cave dwellers carved out small sleeping niches for themselves in large caverns, in order to satisfy the need for change to more intimately scaled environment. We derive pleasure from going through fun houses, where our image is distorted to unrealistic scales in mirror images, and we enjoy the stimulation, even if it is a somewhat uncomfortable one, of going through mazes and labyrinths. A speciality developed by interior designers from the baroque period through the eighteenth century was a device called "Trompe L'oeil", meaning the fooling of the eye. Interior walls and ceilings were painted in highly realistic scenes depicting large-scale exterior views; and even on the fronts of furniture, deceiving perspective views were painted or inlaid in wood in order to bring an unexpected change of scale to the eye of the onlooker.

This change of scale can be accomplished by many means. The interior of the Four Seasons Restaurant on p. 49, for instance, shows the large-scale interior broken up into smaller-scaled spaces for intimacy of dining. Diners are part of the overall space, but have the luxury of privacy and personal scale, once they are seated at a table.

The need for "personal" environment relating to man and man's activity can best be understood by considering some extreme examples. When we fly at 30,000 feet in an airplane, the scale of everything seen on the ground appears so small that we lose touch with the reality of objects. Many people are nervous about heights and hesitate to look out of a window in a twenty-story building. But the same person who experiences fear of heights is rarely bothered by the view out of an airplane, because the immediacy of the objects on the ground has transcended normal perception of scale. Our reaction to the scale of a small house is quite different from our reaction to a large high-rise building. We accept and expect details and materials in the small structure that are in a meaningful scale to man or that provide the "human touches". The impersonal scale of huge structures was not fully understood by the early builders of skyscrapers, and some of the sculptural ornaments on top of late Victorian buildings strike us as rather funny today— that is, if we can spot these details at all without a telescope. Architects have learned to handle the scale of very large structures in proportions appropriate to their size. The majestic simplicity of a Seagram Building is a perfect example of Mies van der Rohe's mastery of scale and proportion. The human touches related to ordinary scale, such as the pool and fountains in the plaza area, are where people can enjoy them and where people can enjoy the environment. It is interesting to note that although the Seagram Building represents almost the epitome of the great mid-twentieth century skyscraper, its monumental scale also makes it rather forbidding. As George Nelson, the renowned designer has said, it seems a structure designed for use by sophisticated computers, and when an employee appears visible against the large glass areas somewhere on the upper floors, one almost feels as if an intrusion had been perpetrated.

We have mentioned the psychological and physiological influence of interior scale on people, and in that connection have discussed the uplifting and spiritual character of cathedrals and some churches. A different situation is true in interiors familiar to all inhabitants of large cities. Underground transportation is rarely pleasant. Passages leading to subway stations or connecting stations are extreme examples of depressing

**The Seagram Building,
New York.
Mies Van der Rohe and
Philip Johnson, architects.**
(Photograph courtesy of
Seagram and Sons Inc.)

and unpleasant spaces. The enormous length of these sub-
terranean tunnels, their narrow widths, and extremely low
ceilings create physical discomfort even without the mass of
humanity usually rushing through them. It is no coincidence
that underground passages in many cities throughout the
world are breeding grounds for crime. The depressing scale of
that environment brings out the worst in human nature. A
cheerful note has been sounded by recent subway systems such
as the ones in Montreal and Toronto. Both cities have found

New York City subway.

Montreal subway.

House interior.

it possible to create a variation of scale, and many other design improvements.

Many interior designers may never be faced with major decisions on the basic scale of spaces that they are called upon to design. Often the only important scale considerations are the selection and specification of furniture and furnishings. It is amazing that even this basic design consideration is so frequently ignored. A room such as the one shown here is not an unusual sight in the typical American home, or worse—

Strozzi Palace, Florence. (Photograph by John Pile)

in many public spaces. If we understand the significance of scale in all environment, to design the interiors in scale with the building in which they exist, and above all, to relate them to the scale of man, becomes a simple rule to adhere to.

3

TEXTURE

We are critical at times of certain interiors, or in fact of any number of objects, and state that they "lack texture". This, in a precise interpretation of the word, is incorrect. Everything has texture. But texture is a matter of degree or scale. While even the smoothest surface has texture, sometimes it has so little that one could only notice it under a magnifying glass. The use and combination of various textures in an interior are not usually subjected to minute inspection, but they are perceived at close range and are subject to inspection by touch. How strongly minute differences in texture can affect our senses can be noted by the borrowing of this term when referring to the taste of wine. Connoisseurs refer to the small variation of taste and quality by talking about the "texture" of a particular wine. It is obvious that meticulous handling of textures is a very important aspect of interior design. Large blocks of stone may form a beautiful and appropriate texture for the exterior of a large building. In seventeenth- and eighteenth-century architecture, the further emphasis of the textural quality of stones was brought out by rustication, a method of setting stones with deep reveals between joints. To use that effect, or just very large blocks of masonry in an average-sized interior space, would be extremely uncomfortable to the inhabitants of the space.

One of the clearest demonstrations of scale effect upon texture can be seen in architectural or interior scale models. A piece of upholstery fabric might be perfect for a sofa in a room, but if one were to use the same fabric in a scale model of that room at something like one-twelfth of full size, it would be

Natural Textures: Elephant's tail, Wood,
Cliff in Utah, Fungus on tree.

completely out of character and out of scale. It would, in fact, appear in the scale model as if the sofa were covered in a kind of a shaggy textured rug.

One could say that scale is one of the first considerations of texture. An equally important fact about textures is the reflection or absorption of light. Very smooth materials reflect light to the point of returning images; smooth water, glass, polished metals have almost mirrorlike surfaces, and unless a mirror effect is desired, a space surrounded with such materials could be a very disturbing environment. Deep and heavy textures, on the other hand, especially if they happen to be dark colors, absorb light and distort it. A white plaster wall covered with a deeply textured white carpet would appear much darker than the original texture. One can, in fact, quite easily experiment with the effect of light on texture by comparing a number of fabrics or carpets of identical color and even identical yarn. Each material would appear to have somewhat different coloration because of the varying textural quality and the difference in the reflection of light.

The third most important consideration of texture is the sense of touch. Even if we do not as a rule walk around touching everything we see, our eyes have learned to interpret textural qualities with all our senses. To touch a soft wool fabric is pleasant; to touch a soft fur gives an almost sensuous pleasure; but to touch sandpaper or a browncoat of plaster is a decidedly unpleasant feeling. In the textile field, the "feel of hand" of a fabric is considered an important criterion for judging fabrics. Fabrics which appear quite similar from a few feet away may radically differ because of the sense of touch— really a rather minute difference in texture. For instance, pure silk fabric feels pleasant to the touch, yet fiberglass fabric, although quite similar in appearance, has a peculiar and to most people unpleasant, tactile quality.

Understanding the basic attributes of texture brings us to a closer understanding of our own reactions to varying textures. The desire and the need for varied textures in our surroundings is a basic human need. Nature is full of the most delightful textural effects, and environment without variation (such as the desert or the snow-covered regions of the Arctic) has serious and disturbing effects upon us. Environment of too many and overly powerful textures would be equally disturbing. Exhibitions or trade fairs are often examples of conglomerations of many unrelated and unplanned textures and design elements that result in very disturbing and even physically exhausting surroundings. It is therefore the designer's chal-

Considerations of texture:
1. scale
2. reflection + absorption of light
3. sense of touch

I. Miller shoestore, New York. Victor A. Lundy, architect.

lenge to create textural effects that are well-balanced in scale, and appropriate.

The interior shown here is a shoestore designed by Victor A. Lundy for I. Miller in New York. The dominant texture is created by strips of wood laminations with deep reveals between the strips. The rear wall of the store is mirrored. The floor-covering and upholstery materials are incidental to this conscious play of two strong textures against each other. The form created by the wood strips is a very powerful one, and the effect of the store interior is extremely elegant, through use of both form and texture. It is an interior with exceptionally strong character, in spite of the fact that little important furniture has been used; yet the existing space was no more distinguished than any other average store interior.

If one can make generalizations at all, one might borrow here a famous saying by the architect Mies van der Rohe. He once stated that "less is more". This principle might serve us well in many aspects of design, but can be an extremely useful

Lobby, Seagram Building, New York.
Mies Van der Rohe and Philip Johnson, architects.
(Photographs courtesy of Seagram and Sons Inc.)

principle to keep in mind in connection with textures in interiors. We might compare Mies's own creation, the Seagram Building lobby, with the lobby of almost any other building along Park Avenue in New York, where there are many huge high-rise office buildings within a few blocks of each other. We mentioned the Seagram Building earlier as a very excellent design example. The lobby has wonderful proportions and creates an imposing entry into a distinguished building without resorting to the use of any furnishings or decorations. There are only three basic materials used throughout, of little textural variety. The floor is terrazzo, the walls are travertine veneer, and the ceiling is mosaic tile. The other texture present is that of glass, but since the purpose of the large glass areas is to relate the entry to the exterior plaza, the glass in this case hardly counts as a texture. Unlike the mirror wall in the I. Miller store, the glass does not reflect anything, at least by day, and the forms visible through it negate its existence. The typical building lobby in less distinguished structures is most often overdesigned, and in many cases appears to be a kind of exhibition of architectural materials. It is not unusual to see as many as four different kinds of marble used together with mosaic tiles, wood panels, mirrored walls and glass, etc. Added to this usual conglomeration of materials, one finds a collection of lighting devices competing with each other on the ceilings or on the walls, and in just about every lobby one can be assured

(Cartoon by Robert Day, Look Magazine, April 1968)

"Oh, Linda, I'm home! Linda! Where are you?"

to find several of the ubiquitous planters with horrible artificial plants. However, building lobbies in office buildings are most certainly not in the category of offensive or overtextured interiors compared to the many really bad interiors we are exposed to in other areas. We suggest comparison to the lobby of the Seagram Building and analysis of some standard building lobbies precisely because the differences are more subtle and would normally not be noticed by the layman. Everyone has experienced gross examples of overdesigned and overtextured interiors. The cartoon on this page makes a very clear statement and need not be explained further.

The quality of textures in general is very much related to the honest expression of materials. One can, in other words, make certain judgments about textures regardless of whether they are used in combination with others, and regardless of whether they are used inside or outside a building. Most of us like the natural quality of wood, its texture, and its pattern. Much of the furniture of the past two hundred years was finished with high gloss polish. This, in a way, created an alien film over the natural grain of the wood and through its shiny reflective quality gave a kind of double image. Most trained designers today prefer the natural quality of wood brought out through dull finishing processes. Cultures with strong craft orientation, such as those of Japan and the Scandinavian countries, rarely used the glossy polishes so fashionable in nineteenth-century Europe and the United States. A simple comparison can be made between the beautiful texture created through the effect of time and of the elements on weathered wood, and the attempted duplication of that effect by sandblasting processes on plywood. Needless to say, the latter does not come near the quality of the natural material. The honest use of the most ordinary materials can give much visual delight. Many beautiful buildings have been created in concrete. Le Corbusier often left the texture created by wooden formwork on his buildings exposed, and many designers have since used similar techniques.

To a certain extent we associate particular textures with elegance, and others with informality. Our associations are, however, somewhat influenced by the fashions and mores of various eras. The use of exposed concrete or old rough textured brick would not have been considered appropriate by the tastemakers of a generation ago, but is quite acceptable to us today. Certain fabrics such as silk and velvets have always been associated with elegance, while rough textured tweed fabrics or burlap-type fabrics are generally considered textures for informal use.

Because of changing fashions and attitudes, it would be risky to establish and accept rules. A careful examination of the intrinsic quality of materials would seem to be a better guideline. There are for instance literally hundreds of imitation brick wallpapers and vinyl materials on the market. Not one of the many imitations comes close to the textural quality of real brick, and these as well as all imitations are always rejected by the sensitive designer. It is a most peculiar trend that manufacturers of vinyl floor coverings, a material available for about twenty years, still have not found the courage to produce this excellent material in an honest expression of its natural texture and inherent qualities. The large majority of vinyl floor coverings are trying to imitate some texture other than what they are. Some of the plain vinyl flooring materials are quite handsome but they usually represent just a small segment of the products marketed by the manufacturers.

The key to the successful use of textures in interiors is above all in the careful combination of differing textures for whatever uses and character the designer wishes to achieve. No rule is ever going to substitute for the sensitive and trained eye of the interior designer.

The last point we must keep in mind is the maintenance factor of materials. No matter how exciting, honest, or beautiful a certain texture might be, it would not be appropriate for a bathroom if it cannot be washed with ease. No matter how elegant one wishes to make a high traffic area, such as a building lobby, one can hardly use a deep pile carpet, for that carpet

Concrete texture in interior.
(Photograph courtesy of Ashley, Myer & Associates, Inc. by Louis Reens)

will wear out in less than one year. For office interiors, schools, and other public buildings, maintenance and cost factors often limit the choice open to the designer. But keeping in mind that wonderful effects can be created by the combination of different textures and even the use of such indestructible materials as concrete, we can see that the limitations imposed by functional considerations can be more than met by the designer's imagination.

4

COLOR AND LIGHT

It must be apparent by now that good design is never the result of a series of unrelated decisions based on an arbitrary manipulation of form or scale or texture. All these facets are strongly interrelated. None is more interdependent than color and light. Color is in fact a quality of light reflected from an object to the human eye. It causes the different color cones of the retina to react, thus making visible color phenomena in the objects. Color is a property of light that depends upon the wave lengths of light in the visible spectrum; red, for instance, has the longest wave length. When light falls upon an object, some of it is absorbed. That which is not absorbed is reflected, and the apparent color of an object depends upon the wave length of the light that it reflects. A red object, for example, appears red because it reflects only the long waves perceived as red light. The physical attributes of color and light are well-known facts, but are too often ignored in interior design. A dark or intensely colored wall surface in an interior may absorb most of the light that falls upon it, with a resulting loss of brightness.

Scientists have done much valuable work on the analytical aspects and other phenomena of color. A good deal of research on color and its effect on human emotions has been done by psychologists. Several authoritative systems for classification and naming of colors have been developed. Foremost are the systems developed by the German color scientist, Ostwald, and the American system developed by Munsell. Helpful as these systems are for understanding color in an analytical way and for industries such as dyeing, printing, or manufacturing of paint, they do not hold significant value for the designer in the solution of problems concerned with a total environment. To base a "correct" color scheme on a scientific color system would be somewhat like writing poetry based on the knowledge of the alphabet. At best, designers can work with color systems in terms of communicating verbal description of color to manufacturers or painters. The worst approach for a designer is to use a set of rules on color out of context and to use color as if it existed in a vacuum. But even communications present serious difficulties, since color names without color samples do not convey a clear visual image. The color names invented for advertising purposes year after year by manufacturers of paints, textiles, and finishing materials are rather amusing, but meaningless as a tool of communication.

While we are discussing color as an abstract concept, mention should be made of the fact that in itself there is no such thing as a "bad" color. The quality of color depends on how and where it is used. Many people have strong color preferences and prejudices, and indeed certain colors or combinations of color are highly inappropriate for certain functions. But if one analyzes a great painting, for instance, into its component colors, one can find hundreds of hues, values, and chromatic variations. The fact that these colors are contained in a fine painting would not necessarily make them suitable as paint colors for interiors or as dye colors for fabrics. Yet even if an individual color isolated out of context seems sickly in itself, or if two out of hundreds of colors seem to clash, the proof to our thesis is in the fact that even the "bad" colors may be contained in a recognized masterpiece of painting. Another basic fact we must keep in mind is that every single material has some color, just as we saw that every material has some texture. Building materials such as stone, brick, slate, or wood have very definite colors; within one family of materials such as wood or stone there can be hundreds of color variations. The natural and honest colors of most materials, when used in their true expressive sense, are often far more beautiful than any artificially applied paint colors. A Frank Lloyd Wright interior is a good example of an often exciting and colorful space without the use of a single paint or dye color. Likewise some of Corbusier's interiors are subtle compositions of natural materials in their natural colors which provide more sparkle than many a lesser space in which strenuous efforts to combine painted and dyed surfaces appear just for what they are—a forced exercise in color combinations, without realization that the three-dimensional effect of the total space should provide the color and contrast of textures as a total entity.

We perceive color contrast or differentiation between lights and darks more readily and more strongly than mere color variations. If we look at a simple shape like the cube pictured here for instance, we cannot mistake the shape of the object for anything but a cube—even if no line has been used for delineation. But the same cube presented as a line drawing without any shading whatsoever is less apparent to the eye as a cube, and can be interpreted as a series of parallelograms, as a cube, or as an interior view of a cube. It is indeed the reflection of light, the contrast of light and dark, the emphasis of shades and shadows that makes a space come to life, and that is more significant for a strong architectural interior than a decorative choice of wall and floor surfaces.

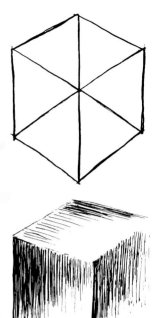

Popular decorating magazines, manufacturers of home-furnishings products, and fashion magazines attempt year after year to prescribe a fashionable or "correct" set of color schemes. A great many cliché-ridden rules on colors for interiors have been published attempting to pronounce a "correct" color for certain areas, such as kitchen, living room, or office. None of these "correct" colors is meaningful, as shown by the very fact that they change year after year. If there is any basic color that one could recommend as a sound one for most interiors (where no natural materials with indigenous colors have been used) it would be white. This is by far the best background color for almost all purposes, and it is the one color with the best quality for the reflection of light.

We do not mean to imply that color is not an important part of interior design. The experienced designer can create exciting effects with color accents, fabrics, and materials; and bold colors in the hands of experts can make a stimulating environment even within a rather ordinary architectural space. But the stress must be on the relation of one color to another, on the contrasts created, and above all on sensitive attention to the overall design. Since color is in fact reflected light, one can observe the influence of light or color on interior spaces by studying the effect of both daylight and artificial light on the character of interior spaces.

A space flooded with uniform light might be a good work environment, but is not necessarily a pleasant interior. The lighting system known as "luminous ceilings" can, through the careful work of an illuminating engineer, be designed to give a strong and steady light on the work surface, with hardly any shadows cast at all.

For office work, or drafting, this might be desirable, but for relaxation, dining, or living, it could be rather dreadful. A space illuminated by large picture windows on all sides of the room will provide good and clear daylight, but little interest. Daylighting consideration must also be tempered by the climate, season, exposure, and geographical location. The movement of the earth around the sun provides a natural variant, but one which in certain locations must be carefully controlled through shading, overhangs, or curtains. The size and location of windows—whether picture windows, clerestory windows, or skylights—should be very carefully designed in relation to the function of the interior space, and even in relation to the planned furniture arrangement. This unfortunately happens only if an interior designer works closely with the architect, or if the architect pays careful attention to interior design.

A certain amount of light variation within a space is highly desirable unless the specific task (for example, surgery) demands specialized illumination. We made a similar statement about the use of textures, and repeated this view in discussing color. A delightful residential space might have standard windows, high windows, and a skylight. This is not just variety for the sake of variety: it creates highlights, shades, and shadows, and it also creates the kind of natural light that brings out the visibility of texture and color. The same space lit uniformly by either daylight or artificial illumination would appear dull and cold.

One of the essential basic controls of light is the elimination of glare. We have all experienced the blinding effect of looking directly into sunlight or into a strong source of electric light. Daylight control of glare can be achieved with roof overhangs, with sunbreaks, or with any number of interior controls such as blinds, shades, and curtains. Unlike the shape and form of a building or interior, the quality of light inside a building is not a static component, and the designer must provide flexibility to meet changing needs and conditions. The controls needed for electric lighting are numerous and technically rather complex, and will be discussed in more detail in another chapter. The visual effect of light on form, texture, color, and all other aspects of design is, however, a reality in either daylight or artificial illumination.

One of the considerations one must keep in mind in dealing with light and color is the character or the atmosphere of a space. Although much has been written about the psychology of color, and some serious experiments have been done on the effect of color and light on the inhabitants of interiors, no firm facts and guidelines are available to the designer as yet. The emotions that can be evoked through controlled environment vary considerably from social group to social group. It is not always true that warm colors create a "happy" mood, nor is our

Le Corbusier's Marseilles Block. Notice use of sunshades. (Photograph by John Pile)

concept of warm colors (the reds, oranges, and yellows) a fool-proof guideline for the designer. It might be assumed that these colors would be highly suitable for colder climates, and that the cool colors (blues and greens) would provide a better environmental background in warm climates. Nothing is farther from the truth. In fact, many tropical climates have developed independently from each other's civilizations a strong preference for "hot" color combinations, which are used frequently in their interiors. Psychological associations with colors also tend to vary from group to group. Black, in our society, is associated with death; yet there are ethnic groups where the opposite color—white—is the color associated with death. Our society would in general associate a dark, poorly lit interior with a glum and serious mood, whereas some tropical or Southern societies prefer to counteract the bright exterior sunlight with subdued and rather dark interiors.

This chapter dealing with color and light is the last one in Part Two concerned with the vocabulary of design. In these four chapters a number of terms frequently used in discussing design and architecture have been discussed and explained. It should be quite clear that no rules have been established and that no attempt has been made to present a paradigm on design. If there is a conclusion which can be drawn, and which should, in fact, be clearly understood in summary, it is that all phases and facets of design are important in relation to each other. No book of rules or dictionary on design should ever substitute for creativity. The successful integration of all aspects of design is precisely the function of the good designer.

5

STYLE

Style is a concept very quickly associated with interior design by the layman; yet to confuse creative design with stylistic imitation is one of the age-old pitfalls even for the semiprofessional designer. Style can mean several things. It can denote the personal expression that a designer will bring to every job he does. It can mean the qualitative expression of a design, or of almost any action from literary achievement to social graces. It can also refer to the expression of a particular era or culture such as the Gothic style, or a period of time such as the Victorian era. It is style in the latter sense which requires some rather careful analysis. There is hardly a designer or teacher who has not many times encountered the question, "What style or period do you prefer?" The temptation is to answer this sort of question with a casual or glib reply, but it seems important to explore the whole question of period and styles in a somewhat more searching way.

The briefest glance at history will tell us that none of the arts has ever existed in isolation, but they have always been strongly interrelated. In fact, one sees such strong stylistic influences from one field to another that the term "environmental" design, which has become the fashionable term in our field, no longer seems quite so new. It appears, in other words, as if throughout history, painting and sculpture, architecture and landscape architecture, interior design and furnishings, were always strongly related through similarities in style. The influence of style has always been felt in all aspects of human thought and endeavor; the arts, the sciences, and literature have always developed along similar conceptional lines. In the broadest possible sense one might sum up the recent history

The Parthenon.

of civilized man in a classification of three major eras. First was the age of idealism, typified by Greek classical thought and philosophy. Certainly we can recognize the "idealistic" style in Greek sculpture and art and even in Greek architecture. We can classify the era starting with the early Renaissance as the age of realism. Renaissance painting and sculpture, the concern with the importance of the individual man, and even political thought of the era all exemplify realism in a broad sense. The third major era is our present one, which we might call the age of symbolism. Abstract expressionist painting, and the theory of relativity represent some of the early symbols of the age, which in the recent present have been replaced by the computer, electronic music, and the new math.

Each of these eras borrowed heavily from a preceding one, and each more precisely defined era in the development of the arts has been built upon the foundation of previous thought and development. The further back we go in history, the more objective we can become in our evaluation and critical reaction. Most of us would agree that Greek sculpture was more meaningful and original than Roman sculpture, because clearly the Romans tried to imitate the sculptural concepts established by the Greeks. Upon closer examination one can notice that even the great works of art throughout history were rarely truly original and creative, but were stylistically influenced by preceding styles. The great Parthenon essentially used a wood construction concept interpreted into stone construc-

**Gothic cathedrals
showing flying buttresses
and stone vaulting.**

tion, as shown rather clearly in the fluting of the columns and
in the handling of post and lintel in a somewhat naïve and
spatially limiting way. How much greater in a creative sense
were the subsequent developments in stone when some truly
original designs in vaulted stone construction were built, and
beautiful cathedrals using the principle of flying buttresses
were erected.

When we trace the development of architectural and interior
styles throughout history we meet the strongest influence on
our current "traditions" somewhere around the eighteenth
century. This is strange when one realizes that eighteenth-
century European interior and furniture design was far from
original. In fact some of the most famous designers of that

era showed a spectacular lack of originality. For example, the work of the famous English-Scottish architect and interior designer, Robert Adam, was extremely elegant and decorative with great attention to meticulous details, yet was all based on classical sources. It seems puzzling that Adam and other eighteenth-century designers who borrowed so heavily from previous styles should now be the dominant trend-setting influence in the twentieth century. Another fashionable and popular eighteenth-century designer was the cabinetmaker Thomas Chippendale. Yet an examination of the book he published on his designs, the *Gentlemen's Guide to Cabinetmaking*, will make even his most ardent admirers happy at heart that only a few of his designs have survived into our present time, since so much in the book is really quite ugly.

The periods which are associated with definition of style in interiors are by and large based on furniture design, and we must recognize that furniture making is an art form—a lesser art form perhaps, but one having something in common with painting, music, and writing in that it expresses the ideals and the everyday life of the period in history which named it. To understand period furniture and historic styles, one must always visualize some of the social, political, and religious life of the people who designed and used such furniture.

It is easy to look at the graceful, feminine lines of a Louis XV chair, delicately curved and luxuriously upholstered, and to see it as an expression of an irresponsible court life, where dress, jewels, insincere gallantries, the studied figures of the minuet, and other nonessentials occupied the minds of the rulers of France more than either religious or social issues.

It is also easy to look at our own strong, crudely fashioned early American furniture and see in our mind's eye the life of the settler who fashioned it. Life was rugged, time was precious, and articles of furniture were confined to essentials made from pine, maple, cherry, or oak trees which the involuntary craftsman found around his home. A need for an economical use of space for utility purposes fathered the corner cupboard. "Functional" is the word for dough boxes which served as tables, and for hutch tables which turned into chairs and had storage compartments for the family Bible as well. Such furniture is an eloquent expression of a life composed of hardship, prayer, and work.

Each style throughout history reveals definite social influences, and in all cases strongly reflects the mores of the society at that particular time; in almost all cases furniture styles also reveal an attempt to use the most sophisticated methods of fur-

Louis XV armchair. (Metropolitan Museum of Art,
Bequest of Catherine D. Wentworth, 1948)

niture making and craftsmanship available to the artisans of
the period.

Mentioning the mores of society brings up the subject of
fashion, which is quite different from style. Change, growth,
development, and variety are human needs, and an examination of fashion trends in psychological terms will attest to
these needs in all aspects of human activity.

Added to this psychological need for change, we have also
developed an economical need for change and continually
increased production and consumption, especially in highly
industrialized societies. These factors—the need and desire for
change—cause problems in design and in the visual environment. In theory there is something we might call the "ultimate
design", but we rarely seem to accept any design solution as

**Seventeenth-century
American chair-table.**
(Metropolitan Museum of
Art, Gift of Mrs. Russell
Sage, 1909)

permanent or ultimate. It would seem very difficult to improve upon the basic shape of a spoon. That shape has evolved functionally to fit the mouth, and there seems little likelihood of improving it other than through minor variations and embellishments of the handle. Designers are of course the least likely group of people to advocate the *status quo* in any designed product; the need for change and the definition of "design" as a creative force and activity in the present is clear. Since man likes change and industry needs changes, it can happen—as it has happened in the past thirty years in the United States—that a great deal of very bad contemporary design comes forth. Previously this happened in the early stages of the Industrial Revolution in England, when manufacturers were first faced with the challenge of producing goods in a machine-oriented manufacturing process. It happened again with the post-World War II rapid industrial development and the vastly increased world population. Until not very long ago few industries found it necessary to employ the services of designers, and the profession of industrial design dates back no farther than the emergence of the interior designers as serious professionals. The resulting products were often ugly and absurd, and many products and furnishings came into being in which a meaningless juggling of parts and pointless superficial decorations represented the frantic attempt to create new designs. Housing experienced a similar fate; buildings built without architects, and development houses thrown together by builders and plunked down on the raped and violated countryside were the norm. These comments are not intended to justify the public's predilection for so-called period styles in interiors and furnishings, but they are a partial explanation for the causes of much of the poor design surrounding us.

Interior design is very much a part of architecture, and most interiors are generated by architecture. Twentieth-century architecture did not fully emerge as a forceful, indigenous design expression until the 1930's. Until that time the fashionable contemporary styles were very much in the Victorian tradition. They were copies and imitations of the previous periods. This was reflected in the teaching of architecture and design. A typical school problem for the young designer was to design, for instance, a city hall in "classical" style or a church in "Gothic" style. The amusing fact is that stylistic imitations were contemporary in spite of the intent of the designers to have them represent something from eras bygone. Materials, building or manufacturing methods, and craftsmanship left their recognizable imprint on each period. A "Gothic" church from the year 1820 can be spotted as such, and a "Gothic" church from 1920 has the imprint of that year as clearly as the date on the keystone. The real change towards meaningful contemporary design in our century probably started with the establishment of the famous Bauhaus school in Germany in the 1920's. Since that time architecture and design throughout the Western world have slowly advanced towards a true expression of our times, our way of life, our methods, and our materials.

The process has been, and is, slow in the furniture and interior design field because the typical manufacturing enterprises have for years been nothing but small craft woodworking shops simply blown up into larger scale. The labor force thus consists of artisans whose skills and traditions of craftsmanship are based on handwork, and it is indeed a slow process to change traditions dating back hundreds of years. Manufacturers are likely to state that they must produce what the public demands, but in an industrial economy like ours the demand is really created by the manufacturers and the products they advertise. The preference for "traditional" styles shown by a large part of our population is in part a myth created by industry and perpetuated by interior decorators and retail merchants.

No society in the history of civilization has been more progress-oriented than ours in twentieth-century America. In everything, that is, except interiors and furniture. The typical American man wants to live five years into the future, rather than in the present or in the environment created two years ago. An automobile older than two years should really be traded in against next year's model. When color television became available it was far from perfect, but the public was willing to pay high prices and suffer poor performance because it was new. Kitchen appliances and gadgets, mass transportation and highways, and just about any type of machinery became desirable because they were new. As a progress-oriented society we have conquered space, and we have unleashed the forces of the atom. We have put our trust and our future into the hands of computers, and we are developing airplanes that cannot possibly be of use to society until we solve the problem of sonic boom and adequate airport facilities. One cannot therefore label our particular society as tradition-oriented, as some Far Eastern and Oriental societies were until very recent years. The clinging to pseudo-traditional environment for home life can only be labeled as a puzzling psychological mass phenomenon, and a real paradox in our current life.

A very clear distinction must be made at this point between

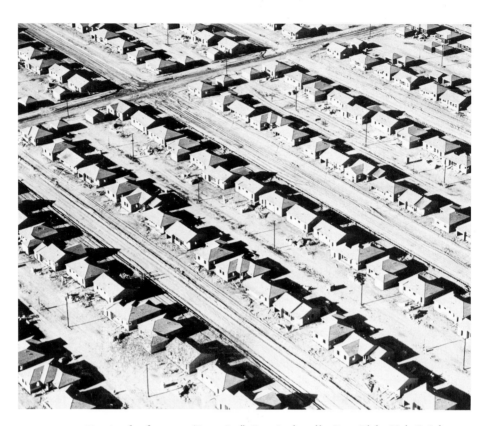

Housing development. (From *God's Own Junkyard* by Peter Blake. Holt, Reinhart and Winston Inc.)

authentic and fake traditional interiors and furnishings. Many of the old surviving pieces and interiors—as early as some Egyptian ones and as recent as some from the Victorian period —are indeed valuable, beautiful, and meaningful. They are, at their best, an expression of the cultural and artistic life of their time. They are beautiful in museums and historic restorations, and they are beautiful in private possession in homes where there is appropriate space and where facilities exist to care for their maintenance. Some period pieces are works of art, and are as valuable as paintings and sculpture. The implied criticism in the foregoing pages refers to the fakes, to the reproductions, and to the period styles invented by advertising agencies in their frantic search for novelties. Styles such as "Mediterranean" or "Italian Provincial" have no historic existence and have no meaning. Some of the so-called styles offered to the unsuspecting public from time to time sound like science fiction in reverse. Through this strange hankering for the past

The library, Kenwood House, Hampstead, London, Robert and James Adam, 1767-68. One of the most admired of the Adams' interiors.

French Rococo interior; a salon of the Petit Trianon at Versailles. (Photograph by John Pile)

**Sunar, Showroom, Houston, Texas.
Michael Graves, architect and interior designer.**
(Photograph by Charles McGrath)

**Open offices surround a garden-atrium.
Corporate headquarters of John Deere and Co.,
Moline, Illinois. Roche Dinkeloo, architects.**
(Photograph by John Pile)

**Knoll International Showroom, Boston.
Charles Gwathmey and Robert Siegel,
architects.** (Photograph by Steve Rosenthal)

**Los Angeles Ticket Office for Pakistan
International Airlines. Designed by
The Space Design Group.**

we have encouraged a trend toward imitating materials out of other materials and out of styles that never existed; much of the ugliness around us, especially in home furnishing products, is the result of this mistaken search for a past that never existed—or that would have no meaning and relationship to our present-day life, even if it did exist.

It is somewhat more difficult to make decisive statements about really good reproductions, except to repeat that it is just about impossible ever to reproduce the past without leaving a clear imprint of the present.

There are, however, questions unanswered in the philosophy of art in spite of the many tomes that have been written about them. Is, for instance, the first cast made of a piece of sculpture the only valid one? How many casts of the same mold constitute original art? Is a Sheraton chair only valid if made in Sheraton's own workshop—what if it were made at Sheraton's time in another cabinetmaker's shop, or what if it were made in his own shop ten or fifteen years after his death? There are no clear answers to these questions. But it seems probable that given a choice most people would prefer to own an original painting rather than a reproduction. It also seems likely that most people would prefer a print that was run in a limited edition of fifty and signed by the artist, to one that was run off from a plate in an unsigned edition of many thousands.

Even if it were possible to create very accurate and exact copies of traditional furniture and interiors, they would be totally inappropriate for today's living and living spaces. Our way of life has changed. Many of the period pieces admired by all were designed for the palaces and homes of kings and nobles. Twentieth-century buildings do not provide the space and setting for these pieces. The scores of servants at the beck of the rulers of old exist in no households today. Very few families have any servants at all, and the modern homemaker does not have the time to take care of elaborate furnishings. An example of the Louis XV period, an expression of life at court, is totally out of place in a suburban home with children romping around, and the homemaker acting as chauffeur, cook, and nursemaid.

This does not mean that some genuine period pieces have no place in today's interiors. It is indeed a fact that many traditional pieces of furniture are as timeless in their beauty and as desirable as paintings and other works of art for the collector or owner. Nor is it implied that a completely personal

Atrium with cafeteria in corporate headquarters of Xerox Corp., Stanford, Connecticut. I.S.D., Inc., interior design. (Photograph by Jaime Ardiles-Arce)

**Habitat 67, Montreal.
M. Safdie, architect.**

interior created in some anonymous or ugly building is not justified at times in overcoming and defying a dull and meaningless architectural envelope. But when interiors are designed inside good buildings, an alien and artificial style violates the existing character. It is not unusual to spot eighteenth- or nineteenth-century curtain arrangements spoiling the façade of a well-designed contemporary high-rise apartment building, and enhancing the building façade with as much success as a jet plane flying over an open-air concert. One of the most exciting developments in recent architectural history was the Habitat project at the Montreal World's Fair. It was sad to see many model units furnished in pseudo-traditional "Quebec Provincial" style (Moshe Safdie, the architect of Habitat, objected to the furnishings as well). But it was encouraging to note the comments by visitors, who without fail objected to the inappropriate furnishings in the display.

Much of the foregoing discussion refers to interior design of residences, and obviously we must accept everybody's right to live in as personal or stagelike an environment as desire or fashion might seem to suggest. One does not, however, have to agree completely with Shakespeare's saying that "all the world's a stage" when it comes to public interiors. There exist many hotels, building lobbies, banks, or stores that have been built in recent years inside the most advanced contemporary buildings but that attempt to be quaint or elegant traditional interiors. All of these artificial copies of past styles are doomed to failure and are often ludicrous as well as ugly. Many of the illustrations of public interiors in Part Four show with great clarity that elegance and splendor in a twentieth-century building is far more successful if the interiors are handled in the manner appropriate to the architecture and technology of this century.

In summary we should reiterate the importance of an understanding of the development of styles in interiors by pointing again to the influence of one period upon another. The knowledge of history is essential for the designer. A conscious understanding of stylistic developments can be an important tool for the designer. But we must strive to keep history and present apart, as clearly as creativity and imitation. And when one has learned to understand the validity of traditional architectural and interior styles, and to recognize their good and sometimes their bad features, one can really sum up the discussion with this statement: There are no periods and styles that are better than others. There is in essence no such thing as traditional design or modern design. There are only two kinds of design that matter—good design and bad design—and there can be no argument about which one we prefer.

6

HISTORIC FURNITURE

It may seem strange to find a chapter devoted to historic furniture following the chapters devoted to a discussion of the vocabulary of design. The reasons for the confusion of style and design are made clear in the preceding chapter. Historic furniture is indeed of great importance to interior design. In order to stress this importance as factual information rather than an element of creative design we present this chapter as one of the significant elements of the interior designer's vocabulary. While we mentioned in our discussion of style that the strongest influences and greatest popularity in current uses of traditional furnishings derive from somewhere around the eighteenth century, obviously the history of furniture starts with the earliest manmade structures. The singling out of the eighteenth century is really a pinpointing of the strongest influences on contemporary design as it occurs today, and at the same time a reflection of the popularity of the traditional styles used in our era. For the sake of historic accuracy, one must begin to consider the early seventeenth century as the period from which our furniture today descends. As a source of influence and inspiration, the interior designer must be familiar with these beginnings of furniture design which developed in cycles and which will be explained in chronological order in the following pages. As a matter of historical facts, a designer must have the knowledge to recognize the important periods and be familiar with the significant details that distinguish each period.

In a rather general classification one can separate period furniture into two major categories: formal and informal styles. Formal furniture designates the furniture that was once designed and executed for life at court or for the spacious homes of wealthy nobles and landowners. Preferences of reigning monarchs and their courts traditionally dictated styles, and for that reason major periods often bear a monarch's name (Georgian, Louis XVI).

The informal periods usually comprise the simpler pieces of furniture made by local craftsmen in their rural areas, where they plied their trade with limited tools, using local woods. Provincial styles and Early American furniture are examples of informal periods. The lines of such pieces often follow the more sophisticated styles, and were inspired by an occasional "imported" piece to the rural districts, or were based on "city" furniture remembered by a craftsman or country squire from his trips to the city.

It is clear, therefore, that no precise distinction can be made between formal and informal periods. It is also clear that upon an examination of periods by dates—dates that indicate the years during which any particular period flourished—one notices that many dates are overlapping, particularly during

Room from the Derby House, Salem, Mass., by Samuel McIntire, 1795–96. (Photograph by John Pile)

The library, Kenwood House, Hampstead, London. Robert and James Adam, 1767–68. One of the most admired of the Adams' interiors.
(see figure page 85)
(Photograph by John Pile)

the Georgian period. In France the periods designated by the names of the rulers Louis XV and Louis XVI were flourishing at the same time that the Georgian designers were creating furniture styles in England. It is inevitable, therefore, that each influenced the other: that is, that Sheraton borrowed details from the French; that the English Regency furniture was similar to the French Empire furniture; that Duncan Phyfe in America was inspired by a little of everything that preceded him. Each period overlaps another somewhat and, therefore, it is difficult to be hard and fast about dates and details. For a quick judgment as to the period of any piece of furniture, probably the most characteristic part of the piece will be its legs and feet. Scrutinize these and then look at the decorative details, and you ought to be able to make a fairly accurate judgment. No one leg or detail is completely typical of any one period, however. The charts following on the next pages will point out the typical details that are the characteristics of each period.

Since the charts begin to list periods from the start of the seventeenth century only, we must make brief mention at least of the preceding eras. The first important major period for the

An early 19th Century interior with a sense of simplicity suggesting modern work. A room in the Sabathday Lake, Maine community of the American Shakers. (Photographs by John Pile)

development of free-standing furniture lasted from about A.D. 1100 to 1500 and can be described as Gothic. Furniture throughout Europe was similar. It was heavy and ornate and much of it was ecclesiastically inspired, and in fact was often made in monasteries. The sixteenth century saw the flourishing of the Renaissance, the revival of classic culture. Furniture making prospered and became one of many respected crafts, but because of the era's interest in classical origins, most Renaissance furniture throughout Europe had rather similar characteristics. England, which was more distant from the mainstream of Renaissance thought and development, developed Tudor and Elizabethan furniture, combining some earlier Gothic concepts into the newer styles becoming fashionable on the European continent. Mention was made earlier of the fact that furniture history is as old as recorded history; indeed some few examples from early Egypt have survived, and Greece, Rome, the Near East, and the Orient have all developed some interesting and beautiful furniture. Our twentieth-century design, however, has barely been affected or influenced by these periods, or if at all, only in indirect ways such as the Oriental influence, for example, which came to European furniture in the form of Chinese Chippendale.

Therefore the following charts do not attempt to present a complete history of furniture, but rather to pinpoint the key English, French, and American periods, and to show them in chronological order with mention of major significant characteristics.

PRINCIPAL PERIODS OF ENGLISH FURNITURE

Period	Typical Details	Typical Woods and Pieces	General
Jacobean 1603–1649 (James I, Charles I)	Heavily ornamented Carved paneling Turned legs	Mostly oak Heavy chests, tables, and chairs	Tapestry and needle work used frequently for upholstery
William and Mary 1689–1702	Hooded tops, lacquer, tear-drop, tulips Trumpet-turned leg, baluster leg, bun foot	Walnut and oak Cabinets, small chairs, occasional tables (for style of tea drinking)	Dutch influence strong Marquetry became popular
Queen Anne 1702–1714	Cockle shell (carved) Flame finial, caning Cabriole leg, bun foot	Walnut, some mahogany Wing chairs, tallboys, secretaries	Some Oriental influences
Georgian (Chippendale) 1714–1765	Piecrust table tops, Chinese lattice and fret work, Rococo ornament Cabriole leg with claw and ball foot	Mahogany Camelback sofas, mirror and picture frames, china shelves and cabinets, chairs	Thomas Chippendale was successful cabinetmaker to society. Combined Gothic, Chinese, and Rococo details
Georgian (Adam) 1760–1792	Classical ornaments (wheels, lyres, urns) Straight and tapered legs, square or round, fluted or reeded	Mahogany, satinwood, and painted wood Console tables, chairs, sideboards, knife urns	Robert Adam and brothers, architects who designed many elegant country homes, developed furniture to match delicate decorations

Period	Typical Details	Typical Woods and Pieces	General
Georgian (Sheraton) 1780–1806	Inlays, swags, fan motif Slender round legs--reeded, spade, or collar feet	Mahogany, rosewood, and satinwood Cabinets, secretaries, sideboards, dressers, chairs	Thomas Sheraton was a cabinetmaker and scholar, preacher, and teacher
Georgian (Hepplewhite) 1770–1786	Wheat and Urns, shield backs and oval backs, Prince of Wales plumes Slender tapered legs, straight foot	Mahogany and satinwood Chairs, sideboards, and consoles	George Hepplewhite, like Chippendale and Sheraton, a cabinetmaker in Georgian period
Regency (George IV as Prince of Wales) 1810–1820	Floral designs Chinese motifs Legs usually straight and sometimes fluted	Mahogany, rosewood, also black and gilt paints Chairs, tables, sofas and beds	Prince of Wales strongly influenced by classical period in France of that time
Victorian 1830–1901	Much of everything Carved and turned pedestals, spool turnings, sweeping curved backs on sofas	Variety of woods, but much mahogany, walnut and oak Occasional tables and stands—round and oval	Growth of industrialism. Eclecticism. Queen Victoria's husband, Prince Albert, set much of the "taste"

Two typical examples of chairs designed by Thomas Chippendale.

An ornate Georgian library of 1748 from Kirtlington Park in England, now installed
in the Metropolitan Museum of Art in New York City. (Photograph by John Pile)

A Victorian parlor; the home of Thomas Carlyle in London. (Photograph by John Pile)

PRINCIPAL PERIODS OF FRENCH FURNITURE

Period	Typical Details	Typical Woods and Pieces	General
Louis XIV 1643–1715	Large-scale furniture	Oak, walnut, chestnut	Baroque style decorations
	Heavy carving and ornamentation, palm leaves, scrolls	Large sofas, consoles, armchairs	Ormolu (gilded bronze) became popular
	Straight lines predominate		Building of Versailles
Louis XV 1723–1774	Ornamental veneers, marquetry, plaques, lacquer	Mahogany, oak, rosewood, tulipwood	During early years of Louis XV "Regence". When Louis began reign he encouraged more luxurious and delicate designs (Rococo style)
	Curved and carved forms	Chaise lounges, fauteuil (large armchair), bergere (small armchair)	
	Cabriole legs, scroll feet		
Louis XVI 1774–1793	Classic details, inlay, and painted decorations	Mahogany, beech, walnut	Marie Antoinette was Queen
	Straight tapered and reeded legs	Chairs, daybeds, tea tables	Rococo continued
			Furniture development parallels classic style of Adam brothers
Directoire 1795–1804 ⎱ similar ⎰ **Empire** 1804–1815	Simpler and purer style of Directoire became more ornate under Napoleon	Mahogany, rosewood, oak	Napoleonic era
	Tapered Pillar legs and round legs—ball feet	Roman chairs, gondola chairs, sofas and beds	Egyptian motifs and Napoleonic Bee were popular

French Rococo interior; a salon of the Petit Trianon at Versailles; See also page 85. (Photograph by John Pile)

PRINCIPAL PERIODS OF AMERICAN FURNITURE

Period	Typical Details	Typical Woods and Pieces	General
Early American (Pilgrim) 1620–1720	Sturdy and crude construction. Utility was first consideration. Primitive details	Maple, oak, or any locally available wood Benches, cupboards, chests, tables Dual-purpose pieces	Serviceability was a prime requisite. Furniture reflects Puritan and pioneering spirit
Georgian 1720–1790	Details echo the styles of Queen Anne, Chippendale, Sheraton, and Hepplewhite	Walnut and mahogany	Gradual introduction of more accurate copies of prevalent English styles
Federal (Duncan Phyfe) 1790–1830	Lyre motif, also Eagle French Directoire and Empire influence Brass terminals on reeded and curved legs	Mahogany Chairs, tables, sofas	Period covers era between late Colonial and Victorian. Duncan Phyfe (cabinet-maker) strongest indigenous influence

An ornate Victorian "two-seater".

Other Noteworthy American Periods

Pennsylvania Dutch 1680–1850	Similar to Early American		German influence
Shaker 1776–1850	Slatbacks, good craftsmanship	Pine and maple	Shakers were religious sect deriving from Quakers
Victorian 1830–1901	Similar to English Victorian		

III

ARCHITECTURE

Interior design as an art and as a profession is intimately connected with architecture. In fact, it is a subdivision of the architectural profession that has become so specialized as now to be regarded as a separate field. Interior designers are not required to have the same complete education in structural techniques as architects, nor are they under the same legal licensing requirements as architects because their work does not deal with the aspects of building that affect structural strength and safety. Nevertheless, many architects elect to specialize in interior design and all good architects must have an understanding of what interior design is if they are really to make their buildings complete internally.

Whenever a building is well-designed architecturally, the interior designer has an obligation to make his work augment and support the work of the architect. There are, unfortunately, all too many bad buildings, both old and new, and the interior designer often finds that his work will go into such buildings. Even then, however, he needs architectural understanding to grasp what is wrong, and to help him find ways to minimize the effects of the architect's mistakes within the interior spaces. In many cases the interior designer may be a part of the architect's organization, or may be an independent professional working closely with the architect as a consultant. In such cases, communication between architect and interior designer can be easy as long as each understands the aims and the language of the other. Where the interior designer is working on a project in an older building, in remodeling, and in situa-

The sanatorium at Paimio, Finland designed by Alvar Aalto in 1932. (Photograph by John Pile)

tions in the rented spaces of large office or apartment buildings, there may be no direct communication with the building's architect, but the interior designer still has an obligation to understand the architecture of the building so that his work enhances what may be good and counters anything that may be bad in the situation given to him.

Architecture has been recognized as both art and profession for a very long time and has a vast serious literature dating back at least as far as ancient Rome. Every interior designer needs to be knowledgeable about architectural history and theory, and to know about the aspects of modern practical matters that affect his part of the total architectural field. This book cannot possibly include more than a brief summary of the territory which must interest the interior designer. The bibliography at the end of the book suggests some of the excellent books which the reader may want to explore. It is suggested that a well-illustrated architectural history (such as Nikolaus Pevsner's Outline of European Architecture, *1943) and some book about modern architecture (such as J. M. Richards'* Introduction to Modern Architecture, *1940) might be kept at hand while reading Part Three to provide additional illustrations and information.*

1

FUNCTION AND PLANNING

As an art, it is clear that there are several things about architecture that make it very different from painting, sculpture, or music. The most obvious difference is that a building must serve a practical purpose—indeed, from the point of view of the owner and user, that is generally the only reason for building at all. The painter, sculptor, or musical composer can usually afford to buy their own materials and produce their works entirely on their own, and no one asks that they serve any purpose except an artistic one. The architect can do nothing, in most cases, until a client comes to him ready to pay the cost of building; and then the client comes not to obtain a work of art, but to get the house, factory, office building, hospital, or school that is needed so that it can be put to use. He is usually willing to make his building a "work of art" as well, if he can be sure that this will not cost money or interfere with practical workings, but the fear of those possibilities leads many clients to seek out architects who minimize their creative role as artists. Every architect must, of course, be a practical man. His client needs him as an expert in functional planning and in the technology of building, and it is these aspects of his work that lead to buildings that work well and last well. Faults in these parts of an architect's work are the faults that any sensible man can discover and criticize, and we have all heard jeers at architects who have forgotten a stairway or a door, or whose buildings develop cracks and leaks. Architects, theorists, and laymen all agree that no building can be considered a good piece of architecture if it has serious faults of either functional or structural sort. Because of the complexity of modern building and the somewhat primitive nature of our building methods, no large building can be without some minor defects when it is first completed. It is a mistake to say that an architect is incompetent just because of some leaks and cracks when a building is new, but if there are major problems that cannot be corrected, or if a building actually sags or collapses, we are quite justified in saying that it was an architectural failure, quite aside from whether we like or dislike the design.

Similiarly, good architecture means skillful functional planning. Spaces must be of the right sizes and shapes and must be located with regard to problems of circulation, communication, privacy, and orientation. Suitable lighting, plumbing, and heating must be provided for. In the area of planning, while we can easily recognize bad mistakes (a kitchen too far from a dining room, a bedroom too small to hold a bed), it is less easy to make a clear separation between "good" and "bad" plans. Most houses built by speculative builders are badly planned, yet their owners are quite satisfied with this planning. We are only justified in calling the planning "bad" because it is so easy for any trained architect to discover hundreds of improvements that could be easily made without any additional cost. The planning of the majority of modern buildings probably falls into a middle area, good enough to keep owners and users from protesting, but actually not nearly as good as the work of the most expert of architects. We must also remember that the uses of buildings may change as time goes by so that many plans which were excellent for the program established when the building was new turn out to be unsatisfactory years later. The best planning includes some study of predicted future changes and tries to provide for these, but all predictions are subject to question. The architect of an airport terminal cannot know what conditions will be like in fifty years since no one can guess that far ahead what will happen to transportation equipment. He can only try to make his building flexible in the hope that it will not become obsolete almost before it is finished as has so often happened with this particular architectural type.

Good plan and structure are all we ask of the building projects of technical men such as highway engineers or the structural engineers who design some factories or bridges. That is often all that a client asks of an architect too. But the architect himself, other architects, architectural critics, and sensitive and intelligent laymen expect more. They recognize that architecture is an art as well as a craft and they expect a building to be a work of art. Only the best buildings really deserve this description, but the possibility exists every time anything is built. Anyone can recognize that the greatness of many famous historic buildings is not just the result of their doing their job and standing up well. A pyramid, a Roman amphitheater, or a cathedral are great for reasons that go beyond their doing an adequate job of being a tomb, a stadium, or a church. Not many modern buildings deserve to be mentioned in the same breath with such historical examples, but some do, and these are the buildings that demonstrate that architecture can be an art whenever the architect has the necessary ability and determination.

If asked *why* architecture is considered an art, most people would probably say they suppose it is because a building can be beautiful. While this answer has a certain superficial validity, it does not satisfy the more thoughtful theorist. After all, a bridge, a ship, or an airplane can be beautiful also, but designers specialized in those fields are not considered to be artists in the same way that architects are. It is not an answer that will satisfy the thoughtful architect either, since he knows that *trying* to make a building beautiful is not a very effective way to get good architectural results. Every art, by the use of a particular medium, is concerned with transmitting ideas and emotions that go beyond a strictly utilitarian level. Words are probably our favorite medium of communication in modern life. We use them for every sort of utilitarian purpose from street signs to business letters to news reports. None of these things is thought of as an art, but a poem or a novel can be an example of the art of literature if it communicates thoughts and emotions that go beyond a factual and utilitarian level. A poem may, in fact, not have any clear "meaning" in the usual sense, and still be an effective communicator of emotion or feeling. Painting is the art concerned with using the two-dimensional surface of a canvas as a space in which color and shape can be used for similar communication. Modern painters make it clear that there need not be recognizable images in order for a painting to be a success. The sculptor uses solid, three-dimensional mass in much the same way. If we try to analyze the medium of the architect in a comparable way, we find that it has some things in common with sculpture, but that it is also quite different.

The solid mass of a building affects us in much the same way that sculpture does. We can be impressed, excited, or moved by the sight of a tower or a dome or the form of a factory or cottage. This is not the whole story about architecture, however—in fact, it is not the most important part of the story. The architect does not work in *solid* masses; indeed, a solid building would have very little use. The only important historic buildings that are almost solid are the Egyptian pyramids, and it is not unfair to say that they are more sculptural than architectural in concept. A building is normally hollow and, in order to fully understand it and appreciate it, we must go inside and move from space to space. The better the piece of architecture is, the more important it is to move through it. We are justified in being disappointed in many modern skyscraper office buildings because they offer us so little beyond the sculptural mass of the exterior. Going inside is often uninteresting and disappointing. A cathedral, an opera house, or even a simple residence requires us to know it inside and out if we are to understand it and experience the ideas, emotions, or feelings that the architect built into it.

Architecture, then, is the art that deals with space. It deals with outdoor space through placing buildings in relation to one another and through the special problems of town or city planning. It is interesting to notice that the art that deals only with outdoor space is given the name of landscape architecture in recognition of its similarity to architecture. Architecture itself, however, deals with interior space also, and it is clear that the most exciting and interesting buildings are always those with exciting interior space concepts. Nothing could make more clear the central role of the interior designer in the field of architecture than the realization that it is the interior spaces that are most central to the expressive possibilities of this art.

Being an art of space, and particularly of interior space, gives to the art of architecture another special characteristic. To study a building, one must move about it, around it, into it, and through it—a process which takes time. A painting can be looked at all at once from a fixed point: one color picture captures it in total. Sculpture, at best, leads us to move around it also, but no sculpture (except for some recent experiments that are very like architecture) asks us to step inside and move about. To really "see" a cathedral can take hours and illustrating it might take dozens of photographs that would still fail to give us the full impact and feeling of the space itself. Architecture is then also an art concerned with movement, which must take place in time. Modern physics has made it clear that space and time are intertwined or can even be thought of as differing aspects of the same thing. It is certainly clear that one cannot experience space without spending time. It is interesting that Sigfried Giedion gave the title, *Space, Time and Architecture* (1941) to his book, which has come to be regarded as one of the best theoretical books about architecture written in modern times.

Having said this much about what architecture is, it might be useful to try to describe how an architect goes about designing a building. It is usually his client who initiates the process by having a specific need that leads him to an architect. The client requires a house, a factory, a shop, a school, or some other building to supply a specific need. The first step that the architect must take is to prepare what he will call a "program". The program is a statement in words in the form of a list of the detailed requirements for the new building. The making of a good program is basic to producing a good building, and it has only recently come to be realized that a bad or thoughtlessly made program stands behind much poor architecture. The client will often have attempted to make a program. He will, perhaps, say to his architect, "I want a center-hall colonial with three bedrooms, a separate dining room, and a two-car garage". Taking such a program at face value will lead an architect to produce an indifferent or bad house. He must persuade his client to allow the making of a new program that will be based on the actual nature of the client's family, its living habits, and future plans. It may turn out that there is no reason to make the house an imitation of a colonial design at all. This requirement may have been mentioned only because that was the only kind of house that the family knew about which seemed pleasant and cozy. The center hall might better become part of the living area, the separate dining room might really be a need, or might be a space that could be omitted entirely. The two-car garage might better be an open carport or might need to be an enclosed three-car garage. In any case, it will usually develop that the client's own program includes items that have been noted down quite thoughtlessly because the alternatives that exist have not been considered. A good program prepared by the architect will not fix anything that need not be fixed, but will include every fact that should influence the design of the building. It will include the special tastes and preferences of the owners and users, the detailed needs for spaces, equipment, and facilities; but it will not call for stock elements borrowed from other buildings, other periods, or arrived at without real understanding of genuine rather than imagined needs. A really good program tends to get the design process started in the direction of an outstanding design solution.

From the program, it is possible to extract a list of specific spaces that will be needed. Either there will be a clear area requirement for these spaces, or it will be necessary to give each space an area estimate based on the use that the space will have. It is tempting to call this a list of "rooms", but the term "room" leads us to think of a boxlike space with four walls and a door, which is often not at all the best kind of space for a particular use. Area requirements derive from such considerations as the number of people, the size of equipment, and the type of activity that will go on in a particular space. In a factory, this might mean the size and shape of machines; in an auditorium it will have to do with seats and aisles; in a house it may be a matter of considering size and shape of furniture together with people's need to move about and feel neither cramped nor lost in empty space.

Area requirements can be translated into blocks of space which can be drawn out on paper even though the exact shapes are still not set. Planning is largely a matter of arranging such blocks of space so that their relationships work out well from a practical point of view. This means placing things that have an interdependent relationship close together (kitchen and dining room, front door and coat closet) and making sure that the patterns of circulation or movement are smooth and direct. Spaces that will need daylight must be located so that they are near outside walls or can have skylights. "Orientation" means facing windows so as to take advantage of good views while avoiding unpleasant ones, and remembering that the sun will reach south-facing windows all day, never reach windows that face north, and reach east- and west-facing windows in morning and afternoon respectively. It may be desirable to group quiet activities and noisy ones and to provide some way of isolating each category. Entrances and exits must be of adequate size, well-placed, and properly protected by vestibules and control points. As areas are organized on the basis of such considerations, a building shape begins to develop. It must relate well to the site and to neighboring buildings. Often many different shapes are possible for the complete building, but each will relate to a particular system of internal area plan. If there is to be more than one floor level, the problem becomes more complex since spaces must be related in a vertical as well as a horizontal dimension. Each floor level is developed in plan on a flat sheet of paper, but the vertical relationship must be carried in the designer's mind with the aid of drawings called "sections", which show the proposed building sliced through. Stairs, elevators, escalators, and shafts for pipes and ducts must move through a multistory building, and must be placed where they will work well and not cause dislocations in the planning of the individual floors. In very tall buildings, the decisions about where things will be placed in the vertical direction may come before the detailed planning of the individual floors.

The architect must not go too far with planning before he begins to think about construction. Roofs and floors can only be held up by walls or columns, which must be placed in the plan where they will be most convenient and useful. It is not wise to plan a building completely and then call in an engineer to solve the construction problems (as was sometimes done in the past) because the plan may create problems that are impossible or at least very costly to solve and also because this leads to architecture in which the structure plays no important expressive part. The best buildings use the structural framing, walls, and roof systems as a part of their design and do not disguise these elements as if they were a necessary evil. Structural planning leads to thinking about questions of cost in a very direct way. Big open areas without columns are more costly than spaces with columns at regular intervals, but may be important for special purposes (an auditorium or an airplane hangar, for example). Steel construction makes it troublesome to space columns irregularly, while this is easy in concrete; as a result, concrete framing is usually preferred in apartment-house construction, where regular spacing of columns can make room planning difficult. High buildings are generally more costly per cubic foot of space than low ones because of the cost of elevators and stairs and the space that they occupy, but where a site is limited (as in crowded cities), a high building may be the only way to make economic use of a space. City building is regulated by very strict rules about the sizes and shapes of buildings (called "zoning laws") and by equally strict and complex rules about fire safety and structural solidity. The architect, in planning, must hold all of these interrelated matters in mind and juggle their often conflicting pressures in a way that will lead to a building that will be practical, solid, and economically logical.

Complex and difficult as all this may sound, it is still not the whole story. Along with solving all these practical problems, the good architect will keep in mind the goal of making his building a "work of art" as well. This means that he will evaluate every idea not only on the basis of how it will work, but also on the basis of how it will *seem*—that is, how it will look and feel to the people who will see and use the building. Many buildings that work quite well in a practical sense are still bad pieces of architecture because they are not worked out in this expressive sense. They confuse us and disturb us because their forms and spaces do not make us see and understand, and so enjoy, the solutions to practical problems that they offer. The best architecture always manages to be equally successful in solving practical and technical problems, and visual, expressive, and psychological ones—the solution of which makes a great building a great work of art.

2

HISTORIC DEVELOPMENT OF ARCHITECTURE

Historical architecture provides innumerable examples of this kind of synthesis of functional and expressive design. The program requirements for a tomb, a temple, or a church are fairly simple; but those for a huge public bath, a monastery, a castle, or a palace are as complex as those of most modern building situations. The technical systems of building were more limited, but the exploitation of available techniques in dome, vaulting, and similar structural systems were as adventurous as any modern engineering techniques. The architecture of an ancient Greek temple group, a medieval town, or an American colonial village are each so skillful and consistent that they are readily understood and enjoyed by almost everyone who visits the preserved examples. It is a curious fact of architectural history that this firm grasp of the basics of architecture began to be lost as our own era developed.

Architects, like all other artists, have always been borrowers of ideas from other times and places. Greek architecture borrowed from Egypt, and the Romans were heavy borrowers of ideas from Greece. Romanesque architecture is full of Roman elements and developed into Gothic. Renaissance architectural ideas were largely a matter of rediscovering the ancient classical work of Rome, while Georgian work in England and its colonial versions in America were actually part of the later phase of the Renaissance. Throughout all these borrowings, however, the new work was always original and characteristic of its own time, however much it may have borrowed from a past era. A Greek temple does not resemble anything Egyptian. The Romans' technical developments and new build-

The great pyramids at Giza, Egypt.
(Photograph by Irving Harper)

ing needs made it impossible for them to settle for duplications of Greek architecture even if they had wanted to do so. Gothic architecture is strikingly original, and the work of the Renaissance, much as it used ideas and details from classical antiquity, produced work that was also totally original and characteristic of its particular time. Beginning around the year 1800, however, architects began to think in terms of "revivals" of past styles. The Greek revivalist wanted to bring back Greek archi-

Inside the Greek Doric temple at Paestum, Italy; now usually called "The Temple of Poseidon".
(Photograph by John Pile)

tecture in its entirety in the sense of the complete designs of the complete buildings. He did not hesitate to build houses, banks, churches, and capitols in the form of Greek temples. Such architects felt that by imitating beautiful old buildings as exactly as possible, they would surely produce beautiful new buildings; and they were quite willing to ignore the fact that the programs and the structural techniques of 1830 or 1840 were totally different from those of Greece in 400 B.C. If Greek architecture could be revived, so could Gothic, even if this meant imitating a stone architecture in wood and plaster. In this way the attention of architects moved away from solving problems of planning and construction and toward the designing of imitative exterior treatments more like stage scenery than like actual building.

The term "eclecticism" is usually used to describe the work of the architects who devoted themselves to making every

An American Greek Revival building (The Nantucket Atheneum).
(Photograph by John Pile)

A Gothic cathedral interior (Lichfield).

The Greek Revival U.S. Treasury Building, only 145 years old, carefully reproduces the Greek Ionic order. (Photo courtesy Armstrong World Industries, Inc.)

building an imitation of some historic original. The eclectic architect often was willing to work in a variety of styles and did not hesitate to produce a Gothic church, a Roman bank, a colonial town hall, and a Tudor country club. Most American architecture produced between 1900 and 1950 was of this kind; some architects are still practicing in this way and many laymen have not yet noticed the absurdity of this kind of pseudo-architecture. Everyone would agree to the absurdity of building a modern ocean liner disguised as a sailing ship or an automobile trimmed to look like a chariot or stagecoach, but Gothic colleges and colonial cottages are most common. Curiously enough, it seems to be in interior design that this idea hangs on most persistently. It is not at all uncommon for the tenant of a modern apartment house to insist on a "French" living room or an "Empire" bedroom, entirely furnished with things that imitate those of some distant time and place.

Chicago Tribune Tower
(note dummy flying
butresses). (Photograph
by John Pile)

Glass and iron train-shed
(Victorian Station,
London). (Photograph by
John Pile)

While architects were devoting their interests to the archeo-
logical fantasies of eclecticism, enormous developments were
taking place in science and engineering as a result of the new
ideas of the industrial revolution. Steel, concrete, and glass in
huge areas became available, and new systems for building
to great heights and with vast spans developed. Since these
things had no historical precedents, most architects ignored
them or used them only timidly in places where they would not
show, using historical disguises wherever possible. A railroad
station, for instance, might have a huge open glass and iron
train shed at the rear, but the front would still imitate a Greek
or Roman building. A skyscraper might have a steel frame and
elevators, but its exterior would still be an imitation of a Gothic
tower. As a result of its isolation from modern problems and
structural techniques, the profession of architecture went into
a broad decline. Architects became fussy stylists and decorators, and knew and cared nothing about the most exciting
developments of their era. Architectural schools taught little
except a technique for skillfully stealing and adapting historic
plans and details to new uses.

There were several isolated stirrings against this direction.
These developments were, perhaps, ahead of their time as they

Antonio Gaudi: The church of the Güell Colony, Santa Colona de Cervelló, Spain.

The Glasgow School of Art
by Charles Rennie Mackintosh,
completed in 1899. (Photograph
by John Pile)

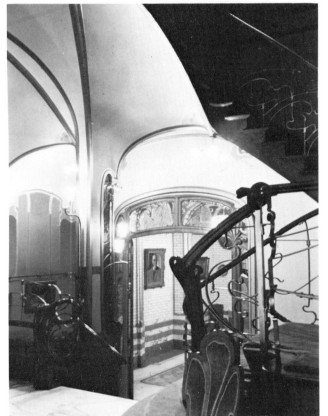

An interior of Victor Horta's own house in
Brussels; Art Nouveau of 1898.
(Photograph by John Pile)

The vast central hall of the Amsterdam Stock Exchange designed by H. P. Berlage, 1897–1903.
(Photograph by John Pile)

remained isolated and seem "failures" in their own era. Each of these historic abortive beginnings has captured great interest in recent times because they pointed toward a direction that has since flowered. In England, William Morris organized a rebellion against mechanization of design production and, in the process, focused on the simplicity and honesty of earlier design. His movement is usually called the "Arts and Crafts Movement". Because Morris concentrated on the excellence of Medieval design, it was easy to misinterpret his aim as being merely a Gothic revival, but in fact it was a first statement of the ideas that went into the eventual development of a truly modern design orientation.

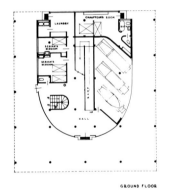

GROUND FLOOR

MAIN FLOOR

**Villa Savoye, Poissy,
Le Corbusier, architect,
1929–31.** (Photograph
courtesy of The Museum
of Modern Art, New York

"Art Nouveau" is the term usually given to another movement of the late 19th century that turned from historic imitation toward originality. Hector Guimard in France and Victor
Horta in Belgium turned to forms of nature for inspiration and
created a kind of design that is easy to recognize and char-
acterize. Their own work depicted a creative and lively style,
but one that was also easily misunderstood—in this case as a
simple fashion in decoration. Art Nouveau lost its momentum

and was soon dismissed as a side issue in design. With the perspective of the intervening years, it is now clear that it was a movement with real strength that could have led to a truly modern design vocabulary had it not expired due to changing public tastes. Ideas in connection with Art Nouveau appeared in a number of unrelated places. In Vienna Josef Hoffman developed a movement usually called the "Vienna Secession", which differs from Art Nouveau in having less concern for the curving forms of nature and more devotion to straight lines and rectilinear forms. In Scotland Charles Rennie Mackintosh and in Barcelona Antonio Gaudi each developed an individualistic style free from historicism. In his own time, each seemed an isolated and eccentric phenomenon, but each of these men and Louis Sullivan in the United States as well, now seem to have found their own way to an expression related to Art Nouveau, but also containing predictions for the directions that architecture and design were about to follow in the 20th century.

3

PIONEER MODERN ARCHITECTS

The term "modern architecture" is usually used, not for all building being done at present, but rather for describing the kind of architecture that developed in rebellion against the historical obsessions of the eclectics. Eclecticism was so firmly established as the norm of the architectural profession in the early part of the twentieth century, that it took unusual clarity of thought and great courage to break away. The men who made the break first were each men of unusual character and great courage. Although they were aware of some stirrings of rebellion against the eclectic point of view (in the work of such men as Auguste Perret and Peter Behrens in Europe, H. H. Richardson and Louis Sullivan in the United States and in "movements" connected with developments in modern art such as "De Stijl" in Holland with its emphasis on geometric form), each of the outstanding pioneer modern architects really "invented" modern architecture independently. Although they came to know of each other's work, they did not form a group or "school", and it seems clear that modern architecture would have appeared if only one of the pioneers had existed. The list of names of these pioneers is short, although there might be some disagreement about exactly which men belong on it and as to whether the list should number only three, four, or as many as seven or eight. There are certainly four men important enough to require our special attention if we are to have any clear idea about what the ideas of modern architecture are. These are Le Corbusier, Mies van der Rohe, Walter Gropius, and Frank Lloyd Wright.

It is not possible to arrange these names in a logical order of importance or to treat their careers in chronological order

Chapel of Notre Dame du Haut at Ronchamp. Le Corbusier, architect, 1950–54. (Photograph by John Pile)

since the major portions of their careers overlap. Van der Rohe and Gropius were German and both lived and worked in the United States since World War II. Le Corbusier, whose real name was Charles Jeanneret (the pseudonym always used in referring to him means "the crow"), was originally Swiss but lived and worked in France so that he is usually thought of as a French architect. Frank Lloyd Wright, the only American of this group, began practice in the 1890's—long before any of the others—and throughout his lifetime remained disdainful of practically all other modern architects' work.

Le Corbusier, because of his revolutionary and, in their day, shocking ideas, had very few actual building commissions in the early part of his career. He turned to writing as a means of making his ideas known and produced a number of books and pamphlets that were extremely successful in spreading his fundamental thoughts about the functional and artistic bases of architecture that eclectics were ignoring. He called attention to the surprising beauty of ships, the early automobiles of the 1920's, and such buildings as grain elevators and factories, and compared them with the great buildings of historic architecture. He called attention to the new possibilities of modern steel and concrete construction and huge glass areas, insisting on the elimination of meaningless decoration so that big, clear, simple surfaces could be seen in their pure geometric relationships.

His early work (in the 1920's and the early 1930's) established the very specific character of much modern European work, which is often given the name "international style" by critics because it had no association with any particular region or

nation, but came into use in many different places. These building forms are usually of very simple geometric mass with flat roofs, large openings, and smooth white exterior wall surfaces. Steel and concrete structure makes solid walls unnecessary so that big open spaces are possible with a minimum of obstruction. Furniture and equipment are built-in, insofar as possible, so that interiors are uncluttered to the point of seeming barren.

Although Le Corbusier—through his admiration for machinery, ships, and airplanes—developed a highly respectful attitude toward functional pressures ("a house is a machine for living in", he wrote), he was also very sensitive to the abstract formal possibilities of architecture. He was close to French cubist painters and was himself a distinguished painter. Many of his buildings have some of the qualities of modern sculpture with, of course, the added qualities of internal space. He believed in using complex geometric systems of "regulating lines" to establish formal, proportional relationships in his designs and gradually developed a special system of measure and proportion to which he gave the name "Modulor". In the course of his lifetime, as he came to have more commissions, a new strain of freer and more expressive character developed in his work. It became less rigorously logical, and more sculptural and poetic. Some later buildings (such as the famous chapel at Ronchamp) are almost entirely sculptural in character, while others retain the cubistic geometry of earlier work. Although, with increasing fame, Le Corbusier had more important commissions, many projects were denied him because of the combination of his adventurous ideas and

Monastery of Ste-Marie de la Tourette. Le Corbusier, architect, 1959.

**The chapel of
Notre Dame du Haut at
Ronchamp. Le Corbusier,
architect, 1950–54.**
(Photograph by John Pile)

uncompromising determination to carry through projects in his own way.

As Le Corbusier's writing and work gradually came to be known throughout the world, younger architects and students became his admirers and disciples. His works were fully and widely published, and certain of his important buildings are well known in detail to every modern architect. It is probably the combination of theoretical logic expressed both in writing and building, combined with an intuitve artistic inventiveness, that tends to make his work influential among other architects to a degree that is out of proportion to the actual number and size of his works. No one can really understand what modern architecture is, without studying and understanding the major works of Le Corbusier.

Walter Gropius' particular importance arose from his influence on the development of modern architecture and design through the school of design called the Bauhaus, which operated in Germany, first at Weimar and then at Dessau, from 1919 to 1933. Under Gropius' direction, it became the first and most important focus for the formal teaching of modern ideas

about design. The school included workshops where students could learn about materials and manufacturing techniques and could actually make working prototypes of their own designs. Architectural students worked on actual building projects and followed through in construction work wherever this was possible. The Bauhaus also stimulated an understanding of the relationship between fine arts and the various kinds of design by bringing together in one place a number of important modern artists, along with architects, designers of furniture, ceramics, textiles, printed material, and even stage settings. Many Bauhaus students and teachers have become influential in their own fields in various parts of the world and virtually every school of art and design has been influenced to some degree by Bauhaus-originated ideas.

Gropius, in his role as director, stood behind this development through his selection of faculty and planning of curriculum. In addition, he was the architect for the Bauhaus buildings at Dessau, which were in themselves a powerful example of the kind of architecture the school was teaching. Gropius' work is, possibly, the most characteristic "international

The Bauhaus, Dessau. Walter Gropius, architect, 1925–26. (Photograph courtesy of The Museum of Modern Art, New York)

Library of Mt. Anthony District High School, Bennington, shown in architect's drawing. The Architects' Collaborative, architects.

**German Pavilion,
International Exposition,
Barcelona.
Mies Van der Rohe,
architect, 1929.**
(Photograph courtesy of
The Museum of Modern
Art, New York)

school" production to come from any modern architect. Its emphasis on totally functional planning—together with the typically characteristic flat roofs, boxlike forms, plain white walls, and ribbon windows—is more predictable and less adventurous than the work of Le Corbusier.

The Bauhaus was closed down under pressure from the Nazi regime in 1933, and Gropius moved first to England and then to the United States. He became the principal teacher in the architectural school at Harvard and exerted enormous influence on a whole generation of younger Americans who are now an important portion of America's architectural profession. Gropius continued to practice in the United States and eventually organized a firm with the name The Architects' Collaborative (TAC). It was typical of Gropius that he preferred not to give the firm his own name, and to be an equal collaborator within it rather than a dominant leader. He always emphasized the teamwork aspect of architecture and did not believe in the merit of the individual celebrity practitioner. The work of The Architects' Collaborative reflects this attitude through its emphasis on a relatively undramatic professionalism.

Ludwig Mies van der Rohe was associated with the Bauhaus for a brief period following Gropius' resignation, but his reputation as an architect is not primarily based on this fact. Mies, as he was usually called by architects, began work in the 1920's and came to international notice with his design for the German Pavilion for the Barcelona International Exposition of 1929. This was a building having no demanding functional requirements since it was intended that the structure itself should be the exhibition. It consisted of a platform and a somewhat smaller flat rectangular roof supported on eight slim

Tugendhat House, Brno, Czechoslovakia.
Mies Van der Rohe, architect, 1930.
(Photograph courtesy of The Museum of Modern Art, New York)

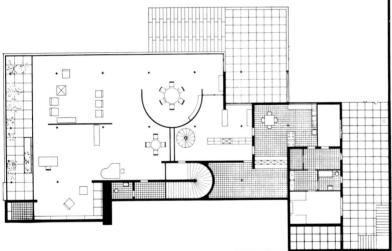

steel columns. Between the floor platform and the roof there was an arrangement of screen walls of glass and marble placed in a free, yet orderly system. Two pools, a sculpture, and some pieces of furniture designed for the building by the architect complete the design. Two ideas that remained typical of Mies's work are clearly developed in this building. One is the concept of "open planning", in which there are no rooms as such and space flows freely from area to area, often flowing also into outside space through glass or openings. The second typically Miesian characteristic is the meticulous concern for the choice and use of materials. The kinds of marble and glass are chosen

Crown Hall, Illinois
Institute of Technology.
Mies Van der Rohe,
architect, 1952.

Farnsworth House,
Plano, Illinois.
Mies Van der Rohe,
architect, 1950.

with great care (the glass is clear, grey, green, black, and etched in different locations; the marble, of several kinds), and the detailing of construction is of the most extreme elegance in order to bring about the visual effect of effortless simplicity. This building can also be described as an example of the "international style", but it is stamped with a very distinctive personal character. Its influence on the development of modern architecture has been amazing considering its small size and purpose.

The Tugendhat house in Czechoslovakia of 1930 is the other early Mies building which exerted a comparable influence. Since it is a rather luxurious residence with all the complex functional requirements of family life, it gave Mies an opportunity to demonstrate how open planning can work with a full functional program. Bedrooms and service spaces are conventional rooms, but the main living space is a huge area with slender columns as the only structural elements. The space is divided by a screen of marble and a curving wall of ebony placed so as to avoid forming rooms, while still giving separation and variety to the space. The outer walls facing the garden are of glass and can be lowered into the basement to make the entire space an open pavilion. The specially designed furniture and the meticulously perfect detailing are also part of the impact of this building. Mies's other early work included some housing of less exciting character and some unbuilt projects, which have come to have great influence on younger architects in more recent times.

Mies came to America to become the Director of Architecture at Armour Institute (now called Illinois Institute of Technology) in Chicago in 1938. In this role he exercised influence as a teacher; he was also in active practice until his death. His plan for the campus and designs for buildings for IIT demon-

strate his way of grouping buildings in an ordered way analogous to the free placement of walls in interior space. His ideas
about tall buildings, expressed in some of the unbuilt projects
of the 1930's, were turned to use in the tall apartment buildings in Chicago in the 1950's. The Seagram Building in New
York (designed in collaboration with Philip Johnson) is generally admired as the most successful statement to date about
what a skyscraper office tower should be. In apartments and
office buildings, Mies's ideas about interior space had little
chance to appear since rented interiors are under the control
of the individual tenants. In the Farnsworth house of 1950,
however, Mies's ideas about building structure and interior
are fully demonstrated in a project of great simplicity and
great elegance. The house consists of simple floor platforms
and roof supported with externally exposed steel. Between
these planes, glass encloses a single space within which an enclosed "island" houses baths and utilities. The means used are
so simple that the beauty of the resulting building seems impossible to explain. No other architect has gone as far in
demonstrating the creative possibilities in using the most
extreme simplicity of means in architecture.

Of the four leaders under discussion, Frank Lloyd Wright is
certainly best known to American readers. His career began

**Twin towers. Mies
van der Rohe, architect.
Toronto, Canada**
(Photograph by John Pile)

**Seagram Building, New
York. Mies Van der Rohe
and Philip Johnson,
architects, 1958.**
(Photograph by John Pile)

**Roberts House,
River Forest, Illinois.
Frank Lloyd Wright,
architect, 1908.**
(Photograph courtesy of
The Museum of Modern
Art, New York)

before the men mentioned above had started practice, at a
time when eclecticism had not yet taken over American architecture. Louis Sullivan, Wright's employer and mentor at the
turn of the century, had developed an individual style of design
in a distinctively American milieu centering on Chicago. Sullivan's career was brought to an end when American taste moved
toward the eclectics' imitations of historic architecture, but
Wright managed to survive and develop his own architecture
in a highly individual way. His early work, preceding the work
of the European pioneers by many years, demonstrates most
of the typical characteristics of modern architecture. There is
no imitation of historic prototypes, planning is based on the
solution of functional problems, spaces are open and freely
interconnected, windows are large and continuous, and the
indoor-outdoor relationship is as open and free as possible.
Wright did not insist upon the boxlike simple forms and
smooth white surfaces, the flat roofs, and large glass areas

**Imperial Hotel, Tokyo.
Frank Lloyd Wright,
architect, 1916-22.**
(Photograph courtesy of
The Museum of Modern
Art, New York)

that are typical of the "international style", nor did he rule
out the use of decoration. The typical early "prairie houses",
as he liked to call them, had low, spreading, hipped roofs, a
great central chimney, and a complex arrangement of rooms
grouped around the massive chimney as an anchor point.
Materials were usually warm and natural (wood, brick, stone)
and used with great sensitivity. Certain of these early houses,
such as the Coonley house of 1908 and the Robie house of
1909, are highly successful examples of modern architecture
despite their early dates. In addition to a very large number
of houses, Wright's early work included a variety of other
building types, including a large office building (the Larkin
Building of 1904) and a church (Unity Church of 1906). In
spite of his successful practice, Wright also felt the unfortunate effects of the eclectic era. His commissions became
fewer and he moved into a kind of semi-retirement when his
name came to be little known in America. He was called to
Japan to design the Imperial Hotel in Tokyo (1916–1922) and
so almost dropped from sight in America. His work came to
be known through publication in Europe and, oddly enough,
Wright's influence was probably more strongly felt there than
in the United States through the 1920's and early 1930's.

The survival of the Imperial Hotel after a great Tokyo earth-
quake brought Wright back to the notice of Americans and
more commissions began to come to him in the early 1930's
(when some news of modern architecture in Europe also

An interior of Frank Lloyd Wright's *Fallingwater.* (Photograph by Yasuto Tanaka.)

become known in America). In the late 1930's, full publication of Wright's work included many new and important buildings and indicated some changes in Wright's style. Although he always denied that he had been influenced by the European moderns (whose work he regarded with contempt), the work itself shows still more open planning, bigger glass areas, more use of steel and concrete, more flat roofs, and less use of ornamentation. Many of the flat-roofed houses and the famous Kaufman house (built over a waterfall) seem to have a great deal in common with the mainstream of modern work in Europe. Other buildings, such as the Johnson Wax Company office building of 1936–39 and the Guggenheim Museum of 1958, are more individualistic in character. In the latter part of his career, Wright had a huge number of large commissions and produced examples of almost every building type.

At his home in Wisconsin he established a complex of studios and dwellings where apprentices (called "fellows") could come to work and study the distinctively Wright way of designing. The Taliesin Fellowship (as Wright named it) has continued to practice since his death in a manner quite characteristic of his own later work.

The originality and imagination of Wright's work, and the early dates at which he introduced so many of the key ideas of modern architecture, make him an immensely important figure in the history of modern architecture. The liveliness and warmth of his work make it appealing to most laymen in a

way that some of the early European work cannot be. Wright's
work is highly individualistic and idiosyncratic—even sometimes eccentric—to a degree that often makes it quite controversial in professional discussion. There can be no question, however, that he was one of the "inventors" of modern
architecture and the only American belonging to the very short
list of men who brought about the needed development of an
architecture suited to contemporary life.

Modern architecture was not, of course, the achievement of
only these four men. In the late 1920's and the 1930's, more
and more converts to the new and logical ideas gradually
appeared. Some of these early modernists are still in active
practice and will be discussed later. Some made a contribution
that was limited to a particular region or that has come to
seem less significant with the passage of time. Certainly the
list of pioneer modernists should include Bruno Taut and
Erich Mendelsohn in Germany; J. J. P. Oud, J. A. Brinkman,
and L. C. Van der Vlugt in Holland; Berthold Lubetkin and
Tecton in England; Gunnar Asplund and Sven Markelius in
Sweden; and Alvar Aalto in Finland. The United States was,
except for Wright, very late in producing any modern leaders.
William Lescaze and Richard Neutra, both from Europe, were
the only other active practitioners identified with the modern
movement during the early 1930's. As knowledge of European
work became current in American architectural schools, and
particularly after the arrival in America of some of the leading
pioneers in the role of teachers, younger architects turned
away from eclecticism to join the line of thinking that had
become dominant in architecture elsewhere. A similar process
went on in South America, Canada, Australia, and Japan.
Russia and the countries under Russian influence have tended
to be oddly conservative in architectural thinking, but within
the last few years there have been evidences that the logic
of modern architecture has led to some acceptance of its principles in those countries also.

In the late 1920s and 1930s, somewhat independently of the
work of the leading modern architects, a more superficial
style of modernism appeared that sometimes seemed to be at
war with the serious development already discussed. It was
often given the stylistic label "modernistic" (which means "in
the style of modernism"), but is now usually called "art deco",
a contraction from the French term "Arts Decorative". The
term refers to a style of decoration using straight, parallel
lines, rounded corners, zig-zags suggesting lightning or electrical energy, and sometimes the aerodynamic forms usually
called "streamlining". The art deco style was a particular

New York's Art Deco
Chrysler Building, 1930.
William van Alen,
architect. (Photograph
by John Pile)

**Interior of the Chrysler
Building lobby.**
(Photograph by John Pile)

favorite of the designers of shops and theaters and, in some
cases it was taken up by the architects of skyscrapers (such
as the Chrysler Building in New York) and exhibition buildings where it served to suggest ultra-modernity through surface decoration. It was in fact used as one more style which
the eclectic architect could offer as a new alternative to classi-
cism or gothicism, but its relation to real problems of architecture remained superficial. There still remains in the United
States a small surviving group of eclectics producing pseudo-
historic architecture of the sort that was the norm of the
1920's. It is made up of some surviving older men and a few
younger ones who have chosen, perhaps rather cynically, to
serve the desires of some conservatively-minded clients. This
is, however, a declining aspect of the architectural profession.
There is, unfortunately, a far larger number of architects who
have joined the ranks of modern architects in terms of superficial style characteristics without having much understanding of the serious purposes of the modern pioneers. These are
the producers of the indifferent to bad works of supposedly
"modern" design that disfigure any number of American cities.
The teaching in the leading schools, the practice of the best
architectural firms, and the work of the individual leaders of
the profession is now, however, firmly oriented toward a
growth and extension of the ideas that were first developed
by the pioneers of the first half of the century.

4

CURRENT ARCHITECTURE

Although all four of the pioneer modernists discussed above were still in active practice well into the current era, we tend to see them as a separate group because they each made such major contributions in their roles as pioneers in the 1930's, 1920's, or before—when modern architecture was still a daring and revolutionary venture. Current architectural practice throughout the world (with the exception of a few curious holdovers from the past) accepts the achievements of the pioneer modernists and builds on their ideas. A few of the leaders of the present day are older men, contemporaries or near contemporaries of the pioneers, but whom we think of as belonging to later generations only because their major work falls into recent years rather than belonging to the early movement. Alvar Aalto, for example, the best-known representative of the very lively architectural profession in Finland, could be made a fifth name on our list of pioneers on the strength of his work in the 1930's. He is, however, an even more important figure in contemporary architecture because he is continuing to work in a way that is constantly changing and developing. Similarly, Marcel Breuer, who was well known for his work at the Bauhaus, is now even better known for his active practice in contemporary New York.

The development of the present-day architectural scene might be described as having two phases (which have not occurred in chronological sequence but which overlap and are still both active). The first phase was a matter of learning about and accepting the ideas of the international-style modernists of Europe. This meant discarding the habit of historic imitation, learning to accept functional and constructive pres-

The altar, pulpit and fittings designed by Alvar Aalto for the church at Imatra, Finland.
(Photograph by John Pile)

sures as the main determinants of architectural design, and learning to understand and use the resulting aesthetic, which sometimes came to be an end in itself. The second phase is concerned with searching out a line of development to go beyond the international style. It tends to be critical of the more dogmatic and rigid tenets of early modernism and, while accepting its logic and value, rejects the idea that modernism is a fixed and unchanging style to be made into a firmly frozen formula. This leads to lines of experiment that move away from the modernism of the 1920's into more personal and individualistic explorations. It can lead to disorganized and pointless "artiness" in some cases, but it is also the direction that keeps architecture a lively and developing art. The ordered works of Gropius and Mies and the early work of Le Corbusier are the guidelines for the first phase; the work of Wright and the later work of Le Corbusier tend to inspire the second phase.

Progress before World War II was largely a matter of the development of the first phase. Modern architecture found acceptance very slow in most parts of the world. Switzerland and the Scandinavian countries were early in understanding (as was Germany until the oppressions of the Nazis); however, good modern work elsewhere was largely restricted to a very few works that became well known in professional circles, but which were little known and little liked by the

public that commissions and occupies buildings. Almost every-where the established profession fought the new ideas and almost every school of architecture became the scene of a long and slow battle between the more open-minded students and younger faculty members who urged that there be some recog-nition of the progress that was underway, and the older au-thorities who insisted on continuing the teaching of the old historicism.

In the United States, a very few men and a very few build-ings were the only representation of the new thinking. Richard Neutra, who came from Vienna, studied briefly with Wright and then established a practice on the West Coast, which is

Johnson Wax Company Office Building, Racine, Wisconsin.
Frank Lloyd Wright, architect, 1936–39.
(Photograph courtesy of Johnson Wax Company)

Whitney Museum, New York. Marcel Breuer and Hamilton Smith, architects, 1963–66. (left) (Photograph courtesy of © Ezra Stoller (Photographer))
Lever House, New York. Skidmore, Owings and Merrill, architects, 1952. (right) (Photograph courtesy of The Museum of Modern Art, New York).

Philadelphia Saving Fund Society Building. George Howe and William Lescaze, architects, 1932. (Photograph by John Pile)

still thriving. Neutra's work has much in common with the best European work of the 1920's and 1930's in Germany and Switzerland. It is usually serene, austerely simple, and can well be described as an American expression of the international style, although in its more recent development it has been more varied and less rigorous than that term might suggest. William Lescaze came from Switzerland to the United States and, together with George Howe, had the good fortune to obtain a commission to build a major skyscraper office-bank building in Philadelphia in the early 1930's. Howe had been a traditionalist but, in the course of the collaboration, become converted to the thinking of the European modernists. The resulting building for the Philadelphia Saving Fund Society, finished in 1932, remained the best and virtually the only modern tall building in the United States until after the war. Later Howe became the dominant influence in modernizing the school of architecture at Yale, while Lescaze continued in active practice.

Marcel Breuer joined Gropius in the architectural school at Harvard as it took its inevitable step into the modern world. The two were partners in a few projects before they separated,

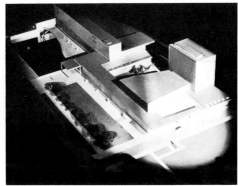

Ford Foundation Building, New York. Kevin Roche, John Dinkeloo and
Associates, architects, 1967 (left). (Photograph courtesy of © Ezra Stoller (Esto)).
Model of unbuilt competition winning design for Smithsonian Gallery in
Washington, D.C. Eliel and Eero Saarinen with R. F. Swanson, Associate
architects, (right) 1939.

Gropius to form The Architects' Collaborative—now a large
and active office in the Boston area—Breuer to establish his
own practice in New York. Breuer's work has moved away
from the norms of the international school toward a more individualistic and more sculptural vocabulary. The new Whitney
Museum in New York serves as a fine example of his current
work. Eliel Saarinen, a Finnish architect who had arrived at
an individual and nonimitative architectural style in his own
country in the early years of this century (he is probably best
known for the Helsinki railroad station of 1904–14), came to
the United States to teach architecture at Cranbrook Academy.
His son Eero, first in collaboration with his father and then
in his own practice, became a leader in developing modern
buildings that moved away from the norms of the international school. The design for a Smithsonian Art Gallery, prepared with the elder Saarinen and Robert Swanson, won a
competition in 1939. It could have been one of America's first
truly beautiful modern buildings but has never been built for
reasons that remain unclear. However, Eero Saarinen, until
his untimely death, had many important commissions, and his
work is particularly distinguished by its lack of any formula.
Each project was considered as a new challenge so that the
Kresge auditorium at M.I.T., the General Motors Technical
Center, the TWA terminal at Kennedy airport, and the terminal
at Dulles are each highly individual solutions to specific problems. Since Saarinen's death, the successor firm of Kevin
Roche and John Dinkeloo has maintained a similarly high
level of practice. The building for the Ford Foundation in

W. R. Grace Bldg.,
New York, Skidmore,
Owings and Merrill,
architects. The tall
office building with
the typical slab form
modified by an outward
curve at the base.
(Photograph by John Pile.)

New York serves as an example of the continuing vitality of this office.

Although we speak of architects as individuals, it must be remembered that no one man can deal with even one large project. When an architect finds himself processing many large projects simultaneously, it is necessary that he have a staff of many architects, designers, draftsmen, and various specialists if jobs are to be produced at a reasonably rapid pace. The relationship between the individual architect and the large staff that he must organize and direct is a particularly problematical aspect of the architect's art. In America, there has been a strong tendency to build large organizations in which no one individual is dominant. This was true in the eclectic era also when such firms as McKim, Mead and White; Coolidge, Shepley, Bulfinch, and Abbott; or Cram, Goodhue, and Fergusson were leaders. The individual partners in such firms were, of course, often leaders, skilled designers, and sometimes colorful personalities; but the firms were large in-

stitutional businesses with hundreds of employees that could survive the resignation or death of any one partner. Such large firms have survived into the modern period, and new large firms have appeared with some of the same impersonal qualities.

Skidmore, Owings and Merrill, for example, is probably the largest producer of high quality work in America. The partner most often credited with its design success is Gordon Bunshaft (whose name is not even part of the firm's identification). There are many partners and offices in several major cities. The work of SOM (as it is usually called) clings closely to a developed form of international school design, with ideas formed by Mies and by Gropius through the many Harvard-trained architects who are members of the firm. Interior design is dealt with through a department that is an integral part of the organization and produces outstanding work sharing the somewhat impersonal and anonymous character of the firm's architecture.

Perkins and Will, a comparably large organization particularly known for its work in the design of schools, has established an independent but affiliated office to deal with interior design problems under the name Interior Space Design (ISD). The West Coast-based firms of Welton Beckett and John Carl Warneke conduct practice on a similarly large and impersonal basis. The consistent logic and highly teachable philosophy of the international-style pioneer modernists has served these large firms well because young designers, trained in these ideas by the leading architectural schools, can move into big offices and become productive in a style and way of working that has already become highly codified and standardized.

This very consistency of modern practice has given rise to

Row houses in Society Hill development, Philadelphia. I.M. Pei, architect, 1964.

Library, Pakistan Institute of Science and Technology, shown in a rendering by Vincent Furno. Edward Durell Stone, architect.

144

The new wing of the Des Moines, Iowa Art Center designed by I.M. Pei. (Photograph by John Pile)

Salk Institute, San Diego. Louis I. Kahn, architect, 1959–66. (Photograph courtesy of The Museum of Modern Art, New York)

worry and protest among architects and critics who see the new uniformity of work, however excellent, as representing a new academy of dullness and conformity. Even laymen notice the monotony of the modern tall buildings of New York and wonder why architects have become so unoriginal. Large projects tend to gravitate toward the large offices, and large offices are more inclined toward design formulae because of the assembly-line routines of their production. Some larger offices are still dominated by an individual who tries to give a personal stamp to each project. The offices of Philip Johnson or I. M. Pei can serve as examples of this category.

Edward Stone and Minoru Yamasaki, in giving personal character to the work of their large firms, have moved in the direction of a highly decorative treatment of external surfaces. While this seems to be an approach that is highly acceptable to laymen and important clients, it has tended to be disappointing to most architects because of the rather glib and superficial ease with which this approach can gloss over complex problems with an icing of surface that can become dull and boring more readily than some more demanding approaches.

Such men as Paul Rudolph, John Johansen, Edward Larabee Barnes, and Victor Lundy are each working in a way that is strongly personal and individualistic, in no way eccentric, and fully in line with the mainstream of development of modern architecture. Each has found his own compromise with the difficult problems of organization capable of dealing with large projects, combined with a sense of a particular man's creative work.

The American architect who stands out above all these others in the view of the international architectural profession, however, is Louis Kahn. Although born in 1901, Kahn had little opportunity to build until he was over fifty years of age. The list of his finished works is quite short, and the works themselves are not well-known or even very appealing to most laymen. Nevertheless Kahn's work is known and admired all over the world, particularly among younger architects and students of architecture, to whom he became almost an idol. His work departed from the stern logic of the international school and included an intuitive, almost irrational, element that made it powerful and meaningful in a way that can best be compared to the similarly arbitrary but powerfully creative strain that runs through the work of Le Corbusier. Kahn's finished buildings are not always well-liked by the people who occupy and use them, but their influence throughout the profession of architecture is undeniable.

It is also necessary to mention Buckminster Fuller in any

Interior of U.S. Embassy,
Dublin, in a drawing
by the architect,
John Johansen.

Technical Institute at
Otaniemi, Finland.
Alvar Aalto, architect,
1959–66. (Photograph
by John Pile)

Plan of Kaleva Church,
Tampere, Finland.
Reima and Raili Pietilä,
architects, 1965–66.

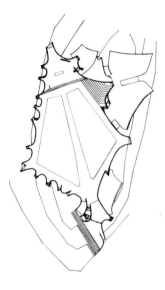

discussion of American architecture, although Fuller fits no classification as clear and short as that of "architect". He is an inventor, engineer, industrial designer, and philosopher in about equal proportions, but his major public successes have been in the invention of new structural systems of extraordinary lightness, clarity, and beauty. Architects remain somewhat aloof from Fuller's contributions, perhaps because they have have not been able to find a way to assimilate them into the norms of architectural practice. These structures are, nevertheless, achievements that have also found international recognition on a scale that goes far beyond the importance that their undeniable practical uses would suggest.

In the United States it is all too easy to assume that the progress of modern architecture can be judged by the buildings that are available for inspection here. Actually, despite the major setback to progress that resulted from World War II and its aftermath, European architecture has moved ahead with a vigor and liveliness that makes American architecture often seem dull and disappointing. The conservatism that held back progress in the United States in the 1930's was never so evident in Europe, and the firm successes of modernism in Switzerland and the Scandinavian countries before and during the war years meant that good modern work came to be the norm in Europe while it was still an exception in America.

In Finland, with a total national population only half that of New York City, there is a rich production of work led by the continuing output of Alvar Aalto, but including work by such younger architects as Timo Penttilä and Reimi and Raili Pietilä that is full of the same kind of poetic and imaginative freedom that made Kahn so important in the United States.

In England, the modern work of the 1930's tended to cling closely to continental international-style precedents. In recent years adventurous developments have appeared, having their origins, perhaps, in the later work of Le Corbusier. The work of Peter and Alyson Smithson is characteristic of what has been called "new brutalism", a somewhat mannered designation for a willingness to use shapes and surfaces that would have been considered crude or "brutal" by earlier standards. The work of Kahn, later Le Corbusier, and the Smithsons plus, possibly, some knowledge of recent Aalto work, seems to have been assimilated in the current work of James Stirling, still only represented by a few buildings.

Italian modern architecture, active in the 1920's and 1930's, was set back by the war, but has moved ahead in the work of such men as Gio Ponti and the partnership of Belgiojoso, Perisutti, and Rogers. Pier Luigi Nervi—although actually an engineer, not an architect—has produced excellent buildings both alone and in collaboration with Italian architects.

Oscar Niemeyer, closely associated with Le Corbusier at one time, is probably the best known of South American architects. His city plan and designs for buildings at the new Brazilian capital of Brazilia are particularly well known. His work is, however, representative of a wide range of lively activity in South and Central America.

Japan, with its strong traditionalism in architecture, has wavered between joining in the mainstream of European and American architecture and finding a more distinctively Japanese vocabulary. The work of Kenzo Tange, also much influenced by Le Corbusier, represents some of the best Japanese work,

Engineering Building, Leicester University. James Stirling, architect, 1964. (Photograph by John Pile)

Pirelli Building, Milan. Gio Ponti and Pier Luigi Nervi, architects, 1955–56. (Photograph by John Pile)

Buckminster Fuller's gigantic Geodesic dome enclosing the U.S. exhibit at EXPO 67 in Montreal, Canada. (Photograph by John Pile)

**Habitat, Montreal. Moshe
Safdie, architect, 1967.**

**A "plug-in city" of the
future in a drawing.
Peter Cook, architect,
1964. An example of the
"Archigram" group's
proposals.**

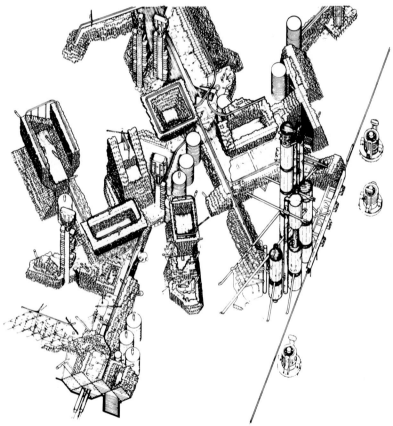

retaining as it does some of the aesthetic sensitivity of traditional Japanese work, while moving into the modern world in terms of technical innovation.

Contemporary architecture continues to feel strong pressures to move ahead into new territory, pushed by the demands of modern problems and pulled by the possibilities of the newest technology. In many different places there is an interest in the development of gigantic agglomerate structures (often called "megastructures") reaching the proportion of entire cities or regions. Moshe Safdie's demonstration apartment building "Habitat" at the Montreal Expo 67 gives us a tiny sample of what such building could be. The "Archigram" group in England through its spokesman, Peter Cook, has been active in advancing ideas that grow out of modern compter technology and modern constructional possibilities. Many of these proposals have a futuristic quality that makes them seem remote from the realities of everyday architectural practice; yet they are clearly more strongly related to the needs of the rapidly changing human population than many of the more conventionally aesthetic and formalistic ideas of the modern architects who have come to dominate the profession, receive the most lucrative and spectacular commissions, and so represent the ideas of the present *status quo*.

Modern architecture is still in flux; there is no possibility of predicting the future directions which are, in the end, determined by the will and imagination of the individuals who deal with the specific problems of building that our society is willing to undertake. No work already built or currently in hand begins to demonstrate the possibilities that modern skills make available. It is clear that the vision of current architects goes far beyond anything that our society as represented by the individual private client or by the institutions of industry and government has, as yet, been ready to sponsor.

5

THE CITY
AND ITS SURROUNDINGS

In the last chapters treating historic architecture and interiors, the work of great masters of the early part of this century, and the current state of architecture and design, most buildings and interiors mentioned were described in positive terms. One might assume from the positive aspects of historic development that the state of design and architecture is getting better and better, and that our environment is in a healthy state. Unfortunately this is far from true. The state of environment, especially in our mass urban societies, is so frightening that it seems important to make some general observations at this point. We have repeatedly stated that interior design is a part of architecture and that architecture is a part of the total environment. As designers we must be concerned with our surroundings, whether immediate and intimate surroundings or the community or country at large. This chapter cannot provide answers, for there are no simple answers to the problems that face us. At best, this discussion can point to some of the questions that we must learn to deal with. At its worst, it might sound somewhat like a warning—a warning to each reader and a warning to each and every member of society, regardless of whether he is involved in design or not.

It is a most peculiar fact that Americans as a nation are not very conscious of their environment, that they are in fact blind to many of the visual horrors that were created in the name of progress in the past half century. More Americans receive a college education than any other group of people in the world, yet even the college graduate is usually illiterate visually. A standard college education might contain a course on music and possibly a course on art history, but hardly ever anything concerned with design or the visual environment. It is not totally surprising, therefore, that most educated and intelligent people accept the state of chaos in our cities and its surroundings without consciously noticing it.

America has grown and developed more rapidly than any other western country and our cities, as exciting as they are, rarely contain the architectural beauty and serenity found so often in historic European towns. The speed with which cities grew caused much of the building and development to happen without overall town plans; even today when at least the design community is conscious of planning needs, it is difficult to achieve meaningful controls, zoning laws, and building ordinances due to our tradition of free enterprise. Many of our huge high-rise buildings and apartment house projects were built with no other criteria than maximum profits for the builders. Our laws and building codes are still inadequate for the protection of the public. Several years ago a real estate firm wanted to obtain the air rights over New York's famous Grand Central Station and build a high rise building literally on top of it. This would not only have ruined a major landmark building, but would have created additional congestion in an already over-crowded part of the city with heavily overtaxed transportation systems. The investors managed to retain one of the world's leading architects, Marcel Breuer, and hoped that his name would dispell the rising protests of many civic groups. Fortunately, the proposal was finally defeated. Yet, the fact that such a structure could be contemplated seriously is an indictment of the public attitude towards the shape of our cities. This example is by no means unique. Between the early 1950's and the middle 1960's several huge office towers and hotels were built west of the famous and well-planned Rockefeller Center in New York. Not one of approximately ten vast strucures was built in a fashion coordinated with one of its neighbors. Individually some of these buildings, specially the CBS Building (designed by the late Eero Saarinen), are very handsome structures. As a group or as a cityscape they represent utter chaos. The visual impact of un-planned cities is only one aspect of concern. The deepest concern must always be man. The result of our congested and chaotic cities has been an enormous increase in air pollution, level of noise, overcrowded transportation systems, congested highways, rise of crime rates, rise of slum areas, and in general nervous tension of all city dwellers.

It is not only the large city that has suffered from a lack of planning and from a lack of visual controls. Our highways throughout the nation are marvels of engineering and give us the means for easy mobility and communication. Yet our cul-

A central public square in Toronto, Canada with the City Hall designed by Viljo Revell, a Finnish architect chosen in an international competition. (Photograph by John Pile)

ture seems more concerned with the automobile and its needs than with people and their needs.

Highways fulfill a vital need in providing means of communication between cities. They are a lesser blessing when they lead into large population centers and encourage drivers to congest the cities instead of using public transportation (which has not kept pace with our current needs). Los Angeles is famous for its system of freeways, but as a city it is no more than a series of suburbs in search of a center. Residents of that city hardly know the joys of walking. In fact it is not unusual for pedestrians in certain sections of Los Angeles to be apprehended by the police as suspect characters, even in broad daylight. Seattle was one of America's beautiful cities until a few years ago. A new highway was built to connect the existing network of roads, and the new road has effectively cut the city into two halves since for the sake of economy most of the highway is built as an elevated structure.

Our automobile culture has created further problems by attracting along our roads and highways hundreds of enterprises to service the automobile and to feed its hungry occupants. Much criticism has been leveled against junkyards and advertising signs, and perhaps the coming years will see improvements in this area. However, the general public doesn't seem to object to the incredibly ugly structures and signs that abound alongside the roads leading into the cities. Almost every town has miles and miles of these eyesores in its outskirts, the classic examples being Route 22 in New Jersey and Colorado Boulevard in Denver. These stretches of roads are the worst examples of visual pollution in our country. Perhaps the only solution to this state of affairs is a strict series of federal laws. Considering the snail's pace with which we are beginning to tackle the even more acute problem of air pollution, this hope seems to be destined for the rather remote future.

The automobile is by now a serious problem in all western cities. Traffic jams and lack of parking seem one of the burdens of our civilization, in France and Italy as much as in England and America. Yet it would be wrong to blame the automobile alone for the chaos and ugliness around us. Some of the problems are of a social nature, many are economic ones, and in our country some of the urban problems have racial aspects.

We have attempted to solve some of these problems through urban renewal programs and many housing laws. The results have often been somewhat like the uncoordinated building activity near Rockefeller Center. No overall city planning has been in evidence and only a few cities have seen delightful visual improvements as a result of major urban renewal. San Francisco's Ghirardelli Square, some of the renewal projects in Boston, and some in Philadelphia are examples that show that renewal can be beautiful as well as effective. Often, however, the wrong approach has been taken. One of the earliest low-cost housing projects in the Midwest was proudly introduced by city officials who pointed out that all the surfaces (exterior as well as interior walls) that might be touched or marred by the public (the residents) were all covered with the same green washable tile so that one could simply hose them down. We have learned much since those days, but cities still have the tendency to tear down block after block or whole sections, not realizing that a community is more than a collection of houses. Jane Jacobs has written extensively on this subject. She recommends an approach to city planning and urban renewal which would preserve the spirit and, in effect, the institutions, establishments, and physical realities which make a community a cohesive body. One could make the facetious statement that the only truly meaningful environments that our society has created in recent years are environments created for animals, namely zoos. Animals are less adaptable than human beings. Unless the proper physiological and psychological conditions are provided, animals perish. Man on the other hand can, and must learn to adapt to overcrowded conditions and to the poisoned air created by automobile exhausts and industrial fumes.

One might ask whether air pollution and noise are problems of concern to designers. The answer must be an emphatic yes. We must learn that our environment is a totality in which neither the individual dwelling, nor the street, nor the air, nor the sound waves are unrelated to each other. We have stated repeatedly that interior design is a young profession, but *all* design is recent in the sense of scientific attitudes. Since no other era has had to cope with the population explosion of our time, the problems of design and architecture in past centuries were less acute. Design was not a matter of life and death and had always been concerned primarily with aesthetics. Today, design is necessary for survival. We are only beginning to notice the needs and have not really come up with the approaches to solutions, certainly not with any answers. Significantly, some of the serious minds who have started to explore the problems of human environment in depth are scientists rather than designers.

Dr. René Dubos, an illustrious scientist in the field of biochemistry presents some thought-provoking theories in his book *Man Adapting* (1965). His thesis points out that man is capable of adapting to his environment more than other living organisms. We know very little, however, about the effect of this adaptability since practically no serious research has been done about it. Dr. Dubos mentions inhabitants of European coal mining and industrial areas, who have adapted to the special pollution in their environment, but who have developed symptoms of premature pulmonary diseases and other health afflictions in large numbers in a matter of a few generations. A number of other examples of environmental influences on man's physiology are described, all of them in theory pointing to the need for serious scientific research. According to Dr. Dubos, the air pollution in some of our cities has reached crucial proportions, which might cause real catastrophes costing thousands of lives if certain weather conditions were to occur. It seems that we are talking a great deal about environmental pollution, but are not really serious about it as a national concern. Our societies like gadgets and economic prosperity more than we dislike environmental pollution; it might take a disaster to make us act.

Another scientist whose ideas show need for much serious research is Edward T. Hall, an anthropologist. In his book *The Hidden Dimension* (1966) Dr. Hall emphasizes the fact that

virtually everything that man is and does is associated with the experience of space. Some revealing experiments and observations of animal behavior under crowded conditions are described which show clearly that the living organism is affected biologically by space or lack of space. Dr. Hall throws new light on man's use of space, on what may be the crucial dimension in everyday living, family relationships, business management, city planning, and architecture.

The aforementioned examples emphasize the vital need for serious research into all areas concerned with man's environment. A few universities and independent groups have started some work in this direction. Some designers and architects work closely with behavioral scientists in teaching or research situations. The funds and facilities available, to date, are pitifully inadequate for the work that must be done and it may take disasters as predicted by Dr. Dubos, or perhaps more violence and riots in our cities (which are disasters partially caused by environment) before our society recognizes the urgency of these new needs. For designers, the recognition of the serious and vital effects of environment on the well-being of humankind presents a challenge and obligation to face up

The central atrium of the Citicorp headquarters building in New York City. Hugh Stubbins, architect. (Photograph by John Pile)

to the social responsibilities of the design professions. These responsibilities include participation in the life of the community on all levels, and they include the mantle of collective leadership for awakening society at large to the many needs of a liveable environment in the years to come.

The renowned Greek city planner and architect. C. A. Doxiadis stated, during a 1966 interview, that the only architecture that matters today is interior design. His reasoning was that so much of our environment is objectionable that people have a tendency to turn inward, away from the outside. There is much truth in this statement, but to base the needs of interior design on that reasoning would be a negative approach. Man cannot live withdrawn into a shell, oblivious to his broader surroundings.

The very basic and global concerns expressed in this chapter should make it eminently clear that the need for design on all levels is a continuously increasing one. No professional concerned with manmade environment can sit back and expect the city planners or architects or any of the other specialists to solve the pressing needs of man and his surroundings. The tasks that must be undertaken will need the concerted action of all designers, and most certainly must include interior designers as important members of the team.

6

ENVIRONMENTAL BEHAVIOR

The previous chapter made mention of several behavioral scientists who have started to explore the problems of human environment. The serious and systematic study of the environment and its effect upon human behavior is probably one of the most revolutionary and rapidly growing fields related to design. It is true that the influence of man's surroundings upon behavior must have been apparent to Adam and Eve, yet the attempt to study, record, analyze and, above all, act upon predictable influences of environment upon human behavior has only recently blossomed into a meaningful aspect of the design professions.

Before the late 1950's, psychologists and other behavioral scientists were aware of the behavioral aspect of man's environment, but until that time designers and architects rarely took scientific findings into consideration in the process of design. Environmental Psychology and Environmental Behavior are still relatively new concepts. The significant change that took place just recently is the awareness of designers and architects that the tools and methodologies developed by behavioral scientists are essential to the design process. Scientists, on the other hand, have realized that the meaningful application of their findings can only be implemented by those who are engaged in the process of physical design. Whether the future will see more collaboration, or more designers trained in the behavioral sciences, or scientists educated as designers is not clear; it hardly seems to matter as long as the need for the joint pursuit of design and the related fields of behavioral science has been clearly proven.

The recognition of this need has been hastened through the vastly increased populations, and the urbanization and industrialization of the twentieth century. Consumerism is another phenomenon due to these same causes, and is in itself another catalyst having brought about new attitudes towards design. Interiors, buildings and cities are for people. And people want to have a voice in the design of their surroundings. Much in the history of design consists of great masterpieces that have been created as monuments to their sponsors (kings, nobles, wealthy corporations) or more frequently as monuments to the designer or architect. An earlier chapter mentioned New York's Seagram building as an example of great design, yet at the same time, as a somewhat inhuman building. Although attitudes and styles in architecture and design will always change, the current trend is based upon the consideration of people, human scale, ecology and environmental concerns, much more than purely stylistic considerations. This is a movement that, we hope, once the importance of it is realized by designer and user alike, will cease to be considered a trend and will remain as an essential design criterion.

Of the many examples one could mention, the most radical design failure was a housing project built as a low-income project in the 1950's in St. Louis. At its completion, the Pruitt-Igoe houses were widely acclaimed by the design profession for design and innovation, including play areas and public corridor-type spaces on several of the high-rise floors. The project was beset by serious crime problems, fear and anti-social behavior from the outset, and finally the situation became untenable. In 1972 a part of the Pruitt-Igoe project had to be demolished in the hope of increasing tenant acceptance through lower density housing. By now the total project has been razed, since no modifications seemed to work towards a more acceptable environment. The problems and failures of Pruitt-Igoe were very complex. They have to do with crime, social, economic and racial problems, and it would be an oversimplification to put the blame for failure upon the designers alone. It does show, however, that the need for joint approaches with sociologists, psychologists, economists and perhaps anthropologists might have prevented the vast and costly failure. The problem is that the designer and the "social scientist" don't speak the same language. Neither can understand what the other needs to know.

In 1972, a book by Oscar Newman called *Defensible Space* (subtitled "Crime Prevention Through Urban Design") was published and quickly became an important reference for planners, designers and behavioral scientists. Newman's study deals primarily with the effects of the physical layout of residential environments on the criminal vulnerability of its inhabitants. It relates the incidence of crime and vandalism to the specific factors that encourage it. Many of Newman's findings were based on careful analysis of data kept by the Housing Authority of New York. In essence, the book shows the increase of crime in high-rise buildings in projects of great density. An exhibition at the Museum of Modern Art in New York in 1973 showed a number of new housing projects, significantly of low-rise and low-density design. It seems that high-rise buildings work best for higher income groups who can afford to pay for the security, which in low-income projects can only be provided by the tenants themselves, through familiarity with each other, and through an ensuing sense of territoriality.

One cannot simply state that architecture and design can control behavior and give rise to a kind of ideal society—an idea that perhaps was very prevalent after the completion of Le Corbusier's famous Ville Radieuse in Marseilles. But certainly it has now been shown conclusively that while design cannot create behavior, it can to a large extent modify and control it. This holds true in work spaces as well as living spaces, although relatively little serious study has been done in those areas. The concept of office landscaping is partially a system that has been shown to influence behavioral patterns within corporations or large groups of office personnel. To provide designers with predictable results will require considerable research on the part of interior designers and behavioral scientists.

In a larger sense, the field of environmental behavior is also a political one. Often an analysis of design/behavioral problems has shown that the building program, or the program leading to the utilization of spaces has not been handled in a sophisticated political way, the result being a rejection of buildings and spaces that might have been otherwise acceptable to the users. In his book, *Design Awareness*, psychologist Robert Sommer states that "if designers want to have an input into the significant questions of who builds what, where it is located, and how it is used—which are essentially political questions—they are going to have to enter the political arena. They will need allies, and the logical place to look for them is among the people who are likely to use the facilities".

In spite of the fact that team work in environmental design has become an accepted norm, it is curious to note that Interior Design is still considered to be a somewhat frivolous aspect of the total process by many planners and policy makers. Perhaps this is due to the fact that the field of Interior Design is still so new as a profession; most likely it is due to the fact that beauty and aesthetics have traditionally been considered superfluous frills by politicians and businessmen. Substitute "user satisfaction" for comfort and aesthetic fulfillment, and substitute "problem solving" for beauty, and the need for serious interior design becomes quickly self-evident. It is puzzling that the extensive recent literature dealing with environmental psychology is primarily concerned with large scale planning, with vast urban problems, with megastructures, landscape architecture and architecture, but rarely with interior design. A significant book dealing with environmental behavior by Constance Perin, *With Man in Mind* (MIT Press, 1970), mentions the interior design profession only in connection with programming. Yet the concept of programming a building or any man-made environment as a process of defining the problem is perhaps the most significant step in the creation of environments responsive to human needs. Interior designers have for some years been interested in pre-architectural programming, and indeed a number of firms specializing in that field have emerged out of interior design offices.

In a discussion of Environmental Behavior one must acknowledge the fact that due to man's ability to adapt, the actual influence of environment upon behavior is difficult to measure in clear and scientific terms. Animals have a considerably lesser range of adaptability, and the manmade environments, specifically zoos, are perhaps the best example of architecture that we are capable of building. Unless such an environment—a zoo or animal habitat—is designed with great attention to temperature, space and physical needs, the animal housed in an inappropriately designed structure would simply die. But since we must accept the fact that design can modify and, to a certain extent, control human behavior, the fact that many of our activities are carried on in interiors seems to point clearly to the need of dealing with the behavioral aspect of what has traditionally been known as architecture.

The greatest need for the input of the social sciences into the design process appears to be in the initial stages of programming. Equally important is the aspect of *design evaluation*, a concept widely discussed in the literature of environmental psychology.

The evaluation of work after completion is something rarely done by designers and architects. Yet a strong case must be made for the need of such ongoing evaluation, perhaps to the point where design fees should clearly include such continuous involvement. In the past, designers were rarely interested in their completed structures once the carefully staged photographs for professional publications had been taken. Yet not only will design evaluation involve learning for the designer and recognition of errors, but it obviously can lead to correction, change and ongoing modification. An anecdote about Frank Lloyd Wright tells of a call from a client to the master reporting a leaking roof and asking what to do about it. Wright's answer was to "put buckets under the leaks". Yet Wright, in his early years before becoming an imperious person, was very conscious of the varying needs of differing clients, and felt that ideally an architect should live with his clients for a while before designing a house for them.

Social scientists have developed methodologies for design evaluation based on careful observation, questionnaires and other testing devices. The evaluation process must be done in several stages, such as upon completion, after a period of months, and probably after a period of years. Ideally, the process will involve a certain amount of modification and re-evaluation after each step in order to provide the maximum benefits to the users.

A number of structured studies have been conducted by social scientists, most of them in controlled institutional settings such as hospitals, schools, dormitories and psychiatric institutions. Meaningful psychological comparisons are in need of control groups for comparative analysis and obviously institutions provide such controls more readily than private residences or work environments. The surprising thing is that in spite of many years of serious and highly revealing research, practically no new design ideas were derived from these studies. Perhaps the need for bridging the gap between the behavioral scientist and the designer is most strongly articulated in this lack. In other words, the ideal approach to such studies would involve the actual implementation as its ultimate goal. The few cases that have been recorded have shown the relative ease with which success and fruition can be brought about. For instance, such minor environmental modifications as carpeting in schools have measurably influenced student behavior. Spatial modification in homes for the retarded have resulted in noticeable behavioral changes on the part of the residents, and studies such as those described in Oscar Newman's book show clearly the resultant attitudinal changes through environmental modification.

The special bibliography appended to this chapter lists a few of the significant books dealing with the field of environmental behavior. In addition, there are several periodicals dealing specifically with the subject. The most comprehensive one is *Design and Environment,* which started publication just a few years ago. The main reasons that motivated a new publication were articulated by its editor, Ann Ferebee as follows:

(1) The natural environment of the entire country was being urbanized and transformed into an inhuman environment.
(2) The conventional architecture of the 60's was contributing to, rather than ameliorating, the problems of human beings.
(3) The conventional "ethic" and "aesthetic" of the 60's was rejected by the young. This was particularly evident in those young people who chose to leave the city and the suburbs and go to live in communes. New aesthetics were beginning to emerge, such as street graphics.
(4) New special client groups were beginning to emerge. Whether from the government in certain NASA programs, or in special citizens' groups, or in "invisible" groups— infants, students, blacks, senior citizens, mental patients. These all began to emerge as special client groups and the question seemed to be: How do we develop data that would give us information about these special client groups?

The recognition of social needs in planning and design is not enough. Equal consideration must be given to ecological, environmental and economic needs. Architects have probably been as guilty as any one group of professionals in their lack of consideration of these problems, and more frequently in causing waste. Many high-rise buildings constructed in the past twenty years were designed without any thought to economic uses of power, consumption of fuel, and electricity. New York City's World Trade Center uses as much power as the city of Schenectady, yet it is impossible for the individual tenants to turn off lights. Heating and airconditioning systems are often causing serious problems to the users of buildings (usually too much) yet there is no way in large structures to open a window. Environments of that nature lack responsiveness to the individual needs, and cause extensive over-use of energy at the same time. Problems dealing with waste disposal, pollutants and other ecologically significant influences are often caused by the designers and architects. It seems safe to predict that design and building economics will become as important over the next decade, as psychological and attitudinal concerns have been for the past ten years.

Another example of joint psychological and economic problems caused by inadequate programming and planning are the hundreds of dormitory buildings erected by universities over the past dozen years. It seems that nobody bothered to find out what students want and need, and at this point, many dormitory structures are empty. Those universities insisting that students continue to live in official student housing find that many of the structures cause serious anti-social behavior, and yet if universities permit students to move off campus, the cost of running the housing units continues for the university; in addition, usually the towns and neighborhoods near universities cannot readily absorb the additional influx of low-income residents (students).

The last two examples of "problems" point out the fact that perhaps we have started to ask the right questions, or have become aware of problems, but certainly we are a long way from dealing adequately and scientifically with the right approaches and solutions. Economic waste, energy waste and environmental or ecological problems in design have not been stratified into specific professional concerns, but it seems clear that all of these aspects concern designers and must involve designers if proper solutions are to be found. It is also important that designers not look towards the behavioral sciences for sudden answers to complex problems, not all experts are competent, and solid research and utilization of research are as rare as good design.

As a summary of this chapter, it might be worthwhile to list briefly those social sciences that have emerged as recognized areas of concern and help to designers:

Landscape Assessment is concerned with the largest spaces, the use and utilization of land and natural resources. Although essential to sound planning and design approaches, it involves planners, geographers and landscape architects, rather than designers who deal with more proximate spaces.

Urban Sociology deals with the determination of social needs on the level of towns and neighborhoods. This is the field that is of primary importance in dealing with mass urban housing, with ethnic and minority groups, and with the background studies, both anthropological and sociological, of large groups of people and their interactions.

Proxemics is probably the field of most direct concern to interior designers. The word has been coined by the anthropologist Edward T. Hall (*The Hidden Dimension* and *The Silent Language*). Hall points out that people's perception and use of space vary from culture to culture. Proxemics also deals with individual differences and perceptions of space within specific groups and cultures; by now, there are many ongoing studies with significantly revealing results that are used by designers.

Ecological Psychology was first pioneered by Roger Barker, a psychologist. Much of his work has centered around schools and has resulted in a concept based on behavioral settings. In other words, unlike the anthropological approach dealing with culture differences, ecological psychology deals with the setting as the determinant to behavior.

Environmental Psychology (or architectural psychology) has been pioneered by Ittelson and Proshansky at the graduate department of psychology at the City University in New York. The technique that has been developed as a prime tool is called "behavioral mapping". Many of their studies were done in mental wards. Compared to Barker, who would observe and monitor a space in order to observe who came and went and what effect such space had on people, Ittelson and Proshansky's method observes the individual and his or her behavior.

These foregoing classifications are obviously somewhat oversimplified in order to present a concise summary of the total field of environmental behavior. Since it is a new field, and a scientific field larger than the main concern of this book—design—we include in the general bibliography a selected bibliography for those readers and students who wish to delve more deeply into the subject matter.

IV

INTERIOR DESIGN IN CURRENT PRACTICE

Most of our lives are spent in interiors, but not all manmade interiors were necessarily designed by designers for their particular purpose. Many factories, transportation interiors, schools, offices, and houses were built without architects and designers.

Maybe there is hope implied in this observation: when our society learns to care enough about its environment, there will be vast visual improvement and also largely increased opportunities for the scope of activities of designers. No business interior of importance is built today without the involvement of a designer somewhere along the line, and it seems reasonable to anticipate that society will eventually expect the care, the planning, and the design that is the norm for those interiors to be brought about as a matter of course for all manmade interiors.

The main activities of interior designers today can be divided into roughly four different categories: spaces for work, spaces for living, public spaces, and special-purpose interiors. The photographs on the following pages and the accompanying captions reflect not only the solutions to specific problems, but also point out the significant design statements in each case. There are certain basic approaches to interior design, and it might be well to consider those in general terms before we examine specific solutions.

Design is above all the solution to a problem. It is not just a matter of combining beautiful forms, textures, colors, and materials. Every interior has some function and purpose, and it is the designer's obligation above all to deal with the required function. An interior that does not "work" might be an attractive stage set or window display, just as a building that does not work might be an interesting piece of sculpture; but if the interior does not work for its stated function, it fails on the most important level of design.

We are concerned with design and must therefore apply designers' criteria in observing the current practice of interior design. Regardless of the type of interior to be designed, there are a number of criteria that should be examined. Depending on whether the interior is for work, living, public use, or some special purpose, the degree of importance of these criteria will vary. Here are some of the key questions a designer must consider and the same questions should be posed by the critical viewer and by the user of the space:

What is the main activity in the space?

How does it relate to other spaces in the same building?

What are the traffic patterns and patterns of circulation?

What are the special requirements for this space? Have they been provided for?

What are the needs for daylight and nighttime illumination?

What about acoustics, heating, and air conditioning?

What consideration has been given to maintenance?

Is the mood or atmosphere appropriate?

Are the materials used the proper ones? Are they readily available? Are they economical?

Does the space strive for an "image" (as in a public building?)

What is the budget limitation? Has it been respected?

What are the clients' special desires and needs?

Does the location of the job and the architecture suggest certain materials or design features? Are there climatic considerations?

What is the designer's intent?

These are just some examples of the questions that a designer must first consider, and that we should keep in mind when we try to understand and evaluate a completed job. The examples of criteria are not meant to be a complete checklist of all possible questions for every and any kind of interior, but they will explain the fact that a space cannot be judged by its emotive and aesthetic impression alone.

1

WORK SPACES

We mentioned that not all interiors are "designed" with a view to the creation of the most functional and beautiful environment. There are many factories, laboratories, warehouses, and workshops that are quite beautiful without the conscious effort of a designer. The reason for this is precisely the fact that these kinds of spaces have been designed with the functional or problem-solving approach alone in mind, and therefore turn out to be beautiful. We discussed this phenomenon in Part One in relation to industrial products, bridges, and engineered objects such as airplanes and ships. The beautiful results often achieved by unconscious design in interiors are effected through the same logical and functional approach that results in some of our best twentieth-century technological achievements of beauty.

The work spaces that are designed with the intent to create beauty as well as efficiency are most frequently offices. It is interesting to note here that in an industrial, technologically advanced society, the vast majority of jobs are so-called white-collar jobs, and jobs classified by economists as "service" jobs. The increased attention that business and industry have lavished upon the environment of its office force is therefore the direct result of a need that did not exist fifty years ago to the degree that it exists today. As a result of this relatively recent need, interior design firms have come into existence whose main activity is the planning and design of offices. In fact, the name that is frequently used to define these design organizations is "space planners" or "contract designers". The latter name derives from the mode of business operation of

Manufacturers Hanover Trust Company Building, New York. Skidmore, Owings and Merrill, architects, 1953–54. (Photographs courtesy of Manufacturers Hanover Trust Company, New York)

these designers as contrasted to the mode of business operation of the decorator of a generation ago. The "interior decorator" used to earn his/her compensation through the sale of furnishings sold to the client at a markup over the wholesale price. In designing and furnishing business interiors, the standard procedure is the more professional one of making a contract with the client in which a professional fee is clearly spelled out for services performed by the designer, and supplying furnishings is included as part of the same contract. Hence the term "contract design". The typical method of work and operation of these and other types of interior design offices will be discussed in a later chapter. For the purpose of gaining an understanding of the specific problems involved in the design of work spaces, it is more important here to examine the needs and points of view of the client.

There is a considerable difference in needs between a small one-man professional office, a local branch office of a bank, and a large corporation headquarters occupying many floors in a high-rise office building. Within the general classification of office work there are equally large differences between the work of secretaries, computer operators, and clerks on the one hand, and executives, salesmen, or administrators on the other hand. For each type of office and for each type of worker within an office, it is essential for the designer to understand precisely the spatial and functional needs of each individual, as well as the interrelationship between individuals, departments, and the public. A whole new method for the scientific solution of large and complex offices has been developed in an

experimental way in recent years. This method, known as "office landscape", was developed in Germany, and has not been used widely in the United States at this date. It is, however, a significant approach to the solution of office design problems and will be discussed briefly in a separate chapter.

Every client who retains a design firm has some idea (by no means precise) of his spatial and functional needs. What image the office conveys is often a decision that must be made by the designer, and it may reflect the intent of the designer as much as the expressed intent of the client. The mores and traditions of our society dictate certain expectations. One would expect the offices or ticket agencies of an airline to reflect the image of up-to-date efficiency, but one would expect a more playful or frivolous image projected for offices or sales areas of toys or perfume. The mood created in a funeral parlor would obviously be a different one from the mood or atmosphere in a nightclub or restaurant. Social mores are somewhat like fashions and change from time to time. Until about fifteen years ago the interiors of banks "had" to be solid, full of marble, fake columns, and heavy, stodgy furniture. With the building of the Manufacturers Hanover Trust Company's Fifth Avenue office by Skidmore, Owings and Merrill in the early

An open "Action Office" interior for the Asiatic Petroleum Company, New York City. **Michael Di Iorio and Co., designer.** (Photograph courtesy Herman Miller, Inc.)

The "open" office of the Chairman of the Board of Dial Financial Corp. John Pile, office planner and interior designer. (Photograph by Norman McGrath)

1950's, a new tradition was created; and the bank—with large glass areas and many exterior-related features such as planting areas or doors with air curtains—has become accepted by and became a desirable model for the banking community.

Designers of work spaces offer many services to their clients before the actual designing begins. Through training and experience, designers have learned to analyze a client's needs and often can offer substantial savings to a firm by advising on the kind of space that might be suitable for expansion and change; or sometimes through efficient planning the design firm can advise the clients to lease a smaller and less expensive space than the one contemplated originally. From negotiating the lease for a work space to the specification of flooring and wall-surfacing materials, countless factors must be considered that are based on functional and economic considerations rather than purely aesthetic ones.

2

LIVING SPACES

The functional considerations which are of paramount importance in the design of work spaces exist in the design of living spaces too, but are proportionately less important. Living spaces or homes are highly personal environments. Design criteria are valid and meaningful in general terms, but obviously each individual tenant or homeowner can make unusual and esoteric decisions and can be perfectly happy living within a strange interior that might seem shocking or poorly designed to the trained designer. To use a crass example, it would seem poor planning and poor design to find the bathroom on the opposite side of the livingroom, away from the sleeping area, or it would seem absurd to have the dining area separated from the kitchen by a bedroom. Yet such houses and apartments have been built, or owners have arranged them in such a way for lack of proper understanding—or worse, for no reason but wanting to be different. As designers we cannot be too concerned with eccentricities of people and must base our criteria on sound principles and norms. It seems, in fact, that basic principles are the only important ones in the design of living environments. The decorations and the choice of furniture and furnishings would ideally (if really good products were readily available) be up to each homemaker. The selection of colors and materials should be as personal an expression as the selection of a dress or tie. The woman who would not ever dare to select a simple piece of furniture or fabric without her "decorator" would rarely dream of asking a professional fashion expert to go shopping with her for a new dress or coat.

The really capable designer does not impose his own preferences on a client, but will guide the client to the creation of a home that reflects the owner's interests and personal preferences within the principles of good design and planning.

There are a good many considerations which all too frequently are neglected in the design of living spaces; in fact the checklist at the beginning of Part Four applies point by point to a home as much as to an office or other work space. Logical planning of one space in relation to another seems elementary, yet many houses and apartments exist—some designed, some built by developers—that seem to intend their occupants to chase up and down the stairs or through long corridors, or that seem likely to create conflict between activities of children and parents. Even more homes have been built without any consideration for the arrangement of furniture within rooms or for the location of doors and doorswings, and in which the location of windows bears no relation to any possible use of the spaces. Storage for the average family should certainly be more than two or three bedroom closets of very limited size. Most living spaces ignore the storage of normal family possessions, such as bicycles and baby carriages, sports equipment and tools, or any number of the many possessions that most families own. The rare exceptions in which living spaces are logically planned are houses or apartments planned through collaboration between architects and interior designers, or by architects who acted as interior designers for the houses they designed.

Obviously a distinction must be drawn at this point between the living spaces that are truly designed and the mass housing in builders' developments or apartments, which unfortunately represents the large majority of existing homes today. But even in these mass housing units, interior design can often overcome the poor architectural features that have been provided. Without undue expense it is possible to provide storage facilities, shelving, and a furniture plan that will solve the basic needs of the occupants. The needs and desires of the average family usually include such trappings of our affluent society as television sets, music systems (from a simple record player to elaborate stereophonic systems), records, books, hobby equipment, facilities for entertaining, and many more. To see the popular displays and advertisements for furniture, one might deduce that ours is an illiterate society with nobody ever writing a letter, reading a book, or doing anything but sitting in front of a large and ugly television set, smack in the center of the living room or "den". The examples pictured on the following pages are living spaces designed by designers, showing care and consideration that may be beyond the reach of the average family. But it seems self-evident that the level of design in any and every living space could be much improved with at least the basic guidance that a designer could provide. Having stated earlier that living spaces should not depend on the interior designer, but should be the expression of their occupants, this might sound like a contradiction. Much depends, however, on the availability of well-designed furniture and furnishings, and to date there is vast room for improvement in this direction. The market offers huge quantities of tasteless and ugly products in home furnishings, and it is probable that until much better design is produced for the mass market, the services of the interior designer will still be highly desirable, as a kind of guide in the wilderness of bad design.

The guidance and direction that the trained designer can offer would seem to be especially important to families of limited means. National magazines like a feature article on the profession of interior design from time to time. Invariably the image of the society decorator emerges—the decorator-designer who deals with nothing less than a penthouse or luxury apartment, and whose minimum budget seems higher than the average yearly income of most people. Families who can afford to spend a great deal of money on their living spaces can buy the most expensive furnishings, which are not necessarily the best, but which at least have a better chance of being of some design quality. They can also afford to make mistakes and discard a sofa or chair after a year or two if they do not like it. Residents of low-income housing deserve and need qualified design help more than anybody; to date the design profession has done but little in this direction. It is to be hoped that our social structure and social values will change to bring about much more design activity for the low and middle-income groups and make it possible to offer this professional service without loss of income to the design profession.

Some of the criteria on our checklist may seem at first glance to be of relatively little importance for the design of living spaces. Lighting, heating and air conditioning are often just afterthoughts in homes, yet are of great importance in terms of comfort, function, and design. Let us take lighting for example. Obviously good lighting is important for work in kitchens, at desks, or for other tasks in a home, but it is ignored for even these obvious needs most of the time. Most people have experienced physical discomfort and strain just sitting in a friend's house and talking. More often than not, this was the result of poor lighting. It can be as much of a factor of discomfort as an uncomfortable chair.

Maintenance too seems at first glance of lesser importance in a living space than in a hospital or hotel. This is not so. Durability of materials is a vital factor for people of limited means. The ease of maintenance of floors, fabrics, or furniture is certainly of great concern to every homemaker, and the specification of appropriate materials for specific areas or surfaces is again something the interior designer knows by training and experience. As an aside we might mention here that maintenance is also related to safety factors, especially in home environment. More accidents occur in the home than any other place, and many are caused by poorly maintained or shoddy surfaces, or are the result of poor planning in the home.

No mention of beauty, decoration, or style has been made in this brief discussion of the design of living spaces. This is a conscious omission. It is unnecessary to point out that works of art and beautiful objects can do more to create a personal living environment of distinction and meaning than anything that can be created with the planning and arrangement of furniture and materials alone. However, the discussion of living space in terms of basic design criteria will help focus on the underlying principles of interior design in terms of a problem-solving approach. The other facts that contribute to the design of living spaces will be treated in more detail later.

3

PUBLIC SPACES

Any attempt to make a clear and precise definition of what exactly are public spaces, in contrast to special-purpose interiors or even work spaces, is bound to show a good deal of overlapping in definition. Basically the term "public" denotes that these spaces are open to all people and that control of the access is in the public domain. Large circulation spaces or ceremonial interiors such as waiting rooms, concourses, and lobbies in the first group (public spaces), and churches or civic interiors in the second group (special-purpose interiors) seem clear and obvious. Spaces such as hotels or department stores could be classified either way, since they are privately owned. What really matters is not the social or economic categories under which one can count these spaces, but the fact that large numbers of the public are encouraged to use the spaces and that many people use these spaces or pass through them out of necessity. This public aspect places a special responsibility on the designer, one similar to the responsibility shared by the city planner, landscape architect, and architect—namely, the design and control of manmade environment and its effect on man.

One of the serious shortcomings in the field of interior design is the fact that practically no serious criticism is ever offered for completed interiors. No other creative profession exists without public criticism in newspapers and magazines. The role of a qualified critic is often a constructive one. Literature, music, art, and drama receive much professional criticism. The amount of criticism in the field of architecture is small compared to criticism in the other arts, and the amount of criticism for interior design is practically nonexistent, unless

**The Lehman Wing,
Metropolitan Museum
of Art, New York City.
Designed by
Roche Dinkloo,
architects.** (Photograph
by John Pile)

an architectural critic analyzes an occasional interior job. We do not wish to digress at this time, but we should point out that one of the main reasons for this serious shortcoming in the field is the fact that neither the public nor the practitioners have yet made a clear distinction between the business and professional aspects of interior design. Business and industry indirectly control much of the popular and professional press, and it is difficult for a publication to take a clear and critical stand on any public interior as long as this state of affairs exists. This fact is mentioned here in connection with interiors of public spaces, since one could certainly argue that a "man's home is his castle" and take living spaces out of the sphere of

The main entrance hall of the Metropolitan Museum of Art, New York City. Designed in Roman Style by Richard Morris Hunt, 1895. (Photograph by John Pile)

public criticism. One could even state that work spaces too are in a way very private interiors, and are therefore above public criticism. Public interiors, on the other hand, affect many people and—like streets, the neighborhood, or the whole city—are a vital and inescapable part of our environment. They must, for those reasons, be designed to work for their stated purpose above all, they must consider human needs, and they must be designed for multitudes of people rather than for a single client or for the satisfaction of the designer.

Again we return to the criteria or questions we listed at the outset of Part Four. Depending on the specific type of interior, certain questions raised take on more importance than others.

The main concourse of the terminal building at Dulles International Airport (Washington, D. C.) by Eero Saarinen.
(Photograph by John Pile)

For example, the question of circulation is of course a crucial one when we deal with spaces handling large groups of people, such as a terminal or lobby. The traffic patterns, clearances of aisles, and clarity of directions may make the difference between comfortable movement through a space, or congested chaos. Proper lighting and attractive and easy to maintain surfacing materials could make even a subway station a pleasant space, compared to the drab and oppressive-looking dungeons that subway stations are as a rule.

We mentioned some types of public and ceremonial spaces in our chapter dealing with scale (II.2); obviously the scale and proportion of a space should be more generous for large masses of people than for small groups. The noise level in a low ceilinged bus or air terminal can be so intense and confusing that even the most luxurious materials and details in such a space would not help to make it pleasant or even adequate for a large group of people. The majestic proportions of a Gothic cathedral, the lofty heights of a church, or even Grand Central Station in New York offer a spatial elegance that in most cases can only be created by the architect. But the willingness of the interior designer to respect and emphasize these basic tenets is often lacking. Many perfectly well-scaled building lobbies or similar large spaces have been cluttered up with

inappropriate furniture and decorative devices. No public space must be designed without keeping in mind the element of large groups of people, for whom the space is designed. It is in fact not fair to judge a public interior from photographs or even in three-dimensions, without seeing people move through the space and use it for the purpose for which it was created. By the same token, it is a serious mistake to deal with these spaces as if they were small living rooms or other highly personal interiors.

A truly creative designer will analyze the public spaces s/he is asked to design and sometimes come up with solutions that are quite different from the problem posed by the client. Eero Saarinen, for example, was asked to design a new terminal for the Dulles International Airport in Washington, D.C. The building that he designed in 1960 is very handsome and is structurally interesting through the use of a cable-supported roof. But the real contributiton made by Saarinen was to go beyond the norm of the typical airport building. Instead of designing departure lounges connected to the main terminal by means of a concourse, he designed mobile lounges. Passengers enter these lounges directly from the main airport building. When all passengers are checked in, the mobil lounge is driven up to the airplane. Disembarking from planes, pas-

An airline terminal building at Kennedy Airport, New York, I.M. Pei and Partners, architects. The structure is a huge space-truss supported on widely spaced columns standing outside the glass walls. (Photograph by John Pile)

sengers following the same procedure in reverse. This idea is not only of great practical use to the passengers, but it also results in a less bulky and less costly airport structure, eliminates walking, eliminates congestion in the corridors and concourses, and allows for practically unlimited future expansion of the airport. As an aside we should point out that airports are probably the largest growing public buildings and interiors in our era, and, with the exception of the Dulles terminal, few meaningful design contributions have been made in the past few years. In every major city here and abroad, the typical sight at any airport is building activity of some kind. It seems almost as if no airport facility is ever finished, creating a kind of perpetual construction that leads to increasing confusion for traveler and airport personnel alike.

Another interesting example in the category of public buildings and interiors is Frank Lloyd Wright's Guggenheim Museum, built in New York in 1959. Here Wright did away with the accepted concepts of museum design and created the famous spiral-shaped building with a continuous interior ramp. Much criticism was voiced against the building, especially that the building dominates the works of art displayed within. Without taking sides in the aesthetic and architectural dispute, we mention this example only to show what the concept of moving people in a continuous stream through an exhibition has achieved and how vitally it has affected the design of the interior as a totally unique concept.

Public interiors often must create an image or a mood that almost dominates all other consideration. Churches have been mentioned several times as examples of ceremonial interiors, but a number of contemporary churches have been built in the last decade that have achieved a strongly spiritual mood without the scale and proportion of traditional church architecture. Just as the image that was "correct" for banks in the past has changed, other public-interior images too have tended to change. Governmental interiors and interiors of courthouses used to require an almost totalitarian atmosphere—monumental, cold, and rather forbidding. Today, in the more successful government structures, both in the United States and abroad, we have learned to accept other moods and expressions. But in all cases, the public interiors of importance strive for a "message" or an image that may be monumental or spiritual, awe-inspiring or inviting. To achieve these strongly expressive buildings and interiors, designers must consider these requirements very much as part of the function, even if the resulting solution is not the most direct or economical one.

4

SPECIAL PURPOSE INTERIORS

This last group in our four basic categories of interiors in current practice is the most complex and is the group for which it is most difficult to state any common criteria of design. Included in the group are such widely diversified spaces as theaters and stage sets on the one hand, and the interiors of airplanes or ships with their rigidly limited and demanding special considerations on the other hand. To evaluate some of these highly specialized jobs, the first question from our checklist that must be raised is: What are the special requirements for this space?

If a space is designed as a store or sales area, the most important requirement would be to facilitate the sale of merchandise or services, with all its implications of display, lighting, and special atmosphere. If the space happens to be a ship's lounge, the first consideration might have to be safety factors, including the use of fireproof material, even before the consideration of seating, comfort, and character of the space. One of the key factors in the evaluation of architecture and interiors is the clarity of expression for a particular purpose. It seems logical, therefore, to expect the interior of a ship to express in terms of character, the fact that the spaces are part of an ocean-going vessel. The concept of making a ship a "floating hotel" or an hotel "a home away from home" is not necessarily a correct one. The idea of designing such special-purpose interiors as railroad lounge cars to look like old-fashioned pubs, and the design of pubs to make them look like parlors, was a very popular Victorian concept, but one that no longer meets the requirements of current practice and thinking. Once again we point out that the expectation of "images" is constantly

The New York City Olivetti Showroom (demolished) with sculptured wall by Constantino Nivola. (Photograph by John Pile)

Main banking room atrium, Bank of Mississippi, Tupelo, Mississippi. Interiors by I.S.D., Inc., Mah & Jones, architects. (Photograph by Nick Wheeler)

Interior of a Braniff Airlines aircraft. Interior design by Harper and George.

changing. But within each period of time, designers must learn to express in their work a true reflection of current thought. This fundamental aesthetic theory gives rise to many debates in the field of special-purpose interiors and no single answer can be given. If a designer is commissioned to design a restaurant serving South American food in New York City, one could expect an interior reflecting the environment of a twentieth-century United States city and of materials indigenous to the area surrounding the location of the restaurant. Alexander Girard was given such a challenge when he was asked to design the La Fonda Del Sol Restaurant* in 1960 and chose to reflect the culture and the artifacts of South America as the prime motif for the interior design. Girard saw the need to give prime consideration to the image of the restaurant, but he solved the design in handsome contemporary terms in spite of the fact that a certain degree of artificiality or a kind of stage-set quality resulted. Professionals do not always agree on where to draw the line between honest expression in design and fakery. The main critical consideration should be the architecture encompassing the special-purpose interior space. If the interior is within a distinguished architectural shell, the design should reflect the architectural concept. It would have seemed incongruous to design an English pub type of restaurant within the strong and beautiful Seagram Building. Philip Johnson's and William Pahlman's design for the Four Seasons Restaurant was therefore a highly proper solution. The archi-

*See photograph on p. 246

The elaborately equipped control room adjacent to a TV viewing room, D'Arcy-MacManus & Masius advertising agency offices, Chicago, Illinois. Interior design by I.S.D., Inc. (Photograph by Steve Grubman)

tectural shell containing the La Fonda Del Sol Restaurant is a less important one, and in fact the space that Girard created within the shell achieves more importance and distinction than the building itself.

A type of special-purpose interior dealt with very frequently by interior designers is the hotel. We mentioned previously that the cliché of the "home away from home" is an outdated concept. The main reason for this dogmatic statement is that one would have to ask immediately, whose home? Indeed it would seem that the special requirements for hotel interiors must include all considerations of comfort and rest, possibly even beyond those of the home. The designer, however, must keep in mind that his client is not one person or one family, but a succession of hundreds of different people throughout the year. Occupants of hotels vary from the honeymoon couple to the traveling college football team, and from the family with children to the businessman who must use his hotel room as an office or salesroom.

The captions accompanying the photographs on the following pages point out some of the special problems and requirements, and the resultant solutions, in various types of special-purpose interiors. The designer of each one had to cope with differing and at times unique challenges. The conclusion to be drawn from an examination of these interiors underlines the thesis proposed in the introduction to this section. Interior design, like all design, is above all the attempt of the designer to find the solutions to problems.

5

OFFICE LANDSCAPE

A new and very special type of interior is the "office land-scape". This curious term, a literal translation of the German *Büro-Landschaft*, describes a system of office planning developed during the last few years in Europe which is attracting considerable attention at the present time. An "office land-scape" interior tends to be quite shocking to most designers on first exposure, particularly when seen in plan, because it seems to violate all the generally accepted principles of good design. In plan it appears that furniture and portable screens have been thrown into a space at random with a chaotic absence of pattern. On closer examination, however, it becomes clear that the originators of office landscape have some very specific and reasonable ideas which lead to these unusual results.

The developers of this method, the Quickborner Team of Hamburg, are, in fact, office management consultants rather than designers. Their study of office operation has led them to the belief that office planning should be based on patterns of communication, with all other values (such as appearance, status recognition, and tradition) either ignored or given a very minor status. Placement of work stations is determined by the flow of communication, which is the vital part of daily office functioning.

It is also basic to the "landscape" idea that partitioning be avoided. Even so-called movable partitions that take time and money to move are considered barriers to communication and flexibility. Without partitioning, change to accommodate changing work patterns becomes both quick and inexpensive.

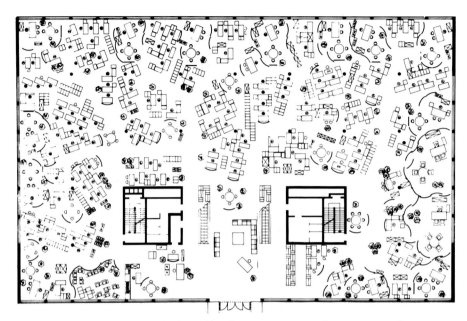

A typical Office Landscape plan. Office for Orenstein-Koppel near Dortmund, Germany. Quickborner Team, planners.

General view of an Office Landscape floor.

Chart showing density of communications flow between departments of an organization. Such charting precedes "Landscape" planning.

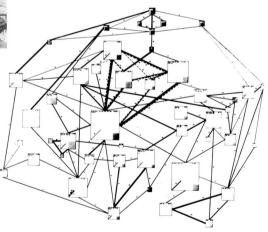

Communication is always easy in an office space without subdivision, there is a saving in space resulting from the sharing of circulation space that would otherwise have to be duplicated in each private space, and the reduction in emphasis on the symbolic values of status turn out to be helpful to office morale and work efficiency.

Without partitions, loss of privacy becomes most bothersome in terms of noise. For this reason, an office landscape requires complete carpeting of floors and elaborate acoustical treatment of all ceilings. It is also a part of the system that all massive furniture with solid surfaces must be avoided because these are also a source of sound reflection. Noisy office machines are removed from the general office space to special isolated locations. Permanent files are also placed in remote locations so that only small open file baskets are used in the regular office space.

Reception area for the U.S. Postal Service built within federal office budget standards. Designed by SLS/Environetics, Inc. (Photograph courtesy of Natalie Parry Associates)

"Landscape" or "Open planning" executive
office space in the corporate headquarters
of the Weyerhaeuser Co., Tacoma.
Skidmore, Owings and Merrill, architects;
Sydney Rodgers Asociates, Inc., Space Planners;
furniture system by Knoll International.

Offices for the Freon Division of DuPont,
Wilmington, Delaware. Quickborner Team,
consultants to Du Pont General Service Department,
planners.

The office landscape planning method begins with a survey of all communication in the office organization—whether by conversation, written memo, or telephone. Every staff member keeps a log of communications conducted for a period of two weeks. These data are then analyzed, in the case of large organizations with the help of a data-processing computer. This leads to a plan placing each work station so as to minimize the length of the most active lines of communication. People who must be in frequent contact are placed close together, those who have little need for contact end up far apart. Departmental organization and official "lines of command" are ignored in order to arrive at an arrangement that will reflect the real needs for proximity. Detailed layout is not geometric (since this would restrict the ease of following the guidance of the communications-dictated plan), but follows certain rules about details so as to avoid, for example, seating any two workers in a face-to-face position.

Once the basic plan has been arrived at, a scale model is built with movable furniture and portable screen elements placed according to the proposed plan. This model is made available to representatives of the working staff who will occupy the office so that criticisms and changes can be considered. In practice, it has been found that few changes result from this

An open plan general office. Dial Financial Corp., Des Moines, Iowa. John Pile, office planner and interior designer. (Photograph by Norman McGrath)

Knoll International, Stephens Office System Plus with Task Lighting. Knoll Task Lighting is a new and revolutionary approach to illumination. The system was designed to individualize the use of light and to provide immediate control of the light source with maximum flexibility for change. There are numerous additional advantages to this lighting system including a reduction in kilowatt hours required for lighting and air conditioning.
(Photograph courtesy of Knoll International)

step, but that it is very helpful in securing the understanding and cooperation of those who will finally use the office. There is also a routine continuing study of needed changes, with a general rearrangement taking place approximately every six months to deal with all the accumulated needs for revision that have developed during that time. Since there are no fixed, architectural elements, such change is quick and inexpensive.

Up to now, most experience with this planning system has been developed in Europe. Reports indicate that there is an increase in work efficiency and that office workers tend to like the "landscape" office better than conventional offices. There can be no question that the cost of construction will be low (because of the omission of partitioning), and the cost of changes is so low as to be almost negligible.

Most American office planners remain skeptical about the value of the system. They dislike its seemingly random patterns of arrangement and question whether the absence of privacy will not be objectionable to most office staff members who

Offices made up of
moveable furniture
modules in the
Center for Training and
Management Development
for the Xerox Corporation
at Leesburg, Va.
Kling Interior Design and
Vincent G. Kling and
Partners, architects.

A round open conference
area in the offices of
the Weyerhauser Co.,
Tacoma, Washington.
Skidmore, Owings and
Merrill, architects,
Sydney Rogers, Associates,
space planners.
(Photograph by Ezra
Stoller, ESTO, courtesy
Sydney Rogers, Associates)

have become accustomed to private offices. As examples of this kind of planning come into use in this country, there will be a fuller evaluation of how well it suits American requirements. In England and in the Scandinavian countries, office landscape seems to have had considerable acceptance in a somewhat modified form in which arrangements of furniture are more orderly and more conventional in spirit than in the German prototypes, and with private (or semiprivate) areas demarked by arrangements of furniture, screen, and storage units in a way that closely approaches the private offices of more conventional practice.

There may well be an assimilation of the original *Büro-Landschaft* ideas into conventional office planning that will lead to results that include the freedom and the economies of this system, while retaining a more traditional visual appearance and offering some level of privacy in the areas where this is a genuine requirement.

6

ADAPTIVE REUSE
AND RESTORATION

The adaptive reuse of older and historic buildings, their restoration and their preservation, involve many groups and many professionals. It has become increasingly evident that a good deal of work connected with these activities is carried out by interior designers, since frequently the work entails interior design more than architectural work, and more than historic research. Whether one calls these activities adaptive reuse (which is the term we chose to apply) or recycling or remodeling of buildings, this aspect of design has become sufficiently important in the field of interior design to warrant a brief overview and discussion of the state of the art.

Historic preservation and restoration of buildings also involve interior designers, in fact, there are a number of knowledgeable experts working hand in hand with architectural historians and architects. Historic preservation refers to the activities of those who attempt to save architecturally significant buildings from destruction. They are moved to this effort by the hope of perpetuating a tangible record of the past. This movement developed in response to the razing of older buildings to make way for parking lots and other so-called improvements. Restoration in its strictest sense deals with historical structures that have fallen into disrepair. Adaptive reuse is an economic necessity. It is obvious that society cannot afford to support more than a small number of beautifully restored and preserved buildings as museums. In Europe, where an awareness of the cultural importance of an architectural heritage has existed long before we became conscious of this need (and of course, Europe has a much greater wealth of historic structures), it also became apparent that the cost of maintaining large numbers of older buildings was not an economically feasible undertaking. The British National Trust, for instance, can not accept the donation of great mansions or country houses unless they are endowed for perpetual maintenance at the same time. Added to these facts of economic reality is today's high cost of building, and inflation. Hence, even builders and developers who in years past might have been tempted to tear down buildings and start new construction, have come to realize that many of our older structures are solidly built, and that adaptive reuse makes economic sense.

The first instance of preservation in the United States occurred in 1816 when the city of Philadelphia bought Independence Hall from the State of Pennsylvania. This was not followed by any other preservation efforts until the middle of the nineteenth century. An attempt to save the old Indian House in Deerfield, Massachusetts in 1847 failed. Efforts to save the John Hancock House in Boston in 1859 also met with failure. The first nationwide preservation effort was organized by Ann Pamela Cunningham to save Mount Vernon in 1853. Developers wished to turn it into a hotel (thus curiously, adaptive reuse was contemplated in preference to preservation). Miss Cunningham sent out appeals to the women of the South: "Can you be still with closed souls and purses, while the world cries 'shame upon America', and Mount Vernon, with all its sacred associations, to become, as is spoken of and probable, the seat of manufacturers and manufactories?...Never! Forbid it, shades of the dead!" Within the week the government of Virginia asked the legislature to consider action. It declined to use public funds for the $200,000 needed, but instead chartered the Mount Vernon Ladies Association. Cunningham succeeded, and moreover, set a precedent for accomplishing the seemingly impossible, which has been the inspiration for preservation efforts ever since. From Mount Vernon sprang the tradition of carefully organized private effort as the means of securing the funds for historic preservation. Following the Civil War and the Centennial Celebrations of 1876, the historic preservation movement was well under way. Efforts sprang from a pious desire to preserve buildings associated with great men or great events such as Faneuil Hall and Old North Church in Boston, or Paul Revere's House, Monticello, and the Hermitage. By 1900, preservationists and the general public were involved in an antiquarian mentality of saving historic houses, buildings, and small districts as museums and shrines. People embarked on a program of historic preservation through restoration, reconstruction, and "re-creation". The emphasis started to shift from purely historical and patriotic, to a cultural and architectural viewpoint.

An American Colonial house at Deerfield, Massachusetts. (Photograph by John Pile)

In the 1920's and 1930's preservation interest shifted to outdoor museums such as Williamsburg. Sparked in 1927 by the Reverend Goodwin, the pastor of the Bruton church, John D. Rockefeller donated over 70 million dollars over a period of 40 years for the restoration of Williamsburg. Some of the buildings are restored, some are reconstructed, point of continuous controversy in the field, i.e., is a reconstruction valid in historic, artistic, and architectural terms, or it is less valid than restoration and preservation? Williamsburg is also criticized at times as being too much of a place of entertainment. Other projects of a similar nature were developed, including Sturbridge Village and Old Deerfield. The latter is probably one of the least commercialized restorations in the country. Unlike the antiquarian restoration of a particular period as done at Williamsburg, Old Deerfield represents the maintenance of a town in which people live, teach, and learn, and where everything from the seventeenth century to the twentieth century can be found along the street.

The Federal Government became involved in historic preservation in the 1930's. In 1933 the National Park Service began the historic American Building Survey, a cooperative effort with the Library of Congress and the American Institute of Architects to document buildings of historic and architectural merit. Under the Historic Sites Act of 1935, the Park Service started a national register of historic places, which initially included historic areas in the National Park system and National Historic Landmarks. In 1949 Congress chartered the National Trust for Historic Preservation. This organization acts as a national clearinghouse for preservation matters, provides legal advice to other preservation groups, and owns a number of buildings. In 1966 the Federal Government passed a comprehensive historic preservation act that broadened and strengthened federal preservation programs. In the same year Congress passed the Model Cities Act which set up urban renewal demonstration grants to make possible for communities to identify, acquire and restore historical structures, and allocate funds to assist those people who were relocated because of urban renewal activities. Since 1966 there have been many changes in H.U.D. programs. Revenue sharing of the early 1970's made funds available for community improvement. The Housing and Community Development Act of 1974 gave Federal support to states and cities in the form of block grants, which potentially make more money available for preservation activities. More recently, tax acts of 1976 and 1978 have given commercial property owners incentives to rehabilitate and restore, in the form of tax breaks.

A 1954 court case resulted in a Supreme Court decision by Justice William O. Douglas which ruled that a city has the right to be beautiful as well as safe and sanitary for its citizens. Such an assumption is basic to the present wide acceptance of the preservation of historic districts by architectural control as a legitimate function of government. However, even prior to that court decision, a number of historic districts were developed–first amongst them in Charleston, South Carolina, followed a few years later by the designation of New Orleans' Vieux Carré as an historic district. Today there are a good many such districts from Boston's Beacon Hill district to Nantucket or to the Lowell, Massachusetts National Park. The fact that the American Society of Interior Designers gave one of its 1980 international design awards to Senator Paul Tsongas for his role in creating that National Park, underlines the importance of these developments for the interior design field. The number of legislative acts and governmental programs from Urban Homesteading to Revolving Funds and Preservation by Deed continue to support and encourage preservation and adaptive reuse. The 1970's saw rapidly increasing examples of adaptive reuse, especially in commerce and in public buildings.

Builders and developers are aware of the fact that adaptive reuse holds real economic advantages. So-called soft costs, such as holding costs during construction, insurance and taxes are less in rehabilitation work because construction time is shorter.

These soft cost savings can mean that an adaptive reuse building can be 30 percent less than it would be for new construction. Frequently, continuous income from current tenants can be maintained during renovation, further reducing the amount to be permanently financed. Hard costs such as demolition are also less. In many adaptive reuse projects, the hard costs of purchasing and remodeling a building to standard improvement levels comparable to a new, large speculative office building, for instance, was 40 to 50 percent of the cost of a new building. Another argument which bolsters the economic benefits of adaptive reuse lies in the rising concern for conservation of energy and resources. While the cost of building materials has been skyrocketing, the availability of materials has decreased. Many raw materials and energy resources exist in finite quantities. Thus an approach such as adaptive reuse is a conservation alternative to the often wasteful energy practices of new construction.

Not every old building is worth saving, and not every location is suitable for major adaptive reuse projects. Three basic assessments need to be undertaken: the assessment of location, the existing physical conditions of the building, and an assessment of the architectural, historical and/or environmental significance. Investors and builders often consider the location of a building of paramount importance. However, experience has shown that through programs such as Urban Homesteading, for instance, individuals have renovated residences in decaying neighborhoods, and have sparked a rather remarkable trend in their neighborhoods, causing others to follow suit, and changing that particular neighborhood within a few years. In a number of inner cities, adaptive reuse has brought forth the new problem of gentrification which means that middle class professionals are moving into impoverished areas, and in the process of upgrading such neighborhoods, displace the low income families who have lived there. Once assessments have been made determining that the renovation of a particular building or series of buildings is feasible, a program for potential new use of the old structure can be particularly helpful. It is difficult for an investor or builder to visualize how a potential use can be imaginatively incorporated into an existing building which was used in a totally different way. The designer is most capable in transforming an existing building shell into an exciting, creative and marketable concept.

One of the best known success stories in the field of adaptive reuse is San Francisco's Ghirardelli Square, already mentioned as a positive example of urban renewal in the chapter dealing with the City and its surroundings. Originally a chocolate factory near Fisherman's Wharf, Ghirardelli Square was an early example of adaptive reuse. The factory and its surrounding area was

The Faneuil Hall/Quincy Market development in Boston. (Photograph by Steve Rosenthal)

made into a focal point for shops and restaurants, and has caused other nearby buildings to undergo similar transformations. Within two decades, the whole district became one of the liveliest and most attractive ones in San Francisco, and new buildings were built in addition to many renovation projects. Another famous success story is the more recent development of Boston's Quincy Market and Faneuil Hall. That project was developed adjacent to Boston's well planned government center area, and the whole district is now a popular attraction for Bostonians and tourists alike. The adjoining warehouses to Quincy Market were also renovated and contain many shops, boutiques, and restau-

rants. Care was taken not to displace the existing outdoor market area, and as a result there are crowds in the area at any time of the day or evening. The whole neighborhood is an excellent example of adaptive reuse combined with excellent planning. Unlike other downtown areas throughout the country, that part of downtown Boston does not become a ghost town after working hours, and the success of the focal areas of renovated buildings continues to generate other adaptive reuse projects nearby.

The Ghirardelli Square project in San Francisco. Wurster, Bernardi and Emmons, architects.

By now, most major cities have some kind of historic district which has been renovated, or is in the process of being renovated. This is done as a general effort to overcome the problems of blighted inner cities, but it seems to have worked all over the world–not just as a result of governmental planning–but due to the real success associated with adaptive reuse. Also in Europe, old buildings and neighborhoods had fallen into disrepair, and for two or three decades people moved out of the cities to the suburbs. Today, most European towns have not only found many

The pedestrian mall of the Faneuil Hall/Quincy Market in Boston.
(Photograph by Steve Rosenthal)

ways to reuse old buildings, but have often created pedestrian malls and districts in these renovated areas, to an extent beyond what would be acceptable to our automobile oriented society.

Certain building types are particularly suitable for adaptive reuse and seem to create much interesting and challenging work for the interior designer. Amongst them are loft buildings, attached houses, such as "brownstones" in New York City, and mill construction buildings in New England. Loft buildings were first used by artists in search of cheap studio and living accommodations. Today, some former manufacturing buildings have been adapted into luxury apartment dwellings, and lofts are frequently as costly as condominiums. Many of these loft buildings have neither historical nor architectural significance, but present to potential tenants the opportunity of large open spaces to be designed to their particular needs. Many of New England's old mill construction buildings (brick bearing walls, wood columns) have been converted to arts and crafts centers, to shopping malls or to apartment houses, but there are still a large number of essentially beautiful and solid structures that are empty or underutilized. The nineteenth century textile and clothing industry spawned many of these structures which now have become sur-

The vast hall of the Washington D.C. Union Station as converted into a tourist information center. (Photograph by John Pile)

The Romanesque Revival building housing the modern Boston Institute of Contemporary Art.
(Photograph by Steve Rosenthal)

plus. Unfortunately many entrepreneurs ignored these wonderful buildings in favor of putting up ugly and poorly built shopping malls. Now this trend has been halted, but not without coming close to destroying many of the charming and architecturally significant shopping areas in small towns. Railroad stations are another building type frequently used for new purposes, but not always in suitable locations. It is unfortunate that American railroads have declined to the point that made many fine stations obsolete. Some stations have been restored, some have been renovated for new uses ranging from residences to restaurants, and some, such as New York's Pennsylvania Station (mentioned in Part I), have been torn down. The conversion of Washington's Union Station into a visitor's center is an example of adaptive reuse that did not work. Both the location of the station and its enormous size prevented it from becoming the success that its designers had hoped for.

There are two basic design approaches to adaptive reuse. One is essentially the preservation approach, where the designer attempts to salvage and restore whatever can possibly be reused. This might include the original moldings in buildings, fireplaces, architectural woodwork and details such as pressed tin ceilings. The other approach is to "gut" the building and pretty much start from scratch. This has been done frequently in residences, such as brownstone buildings, where not many salvagable details had remained. Most of the time, the approach is somewhere midway between these extremes. Since old brick provides a warm and natural texture, the stripping of old brick walls, often covered with many layers of plaster, has become almost a standard procedure in renovations of brick buildings. Renovations that attempt to imitate the past, or to create interesting details where none had existed, usually do not succeed. Even those architects and designers who want to create a true twentieth century expression

The interior of the Boston Institute of Contemporary Art, designed by Graham Gund. (Photograph by Steve Rosenthal)

within an old shell respect some of the old features of architectural interest. The mixture of old and new not only provides an historic continuity, but a very successful aesthetic juxtaposition.

Adaptive reuse is going to be with us for many years to come. Perhaps the one problem that will require governmental regulation is the fact that the success of adaptive reuse often creates undesireable effects such as gentrification, or the fact that the commercial fisherman have been displaced along Fisherman's Wharf in San Francisco. Recognizing that buildings and furnishings from the 1930's have become sought after antiques, and buildings and objects from the 1950's are well on the way to become collectors' items, it stands to reason that adaptive reuse will be a common practice for buildings built in this century, or even after the midpoint of the century. There are dozens of Federal and State funding sources to encourage these activities. In addition there are private preservation programs and funding sources. Coupled with the fact that adaptive reuse pays, it is a part of the design field that promises exciting opportunities in years to come for many interior designers.

7

PERSONAL INTERIORS
AND SUPERGRAPHICS

The beginning of the 1970's saw an increase of highly personal work: interiors without any conventional furniture, interiors and houses rejecting what we generally accept as good design, and the extensive use of supergraphics, both on exterior surfaces and within interior spaces. It is quite possible that this direction in design is a fad that will not leave any permanent traces on the development of design, but usually there are aspects of any fad or fashion that are of some lasting significance. Personal interiors and supergraphics are sufficiently important to warrant a brief discussion.

One can find a number of underlying reasons, and philosophical rationales as explanations for these recent developments. No new design development happens overnight, and the concern for highly personal spaces has been experimented with by many designers for a number of years. One explanation offered is the fact that in a complex and somewhat confusing urban environment, the individual needs a special place of seclusion, a kind of contemplation space, and indeed, several years ago the Museum of Contemporary Crafts in New York featured an exhibition of contemplation spaces. Another explanation is based on the natural desire of creative designers to create space and living or working environments without needing the support or use of manufactured products such as furniture. A third explanation might be the influence of the experimentation done in connection with the space exploration programs. Living capsules, life support systems, and confined environments were an obvious necessity, and some designers were undoubtedly influenced by these scientific

"Supergraphic" giant initials on the window of the Joseph Magnin shop in Costa Mesa. Deborah Sussman, designer. (Photographs by Deborah Sussman)

Wall and ceiling supergraphics in another Joseph Magnin shop, Almaden. Designed by Deborah Sussman.

developments. Even in the world of business the need for highly special, private spaces has been recognized. A number of firms have conventional office environments, or office landscape environments, but provide somewhere within the corporate interior structure a kind of Think-Tank for the express purpose of encouraging people to "get away from it all" and withdraw to communicate with their own thoughts. A related, and highly publicized philosophy in architecture is the work of Robert Venturi and his wife, Denise Scott Brown. The Venturis are highly respected as designers, architects, planners, and writers, and Venturi's most important work is *Complexities and Contradictions in Architecture*. It is difficult to summarize the Venturi philosophy in a few words, but the essence of their message is that there is merit in the popular or common kind of architecture and design that surrounds us, and that designers must learn from the colloquial kind of design that the more theoretical and sophisticated professional would normally tend to reject as "vulgar". Venturi also advocates that buildings should be simple kinds of "sheds" with decorated facades; in essence his very controversial thoughts have often been the exact opposite of what the design and architectural profession as well as the educated public has held in high esteem. Another related movement has been the "Conceptual Art" flourishing around the same period, late 1960's to the early 1970's. Conceptual art to the "traditional" artists or historians was anathema, much like Venturi's philosophy shocked the established architectural historians and practitioners, and much as some of the personal interiors and supergraphics creations shocked the "establishment" in interior design.

It is interesting to note these related developments, and perhaps there is no point in attempting to establish a hierarchial or chronological order of who influenced whom, and who did what first. The forces that shape human behavior and man's creativity are myriad. There are political and social forces at work, and perhaps the long American involvement in Vietnam has been a forceful irritant towards the rejection of accepted social norms. The resultant attitudes of young people have led to the creation of a number of new movements, and the so-called "counter-culture" has in turn contributed another "new" example of architecture and design. The housing preferred by people in communes, or the simple makeshift houses built by many young people, especially in California, are not exactly a new style of design or architecture, but are more than anything a negative response to what has been accepted as "good" by established society.

It would be wrong to ascribe the work resulting in highly personal spaces to revolutionary causes or attitudes alone. In fact, some of the most talented and creative designers have come up with truly distinguished ideas that are as much sculptural and artistic experimentation as social statements. Some of the examples depicted are very sophisticated and highly original design solutions by highly skilled professionals. It is impossible to categorize and classify all the many types of experimental design work in recent years. A book published by Praeger in 1972 was called *Arthropods* by its author Jim Burns, it deals with the work of a variety of designers and design groups in Europe and in the United States. Most projects included in the book are futuristic, often based on conceptual thoughts with shock value, rather than on concepts dealing with real solutions.

The influences of these various forces and philosophies on interior design have not really been revolutionary. The most frequently used "new" idea has been the use of supergraphics. Its name accurately describes its connotations: graphics meaning two dimensional design or a message conveying some kind of meaning; "super" denotes its size. Words, letters and numbers are the most frequently used symbols, but designs, stripes, fields of color and patterns can also be classified as graphics.

Many non-residential interiors have graphic identification systems based on the use of very large numbers, for example, to designate the floor level at the end of hallways or opposite elevators in such buildings as hotels. Usually the numerals extend from floor to ceiling and are essentially handsome examples of numbers, carefully painted on walls. These large numbers provide clear visibility and permit the users of the buildings to know exactly where they are, and, in addition, they provide a highly decorative touch to the environment. The use of numbers and letters as design elements is not really new. Many beautiful book jackets, magazine covers, and building signs have always been successful designs based solely upon the forms of letters and numbers. Type is a beautiful design element when properly used. Some supergraphics tend to place less emphasis on legibility, and more on the combination of letter forms in abstract, decorative and sometimes, playful combinations. Of course, color is a significant aspect of supergraphics, and often letters and numbers used in such ways are in brilliant colors. Architects and graphic designers have also used letters and numbers as exterior decorations on the facades of buildings, and at the same time obtained clear graphic identification for the building's name or street number. Using letters and numbers for residential interiors requires a good deal of two dimensional design ability and sophistication. It is probably not a good idea to use the designation "ground floor" or "living room" in floor to ceiling sized letters in a home, no matter how beautifully done. The use of this kind of graphics is clearly more appropriate in public buildings.

Supergraphics using designs of an abstract nature are of course influenced by contemporary painting employing fields of color, stripes and bold patterns as the artist's expression. Historically, we have used large murals in many interiors; in eras when figurative painting or religious painting was the current fashion, these were the subjects used for murals. When landscapes were the rage, they tended to appear as murals. Simple supergraphics are easy to apply on any normal wall surface, compared to the elaborate preparation of walls required for mural painting techniques. In the past, a major mural by an important artist was also a work of art obviously destined for posterity, whereas the supergraphics used in today's interiors do not pretend to be great works of art. They are simple decorations and fairly inexpensive in their application. Any house painter can follow directions, although many graphic artists or designers paint their own supergraphics on existing plaster or plaster board wall surfaces. The most popu-

"A 20th Century Environment" at the Carborundum Museum of Ceramics in Niagara Falls, N.Y. with spaces created from stretched Nylon fabric. **Designed by Aleksandra Kasuba, artist.** (Photographs by T.A. Watts)

lar designs have been straight linear stripes, or free flowing ones, and simple large, bold and colorful graphic designs. An interesting trend has developed in many buildings where the designers felt that the architectural elements did not have to be respected, or were of such poor design that they should be "destroyed". In other words, often the designs arbitrarily or purposely go over doors, archways, windows and other fixed building elements; some run up onto and over ceilings, some attempt to create a continuous flow of space from floor to walls and ceilings by negating the sharp edges and definitions of planes normally found in interior spaces.

Some supergraphics are intended almost as paintings or murals on one or two surfaces, and some interiors have been painted in very strong colors, patterns, and geometric designs on just about every available surface, thus creating a highly personal environment, transcending what existed before.

Abstract paintings, abstract expressionist paintings, and field of color paintings often look deceptively simple; so do supergraphics. It would be a serious mistake to underestimate the graphic design skills and the knowledge of color required to come up with excellent supergraphics. Some designers have a natural or developed ability in this field. Those designers who have no background in painting or graphics should not attempt to casually suggest large designs in bright colors, lest they ruin some perfectly good spaces. There are capable artists and designers who have specialized in large scale graphics, and have developed it into a real art. Many design firms collaborate with graphic artists and commission super-graphics much like other commissions of art.

The concept of personal interiors, creating highly individual spaces without the use of conventional furnishings is again an idea that is not totally new to our own time. The creation of interiors predicated primarily upon the use of free-standing furniture dates back no further than the 16th or 17th century. Throughout history there have been many examples of great spaces that had no conventional furnishings at all, but created areas, spaces and variety through architectural manipulation of interior spaces. More recently, Frank Lloyd Wright was a master of designing houses with very exciting variations of heights, sizes, and spaces using no furniture or just minimal furnishings.

Perhaps the unique contribution made by some designers in recent years is the fact that they took ordinary, often dull architectural spaces, and created within these spaces highly personal environments, by adding levels, platforms, lofts, and literally nooks and crannies. Much of contemporary housing consists of high rise structures with a series of box-like spaces piled on top of each other in endless repetition. The introduction of levels, providing a change of scale, subdivisions providing a sense of excitement or surprise, and articulation of specific functions such as dining, reading, sleeping, or play through the architectural manipulation of such spaces can measurably enhance dull interiors and can provide highly personal and individualistic spaces. Not every space is suited to this kind of design (low ceilings, limited square footage) and most people are reluctant to invest the expense and effort of permanent "built-in" features. And obviously a space designed with fixed platforms, sleeping lofts, dining spaces, benches and other permanent features is inflexible as well as immovable. Since we live in a highly mobile society, most people prefer conventional furnishings that can be moved

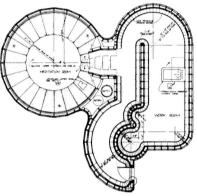

Irregular shapes and padded walls make the "Think Tank" in McDonald's Chicago office headquarters totally unlike any conventional office space. (Photograph courtesy of Associated Space Design by Balthazar Korab.) **The plan shows the circular "meditation room" and irregular work room with their entrance labyrinth. Designed by Associated Space Design, Inc.**

from home to home, or office to office instead of permanent and fixed settings. The best examples of personal spaces are those that were designed as new architectural structures or remodelled structures, such as completely rebuilt interiors of townhouses or brownstones. Some spatial modification of plain interior spaces, perhaps a platform level for dining or sleeping, or the creation of a seating pit, can be extremely successful. The total conversion of existing spaces into highly personal compartments and areas requires high skills, as well as unusual clients.

A number of interiors were created with soft, organic and free-flowing shapes made of sprayed foam, plaster over a wire armature, or through the use of stretched fabrics. The resulting sculpted spaces are even more difficult to reconcile with ordinary rectangular buildings, compared to the modification of such spaces with plywood or other standard building materials. The best examples of sculptural interiors were, not surprisingly, done by sculptors, such as the example shown here.

The desire to create "different" or unusual interiors is understandable. It is questionable whether the attempts to superimpose such solutions on existing buildings makes much sense. It is quite likely that new technological developments will make foam-sprayed structures, air-inflated structures and other new forms become a reality for many future building types. The architecture of fantasy has always fascinated designers, and surely twentieth century technology will enable architects and designers to translate fantasy into reality. Until some truly new forms of architecture become commonplace, interior designers are probably better off to work with buildings rather than against buildings. Much of the experimentation with highly personal interiors is exciting and truly creative, but since interior design by its very nature must usually deal with existing spaces, some well-intended efforts at creativity are doomed to fail if the design attempts to be different at all costs, rather than dealing with rational solutions to problems.

8

TRENDS, FASHIONS, AND NEW DIRECTIONS

Throughout the history of interior design there have been trends and fashions. This is true, of course, in any creative field, but for certain kinds of popular interior design, so-called trends are often created on purpose by manufacturers and merchandisers. These are not the kind of trends that will be discussed here. Throughout this book we have talked about design as a meaningful activity, based upon logic and reason, as well as aesthetics. In fact, we have obviously presented a particular point of view about design and have tried to explain that point of view in rational terms. The underlying principles of design have not changed throughout the history of architecture and design, yet their articulation has varied considerably from era to era. At first glance Victorian design, for instance, appears to us to be confusing, busy, overly ornate, and crowded, as well as heavy–particularly in interior design. Upon closer analysis one can learn to understand that much of Victorian design was an expression of that particular period which included some valid design developments, and which in many ways followed sound design principles, like any other period in the history of design.

A great many of the examples used throughout the book are either current examples, or designs from the first three quarters of the twentieth century. The 1920's, in particular, brought forth the movement (or trend) of modern design as it is and was accepted, and is being practiced in the United States and in most parts of the world. This "modernism" has prospered and was accepted as dogma until about 1970. The architectural style that we referred to as the "international style" already climaxed in the late 1950's; hence it is not surprising that architects and designers have consciously attempted to find new and fresh expressions of design. Some movements have been mentioned earlier. We referred to "new brutalism" in architecture, and we discussed personal interiors and supergraphics in the previous chapter.

It seems clear that by the mid 1970's, and certainly by the early 1980's, many people have simply become bored with what we had thus far accepted as modern design. The term "modernism" is probably unfortunate, since many other past movements were modern for their time–but in due time history will assign a name to what we called "modern design" from the 1920's to the 1970's. Architects are currently very much concerned with the conscious search for new expressions. Interior Designers have always had more opportunity for personal expressions and fantasy, ranging from historic imitations to some of the personal interiors discussed in the last chapter. At this time, many architects are engaged in the practice of interior design, and good interior design can not be separated from architecture. Hence, what some of the leading practitioners of architecture are experimenting with, has already started to influence interior design, and will most likely continue to be a significant influence in the coming years.

The most powerful new trend in architecture is "post-modernism". No definite name has been attached to this movement, although some people refer to it as "new romanticism". The new leadership in architecture rejects the austerity of modernism. They favor an architecture which often alludes to history, and that is considerably more ornate than the style of architecture of the past 50 years. It is often purposely ambiguous to the point of being confusing. It tends to establish peculiar spatial relationships, and it frequently uses offbeat colors. It often appears to be contradictory and to some observers boring. Yet boring is the label that the post-modernists like to ascribe to the modern architecture of the past 50 years. Historical references abound in forms of classical columns and ornaments, yet the movement is definitely not imitative in the way neo-classicism was. Ornaments and historical allusions are used out of context and at times with a kind of tongue-in-cheek sense of humor.

Amongst the leaders of the movement are Michael Graves, Peter Eisenman and Robert Stern, but included in the ranks of post-modernists are such well known modernists as Phillip Johnson. The latter's new AT&T building on Madison Avenue in New York is highly controversial because of its strange, pediment-like top, and its huge arches at the base of the building. Robert Venturi, whose work was mentioned in the previous chapter has also been associated with post-modernism, and the chances are that the new wave will turn into a tidal wave before it subsides. One

No.4 Firehouse, Columbus, Indiana. Venturi and Rauch, architects. (Photograph by John Pile)

can never judge one's own era in an historical perspective, but it is safe to state that post-modernism will turn out to be a passing fashion which will not leave a significant mark upon the development of the history of architecture and design. Yet the movement is obviously going to bring about new attitudes and changes, and as a catalyst–if not as a true style–it will influence design developments in years to come.

Interior Design has always had members of the profession who have worked in an historical vein, hence classical allusions are nothing new. What is new is the fact that some of those interior designers trained in and dedicated to modernism are beginning to embrace post-modernism. Curved walls and curved furniture appear where strict architectural geometry ruled until a few years ago. Pastel colors, often rejected by modern interior designers, not only are used in many current interiors, but actually have found their way as upholstery colors for some of the classic pieces of Bauhaus furniture. Anything but black or natural leather was near sacrilege on such classics as Mies van der Rohe's Brno chairs. But today, their licensed manufacturer, Knoll International, features these and other classic designs in colors such as mauve and celadon green. The same company, for many years a

Knoll International Showroom, New York; Robert Venturi of Venturi, Rauch, Scott Brown, architects: interior design. (Photograph by Tom Crane)

stronghold of "good design" in the modernist sense, (whose furniture was designed by Mies and Saarinen amongst others) commissioned Robert Venturi to design their new showroom late in 1979. At about the same time, two other influential manufacturers of furniture, Thonet and Sunar, had their showrooms designed in the post-modernist manner. Sunar retained Michael Graves for the design of a number of their showrooms, and certainly succeeded in getting a great deal of national attention in the design community. Neither of these showrooms came off as convincing statements of a new direction in interior design, but all three were forerunners of many other important interiors designed in the post-modernist manner.

The polemics in the field of architecture and design are inter-

Ornate ceiling design printed on plastic ceiling panels reflected on polished table tops in conference area, Knoll International New York Showroom. Robert Venturi of Venturi, Rauch, Scott Brown, architects: interior design. (Photograph by Tom Crane)

esting to observe. Respected design firms are becoming defensive about their continued output of "good design" modern. In fact, the very term of "good design" has become suspect in the eyes of some. Hard-core modernists are being accused of being conservative as well as elitists. It is wise to keep an objective and historical perspective on these matters. Modern interior design in the late 1940's and early 1950's was often rejected, based on the fact that the most prevalent examples seen by the public were examples of cheap and usually poor design. No doubt that some valid contributions to the field of interior design will emerge out of what, at this time, is still a fad.

**Sunar Showroom,
New York City.
Michael Graves, architect.**
(see figure page 86)
(Photograph by
Bill Kontzias)

Prior to the arrival of post-modernism two other recent trends were very popular in interior design. Yet within a period of a few years the trendiness has disappeared, but some worthwhile ideas have remained. Minimalism and High-Tech design were the hottest thing around during part of the 1970's. Minimalism never took on great popular importance, but was much discussed by design professionals. Joseph D'Urso was the leading proponent of minimalism, but in some ways, he and others who worked in the same vein, also popularized High-Tech at the same time. Minimalism as implied by the term, refers to interiors that appear almost sparse. Little furniture is used, many of the furniture functions are built in. The composition of such spaces as well as each elevation or wall is very carefully handled. One carefully placed piece of art on the wall might be all that is needed to break up a large surface. The few pieces of furniture used are usually beautiful Bauhaus type pieces. Colors are subdued, or will have a good deal of black and white. Clutter is anathema. D'Urso and other minimalists often used industrial equipment in the most elegant residential spaces and thus introduced High-Tech combined with minimalism. Table bases, hardware, shelving or kitchen components might have been made for industrial purposes. Often these pieces of design are less self-conscious than furniture designed for homes, and are indeed more beautiful.

High-Tech was a movement which was popular in interior design for that reason, but also due to the fact that the costs are frequently very low, High-Tech in a larger sense was and is, a forceful movement in architecture, and there are still a number of proponents who continue design along those directions. Probably the best known building that can be classified as High-Technology is the Centre Georges Pompidou in Paris, France. The building is one of the most controversial ones in Paris. It is a museum, exhibition center, center for industrial design, and library. All the building's mechanical services are exposed; all the structural members are clearly visible and articulated, and all the escalators and stairs are expressed on the outside of the building. It appears to be something of a cross between a very large erector set and a futuristic machine. In spite of this unusual design, the building is enormously popular with large segments of Paris' population and with tourists. It is fronted by a large plaza, and that area has become a center for performers, for young people, and for those who come to watch the street life. A number of high technology buildings have been built by American architects, some of them industrial or institutional buildings, or structures such as fire houses. Of course, the movement is not entirely new. Joseph Paxton's 1851 Crystal Palace was an earlier example of the use of industrial products, developed for the pro-

The Crystal Palace housing the Great Exhibition of 1851 in London as shown in a contemporary engraving.

Eaton Center shopping mall, Toronto, Ontario. Bregman, Hamann and Zeidler, architects. (Photograph by John Pile)

duction of greenhouses, into a significant building. Charles Eames designed his own house in 1949 out of mass-produced materials and building components.

It is interesting to speculate about the direction of design and exciting to observe that many new ideas abound. It would be nice to be able to state unequivocally where design is going. Obviously this can never be done. Currently the fashion is definitely leading towards post-modernism. In 1980, the magazine *Progressive*

Sainsbury Centre, exhibit area. University of East Anglia, Norfolk, England. Norman Foster, architect. (Photograph by John Pile)

Centre Pompidou, Paris. Piano and Rogers, architects. (Photograph by John Pile)

Gallery display area, Centre Pompidou, Paris. Piano and Rogers, architects.
(Photograph by John Pile)

Architecture gave almost every single one of its prestigious design awards to projects that could be classified as post-modernist buildings. In January 1981, the magazine *INTERIORS* gave its Designer-of-the-Year award to Michael Graves, who is indeed the leading post-modernist architect and designer. He was specifically cited for his design of Sunar furniture showrooms. We can safely predict that underlying principles of good design will survive, even if there are those who at times question the validity of anything accepted in the past. This is the difference between fashion and trends on the one hand, and rational approaches to design on the other hand. Some of the ideas that may be in vogue at any given time will probably leave their mark upon the history and development of design. Whether post-modernism, minimalism, high-tech and other movements to come are truly important contributions is too early to tell. But it is exciting to watch. The continuous creative developments happening at all times makes design a rewarding field–and fun.

PHOTOGRAPHS

Receptionists' area in the offices, of L.C.P., Inc. The leaded glass window is part of the traditional architecture of the Tudor City buildings in New York where the offices are located. (Photograph by Robert L. Beckhard)

Openly planned Operations Area. Alexander and Alexander, Inc., Insurance Brokers, New York City. Interior planners/ designers: I.S.D., Inc. (Photograph courtesy of I.S.D., Inc. by Gilles Larrain)

Entrance to the Houston, Texas offices of I.S.D., Inc. designed by that firm.
(Photograph by Robert Muir Associates)

Minskoff Offices. Luss/Kaplan. Gerald Luss, designer. Detail of office. Meticulous detailing and organization of files, storage, and closets into one total storage wall.

Lobby area in the office and plant of Channing L. Bete Co., Greenfield, Massachusetts. Juster/Pope, architects and interior designers. (Photograph by D. Randolph Foulds)

Open offices surround a garden-atrium. Corporate headquarters of John Deere and Co., Moline, Illinois. Roche Dinkelo, architects. (Photograph by John Pile)

Office area with bright
colors and supergraphics.
Chubb Pacific Indemnity
Group, Los Angeles.
M. Arthur Gensler, Jr.
and Associates, architects
and interior designers.
(Photograph courtesy of
© Jeremiah O. Bragstad)

Private Patient Room,
Stamford, CT Hospital
new main building.
I.S.D., Inc.,
interior designers,
Perkins and Will,
architects.

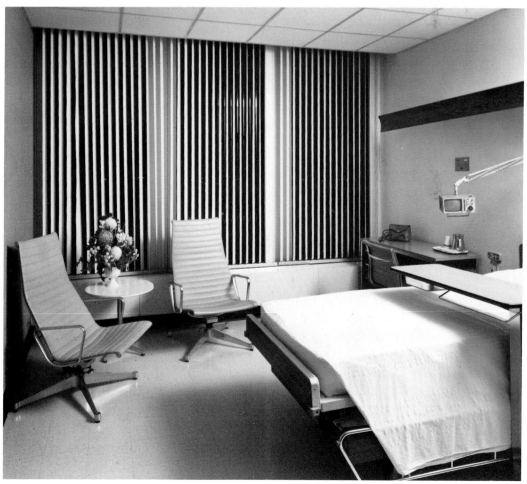

Boston City Hall. I.S.D., Inc., interior designers. Kallman and McKinnell, architects. A full-sized mock-up of a typical secretarial area.

Councillors' Committee Room in the Boston City Hall. I.S.D., Inc., interior designers. (Photograph courtesy of I.S.D., Inc. by Alexander Georges)

Dining room in the office building
of the General Reinsurance Corp.,
Greenwich, Conn. Skidmore,
Owings and Merrill, architects;
L.C.P. Associates, Inc., interior
designers.

A close-up view of the table setting
in a small private dining room of the
First National Bank of Memphis.
Interior design created by I.S.D., Inc.,
the interior design devision of Perkins
and Will, architects. Frequently the
interior designer must be concerned
with all aspects of design–from the
handling of space to the furniture,
works of art, and accessories and,
in the case of restaurants or dining
spaces as shown here, the design
and/or selection of china, glassware,
and cutlery.

Ford Foundation Building, New York. Kevin Roche and John Dinkeloo, architects. Warren Platner, interior designer. This view shows a private office with furniture designed by Platner.
(Photography courtesy of © Ezra Stoller (Esto))

Neumann House, Croton-on-Hudson, New York. Marcel Breuer, architect, 1953. An example of Breuer's work exemplifying the open planning of houses and using the fireplace as a sculptural element in the space

Camino Real Hotel in Mexico City. Interior design by The Knoll Planning Unit in cooperation with the architect. This view looks from a guest room to its adjoining terrace.

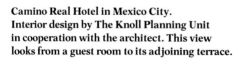

Interior view of the Ford Foundation Building, New York. Kevin Roche and John Dinkeloo, architects. Warren Platner, interior designer. Inner offices overlook a sculptured garden. (Photograph courtesy of © Ezra Stoller (Esto))

Lobby with a view to the
ocean, Cerromar Beach
Hotel, Dorado Beach,
P.R. Leeds Associates,
interior designers;
Toro-Ferrer and Associates,
architects.

John Marshall Hotel,
Richmond, Virginia.
Pedestrian Entrance
Stair; renovation. I.S.D.,
Inc., interior design.
(Photograph by
Mark Ross)

Library lounge at the
Emma Willard School,
Troy, N.Y.I.S.D. Inc.,
interior designers; Edward
Larrabee Barnes,
architects. (Photograph
courtesy of I.S.D., Inc. by
Joseph W. Molitor)

Xerox showroom, New York, Eliot Noyes,
architect. A particularly interesting way of
handling space in a sculptural manner without
conflict with the equipment on display.
(Photograph courtesy of © Ezra Stoller (Esto))

Air France ticket office, New York.
The Space Design Group, Inc., designers.
This office is a perfect example of the synthesis of elegance,
function, a reflection of the national character (the image
of France is expressed through major works of art), and
a fitting projection of confidence and precision so important
to the airline industry.

Lobby, Penn Mutual Tower, Philadelphia. Mitchell/Giurgola, architects.
(Photograph by John Pile)

Singer Company showroom, New York. Victor A. Lundy, architect. The masterful handling of laminate wood creates an almost theatrical environment, yet the design is so clearly stated that it does not compete with the existing structure and creates an honest expression of its own.

Another view of the Xerox showroom, New York. (Photograph courtesy of © Ezra Stoller (Esto))

American Republic Insurance Company, Des Moines, Iowa. Skidmore, Owings, and Merrill, designers, The challenge of the complexities of a computer installation have been met in an expressive, handsome and orderly design statement. (Photograph courtesy of Skidmore, Owings and Merrill by Ezra Stoller)

Main banking room—Waterbury Savings Bank, Waterbury, Conn., remodeled by I.S.D., Inc. The elements of traditional architecture preserved from the original bank building are set off by modern furniture, equipment and lighting. (Photograph courtesy of I.S.D., Inc. by Louis Reens)

Living room of Charles Murphy apartment, Chicago. Benjamin Baldwin, designer. Three antique chairs compose elegantly with the otherwise simple and understated interior. (Photograph courtesy of © Jon Naar)

Entrance lobby, Westinghouse Nuclear Energy Systems Offices, Monroeville, Pennsylvania. I.S.D., Inc., interior design; Deeter, Ritchey and Sippel, architects. (Photograph by Balthazar Korab). See also page 250.

Living room of Malkin apartment, New York. Arnold Friedmann, designer. Sculpture niche and heavy beam housing audio equipment and lighting were created to overcome the problems of a typical builder-designed apartment building. (Photograph courtesy of © Irvin Simon)

Library of Charles Murphy apartment, Chicago. Benjamin Baldwin, designer. The design of the storage wall gives careful consideration to the many needs of storage for books and records and the housing of a music system. (Photograph courtesy of © Jon Naar)

Living room of George Lois apartment, New York. This room in an apartment house, created by combining two adjacent apartments, was obviously designed to allow the owner's art collection aesthetic dominance over the space and the furnishings in it. (Photograph courtesy of © Jon Naar)

La Potagerie Restaurant, New York. Designed by George Nelson and Company. Tiles used for the exterior are carried inside as well. Red-orange signs and trays set off the hearty, natural sense of the growing plants and displays of bread and other food stuffs. (Photograph by Norman McGrath)

Ford Foundation Building cafeteria, New York. Kevin Roche and John Dinkeloo, architects. Warren Platner, interior designer. This employee cafeteria matches the rest of the building's interiors in elegance and careful handling of materials and details. Notice the luxurious materials used on serving counters. (Photograph courtesy of © Ezra Stoller (Esto))

Herman Miller showroom, New York, George Nelson and Co., Inc., designers. This showroom actually represents a collaborative effort on the part of three notable designers: the Nelson office, Charles Eames, and Alexander Girard. Their designs have made Herman Miller products synonymous with the best in contemporary furnishings in the United States.

T & O (Textile and Object) shop for Herman Miller, New York. Alexander Girard, architect. This shop was created as an outlet for fabrics and decorative objects, the latter being primarily folk art objects collected by Alexander Girard. A delightful and sprightly shop with a special lighting system using many tiny bulbs designed for the space.

La Fonda Del Sol Restaurant, New York. Alexander Girard, architect. A restaurant specializing in South American food where the architect created a total design including the display of folk art, the design of special furniture in collaboration with Charles Eames, and the creation of all graphic materials as well as uniforms worn by the staff.

Franklin Simon Shop, Atlanta. Designed by George Nelson and Company. Unusual lighting and ceiling give a feeling of liveliness and glitter in what would otherwise be a drab store interior. (Photograph by Alexandre Georges)

The serving counter of
"The Terrace Floor" employees'
cafeteria at Johns-Manville
headquarters in Denver.
Interior design by
The Space Design Group.

Library area in
a building for
The Emma Willard
School
designed by
Edward Larrabee Barnes
with unusual diamond
windows that set the
character of the space.
The interior designers
were I.S.D., Inc.

Whitney Museum of American Art, New York. Marcel Breuer and Hamilton Smith, architects. Interior of third-floor gallery in this landmark building created by Breuer shows the majestically proportioned space for exhibitions and the ceiling grid which provides maximum flexibility to permit changing exhibitions. (Photograph courtesy of Marcel Breuer and Associates by Ezra Stoller)

Philadelphia National Bank, main banking room with information counter in the right foreground. Designed by The Space Design Group.

Entrance lobby, Westinghouse Nuclear Energy Systems Offices, Monroeville, Pennsylvania. I.S.D., Inc., interior design; Deeter, Ritchey and Sippel, architects. (Photograph by Balthazar Korab)

Lounge, American Academy of Arts & Sciences, Cambridge, Massachusetts. Louis M.S. Beal and Joseph Rosen of I.S.D., Inc., interior design; Gary Kallmann and Michael Wood of Kallmann, McKinnell & Wood, architects. (Photograph by Jaime Ardiles-Arce)

Reception area with paintings from corporate art collection. Dial Financial Corp., Des Moines, Iowa. John Pile, office planner and interior designer. (Photograph by Norman McGrath)

An office system suited for use in open or conventional plan offices. Designed by Bill Stephens. (Photograph by Ezra Stoller ESTO, courtesy Rogers Associates)

The Solomon R. Guggenheim Museum, New York. Frank Lloyd Wright, architect. The exterior view of this famous building clearly expresses the space of the interior. The interior view shows the spiral galleries around the center space with its grand proportions flooded with natural light from the skylight.

Jack Lenor Larsen designed woven murals of hand-spun wool for Louis Kahn's First Unitarian Church. The panels are shaded progressively through soft reds, blues, and gold. Hung on the grey windowless walls, the murals are lit from above by skylights and their subtle iridescent quality complements the elegance of the architecture.
(Photograph courtesy of Jack Lenor Larsen by Bill Helms)

Lobby of Vivian Beaumont Theater in Lincoln Center, New York. Eero Saarinen, architect. Jo Mielziner, collaborating designer. Stairs lead down to orchestra level and up to the loges. (© Lincoln Center for the Performing Arts, Inc. Photograph by Ezra Stoller Associates)

Lobby of New York State Theater, Lincoln Center, New York, Philip Johnson, architect. Sculptures standing at head of each grand staircase are enlargements in white Carrara marble of small works by Elie Nadelman. (© Lincoln Center for the Performing Arts, Inc. Photograph by Bob Serating)

Escalators in the U.S. Exhibit within a Geodesic dome at EXPO 67, Montreal.
(Photograph by John Pile)

Tabernacle Church, Columbus, Indiana: Eliel and Eero Saarinen, architects.
(Photograph by John Pile)

V

THE ELEMENTS OF
INTERIOR DESIGN

FURNITURE

The central role of furniture in interior design is too obvious to need any explanation. The arrangement and selection of furniture is understood by any layman as one of the main tasks of the interior designer, ranking with the selection of colors and finishes as basic to the carrying through of any project. Furniture also has special interest for almost everyone because it is a particularly personal kind of product. In addition to seeing it, we touch and feel a piece of furniture and it can offer or limit physical comfort in a very specific and tangible way. The interior spaces of architecture influence our physical lives also, but the direct tactile relationship with furniture makes the contact more personal. Only the implements that we work with our hands, and our clothing come as close to us in a physical sense. It is probably for this reason that people form strong attachments to particular pieces of furniture (a favorite desk, chair, or bed) and have such strong feelings of liking or disliking for particular designs. The architect and designer tend to have a strong interest in furniture selection and design because they understand that furniture mediates —forms the direct line of contact—between the building and the individual.

In an historic sense, furniture is a fairly new invention. The highly-developed types of ancient Egypt and classical antiquity were lost and forgotten during the Middle Ages, when furniture was little-used. The traditional lack of furniture in the highly developed civilization of Japan proves that it is not a genuine human necessity. In western civilization it reappeared as a luxury available only to the medieval wealthy and aristocratic.

A typically Victorian furniture design. A parlor organ exhibited at the Philadelphia Centennial Exhibition of 1876.

A chair was as much an emblem of rank for a nobleman or a bishop as it was a means of comfort. In the latter part of the Middle Ages, and increasingly during the Renaissance, better developed, more useful, and more comfortable furniture appeared. By modern standards, furniture remained scarce, however. Average people made do with a few crude tables and stools. Poor people took it for granted that a bed was simply straw on the floor (often bare earth). Only the privileged classes had the elaborately decorated and carved chairs, chests, and beds that we admire in museums.

Beginning in the Middle Ages and extending into the Victorian era, the design of furniture for the use of the wealthy and aristocratic became a matter of developing decorative styles having a relation to the character of architectural and interior design of the period. These are the period styles discussed in II.6. As more simple furniture came into use in average men's houses, its design tended to be a modification and simplification of the rich and elaborate designs made for

Bentwood chair first produced by Thonet in 1870. It became famous as a favorite furniture choice of Le Corbusier in the 1920's and 1930's.

Chair designed by Charles Rennie Mackintosh in 1902–03, now in production again. (Photograph courtesy Atelier International, Ltd.)

Josef Hoffmann chair, c. 1900.
(Photograph by John Pile)

palaces and mansions. Both simple and elegant furniture was handmade, with wood as the dominant structural material. Designs were developed by the actual cabinetmaker or craftsman as part of his handwork process, often with some suggestions or directions from the architect or owner of the place where the furniture was to be used.

Beginning in the early part of the nineteenth century, a numbe of changes began to take place that altered the circumstances which had controlled furniture design for hundreds of years. People began to own more objects (and more varied ones) and to use these in more specialized ways in their daily lives. Such objects as the kitchen cabinet, the office desk, or the sofa bed began to appear, with their very specific and demanding design requirements. At the same time a major portion of the population of the western countries moved into a middle-class status sufficiently affluent to make possible the ownership of an assortment of functionally specialized and quite luxurious furniture. The Industrial Revolution, with its development of factory production methods, made it possible to provide the desired furniture at reasonable cost, but it put an end to the craft tradition of furniture design and construction. The Victorian era is famous for its wild profusion of ornate, but unsightly furniture in which meaningless decoration, now easily produced by factory machinery, was piled up in chaos. Even this chaos, since it had a considerable degree of originality, was preferable to the gradual changeover in taste that came with the eclectic era in architecture.

Architects whose work was limited to careful copying of past styles required furniture that carefully copied past styles to match. Factory production was refined and adjusted to make it possible to produce "antique reproductions" on an assembly-line basis. Since factory reproductions of handmade products always involve some simplifications and changes, this meant that such reproductions were always rather poor copies. In the case of the best reproductions, handwork is still used in traditional fashion with a result which is closer to the original but still a copy having no originality or relation to its own time. As the pioneer modern architects developed a way of building that was based on the materials, techniques, and thinking of the industrial era, they quickly came to realize that there was almost no furniture available that belonged in their buildings. Three ways of dealing with this problem appeared and all three were sometimes used in one building. All three approaches survive in the current practice of modern interior design.

A first step was to try to reduce the need for furniture to

Adjustable chaise of 1929 by Le Corbusier in collaboration with Pierre Jeanneret and Charlotte Périand. (Photograph by John Pile)

Tubular armchair designed at the Bauhaus by Marcel Breuer.

The "Barcelona" chair of Mies Van der Rohe. (Photograph by G. Barrows)

Mies van der Rohe cantilever chair with steel bar frame of 1929–30 in a version in current production. (Left) (Photograph courtesy Thonet Industries, Inc.)

Tubular armchair by Le Corbusier, 1929. (Right)

a minimum through the use of built-in equipment. Even the ordinary closet is actually an example of this approach (and a fairly modern invention, as well). It replaced the earlier costly and often elaborate wardrobe with an integral archi-tectural element. The built-in cabinet and drawer chest became a common part of a modern house, and it was a common ambition to deal with all storage problems by this means. This is an approach which has come to have almost total acceptance in the case of kitchens, but it tends to be limited in other areas by the feeling that moving to a new house or changing the use of a space can mean excessive dislocation when the furniture must remain fixed in place.

Although an occasional table, couch, or bunk can also be built-in, there is a clear need for some movable furniture for the more typical seating, desk, table, and bed requirements. The early modernists were able to locate a few designs developed with the progress of the Industrial Revolution that were created outside the obsession with historic imitation. The simple bentwood furniture of Thonet and his imitators, for example, or the utility bases produced for restaurant tables, turned out to be useful and handsome, and fit into a modern building very well. Almost all of the early modernists, however, were in addition driven to the more difficult task of designing furniture in ways that made sense to them, furniture that would be certain to fit into the new kinds of interior space that they were creating. Some of the most distinguished of modern furniture was designed by the pioneer modern architects to solve specific problems in their buildings.

Le Corbusier and Mies van der Rohe each produced a number of designs having no historical references, using such "new" materials as steel and glass and, in some cases, introducing impressive functional advantages (as in the case of the adjustable chaise designed by Le Corbusier). Gropius, although he did not himself design furniture, was closely connected with the development of new designs at the Bauhaus, where Marcel Breuer was particularly successful in arriving at tubular metal design solutions. Some of these became production items manufactured by the same Thonet who had been known for the development of the earlier bentwood products. Many of these designs of the late 1920's and 1930's have become recognized masterpieces widely used in modern interiors at the present time. Alvar Aalto in Finland made a special contribution through finding ways to use wood that were contemporary in spirit and highly suitable to factory production. Bent plywood furniture of Aalto design has also continued to be an important part of the available range of contemporary furniture. Wright designed furniture for many of his buildings in a highly individual and distinctive style. It remains, however, a somewhat controversial aspect of his work, regarded by many critics as quite unsuccessful. His furniture is certainly not as adaptable to general use as the designs of the other early modernists, but taken in the context of the interiors where it was intended for use, it is also an important departure from the shoddy norms of American production furniture.

On the basis of the work of the pioneer modernists, a substantial variety of modern furniture came to be available in regular production and distribution in Germany and the Scandinavian countries during the 1930's. In America, however, except for a few imports and a few tiny and struggling pioneer manufacturing efforts, modern furniture remained almost totally unknown until after the end of World War II. Since then, the increasing proportion of building expressive of modern architectural ideas has created a demand for good modern furniture with a correspondingly energetic source of supply.

Designers of modern furniture have again and again been stimulated by the introduction of new materials. Le Corbusier and Breuer delighted in using chrome-plated steel tube, Aalto and Eames molded plywood in simple (bent) and complex

Lounge chair of
molded and bent plywood
designed by Alvar Aalto
in 1934. From the
Collection of the
Museum of Modern Art;
gift of Edgar Kaufman, Jr.
(Collection, The Museum
of Modern Art, New York)

Armchair designed by
Charles Eames. The
body is of molded
plastic (glass-reinforced
polyester). The same chair
is also available with an
upholstered seat pad and
different bases.

(molded) curvatures, respectively. Still more recently, plastics have become an obvious possibility as a furniture material. Both Charles Eames and Eero Saarinen, after an early collaboration in a Museum of Modern Art competition submission, separately explored the use of glass-fiber reinforced plastics. The resulting chairs of both designers have become widely known and used and almost seem to symbolize the concept of "futurism" in furniture. Glass reinforced plastic is an ideal furniture material because of its high strength, but molding it requires expensive tools that make manufacturers hesitant to introduce new designs based on this material.

Other ways of using plastics in furniture that do not require costly tooling include heat-forming of flat sheets of acrylic and heat sealing of thin plastic membranes. The first method can easily produce furniture that is transparent—a characteristic often of doubtful merit in furniture, but one that can be spectacular visually. Heat-sealing of thin membranes makes possible inflated furniture; an idea long familiar in such utilitarian applications as the air mattress, but only recently exploited for chairs and sofas. Such furniture is, of course, easily portable when deflated and usually very inexpensive. Unfortunately most products of this type developed so far seem to have been conceived as "novelties" with a short life in terms both of durability and design character. There remains the possibility that good design and careful manufacturing may still lead to air inflated furniture of high quality.

The technique of mixing air bubbles into a material has been commonplace for many years in the making of foam rubber and led to the development of foamed plastic as a natural alternative. By control of the chemical formulation used, the resulting foam can be soft or quite hard. The molds needed for forming can be quite inexpensive and other materials (such as metal or wood) can be imbedded in the foam to add strength. This way of using plastic minimizes quantities of material needed to make an object of a particular size and so reduces weight and cost while encouraging great flexibility in the use of varied shapes.

An interesting variant in foamed plastic use was developed in Italy. A complete chair of plastic foam is placed between sheets of air-tight plastic membranes and the air evacuated from the resulting "bag". Normal air pressure causes the foam chair to collapse into an almost flat "pancake". After the plastic sheet is sealed, the flattened chair is easy to store and ship. After delivery, the owner simply removes the air-tight cover and watches the chair re-expand to its normal size and shape.

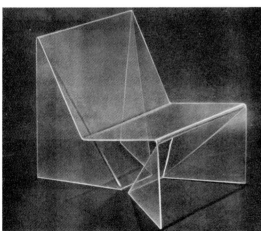

Eero Saarinen pedestal-base chairs with plastic seating shells.

Chair with molded plywood seat and back, and steel frame. Charles Eames.

A single sheet of transparent acrylic plastic has been heat-formed into a shape that makes a usable chair. Designed by Neal Small.

Covering is an elastic fabric that is slipped over the chair after it has assumed its normal form.

Unfortunately, the most common uses of advanced plastics technology are in the making of shoddy reproductions, usually wildly inaccurate and excessively over-decorated, of what pretend to be antiques. Even wood grain and worm holes can be mass-produced in this way! Increasing use of plastics in both imaginative and foolish ways has been stimulated by the increasing cost of wood resulting in the increasingly rapid exhaustion of good wood supply. Ironically, since plastics are

A seating system using three types of molded plastic foam units–straight, concave and convex. In combination, curving sofas of any length can be formed. Designed by Don Chadwick.

largely made from petroleum derived chemicals, similar problems of raw material and supply and rising cost are confronting the plastics industry.

Modern architects and interior designers tend to seek out products that use new materials (especially when the materials are used well) almost as a matter of principle—a feeling that whatever is newest deserves some special encouragement, perhaps, to offset the apprehension of the average man toward that which is new or uncommon. As a result plastic furniture is an increasingly frequent element of modern interiors.

It is still a fact, though, that the best efforts of the best American architects are, with the exception of a very occasional private house, almost entirely confined to commercial and institutional building, while residential building remains in the hands of speculators and promoters whose architectural ideas gravitate toward the bottom level of what is supposed to be popular taste. As a result, the best furniture manufacturers and almost all those who have been concerned with making good modern furniture, have devoted themselves to products for office and public-building use. The manufacturers producing the designs of such distinguished American designers as Charles Eames, Jens Risom, Harry Bertoia, George Nelson, and Florence Knoll are little-known to the average American consumer and so, although many of their designs are suitable to residential use, in most cases actual use is largely in offices and institutions.

As a result of this situation, the furniture well-known and readily available to the American public through retail furniture stores, department stores, and mail-order houses is largely a shoddy chaos of badly designed historic imitations, examples

An inflated chair of thin plastic membrane heat-sealed along the edges so that it can be blown up like an air mattress. Designed by Phil Orenstein.

"Ball chair" from Finland designed by Eerio Aarnio. The shell is plastic, upholstered on the inside.

Plastic table and armchair by Vico Magistretti. (Photograph courtesy Castelli Furniture, Inc.)

Plastic foam is cut into blocks covered in elastic fabric. The units can be piled together for storage or shipping, but separate to form seats and ottomans. Designed by Sebastian Matta.

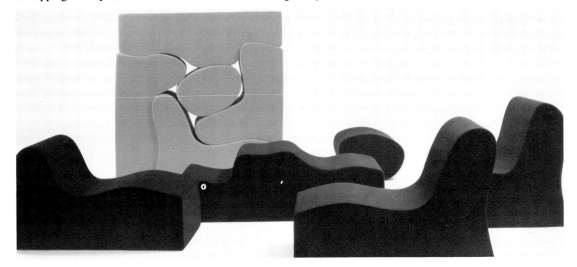

of imaginary historic styles which in fact never existed (such as "Italian Provincial", "Mediterranean", or "American Transitional"), and "modernistic" designs having no relation to the work of serious modern designers and distinguished only by their eccentricity. Such furniture is "styled" on an annual or semiannual basis by anonymous designers who are in fact little more than draftsmen prepared to modify last year's designs to suit a constantly changing style market. Some better designs are available to consumers for certain specialized purposes (outdoor and camp furniture, for example) and through special lines of distribution that specialize in better modern products for a variety of household uses, but the average consumer still has little knowledge of the vast variety of excellent furniture that is well-known to architects and professional interior designers and would be surprised to hear that America is particularly backward in this way among the nations of the world. Some improvement is expected as more people are exposed to better design quality in office and business places and as there is an increasing awareness of the excellence of European imports, which represent the far higher standards that are the norm in Italy, England, the Scandinavian countries, many of the other European countries, and Japan.

A working professional designer has several specific responsibilities in regard to furniture. He must, first of all, know what is available from the manufacturers and importers who are prepared to offer good modern furniture. He must also establish standards of excellence that will help him to sort out products of genuine merit from the innumerable imitations and shoddy, careless designs which are offered to the professional market and which sometimes emerge mixed into the lines of even the best manufacturers. It can be offered as a general guideline that good contemporary furniture is never a direct imitation of some other design, and is almost never (although there may be a few exceptions) the anonymous work of factory-staff design offices. New designers and new furniture firms appear from time to time to join the comparatively short list of established companies with high design standards. Following these developments and making sound judgments of the merit of new work is an important aspect of any interior designer's work.

Among furniture designs, which are in themselves of substantial merit, it becomes important to make selections based on the detailed requirements of a particular use situation. It is easy to agree that all furniture should be functional, comfortable, durable, and of appropriate character and scale for a particular situation, but each situation turns out to have subtle

Chair with wire structure supporting upholstery pad. Designed by Harry Bertola.

Executive desk group designed by George Nelson. Desk chair is a plastic shell by Charles Eames.

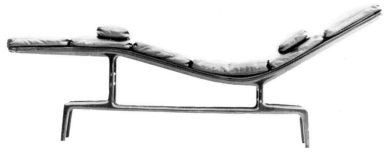

Chaise with leather padding supported in a frame of cast aluminum. Designed by Charles Eames.

Poul Kjaerholm design. This "hammock chair" uses a stainless steel frame to support a body which may be surfaced in either leather or the hand-woven cane shown. The angle of the body can be adjusted and the head-rest placed at any height to suit individual preference.

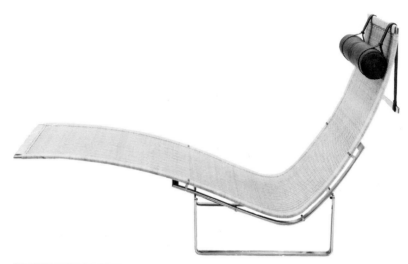

Sofa designed by Morrison and Hannah. The seat and back are suspended in a frame with cast aluminum ends and extruded aluminum lengthwise members.

differences that make the selection of the best object for it a complex matter.

Comfort, for example, turns out to be a complicated criterion. Human beings vary so in size and shape that it is as difficult to find a chair that will be comfortable for everyone as it would be to find a shirt or a shoe to fit everyone. Aside from the variations in human form, comfort is itself a variable thing in different situations. Suitable comfort of dining, desk work, waiting in a public lobby, or dozing for an afternoon at home are each different to a degree that is not always understood by

those who ask that every piece of furniture be totally "comfortable". Durability is also a desirable characteristic, but means something different in an executive office, an average home, a restaurant, an airplane, or a city subway. The qualities of suitable character and scale are even harder to define in any clear way and are therefore even more subtle; yet it is success in choices involving these values that is most central for the sound choice of furniture to serve in each special situation. Finally, it is necessary for a designer to have a sense of appropriateness concerning materials and finishes. Wood, the traditional material of the cabinetmaker, is now more common in the industrial form of plywood than in the traditional solids and thin veneers that were the materials of the antique periods. In addition, metals and plastics are now available that have special usefulness in some situations. As wood becomes more scarce and more costly, these modern materials become more important for purely economic reasons, quite apart from any other merits that they may have.

Comfort, scale, character, and the sense of materials and finishes are the subtle values that determine how a piece of

Office swivel armchair designed by Charles Pollack.
(Photograph courtesy Knoll International, Inc.)

Chair by Charles Eames with soft leather covered cushions supported in a structure of aluminum castings.
(Photograph courtesy of Charles Eames)

President's Office, Benton & Bowles, Inc., New York City. This is an excellent example of a successful combination of the designs of different periods. The Space Design Group, interior designers.

furniture will fit into a particular situation. These are considerations which are impossible to fully judge from a catalog or magazine photograph. Even when looking at an actual sample in a showroom, it turns out to be a complex matter to visualize how a particular item will look when it is in place in a different setting, in company with other furniture, and possibly in a different finish and covering material. A chair that has been selected from a sample having a frame of black-stained wood with a red fabric covering can look very different if it is ordered with a light natural oak frame and black leather covering. The ability to judge such relationships on the basis of mental visualization is one of the special skills that every designer needs to cultivate.

It should also be mentioned that there is no reason why genuine antique furniture, and furniture and objects from remote cultures (a Hong Kong rush chair, an African stool) cannot be used in modern rooms in combination with good modern furniture. It is often said that really good designs look well together no matter what their time or place of origin. This is a generalization that somewhat oversimplifies the problems of relating character and scale. It would be strange to use a clear plastic stool with an elaborately veneered eighteenth-century desk, or a Louis XVI chair at a Victorian rolltop. The problem is not so much a matter of the different time and place of origin of these objects; it is a matter of inappropriate character. There can also be clashes between things which are similar in character, but different enough to be disturbing. An American colonial Windsor chair might not relate well to a modern Danish chair of a similar type designed by Hans Wegner, even though each could be excellent in some other context. These are difficult judgments that must be made through mental comparisons since it is rarely possible to bring the actual objects together in their final place of use as an advance experiment.

Every interior designer also needs some skills as a furniture designer. There will always be occasions when it is best to have certain units built-in (closet fittings, kitchen cabinets, or bathroom vanity counter, for example). Built-in or built-to-order bookshelves, room dividers, work counters, or dressing-storage units can be very handsome and can solve problems that no stock furniture will quite deal with. In commercial and institutional work there are frequent needs for counters, stock storage and display units, banquette seating, and other special designs that move the interior designer into the field of the more specialized furniture designer. The technical aspects of such designs are not particularly complex, especially if the work of construction is to be done by experienced and skilled cabinetmakers and upholsterers, so that the designer who feels confident that s/he knows what is needed in terms of shape and dimensions, can be fairly certain of dealing with such items successfully.

Seating and, particularly, chairs present a more difficult problem. The complexities and subtleties of scale, proportion, comfort, and strength are such that it becomes very difficult to design a really satisfactory chair, and almost impossible unless a number of experimental prototypes are built as part of the design process. For this reason, it is generally best to use chairs of known merit, which can be seen and tried in advance, rather than to take on the difficult and troublesome task of arriving at a new chair design. Almost every designer seems to want to

Office swivel chair using caning in a wood frame. Ward Bennett design. (Photograph courtesy Brickel Associates, Inc.)

Molded plywood framed chair by Bill Stephens. (Photograph courtesy Knoll International, Inc.)

Chair with structure of aluminum extrusions. Gae Aulenti design. (Photograph courtesy Knoll International, Inc.)

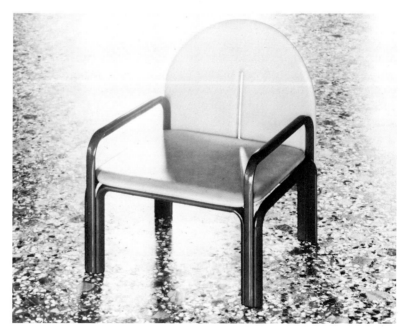

try to design a chair—perhaps because of the excitement that is felt over the famous successful designs by such men as Breuer, Mies van der Rohe, or Charles Eames. There is no reason why this adventure should not be undertaken if the designer is prepared for the many experiments and long period of developmental time that are the norm of chair design (up to 200 samples in one famous case and as long as eight years in another). Clearly this is not an assignment to be made a part of a normal project, but rather a major effort deserving as much thought and care as any other large design project.

Every designer discovers that the area of furniture selection is one of particularly strong, personal interest for the client. Everyone has enough personal knowledge of furniture and enough experience of furniture shopping to be interested in the matter. Unfortunately, the poor design quality of the products that are generally available to consumers and, therefore, to be found in most homes and offices, means that the average individual has had little opportunity to develop any sound knowledge of what good furniture is. A few magazines and newspapers and a few retail shops specializing in modern contemporary design are beginning to make more people aware of what high standards in furniture design really are, but in many cases the designer finds it necessary to carry out a kind of educational program for his client in order to expose him to the good things that are available and thus to develop tastes and preferences that go beyond the level of the average shoddy furniture store. Fortunately, most clients enjoy participating in the process of furniture selection and discovering new and exciting products that they would otherwise know nothing about. Even when a client is little aware of other, possibly more important, aspects of an interior design project, he will invariably be appreciative of comfortable and handsome furniture.

2

INTERIOR MATERIALS

The available choice of interior materials such as textiles and surfacing materials is vast and can be confusing. In the larger cities many specialized firms maintain showrooms for fabrics, floor coverings, and all the other available materials. Every furnishings store, every department store, and even mail-order catalogs offer hundreds of materials. For the layman the selection of fabrics and other materials becomes, therefore, a very difficult chore, simply because of the overabundance of choice. For the homemaker faced with thousands of patterns, colors, and textures in a large fabric showroom, the selection of a single piece of fabric can turn out to be a traumatic experience. The sheer size of the American market of home furnishings is one of the reasons why many people seek the guidance of professional interior designers, whereas in less affluent countries with limited choices of products, the selection of materials such as textiles turns out to be less of a problem, because of limited selections.

The tendency of the nonprofessional in selecting materials is usually to select by appearance and personal preference only. The tendency of many architects is to select materials that are functional and proper in terms of wearability and maintenance only. All too often materials selected and specified for functional considerations alone turn out to be dull and lacking aesthetic value. The interior designer must be familiar with the intrinsic practical values of materials, and at the same time have the sensitivity, taste, and aesthetic judgment to select the most appropriate material for the job, with due consideration of all these factors involved.

The purpose of this chapter is the presentation of a discussion of various interior materials in terms of design and suitability. We shall make no attempt to delve deeply into the history of textiles or carpeting, nor shall we attempt to list every single available material for wall covering or floor covering. Many historical and technical books exist on these subjects. Our purpose is in a way an extension of the previous chapters on form, texture, and scale, for after all these are the design criteria that must be applied in the selection of materials for the success of the total interior. The factors of suitability of materials in terms of wearability and maintenance also bears close watching. Sometimes the most costly and beautiful fabric, such as handwoven silk for instance, would turn out to be the worst possible design choice despite its intrinsic beauty (silk when exposed to direct sunlight will disintegrate in a very short period of time). Another general consideration should be the suitability of materials in terms of the use of a space and its intended atmosphere or mood. Dark colors and heavy textures would hardly seem the appropriate choice of materials for a children's play area, and similarly the use of plastic laminates, vinyl fabrics, and asphalt tile floors would hardly seem right for the creation of an opulent mood in a luxury restaurant.

TEXTILES

In a very general way there are three major aspects to textiles that determine their appearance and suitability for a particular interior use. The designer is concerned with the *fiber* content, the *weave*, and the *pattern*. In order to simplify our discussion of fabrics as an important interior design element, we are going to skip over much technical language and we shall simplify classifications.

Fibers are natural or manmade. The key natural fibers are cotton, wool, linen, and silk. To make value judgments about their relative design merits would seem like comparing apples to pears instead of apples to apples. *Silk* is considered the most elegant of all natural fibers and has historically been a kind of "gold standard" for fabrics. But we mentioned the fact that silk does not stand up well to direct sunlight. Since it requires more care than most other fabrics, it is therefore not a very popular fiber for much of contemporary interior work. Also, it is still a very costly one.

Wool, since it, like silk, derives from animal life, is also relatively expensive. Depending upon its weave, it can be made into extremely strong fabrics and, especially for upholstery materials, the strength and weight of wool fibers have made it one of the most suitable and popular fibers with today's designers. Whether the popularity of a fiber like wool is predicated on the fact that it is a natural fiber and therefore harder to obtain than a nylon or rayon fiber is an interesting point. Designers, as well as the public in general, prefer the unique to the common. Wool is not really in short supply, but since it is processed from the fleece of animals it obviously becomes an expensive raw material. Pure wool fabrics, whether they are woven in a smooth- or rough-textured weave, are not only handsome to look at, but are pleasant to the touch and can be easily handled for just about any shape of upholstery.

Both *cotton* and *linen* are made from vegetable fibers. They are both durable and pliable. They are used more for curtain material than heavy-duty upholstery; unless cotton and linen are interwoven with other fibers, their use tends to be restricted to light-duty interior purposes.

Manmade fibers today abound under a large variety of trade names and new synthetics are continuously being developed. In their generic families these synthetic fibers fall into the following categories: *Glass fibers* (fiberglass) are made into a large variety of fabrics from sheer batistes to heavy textured weaves. Fiberglass fabrics are easy to care for, fireproof, and inexpensive. In spite of the fact that many weaves and patterns are made in fiberglass to resemble cotton, linens, or silk, there is a decided and noticeable difference which certainly appears obvious to the sensitive eye of the designer. The touch or "hand" of fiberglass fabrics is quite different from other materials, and is somewhat unpleasant.

Acetate is a fiber made by many manufacturers under a variety of trade names, but is as a rule combined with rayon or cotton. It has a rather lustrous hand, but needs much more care and careful maintenance than fiberglass. *Acrylic* is somewhat like wool in appearance and feel. Under the trade name of Acrilan (Chemstrand Corporation), it is best known for use in carpets, but under the name of Du Pont's Orlon, it is used widely as a fiber for textiles. *Modacrylics* are modified acrylics and are noted for flameproof qualities amongst a number of other ease-of-care features. The most common trade names are Dynel and Verel. *Nylon* is perhaps the best-known synthetic fiber and derives its fame from use in stockings and other garments more so than from use in interiors. In recent years nylon has been made as a stretch fabric by producing the fiber in a partially drawn form, in other words making it elastic. Nylon is a strong fiber with hard-wearing qualities.

Polyester fibers are best-known through their uses in durable press fabrics. The fiber is used widely in the home-furnishings industry too. In most cases polyester fibers are blended with other fibers for use in curtain or bedspread materials. *Rayon* fibers are well-known for their extensive use in blends with polyesters and other fibers. Rayon fibers are used in dress fabrics as much as in interior textiles and are marketed, under a variety of trade names, by just about every major manufacturer of chemicals or fibers. *Saran* is noted for its excellent ease of care and nonflammable qualities. Like *spandex,* it is one of the newer fibers developed through industrial research. Saran and spandex are the last two examples in this listing of manmade fibers, but we must repeat that our list is by no means a complete or definitive one. We have, however, given here those names of fibers that seem to be the most frequently used in interior textiles, and are therefore the most important fibers at this time.

Weaving is an ancient art. Fundamentally there is not much difference between the very early historic handlooms and the power looms found in major textile plants today. The power loom was invented in the early nineteenth century, and, with relatively few minor changes, is still in operation today. Textile mills are now experimenting with a new type of weaving machine that is called the "shuttleless loom". When perfected and put into wide use, this new process of weaving should provide designers with many new and exciting fabrics at, hopefully, a lesser cost than some of the traditional weaves. Basically weaves can be classified into three general types: plain weaves, which include plain and basket weaves; floating weaves, which include twill and satin weaves; and pile weaves, which include both cut and uncut weaves. There are additional weaving techniques of lesser importance, and some fabrics used in interiors are actually knitted rather than woven.

Textile technology is a highly complex science, and proper engineering in the construction of textiles is as important for the durability of fabrics as attention to construction details in the erection of a building. The durability and dimensional stability of textiles is not just a matter of the appropriate fiber nor a matter of cost of the fabric, it is a combination of many factors. Because textiles are complex, interior designers must be aware of one of the greatest dangers in this (or any) field: action based on little knowledge. Few designers can be experts in all related fields and for significant decisions in the selection and specification of fabrics, designers would be well-advised to seek the counsel of reputable manufacturers and experts in textile technology. The selection of materials for small jobs does not carry the responsibility of specifying hundreds of yards of fabric for larger contract installations. It is annoying to any client if the fabrics in his space do not stand up to their intended use after a year or two. But if the designer specifies the wrong fabric for a very large job, the mistake can run into thousands of dollars, and the appearance of deteriorating fabric will make the most carefully designed interior look shabby.

The *pattern* of textiles, especially in twentieth-century terms, is frequently the indigenous pattern created by the weave of the fabric. In traditional textile terms, reference to pattern usually meant an historic style. Beautiful and artistically significant patterns were developed throughout the history of the decorative arts, ranging from early Egyptian and Chinese patterns through Byzantine, Persian, Renaissance, and eighteenth-century designs. Each era, including our own, has developed fashionable and popular patterns. The current preferences are for abstract and geometric patterns, or possibly for some of the designs based on, or influenced by, the Art Nouveau movement of around the turn of the century. Frequently, however, the contemporary designer prefers the patterns created through weaves. In spite of the almost total industrialization of our society (or maybe because of it) there is much interest in some of the very handsome handwoven textiles produced for contemporary interiors. The extensive use of glazed areas in modern buildings and the increasing integration of interiors with exteriors has all but eliminated the use of heavy, lined draperies made of heavily patterned printed fabrics. Lightweight casement fabrics (a type of "plain weave") over large glass areas, fulfill the function of cutting down on glare and providing acoustical softeners, and add visually to the success of interiors without destroying the intended relation to the exterior world. These casement fabrics are an example of strong pattern created through the inherent pattern provided through the materials' construction. Textile patterns are created (in addition to textures) through a variety of printing processes and through Jacquard weaving. The most intricate patterns can be created on Jacquard looms. The Jacquard loom was invented in Napoleonic times, but is still used widely today for patterned textiles. Many contemporary fabrics use that method.

An understanding of textiles can help in the appropriate specification of fabrics, but a consideration of textiles based on fiber, weave, and pattern does not take into account the stability of color and the fabric's resistance to soiling and to flames. Fabrics often provide the dominant color area in interiors. Obviously the designer must be concerned with the permanence of color if the color is planned as a design feature of the interior. Some poorly made fabrics fade quickly when exposed to strong light. Reputable textile manufacturers will choose dyes and chemicals carefully, will employ expert dyeing techniques, and will certify their products for colorfastness. There are standard tests specified by the Bureau of Standards for colorfastness. The knowledgeable designer will make certain to be assured of such certification wherever there might be a danger of color fading. As objectionable as faded fabrics are fabrics that appear dirty after a short time of use. The maintenance factor for all materials used in interiors must be carefully considered. Any material selected for appearance only may turn out to be a detriment to a carefully designed job if it does not stand up to its expectations. In spite of the extensive publicity given to the new soil-resistant finishes available for textiles, they do not perform miracles. Sooner or later all fabrics and most other materials show wear, although some processes such as Sylmer finishing on textiles provide at least some degree of protection for waterborne soil.

It is not possible to state an easy rule for the selection and specification of fabrics, and the foregoing discussion of textiles can at best provide criteria based on the function of fabrics. The designer who selects fabric based on aesthetic consideration alone does only half a job and possibly a very poor one. Each job requires different treatment, depending on both aesthetic considerations (reflecting the character of the total space) and practical ones (reflecting the use for which the space is intended). The sensitivity needed to understand the successful combination of all these factors must be carefully developed and must, in our society, be supplemented with a considerable knowledge of the availability of the best products on the market.

FLOOR COVERINGS

In spite of the fact that a vast choice of fabrics exists, they fit at least under one generic heading. Flooring materials, however, can be anything from rough concrete to luxurious oriental rugs, or from terrazzo to exotic wood flooring. We are primarily concerned with floor *coverings* in this section, and obviously concrete and terrazzo are not materials that really belong here. But this is precisely the reason why we mention these more structural materials. As far as the public and industry are concerned, flooring in interior design means carpeting, rugs, and resilient tiles only; and unfortunately too many designers have accepted this arbitrary limitation—which is somewhat like being asked to compose music for one string on the violin. In the best approaches to interior design, the specification of flooring is considered in the planning stages of a building and therefore is not limited to the cosmetic surfacing of existing structural floors. With sufficient knowledge, even an existing building can be redesigned for the installation of floors ranging from slate or marble to terrazzo or quarry tile. All these materials have been discussed as architectural materials and they are indeed more permanent, more costly, and more complex in installation processes. However, it is important to remember that the floor coverings discussed in this chapter are just one type of material and are by no means the only one for the consideration of the designer.

To many people *carpets and rugs* represent beauty, luxury, or some kind of status symbol, regardless of the purpose of a particular interior. But perhaps the most important question to be posed in the specification of floor coverings is the question we have raised a number of times, what is the purpose of the space? Carpeting has certain features absent in other flooring materials. It has acoustical properties within the space in which it is used, reducing the transmission of sound between rooms. It provides safety features against falls or breakage. It has excellent maintenance features in terms of ease of maintenance and cost. It is the one flooring material with unlimited possibilities of color and pattern. In psychological terms, it is the flooring material which can create the warmest and most intimate mood.

The earliest known woven floor coverings were made in the Far East and in Egypt probably as early as 3000 B.C. Over the centuries, wool has been the accepted fiber for carpeting. Other materials such as "fiber rugs" (paper pulp twisted into yarn), flax, cotton, and rush have also been used in making rugs, but are of minor importance compared to wool. During World War II, however, wool was in short supply, and since that time many synthetic fibers have been developed. Among the most popular fibers used for the manufacture of carpeting are the acrylics, nylons, polyesters, and a number of other synthetics. A generalization about the relative quality of these fibers compared to wool would be a poor way to judge quality and wearability. For all woven floor coverings, the type of the yarn, the quantity, and the construction determine the quality. The

determining factors in manufacturing are the pitch (number of face yarns per inch), the pile height (the height of the yarn above the backing), the ply of the yarn (number of individual ends of yarn twisted together), and the method of weaving or tufting. Ultimately these factors are reflected in the price, and the cost of carpeting from a reputable manufacturer is a very good indication of its quality.

The traditional weaves for carpeting are Wilton, Velvet, Axminster, and Chenille—terms which refer to the construction of the weave. Tufting is a process of needling the yarns through the backing of the material and it is a less costly method of weaving. It is today the most popular method of manufacturing and accounts for 60 percent to 70 percent of mass-produced carpeting. The most expensive rugs are the handknotted "Oriental" rugs originating from the Middle East. Some manufacturers produce custom-tufted contemporary rugs, but these —like their Oriental cousins—are extremely expensive. Within

Executive lounge (below) and corridor area (above) in Weyerhaeuser Corporate
Headquarters, Tacoma. Skidmore, Owings and Merrill, architects; space planning
by Sidney Rodgers and Associates, Inc.; furniture by Knoll International.
(Photographs courtesy of Knoll International)

these basic categories there are a great number of varieties of weave. The looped carpets, for example, are quite popular since they are strong and are easily maintained. Several new processes have been developed in recent years for printing designs on carpeting through a method of magnetized dyestuffs which are drawn through the tufted materials electrostatically. Some of these new materials are produced in huge quantities at very reasonable costs, but unfortunately the attempt to keep the prices down and make material suitable for vast commercial areas has ignored many of the better design qualities.

The public imagines that carpet represents a kind of status symbol and has not developed the ability to differentiate between well-designed carpeting and the many inferior products on the market. Nor is carpeting the answer to every interior need in spite of its many advantageous features. Many large businesses have evolved a sort of hierarchy of status for their executives, with carpeting as one of the chief criteria. Top executives expect wall-to-wall carpeting (in addition to other status symbols, such as corner offices of large dimensions). In some cases the second-echelon executives find their offices carpeted with the same materials but cut a few inches short from the walls as "area rugs", in order to differentiate these offices as lesser spaces. Among homemakers a similar myth has surrounded the use of rugs and other floor coverings. It is not unusual to find shabby and ugly rugs used over perfectly beautiful wooden floors simply because the rug has become a symbol. In remodeling some of the homes constructed during the last century, very elegant floors were found to be covered with layer after layer of inferior linoleum and similar floor coverings.

Linoleum is one of several types of synthetic floor coverings that has become increasingly available and popular in the past two decades. These are generally referred to as *resilient floors*. There is an abundance of choice in resilient flooring materials, ranging in price from very inexpensive asphalt tile to the fairly costly vinyls. The installation is simple and inexpensive; however, some of these materials cannot be installed on floors that are either on-grade or below grade. Broadly speaking, the resilient flooring materials currently on the market are (ranging up in price) asphalt, vinyl-asbestos, linoleum, cork, and vinyl. Until a few years ago rubber tiles were widely marketed, but problems of cost, color, and maintenance have almost eliminated the production of that material. Linoleum and vinyls come in the form of sheet material as well as in the form of tiles. In interiors where seams or patterns created by tiles are not desirable, the choice is often determined by that factor. Pure vinyls are the most durable materials and come in an almost unlimited range of colors and designs. Many of the designs on the market are highly questionable. The public (or the manufacturers) seem to have a predilection for imitating natural materials such as stone, brick, or marble, in vinyl. Especially since the material takes color so well and is adaptable to any design or pattern, there exists this very dangerous temptation to make it look like something it is not. In its natural appearance it is plain and can be quite beautiful—in a large variety of colors. One must remember, however, that a perfectly plain floor will show every speck of dirt and every mark made by the heels of shoes and is therefore not a very practical floor for areas of high use and traffic. There are a number of textured vinyls which reflect the plastic quality of the indigenous content of the material, and are, therefore, an honest expression of it, thus making it both acceptable to designers and practical for maintenance purposes.

Cork is the only *natural* material in this group of resilient floor coverings. It is the most resilient and has acoustical qualities as well. Cork is not suitable to heavy-duty use and will show indentation marks. It is necessary to keep cork floors waxed in order to preserve the surface, and a well-used cork floor can become a rather rich and beautiful-looking material with the deepened natural hue caused by many applications of wax, even though some marks of indentation may be visible. Some cork tiles are made with a protective coating of highly glossy vinyl, but this hard and reflective surfacing destroys much of the natural beauty of the material.

Linoleum is a synthetic material, made from a combination of ingredients, mostly in sheet form. It predates the availability of the other synthetic flooring materials and has been widely used for heavy-duty areas such as schools and other public buildings and even as flooring for battleships (hence the term "battleship linoleum"). The plain colors, although limited in range, are usually the most successful "designs" in linoleum. The many ugly patterns, the floral designs imitating rugs, and the absurd imitations of such materials as flagstones need not even be discussed.

Vinyl asbestos is only about 25 percent more expensive than asphalt but has many advantages to the designer. It is softer underfoot; through the combination of vinyl and asbestos, it has more possibilities for color and pattern; and it is grease-resistant as well as easily maintained in general.

Asphalt tile is the most widely used resilient flooring, simply because it is the least expensive. It is used in industrial plants, in housing projects, and in countless other types of interiors. Most asphalt tiles have a marbleized appearance, a result of the mixing process of the raw material, rather than a conscious attempt to imitate real marble (which it does not). Asphalt is quite brittle and hard underfoot, but it certainly is one of the most useful and practical materials ever invented by man for use as flooring.

Each year new materials or new combination of materials are produced, thus the listing of the above basic types of resilient floor coverings is not meant to be exhaustive. In recent years some of the vinyls were backed with felt or rubber in order to form a very soft and resilient flooring, and similar processes were used with ceramic tiles. There are also continually developments of materials in new forms, which make some architectural flooring materials available as decorative ones. For instance, there are prefabricated wood tiles in parquet patterns in almost any kind of wood; some of these wood tiles are made to be installed just like resilient floor tiles, over existing floors. Similarly, there are prefabricated ceramic and quarry tiles which no longer require installation over especially constructed subfloors and wet cement, but can simply be installed with mastic over wood or concrete. Even marble floors come in thin tiles, ready to be glued over existing floors with no more preparation needed than the one usually followed for asphalt or vinyl-asbestos tile. Experience has shown, however, that none of the simplified processes is a substitute for the tested methods of more traditional building. Some travertine floors in lobbies of office buildings, for instance, have been heavily used for over fifty years and have never required replacement. On the other hand, in some cases travertine tiles used in residences have started to crack and come loose after only a few months of use.

The selection and specification of flooring materials is one of the aspects of interior design requiring a fair amount of technical knowledge and practical experience. A good designer will seek the help and advice of experts, especially if the interior is to be for public use and involves the investment of large sums of money.

WALL COVERINGS

Earlier we explained the difference between the architectural materials used as flooring and the more decorative materials used as floor coverings. A similar distinction should be made between walls and wall coverings. Every wall is a material in itself and ideally no material, if properly used, need be covered up. Many buildings today, even some rather elegant structures, use concrete in its natural texture (showing the formwork left by wooden forms as a conscious expression of the material). Twentieth-century designers are very much aware of the honesty of materials and are concerned in expressing these materials. This was not always true in the past. The nineteenth century especially saw the popularity of a rather high degree of fakery in design, and our concern with the true expression of materials is in part a revolt against this tradition of previous generations. Today, for instance, we consider brick walls rather desirable. Old town houses often reveal beautiful brick below the plaster and numerous coats of paint; those people who are interested in design and care about it are quite willing to spend the time and money it may take to strip old plaster walls down to their true surface.

The material most readily associated with wall coverings for interiors is of course wallpaper. There exists a long tradition of decorative wallpapers, and some of the early Chinese papers especially were a strong influence and inspiration for subsequent western papers. Until the seventeenth century, the most popular wall coverings were tapestries or wood. The tapestries were used primarily as a protection from the cold. Better building technology, and heated interiors eliminated the need for costly wall hangings. The eighteenth and nineteenth centuries saw the greatest popularity of scenic wallpapers and handblocked or screen-printed papers on almost any subject. There are still countless wallpapers on the market today. They range from small geometric patterns to mass produced "murals". Most good designers have little use for wallpapers, and even the public is less likely today to "enrich" a room with some poorly designed pattern. A well-planned interior, conceived as a total design, does not need the superficial decoration of a printed paper and might, in fact, be destroyed in most cases through the superfluous pattern and color. Even very simple residential interiors are usually more successful with plain walls or walls made of natural materials. Decorative touches and personal expression by the room's inhabitants can be far more interesting through the use of paintings, prints, or other meaningful artwork, rather than through the use of commercially made, mass-produced papers.

If a space is planned for a special purpose and if the use of a strong pattern or color is desired, a well-designed wallpaper can be a meaningful asset. Often a strong paper is better on one wall only, instead of surrounding the whole space with a domineering pattern. Because of the reaction against the last century's overuse of wallpapers, few contemporary designers of talent have tried their hand at the design of wallpapers. There is currently a renewed interest in pattern and "super-graphics", and it seems quite likely that in another few years wallpapers might become available in better designs and therefore create a new interest and find increased acceptance. In some European countries, wallpapers are already used more widely than here. The basic disapproval implied here applies to the general run-of-the-mill commercial wallpapers carried in wallpaper and paint stores, as well as to the many expensive wallpapers available in the so-called decorator show-rooms. Some of the surviving antique wallpapers are as mean-ingful and as beautiful as other old furnishings. They are often works of art, and reflect the values and the culture of bygone eras.

There are a number of very handsome wallpapers which serve a specific purpose and which have some intrinsic quali-ties of their own. These are the textured papers often made from natural materials such as Oriental grasscloth and shiki silk papers. Not only are these papers made from natural materials, they also have acoustical properties and a certain degree of interest and warmth through their indigenous tex-tures. Many domestic papers use similar processes in the lamination of linen, burlap, or similar textures on paper back-ing. They often provide an attractive background, and if treated with Sylmer or plastic coating, provide a wall surface superior in maintenance to painted plaster.

Plastic coated or vinyl wallpapers are useful wall coverings in kitchens and bathrooms. They are washable, and they stand up better than painted surfaces to steam from hot water or to grease from cooking. Unfortunately the vast majority of these highly practical surfacing materials are poorly designed and abound in ugly patterns. The best of these wall coverings are vinyl-coated fabrics, rather than coated papers. A number of vinyl-coated fabrics are on the market for institutional and public space use primarily. These materials are highly appro-priate for use in building corridors, in all high traffic areas, in hospitals (they are completely washable), and in hotels. Vinyl-coated fabrics come in different weights; the heavier the antici-pated traffic and use, the heavier the material. The cost of some of the heavy vinyls is quite high, but is justified by the fact that the material can withstand countless washings and scrub-bings compared to painted surfaces or almost any other sur-face material. The design of these materials is quite good in many cases. Because the specifiers are architects or architecturally aware interior designers, manufacturers have to resist the temptation to produce these vinyls in floral patterns or other "cute" designs, which would not be acceptable to the designers.

Fabric wall coverings were very fashionable during the last century, either in hangings or in stretched panels. When fabrics are used for wall coverings today they are, in most cases, laminated to a paper backing for ease of installation. Almost any fabric can be used as a wall covering that way, but the cost is rather high. There are a number of excellent readily available materials, such as felt wall coverings, which have strong acoustical properties and are manufactured for sound control primarily.

Depending on the budget of a job and the designer's imagination, there is practically no limit to the materials that might be used for wall coverings; leather, metallic materials, or any number of plastic laminates have all been used for certain special-purpose interiors. Cork is frequently used for practical purposes, as tack space, or for its sound-absorbing properties, as well as for its appearance. The heavily textured Portuguese cork, originally marketed as insulating material for refrigeration, is a particularly handsome material. In recent years a number of designers have used carpeting as a wall-surfacing material. Undoubtedly, as industry comes up with new materials, designers will find new uses for them, whether as wall or floor coverings or for use anywhere else in our environment.

It is obvious that the qualities of all the materials discussed have certain criteria in common. An understanding of each individual material is important, but is not sufficient for an interior designer. What is important to the designer is the combination of all the many parts and components into a cohesive whole. Each space has a certain character, whether consciously planned or not. Often that character or atmosphere is deadly and depressing, but a particular mood exists nonetheless. Color, materials, and textures do much to set this mood, especially if the space has little architectural interest. We discussed these concepts in Part Two, which was devoted to the vocabulary of design. There we pointed out that truly well-designed architectural interiors do not depend heavily upon decorative materials and colors, but create their own strong atmosphere through scale, the handling of architectural form, and the structural materials used. We have shown several examples of such interiors (see pp. 227-256). For interiors in lesser architectural shells, for the average office interior, and for the average home, the tools at the disposal of the designer frequently consist of the sensitive handling of materials and color.

Most interior designers analyze the function of a space, decide together with the client the character most appropriate, and keep this image in mind when they set out to plan and design the interior. Even with a fairly clear aim towards color and material, the designer cannot simply describe and specify a particular floor covering, wall surfacing, or fabric. For every material needed, a number of similar ones or a number of alternate materials are studied and collected. For a space containing no more than half a dozen different materials, it would not be unusual for an interior designer to put together as many as twenty to thirty materials before making the final choice. In our society, with the vast resources and choices at our disposal, it rarely happens that a particular carpet or fabric cannot be found to exist. In those cases where a strong idea or preference necessitates a particular shade or color, or a certain kind of texture, the interior designer may design or specify a material to be made to order for a particular job. Once the designer is satisfied that enough choices have been put together for the final selection, including special materials where appropriate, the final selection can be made. The experienced designer will look at his semifinal choices under several conditions of light. If the materials are to be used in a space with all fluorescent illumination, that kind of light will obviously have to be considered in the final selection. Most designers combine their final choices on a sample or materials board for presentation to the client as well as their own use in making the final judgment. Ideally the materials combined on a board will reflect somewhat the sizes or areas of surfaces in the proportion of the samples and cuttings. A 2 inch by 2 inch carpet sample for a wall-to-wall installation, next to a 6 inch by 6 inch cutting of a fabric to be used on one chair, would throw the distribution of colors out of focus and give the wrong image on a sample board. The background color of such a sample board ideally reflects the color of the walls. Most interiors have the majority of walls or ceilings in white, so that a white sample board is usually an adequate background.

Since all surfacing materials have certain criteria in common, it is natural to talk about a "range" of material and colors in one space or in a series of spaces. There are no ironclad rules about this range or affinity of materials other than common sense and above all the experienced eye of the designer.

The function, wearability, and maintenance factors of materials can be found out easily; if an interior is planned for public use and all materials are hard wearing and sensible, it would obviously be wrong to select an inexpensive cotton velvet cover material for the furniture, no matter how beautifully the color might work with the other materials chosen. If all the materials are elegant textures, smooth and silky, soft to the touch, and luxurious to behold, a sudden introduction of a burlap curtain material would be a serious mistake. Or, if the job is the design of a dormitory for boys, the most sensible and handsome selection of materials would be ruined if the designer decided that he must give in to his craving for pink bedspreads. These principles stated here may appear obvious, yet it is sad and surprising to see how often the most elementary considerations are ignored and how often serious mistakes occur because a material was chosen out of context from all the other materials in a space. If a rule must be given, maybe one should remember the famous quotation from Mies van der Rohe, used earlier in this book: "Less is more". Too often a job can be ruined by too many materials, too many textures, and too many colors, even if all the materials used are in some way cohesive. One of the hardest achievements is to know where to use restraint and when to stop.

This chapter has discussed some of the key elements of materials used by interior designers. No attempt was made to discuss every possible material and interior component. An acquaintance with many materials and their properties is helpful and desirable. But more important than an encyclopedic knowledge of all conceivable materials, is the ability to discern the good and the bad features of materials and the ability to visualize how all the components in one space will act together to form a strong and cohesive whole as one expression of design.

3

LIGHTING

In our chapter devoted to color and light (II.4), we discussed some aspects of light—briefly taking up the matter of daylighting and artificial lighting in their relation to color and as a design element in interiors. In this chapter we are primarily concerned with artificial lighting. Until a few decades ago there was no electricity. In these recent decades, however, electric lighting has become the only form of artificial illumination that we use in interiors and has become a major science in its own right. Candles, oil lamps, or gas light might be used sometimes for effect or atmosphere, but are never considered as a prime source of illumination in any industrialized country.

There are three major aspects to lighting: function, aesthetics, and health. The health factor in lighting is not just a matter of providing adequate amounts of lighting for different tasks, although even that basic necessity is all too frequently ignored. Many people are unaware of the strain on eyesight caused by poor lighting or the resulting fatigue, physical discomfort, or headaches. Designers are aware of the recommendations for proper levels of illumination for office, factory, or school; and the lighting in spaces for work tends to be better for that reason. Laymen frequently try to perform delicate tasks such as sewing or writing under conditions that are at best adequate for conversation or dining. Even children are often given most inadequate decorative lamps for homework or reading because their parents do not realize the harm that can come to their children's eyes due to poor illumination. The human eye is an amazingly adaptable organ. Most of man's

370 individual lighting units become the entire ceiling in the entrance lobby of the Whitney Museum in New York. Marcel Breuer and Hamilton Smith, architects; Michael H. Irving consulting architect. (Photograph courtesy of Marcel Breuer and Associates by Ezra Stoller)

indoor activities are carried out under lighting conditions which are but a small fraction of normal daylight. Most indoor lighting for work or reading is just 3 to 6 percent of the daylight level. We have all experienced temporary discomfort and blinding when stepping into bright sunlight from a darkened room. Yet, after an interval of time, our eyes will adjust to the new conditions. The vast range of natural conditions can be understood when we realize that the difference of brightness between a moonlit night and a sunlit snowscape can be expressed in the latter being several million times brighter than the former. In spite of the adaptability of the human eye to varying conditions, illuminating engineers with the help of scientists and physicians have determined the optimum conditions for a variety of tasks. Thus designers can obtain a great deal of specific information for the determination of functional lighting design. There exist many handbooks and textbooks on lighting, and it is not the purpose of this chapter to provide a digest of all the technical information needed for proper lighting design. We shall attempt here to explain some basic principles and a few of the technological factors to show the importance of lighting as an integral aspect of interior design.

The level of lighting is expressed in lumens per square feet. 1 lumen/ft^2=1 footcandle (the amount of light given by one candle at a distance of one foot from the point of measurement). The Illuminating Engineering Society publishes recommended levels of lighting intensity (which have been going up considerably in the past few years) stated in footcandles. General office work, for example, should be 100 footcandles on the task; reading, 60 footcandles; sewing on dark cloth, 150 footcandles; and the general level in passage areas such as escalators and stairs should be 20 footcandles. The footcandle level expresses the quantity of light, but the designer must be equally concerned with the quality of light.

Brightness of the source of light (measured in footlamberts) can be controlled by shielding the lamp from direct view. Excessive brightness is the definition of glare and is always disturbing to the eye. Diffusion of light is another important consideration. A bright, intense light is much more tiring to the eye than a softly diffused light. Diffusion can be achieved directly by shielding the source of light as the luminaire, especially by means of prismatically cut glass or plastic. Diffusion can also be achieved through reflecting light to the work surface from a white wall or other light surface. Light can be controlled with a great deal of precision. The curvature of reflectors, the prismatic grinding of diffusors, and the design of the lamp itself provide complete accuracy to the illuminating engineer or designer who is knowledgeable about these factors. One of the properties of light is the fact that when striking any surface the angle of incidence equals the angle of reflection. This permits lighting designers to manipulate the glare and brightness factors, and to control the incident direction of light in order to emphasize the shape and texture of objects. Overhead lighting devices are the simplest, since vertical sources of light are naturally shielded from the eye by eyebrows and eyelids, and people do not as a rule engage in activities which cause them to look towards the ceiling. A uniformly diffused ceiling system may have the effect of avoiding glare and brightness, but it may also create a light without shadows and highlights, which will make objects in the space appear flat and without texture.

It is always important to avoid drastic contrasts in the intensity of light. A perfectly well-designed reading light used without another source of illumination in the same space will create too strong a contrast for the eye every time the reader looks up. The ideal work surface, or the lighted page for reading, should be slightly brighter than the surrounding room, but not bright enough to cause an extreme contrast. Any abrupt change in illumination is disturbing. A gradual dimming of high-level lights is much more agreeable than the sudden switching on or off of strong lights. Dimmers have the added advantage of providing several levels of illumination for several different activities or functions in the same room.

One of the most important attributes of artificial light is its effect on color. In interiors, we use two basic types of lighting: incandescent and fluorescent. Incandescent (or tungsten) light is somewhat redder than daylight, but all the colors of the spectrum are present. Fluorescent light has an uneven spectrum so that colors appear somewhat distorted. There are a vast variety of fluorescent lamps, and manufacturers claim to have improved fluorescents to the point of real daylight accuracy or other desired effects. As a rule the best lighting effect in terms of color accuracy—as well as softness, diffusion, and highlights—is one in which a mixture of lighting has been used. Whether the mixture is of incandescents and fluorescents, of direct and indirect, or of a variety of types of fluorescents depends upon the effect the designer wishes to achieve. A further consideration is the use of color—and its reflective value—on all walls and surfaces. One of the most important and yet most neglected aspects of lighting is the human complexion. As a simple experiment one can use a "daylight" or "cold" fluorescent lamp in front of a mirror against a blue background and contrast that combination with an incandescent lamp in front of a mirror against a red or orange background. In the first case the face of the viewer will appear ghastly and almost sickly. In the second combination the viewer will appear healthy and tanned looking. The proper design of lighting involves, in other words, not just consideration of the space and its objects, but above all consideration of the human occupants for whom the spaces are designed.

LIGHTING DESIGN

For the design of a lighting scheme the first consideration must be the function of the space and the tasks to be performed in it. We gave a few examples of suggested intensity of lighting for particular tasks, such as reading or sewing. Highly demanding work like surgery or drafting will require shadowless light, as well as considerable intensities. For certain spaces, the atmosphere or the character of the space can be achieved through proper lighting. A luxury restaurant or night-club requires different considerations from a cafeteria or a discotheque. And even the lighting for a residence presents very different demands, varying from kitchen to dining room, or from the area for homework to the lighting near the fire-place.

We mentioned the two basic types of lighting used in inte-riors, namely, incandescent and fluorescent. Both types can be used as direct or as indirect lighting (and in some combina-tions illuminating engineers refer to certain systems as "semi-direct" and "semi-indirect"). A third basic consideration is whether the lighting equipment is architectural (built-in) or portable.

One cannot state that a direct lighting system is better than an indirect one or the reverse. Direct lights can be recessed ceiling fixtures such as spots or floods; they can be recessed or flush-mounted fluorescent luminaires; or they can be portable lamps, such as reading lights or bullet-shaped lights. With properly engineered reflectors and diffusors, direct lights are by no means restricted to a spot or beam. In fact, the increased efficiency in the design of luminaires seems to make direct lighting more popular with lighting designers. With indirect lighting a certain amount of energy or intensity of the light gets lost, even if the light is reflected back from a white or very light surface. The best-known indirect-lighting devices are cove lights or lighting valances and the type of luminaires which throw light on to a white ceiling in order to have it reflected back to the work surfaces. More often than not a well-designed lighting scheme requires built-in features and must therefore be planned as an architectural feature in a space. Any lighting scheme which is planned as an after-thought, once the space has been designed, is likely to fail and can often ruin a space. This is not only a matter of building-in coves or recessed spots, or wall washers and similar special-purpose devices, it is a matter of wiring, which must obviously be planned ahead of time lest the wiring be run in exposed tubing on the finished surfaces. It is also a matter of the proper location of each and every single source of light. If a lounge in a dormitory has a number of game tables or writing tables to be lit by recessed ceiling lights, the precise location of the tables must be known in order to specify the location of the lights.

The technical and mechanical knowledge required for lighting design is complex, but designers who are not familiar with all aspects of this required knowledge can consult illuminating engineers, electrical engineers, or lighting consultants. The aspect of lighting design that is primarily up to the interior designer and architect is the *character* of the space that s/he intends. Lighting can be just adequate and functional; it can also be exciting, sparkling, and dramatic. Perhaps the best example of exciting lighting can be found in the theater. Many theatrical productions have been staged successfully without traditional sets, but have conveyed the changing mood and setting of a play through expertly designed lighting. We know of the psychological need for variety and change in our surroundings, and we discussed this aspect of design in an earlier chapter. This need for variety is also evident in lighting. If one can state any rules about good lighting design, one should certainly emphasize this need for change and variety. A space will be more attractive if it contains highlights and shadows, not only to create different levels of illumination at different times, but at all times. Any room in a home, for instance, will be enhanced if, in addition to adequate and appropriate lighting, there is a "pool" of light in some area for no other reason than visual delight. This might be a small spot trained on a plant or a painting, or it might be exterior lighting seen through the windows of the room. This is true in working spaces as well. A large office lit with an evenly diffused luminous ceiling system can be very efficient, but will also be monotonous and deadly if not sparked up with some area lights of differing intensity.

Detail of Philip Johnson's New York State Theater showing special light fixture.

For certain interiors, such as stores, lighting becomes a design tool in itself. Research into merchandizing techniques has resulted in considerable knowledge about the public's buying habits. Every store uses point-of-sales displays aimed at "impulse" buying. If such a display is lighted with a high-intensity spot, many more people will notice it and will, as a result, buy. We all respond to displays in stores or windows that somehow seem to attract our attention. More often than not, the object that we look at first is one which has been spot-lighted. It is standard procedure in stores to use much higher intensity of light for counters and displays than the level used for aisles and passages. Another type of interior with specific lighting needs, or traditions, are formal spaces of festive assembly such as theaters, opera houses, or ballrooms. The sparkle created through the reflection of light on crystals or glass is unequalled in its effect. Traditional crystal chandeliers

were first used with candles and are still today the most successful lighting devices to create an atmosphere of sparkling
elegance. Today's designers shy away from copying the hand-
made crystals used on seventeenth and eighteenth-century
chandeliers, and a number of good contemporary luminaires
have been developed which have the same effect of elegance.
The special fixtures designed by Philip Johnson for the New
York State Theater at Lincoln Center are a good example of
this trend.

PORTABLE LAMPS

A word of clarification about the terminology used in this
chapter might help to alleviate some possible confusion. In
architectural lighting, designers and illuminating engineers do
not refer to "bulbs", but use the proper term, "lamp". While
"lighting fixture" is not a wrong term, we prefer to use the
technically correct term of "luminaire". The term "portable
lamps" refers to all movable lighting devices such as desk
lamps, reading lamps, floor lamps, and table lamps, and includes also wall lamps or wall brackets.

**Floor lamp designed by
Anders Pehrson.
Georg Jensen, Inc.**

**Table lamp designed by
Yki Nummi from
Georg Jensen, Inc.**

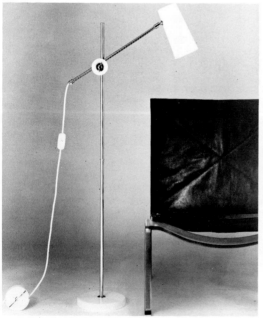

For some strange reason the design of portable lamps has brought out the worst instincts in manufacturers and in the public, who have accepted some of the monstrosities put on the market. Many aspects of interior design and furniture design have suffered low points throughout various eras. It seems that this era concentrated more bad taste and ludicrous "design" on lamps than on any other aspect of home furnishings. Essentially a portable lamp should be an area light, consisting of the source of light properly shielded, placed at a certain height and direction for a specific task or effect. Lampshades run a close second in vulgarity to some of the horrors that were developed under the name of lamps. Actually a lampshade is an excellent diffusor and shield against glare; in its proper size and in a translucent material it does precisely the job it was designed for. The "decorative" lampshades that abound in stores are often opaque materials which successfully prevent any light from penetrating, and are in many cases ugly materials made into peculiar shapes. The bases for lamps, especially table lamps, have been made in almost every material and shape, ranging from china and glass, to wood, ceramic, and metal. The tradition of using beautiful vases as lamp bases is of debatable merit, no matter how beautiful the vase. The tradition of brass, bronze, or silver candelabras seemed a valid expression of the craftsmanship of past centuries, when candelabras were used to hold candles; but it seems silly to use these traditional candleholders indiscriminately as bases for electric lights. We cannot argue with the intrinsic beauty of many antique or even contemporary lamp bases. But we would argue that if these objects are works of art, they would be more beautiful and more enjoyable in their own right rather than converted into some use for which they were not intended. The frantic search for novelty on the part of manufacturers has brought forth such awful lamp bases as a nude figure of a woman made even more "functional" by imbedding an electric clock in her belly.

These comments do not imply that the only acceptable lamps are efficient and mechanical looking devices. The criteria of evaluation for lamps should start, however, with the function for which the lamp was designed, rather than with the attempt to create the reproduction of a work of art or a piece of sculpture that is bound to fail on all aesthetic principles. There are today many excellent lamps that were designed both in America and abroad. Some of them are highly decorative and some, through use of good materials and craftsman-

Lamp for Habitat, Inc., designed by Paul Mayen.

Library lamp by Anders Pehrson. Georg Jensen, Inc.

**Pendant lights by
Vilhelm Wohlert
and Jorgen Bo.
Georg Jensen, Inc.**

**A hanging light using a
black center collar with a
brass tube projecting
above and below.
Designed by
Jo Hammerbog.**

**A small adjustable lamp
made in bright lacquer
colors. Designed by
Tobia Scarpa.**

ship, are very elegant. The choice of portable lamps ranges from the type of lamp which is designed to create a small pool of light as an accent in a space to the highly efficient floor lamps, table lamps, or reading lamps which can illuminate large areas of a room or which can give excellent light for reading or work.

Lamps to be mounted on ceilings or hung as pendants have shared the fate of other portable lamps in recent history. The attempt to create a beautiful object hung in space has more validity than the arbitrary use of *objets d'art* as bases for portable lamps. We mentioned the handsome effect of crystal chandeliers in festive environments. The tradition of a pendant fixture in a dining space is therefore rooted in both function and beauty. Knowing something about the infinite possibilities of lighting design should make it very clear that a chande-

lier or pendant is by no means the only way to light a dining table. But at least there are enough well-designed pendants available today for those designers who wish to use them as a source of light and as a design element in space.

In an age that Marshall MacLuhan calls the "electric age" one hardly needs to emphasize our dependence upon lighting and electricity in general. Many contemporary interiors are built without windows and are therefore in need of constant artificial illumination. All interiors are used approximately half the time with dependence on artificial lighting. Lighting, apart from its functional and physiological aspects, is largely responsible for the particular mood in an interior. The design of lighting is anything but a matter of mood and is a subject of prime importance in any manmade space.

Wall lamp by Paul Mayen, Habitat, Inc.

Wall lamp by Yki Nummi. Georg Jensen, Inc.

4

ACCESSORIES

Most architects and many interior designers tend to look upon the selection of accessories as an unimportant or even somewhat distasteful part of a job. The term "accessories" is admittedly a somewhat vague one and can mean a great many things, from pictures or prints to antique glassware and china. It also evokes the image of vast arrays of junk which have been sold for years and years in giftshops and in special departments for accessories in home-furnishing stores. Most of the poorly designed merchandise that people tend to associate with this subject is being marketed for the home. It might be helpful if we leave the home for a moment, and first discuss accessories for nonresidential interiors. (We shall discuss paintings, sculpture, and art in interiors in the following chapter.) Our definition of "accessories" refers to all the small movable objects that make an interior complete.

A certain amount of accessories in offices, restaurants, lounges, or similar public spaces are highly functional and necessary objects. The most common one (in spite of the public awareness of the dangers of smoking) is still the ashtray. There is hardly a work space or public interior without several ashtrays ranging from table ashtrays to floor urns. It would appear that the design of an ashtray is one of the less difficult assignments for the industrial designer or other designers who may have tried their hand at it. An ashtray must hold ashes; it should have a space to put down cigarettes; it should stand firmly without spilling its contents; it should be designed to prevent the slightest breeze from blowing ashes out of it; ideally it should be sturdy enough to withstand the "knocking" of pipes; it should be fireproof; it should not

Ash receiver. Habitat, Inc.

Planters. Habitat, Inc.

break easily; and lastly—it should be good looking. Easy assignment—or is it? Readers who smoke heavily can probably
add a few more requirements to the above ones, but just
accepting the ones listed here, the conscientious critic or
shopper would find it very difficult to come upon many ashtrays meeting all the criteria set forth. An ashtray can add
measurably to the total interior if the object has been considered as an integral part of the job rather than an after-
thought. Almost every conference room, for example, has a
very large table, usually made of dark wood; and in fact a
good many conference rooms have woodpaneled walls and
are in general treated as somewhat formal and severe spaces.
If a designer plans to use metal ashtrays in such a conference
room in a brilliant enameled color and in fairly large sizes, the
whole appearance of that particular conference table and
room might be sparked up. It is equally important that the

designer care about the selection of the glasses and water carafe and the usual notepads found on conference tables, lest his care shown in the selection of ashtrays be destroyed with an ugly carafe and poorly designed waterglasses, purchased by the executive's secretary half an hour before the first conference.

Many accessories are in such singularly important positions that they really might need more design care than many other major objects on which so much more attention is lavished as a rule. For instance, clocks. Most places of work have clocks in prominent and clearly visible places. A poorly designed clock, an overly decorated one, or one from which one cannot possibly tell time can be ruinous to an otherwise well-designed space. Handsome clocks are difficult to find—but they exist—and a designer must make the effort to find just the right one. It is as important to the job as the floor covering or the furniture. An object of similar importance is a planter. Most interiors are enhanced with some live plants and many public interiors feature very sizable plants, with resulting large planters. There are extremely beautiful ceramic planters and planters in a number of other appropriate materials. Sometimes they are of such prominence that the interior designer must design them as special objects. Due to the natural requirement of light for plants, they always wind up in clearly visible locations and certainly deserve careful attention. Plants are not accessories in the sense of our definition, yet they are very significant interior-design elements. It must be very clear from having read the preceding chapters that artificial plants of any and every kind are anathema to good designers. There is no excuse or justification ever to use artificial plants. The life expectancy of a real plant is not the life of a building or an interior. Clients might have a tendency to sneak in some artificial plants a year or two after the completion of a job if some plants begin to die, and experienced designers are careful to educate their clients to the fact that plants may wither and simply have to be replaced. The fact that nature rarely creates anything ugly was discussed in Part One, but still one cannot say that *any* plant will be right for *any* interior. The form, the size, the texture, and the scale of plants vary greatly; and the selection of plants is often the key to the design of an interior (for example, the Four Seasons Restaurant).

Spaces for work and public use require many other accessories, but this discussion is not meant to provide an encyclopedic listing of each and every one. As our last example, we might mention a desk. On it, there may be a number of needed objects such as blotters, penholders, memo pads, boxes for paperclips, and paperweights. And next to the desk there is always a wastebasket. Some stores feature very costly sets of handtooled leather accessories of highly questionable design merit. Other stores supply simple but poorly made selections for the same purpose. Price is not the criterion in the selection of these items. Each and every single object must have intrinsic design merits, as well as the kind of appearance that will enhance the total intent of the design.

The accessories that we have mentioned so far are of neutral or nonpersonal character. The personal touches that give a space true individuality can only be provided if the room has a regular occupant. Designers find themselves in the difficult position of encouraging executives to add some of these personal touches to their offices, but most of the time the designers must carefully screen these objects and mementos and often suggest the elimination of some that do not meet standards of good design. With the exception of private offices, nonresidential interiors are usually spaces for use by many different people. Objects and accessories that reflect highly personal interest are therefore not very meaningful in those spaces. It is quite the opposite in homes, where the occupant's personality expressed in some personal touches can measurably add to the character of the interior.

The list of objects that can be classified as accessories for residential interiors is almost endless. People who own collections of any kind will use them in prominent places. Collections and hobbies may include traditional collections of glass, china, silver, or pottery, but often reflect highly esoteric interests of their owners. Some people collect folk art, some collect musical instruments, some collect coins or stamps; and sometimes people have collections of anything ranging from matchbook covers to old buttons. One of America's leading designers, Alexander Girard, is famous for his vast collection of folk art, primarily collected in South America. Girard has developed his hobby into a truly scholarly knowledge and has acquired thousands of examples of Latin American folk art. The 1968 Hemisfair exhibition in Texas featured a pavilion designed by Girard housing a beautifully installed exhibition of folk art, arranged to reflect all phases of life in South America. His design of the La Fonda del Sol Restaurant in New York included the use of folk art as an important theme for the overall design. Many museums own great collections of specific objects that were often started by the donors as accessory collec-

Flower containers made from acrylic plastic tubing cut at an angle and cemented back together with white and clear parts exchanged. Neal Small design.

tions for their homes. These examples show the sometimes serious nature of such interests, and it is obvious that the development of such collections cannot be the province of the interior designer. Designers, however, are often called upon to design the proper housing, display, and arrangement of clients' collections, and most designers cherish such jobs much more than design commissions for clients whose interests and possessions are bland or nonexistent.

A home with no accessories but a few ashtrays would look unfinished or cold, no matter how carefully designed. One can see extremely well-designed settings in furniture showrooms that are just right for that purpose, but that lack personality. Or one can compare a residence without accessories to an hotel room—which is designed in a neutral way—precisely because it should not reflect any *one* personality.

Interior designers must be very conscious of these intimate possibilities for decoration. Clients must frequently be educated to recognize the desirability of accessories as an extension of their own personality, rather than as the imposition of the designer's tastes and interests. Specialized accessory shops were mentioned earlier, and it was pointed out that mass-produced accessories are mostly fakes or poor reproductions of antiques. Real antiques of good quality, *objets d'art*, and original paintings and sculpture have intrinsic qualities but are often beyond the financial reach of homemakers. Fortunately there exist enough objects of good design quality in every price level. It is possible to find well-designed glassware in hardware stores or sometimes in stores where glassware for chemical work is sold. One can find handsome ceramics made by young craftsmen in special shops, and there are many stores featuring imported wares from all over the world in a large array of choice. The designer, or the client with the designer's help, must learn to discriminate between the good and the bad, which is all too often sold side by side. The criteria of design that were discussed in the section dealing with the vocabulary of design apply to the smallest object as well as to the largest building. In some parts of the world, for instance in the Scandinavian countries, the general standards of design are higher and more fully developed than in our country. It would be difficult to acquire junk in a Swedish giftshop, where even the less sophisticated objects are at least nonoffensive in design quality. It is more difficult to find superior designs among the mass of objects sold in our stores, and it requires discrimination and experience to do so.

Beautiful accessories can turn out to be just about any natural or manmade object. The trained eye can find lovely shapes among rocks and stones, or among the shells at the beaches, and some of these found objects can make good-looking accessories. Some of the industrial products designed for specific uses can be interesting and beautiful things when they are recognized as such. A very distinguished designer whose home is filled with many beautiful works of art, displays amongst his many possessions a remarkably beautiful object, which upon closer examinations turns out to be a brush used in cleaning sewers.

A battery-driven electric wall clock with a simple and legible face. Terence Conran design.

There are certain home accessories that are functional necessities much like the ashtrays discussed earlier. Fireplaces need screens, andirons, and tools. Hardware is needed for doors, cabinetwork, and windows (although it is not, strictly speaking, to be classified under the heading of accessories). Bathrooms need towel-bars, soap dishes, and an assortment of related paraphernalia. Kitchens need a huge assortment of tools and equipment; and all the dishes, silver, and glassware used for civilized dining represent a sizable number of objects in any home. All these objects are available in a variety of qualities. The example of portable lamps used in the last chapter could serve as a comparison for the evaluation of design merits. Much like the lamp, every object from andirons to cutlery fulfills primarily a functional need. One must determine the precise function, as well as the suitability of form and material, in order to judge an object's aesthetic success. Pure decoration in silver or china can be of great beauty. The decoration is only meaningless if the silver or china so decorated does not meet basic design criteria. There is a difference between applied decoration and original works of art. Those objects that try to become works of art through being superimposed on other functions, often turn out like the lamp base we described in the last chapter (the lady with the clock). The understanding of basic design principles is essential for the interior designer. On the other hand, the detailed and scholarly knowledge of historic facts pertaining to china, glass, silver, or other decorative accessories is helpful, but not the prime responsibility of the interior designer. Some designers are reluctant to admit ignorance in specialized subjects and do a disservice to their clients if they pretend to be expert in all fields. The architect uses many specialists and consultants and the interior designer must know too when he should call on other experts, whether they are lighting designers or me-

Part of the dining area of "The Terrace Floor" employees' cafeteria at Johns-Manville headquarters in Denver. The dull and institutional character of most company cafeterias is replaced here by the quality of a modern restaurant. Interior design by the Space Design Group.

chanical engineers or historians with special knowledge of the decorative arts.

It is important to draw a clear distinction between residential and nonresidential interiors in this discussion. We stated earlier that a designer must attempt to control the kinds of accessories that might find their way into a carefully planned office or other work space. Those spaces are still somewhat in the public domain, even if used by one person. In a home, the guidance and skill of the designer are needed to give direction and sometimes education to the client. It would appear, however, that the occupant's personality is more important than the designer's trained expertness. Rather than give each interior an indelible stamp reflecting the interior designer's point of view, some homes are more attractive and have more personality if the occupants have approached the collection of accessories with enthusiasm and possibly abandon, which a designer cannot do and should not do. The results may not stand up under critical design scrutiny, but frequently are more meaningful to the owners than a "perfect" job which appears to have stepped out of the pages of a design publication.

5

PAINTING AND SCULPTURE

The interiors of buildings are reasonable places for the display of works of art. There is a tradition, going back to the days of the cavemen, which suggests that wall surfaces invite painting or display of similar visual art. Any picture or other work of art that goes into an interior should be of a high order of excellence in itself, and should be where it is, because it is wanted and needed in that place. Unfortunately, the traditional uses of the fine arts for decoration have led most people to feel that every blank wall surface requires some picture or decoration, so that pointless and worthless pictures are unthinkingly hung in places where they have no effect except to add to a general level of clutter.

Le Corbusier suggested that all wall surfaces should be empty and that a collection of fine pictures could best be stored in some convenient place where they could be brought out one at a time for display. This plan is certainly better than hanging pictures for no reason except to fill space and satisfy some arbitrary notion of what makes an interior "complete". If spaces are well designed in terms of their basic shapes, colors, and materials, it is never *necessary* to add anything simply for decoration. No art is always better than poor art. A blank wall is far more beautiful than commercially produced pictures that attempt to cater to the lowest levels of popular taste. Calendar art and meaningless wall decorations having no artistic merit in their own right, have no place in any well-designed interior.

The best reason for displaying a picture, sculpture, or similar work is a genuine desire to display something of beauty or meaning in a place where it can be readily seen and appre-

American Republic Insurance Company, Des Moines, Iowa. Skidmore, Owings, and Merrill, architects. Paintings enliven an otherwise austere work space.
(Photograph courtesy of Skidmore, Owings and Merrill by Ezra Stoller)

ciated. This is the way fresco painting and framed easel paint-ing came to be part of great historical interiors. Art was often functional (as in instructional religious paintings in churches or in the historical record of a dynasty through portraits) so that it had very specific meaning; and it was also usually the work of the best artists that the time and place made available. It cannot be denied that, at best, such art improves the visual excitement of a room or other space in an abstract or formal way that is quite distinct from the uses which it may have had. We must then also agree that works of art can enhance a space by adding elements of color, texture, and points of interest. There is nothing wrong with using art in this more specifically "decorative" way, if it is good art and is used with skill and discretion.

From the point of view of the working designer putting to-gether an interior, the matter of exercising the "skill and discretion" mentioned above can be quite complex in view of the vast range of possibilities that modern civilization makes available. A first question that must be asked in each actual project situation is whether the client owns any pictures

President's office, C.B.S. Building, New York, Florence Knoll Bassett, designer. Franz Kline's painting "Crosstown" dominates the room.

or other related things that he wants to have displayed in the new space. If so, these must be seen and evaluated. It is all too possible that such things may be of poor (or disastrously bad) quality. A family portrait, an amateurish painting, a souvenir of some place or event, a picture of "our factory then and now", or a framed first dollar earned may have sentimental meaning without being of enough intrinsic merit to justify a prominent position on a wall. Where, by good fortune, the things a client owns and wants to display are truly fine, the designer's problem is only the relatively easy one of providing suitable spaces (suitable in size, scale, location, and character of surroundings) for hanging. Where the things in question are of poor quality, ugly, or worthless, there is the possibility of attempting, tactfully, to persuade the client to give up such treasures. In practice, it is often better to try to find a way to provide display in places and in ways that are appropriate to things that are valued for sentimental reasons. This might mean a kind of museum area (however small) where the things in question do not attempt to pose as great works of art dominating a space. Such problems are most characteristic of the private spaces of residences and some executive offices rather than public, commercial, and institutional spaces; so that, at worst, the occupant of the space who insists on retaining some unsuitable picture can be thought of as having hurt only his own interests.

Once such preexisting items have been dealt with in one way or another, the designer must consider whether there is any need to find other works of art or similar objects to enhance the space and add this particular kind of interest to it. Again, it must be said that nothing at all is far superior to something bad. There can never be any excuse for buying and installing poor art simply to satisfy some imagined need for "culture" or completeness. In some cases, governmental agencies or corporate clients, possibly feeling it a duty to act as patrons of the arts, may *require* that some percentage of a total project budget be used for "works of art". This situation imposes a clear obligation to seek out the best possible uses for such funds. The most interesting and most exciting way to go about introducing works of art into a project, is to shop as a collector might for fine original works. Since the designer is representing his client in this process, he becomes a guide and mentor in starting his client off on an interest in collecting art. Some clients will want to be active participants in decision-making; others may abdicate all responsibility to the designer; but in either case the designer has a clear responsi-

President's office, Chase Manhattan Bank, New York. Skidmore, Owings and Merrill, architects. Ward Bennett, interior design consultant. The painting is "Homage" by Kenzo Okada. The figure in the foreground is a twelfth-century Japanese wood carving known as a "Jizo."

bility to serve his client well through making the best possible choices both in terms of the effect of a particular work in the space where it is intended to go, and in terms of ownership of genuinely excellent works.

Good painting and sculpture can be either old or new. Older, even ancient, work can be entirely appropriate to the most modern interior if it is suitable in scale and character. Genuinely fine historic art is, of course, rare and precious, and works of first quality are increasingly valuable as more museums and collectors bid for them. Not everything old is good, but there is certainly no point in buying and hanging works of little merit simply because they have the attractions of age. It is still possible to find examples of historic art that are worthy of display at possible prices, but it takes skill and knowledge to do so.

Contemporary art is perhaps an even more exciting field to explore because of the real possibility of making discoveries and feeling a sense of participation in a lively aspect of modern life. Modern architecture and interior design have strong

Trustees room at Christian Theological Seminary, Indianapolis, Indiana. Painting by Ben Nicholson I.S.D., Inc., interior design; Edward Larabee Barnes, architect. (Photograph by Warren Meyer)

ties with modern art in terms of history and thinking, and as a result, good contemporary art can be particularly appropriate in the context of a modern interior. Even among currently living artists, those who have arrived at a substantial reputation can command very high prices, so that ownership of good modern work often involves as heavy an investment as ownership of major historic art. There is the added risk and added excitement that derives from the fact that critical evaluations of contemporary work are all tentative and subject to change with the passage of time. The designer who is advising or acting for his client in making selections of contemporary art has a very major obligation to look beyond the rather fickle tastes of the critics and museum directors who make the reputations of living artists, and to consider the real merit of the work quite aside from its current market value. A new or little-known artist may, in long-range terms, be a better selection than an artist whose work is enjoying a fashionable boom that may turn out to have no real lasting meaning.

The designer has an obligation, in any case, to know and understand the work of historic and contemporary artists and to have a point of view that will guide him in advising his clients so that any work acquired will have lasting merit, as well as being useful to the interior at hand in a decorative sense.

Perhaps the majority of clients are not prepared to make the large investments that are involved in acquiring major works of art. Acquiring bad art that happens to be inexpensive is never a reasonable alternative. There is a great range of possibilities in both historic and modern work in such media as prints which, because they are produced in multiples, are far less expensive than original paintings and sculptures. Signed prints by major artists have value for collectors also, while unsigned prints, visually hardly distinguishable, are often less costly but fully as satisfactory in their role as elements in an interior. It is important to understand the distinction between "prints" (or "original prints") and reproductions— a distinction seldom clearly understood by laymen. A print is a work executed by the artist in a form that makes it possible to produce a number of copies. An etching, a woodcut, or a lithograph is of this type—the artist makes the plate, block, or stone, pulls the prints or supervises their pulling, and signs the copies that he approves. A reproduction, on the other hand, is done by modern graphic arts techniques and makes possible the printing in quantity of any color or black-and-white illustration through purely mechanical means. This is the nature of the illustrations in books and magazines—the artists has no role in the process beyond having created the original and there is no limit on the number of copies that can be produced. In a similar way, an original sculpture has been carved or modeled by the artist's own hands. If the model is cast in bronze (or any other medium) under the artist's supervision, each cast can be called an "original cast". If, however, a factory produces duplicates in quantity by production methods, these are "reproductions". Reproductions can be smaller (or even larger) than the original which they reproduce, and can vary in quality from being very accurate and faithful to the original to being outrageous distortions. Reproductions of original prints can easily be so good as to be hardly distinguishable from an original. A reproduction of a painting always involves some loss of texture and accuracy of color and can be, at worst, a poor shadow of the original.

Good reproductions make it possible to know and study works from all over the world in much the same way that phonograph records make it possible for us to hear at home, at our convenience, performances from various times and places which would otherwise be inaccessible to us. It is, of course, possible to frame and hang a reproduction, but there is an element of falseness in doing this that disturbs most sensitive people. If one wants to have reproductions available on display for study, this can be done by display on a tack board or easel in a way that is less pretentious than formal "hanging", which suggests that the work is intended to be an important work of art in its own right. The more strongly a reproduction pretends to be original, the more offensive it becomes because of the implication of deception that is involved. For this reason a poster or calendar which includes a reproduction may be quite suitable for hanging on a wall, while a reproduction on canvas with a false "painted texture", in an elaborate frame imitative of one that might be used in a museum, becomes a tasteless fraud.

Where budget and level of interest preclude having good original works (original prints included), instead of turning to hanging reproductions, it might be wiser to consider other kinds of graphic materials such as photographs, maps, charts, handsome posters, plans, or book illustrations. Such materials do not pretend to be anything that they are not, can have great interest through their content, and, in terms of color and texture, can be as useful as any painting in adding interest to a space.

In much the same way, a whole range of objects can be considered for use in a decorative fashion. Rugs and hangings, clocks and instruments, models and displays of mounted natural materials (shells, dried plants, mounted insects, etc.) can give scale, color, and interest while remaining reasonable and unpretentious. The designer must always be alert to the hazard of using an idea which has become a cliché. Coaching prints have been used in men's clubs and bars, maps and ship prints in lawyer's offices so often that it seems absurd to follow such patterns out of habit. The user of such spaces may still enjoy these items, however, and be quite unaware how hackneyed the choices are. Every designer must evaluate such situations as best he can and decide for himself what level of originality he must seek in a particular situation. The prints of Audubon or Currier and Ives and the paintings of Van Gogh are, at their various levels, fine things, but they can become dull cliché elements through thoughtless repetition in the form of poor to bad reproductions.

There are also such elements as trademarks, seals, flags, and signs that can be used as emblems of current realities (as in

A corridor wall employing colorful supergraphics in the office of
Touche Ross and Co., New York. The Space Design Group, Inc., interior designers.

the case of the trademark of an active business), but which are also dangerously subject to falling into the cliché category. Finding new and imaginative ways to deal with elements of this nature is a difficult, but worthwhile, challenge to the designer who feels the need to use such traditional devices in a way that will not be boring and obvious.

In some major projects, particularly in public spaces where there is a budget for art work, a difficult and interesting possibility of commissioning work for the particular space arises. Selection of a suitable artist can be made on the basis of his previous works, but the new work for the new situation will be a new reality that can be either exciting or disappointing according to the chance of the particular event. To protect against major disappointments (since even the greatest artists produce lesser works at times), it is common practice to commission a preliminary "sketch" or proposal which can be accepted or rejected without friction or unpleasantness. A competition is a more elaborate form of seeking work in such situations, but it is a device that has had such a poor record of success as to have fallen into disuse. Where an original work is being commissioned, the designer has a responsibility to define and explain the need and the context as fully as possible without in any way trying to dictate the exact direction of the artist's work. Good collaboration between architect, interior designer, painter, and sculptor is, unfortunately, a rare thing in modern times. It was common during the famous historic periods and is certainly a goal to be sought after in modern times as well. Major mural painting and fixed sculptures that become a permanent part of a building can be very important and successful elements of design, but because of their cost, permanence, and visual importance, can be very sensitive aspects of a design deserving of special thought and care in selection. Good art has a tendency to be controversial because it tends to express ideas somewhat in advance of the average thinking of its time. It is all too easy to turn to innocuous or mediocre art in an effort to avoid the stresses of controversy that really good art can produce. This tends, unfortunately, to be the pattern of most of the art commissioned for commercial and governmental buildings. Perhaps the designer should remind himself that any work of art that offends no one is almost surely worthless. Unless designer and client have the courage and interest to live through the excitements that usually follow the display of genuinely creative work, it might be best not to venture in this direction at all.

6

SPECIAL CONCERNS

There are a number of special issues that need to concern the interior designer, issues that have sometimes been ignored or taken for granted, but that have come to demand extra attention in recent years. New laws and regulations, new concern for the rights of all individuals, a new consumer awareness often active in legal actions to press for more responsibility on the part of those in authority make it impossible and inappropriate to overlook concern for these matters, even when they may seem to be troublesome distractions to the main interests of designers.

The main concern of designers is to make buildings and the spaces within them do what is expected of them. It is easy to forget that buildings and the spaces within can do other, undesirable things that are unintentional and harmful. The special concerns discussed here are generally matters of avoiding or minimizing these objectionable side effects in which buildings can be dangerous, fail to offer the protections that their users can reasonably expect, set up obstacles to their convenient use by many people with special problems and can place unreasonable burdens on their users, owners and the whole society through failure to consider what will be involved in their continuing operation. These matters can be considered under a few general headings.

SAFETY

One of the primary reasons for the existence of buildings is the protection that they offer from the sometimes hostile circumstances of out-of-door life. It is ironic that, while offering protection from commonplace hazards (such as rain and cold), they can present hazards of their own, sometimes in sudden and unexpected forms. Fire is the most obvious hazard connected with buildings and history is full of stories of disasters involving individual building and even whole cities. Occupants of a one story building can usually escape a fire (although it can damage property and destroy the building itself), but multistory buildings present risks that cannot be ignored. In most modern communities, building codes require buildings to meet certain standards for fire safety, but these do not, unfortunately, guarantee safety as newspaper stories constantly make clear. Primary responsibility for fire safety rests with a building's architects and engineers, but the interior designer needs to understand the issues involved, cooperate in trying to maximize fire safety and often, to go beyond mere compliance with basic rules.

The primary ways of making a building fire safe include:

> Basic construction with "fireproof" materials (usually concrete and steel) so the building itself will not burn. Bad fires in fireproof building regularly prove that this is not enough. The *contents* of a building can burn even when the main structure cannot.
>
> Subdivision of spaces with fireproof walls and doors is the means of confining a fire to one area and preventing its spread throughout the building. Designers are often irked to find that open spaces, open stair-wells, and so on, are either forbidden or must be provided with a complex system of doors or shutters that will close off a space where a fire may start. Doors and partitions may need a "fire rating" to insure that the spaces they define are really safely isolated in case of fire.
>
> Exits are the next most obvious need. When tall buildings are considered, too tall even to be reached by fire ladders, the need becomes obvious as occupants can easily become trapped. In general, the fire codes try to provide two separate means of escape from any space in a building–two enclosed "fire stairs" in most cases; a stair plus an outside fire escape in the cases of older buildings. Two exits from each individual room are hardly practical, but once out of a particular room, the aim is to offer two possible exits in case one might be cut off by fire or smoke. Exit doors must be adequate and well

marked. They must swing outward and have "panic" hardware to unlatch under pressure from within if they are to be effective, particularly in hazardous places such as theaters and restaurants where crowds of people are grouped in a limited space.

Alarms, fire detectors, hose cabinets, and fire extinguishers are devices to warn of fire and help control it at its start. Unfortunately, such devices often fail to work when needed or are not noticed when fire occurs. Sprinkler systems are the most reliable fire extinguishing device that can be included in a building and have a good record for stopping fires almost at once, even in older buildings that may have been built before certain regulations took effect. Sprinklers represent a substantial first cost therefore they are often resisted by building owners and not required in situations where their protection would be valuable. The fact that they are automatic, operating whether a building is occupied or empty and acting at once to localize a fire makes them highly effective.

Interior materials present fire hazards that are often not regulated but that should be of special concern to the interior designer. Most fire codes do not deal with anything that can be classified as movable furniture, but these are the very things which burn in an otherwise fireproof building. Burning upholstery or a burning mattress are common origins of fires which can be deadly to the sleeping occupants of a space even when the building suffers little damage. Most traditional interior materials, wood, natural fibers in carpets and woven materials will burn, but burning does not start easily (think how hard it can be to start a log in a fireplace) and a fire will often smoulder and die out. Many modern materials have objectionable characteristics from a fire-safety standpoint. Some fibers will flame up in a sudden flash while many synthetic materials, without actually flaming, can give off smoke and deadly fumes that may be more dangerous than actual flame. Regulations concerning the safety of interior materials are on the increase, but the interior designer has a special obligation to check the characteristics of carpet, upholstery, and wall covering materials, paneling and furniture materials, particularly when plastics are under consideration.

The basic structural safety of a building, the strength of its roof, floors, and framing are generally not of concern to the interior designer, but it is still wise to be aware of problems that can be created within the interior. Removing supports (partitions or columns), the construction of raised floors and stairs may need review by an architect or engineer even when building codes do not require it. Interior layout can also create heavy floor loadings that exceed the loads planned. Files in offices, for example, are often grouped together in one area–paper in bulk is very heavy and a file room may require special structural reinforcements.

Some everyday interior elements involve risks that contribute to the often noted reality that home accidents are one of the main causes of injury and death. In public places, as well as in homes, the most common accident hazards include:

Stairs and the possibility of falls that they offer, particularly to the elderly, the handicapped, to children and to the intoxicated, are always of potential risk. Easy stair slopes, short runs and generous landings, sturdy rails within reach from any point of the stair's width and non-skid step materials are obviously desirable. A single step or two or three steps at a level change are a particular hazard. If they must occur, special edge marking, lighting and rails need to be considered. Curved and winding stairs or any irregularities in the spacing of steps are also dangerous. The inclusion of a curved stair should be coupled with special concern for the safety of its users. Escalators and elevators present hazards of their own, well known to their makers and usually dealt with to a reasonable degree by various safety devices incorporated in their construction.

Floor materials present risks comparable to those of stairs. Slippery materials, all too popular for their appearance, are a cause of endless falls, particularly in places where water or tracked-in ice or snow may add to the problem. Small rugs and the edges of all rugs and carpets can cause tripping. A small, slippery mat on a highly polished floor is a notorious danger. These are all issues within the interior designer's field of concern.

Bathrooms seem to be designed to group potential hazards. Slippery surfaces, glass and mirrors, hot water and electrical devices come together to set traps for the careless, the elderly, and children. Anti-skid tubs and shower stalls, non-skid floor materials, choice and placement of hardware (faucets, towel bars, and so on) are minimal safety requirements. Big windows, big mirrors and, worst of all, glass shower enclosures are very real risks. Use of "ground fault" electrical outlets, now a legal requirement, reduces shock hazards, but placement of outlets, lights and heaters still requires care. Kitchen risks include some of the same problems of electrical outlets and equipment as in the bathroom, but add the problems of heat and flame at the range. Inflammable materials should not be above or beside the range, and a close-by extinguisher should always be provided.

Electrical safety problems, in addition to those mentioned, are dealt with in some measure by legal regulations and the requirements of the Underwriters Laboratories. The interior designer still needs to be concerned with providing adequate outlets to discourage overloads and positioning outlets to discourage tangles of unsafe extension cords and plugs. Lamps, the cords they trail, and lamp shade materials present hazards of their own.

SECURITY

This is a special safety issue having to do with protection of both people and objects against deliberate human actions. Every society seems to have produced some antisocial individuals who turn into criminals, vandals or other kinds of trouble-makers, but our complex modern world seems, unfortunately, to generate increasing problems in this area. Most older buildings were planned with little thought for security problems except for door and window locks and, perhaps, grills or gates on ground floor windows. In modern cities and, to an increaing degree in rural and suburban areas also, it is necessary to consider what needs to be done to minimize risks of theft through burglary or holdup, other intrusions, and such possibilities as terrorist attacks or riots. Certain building and interior types present special problems. Banks are obviously in need of special security arrangements as are shops that deal in valuable goods. It is unfortunate that some of the attractive elements of modern design, openness, big window areas and easy access patterns can create problems of their own. Conversely, closed and cramped patterns of circulation may create hidden spaces and access routes that create problems for opposite reasons.

In general, architect and interior designer need to give thought to various issues, some of which can better be dealt with in basic planning than through later fitting of corrective equipment.

Defensible space, a concept developed in Oscar Newman's book of the same name,* describes planning worked out to avoid hidden passages, invisible elevator entrances, corridors without supervision and similar situations that are an invitation to intrusion and crime, particularly in apartments and housing projects. The same concepts apply to a considerable degree to offices, transport facilities and other places where easy viewing of space by many people, resident or transient, tends to deter criminal action. It may be objected that the criminal will simply choose a different place to work, but this at least reduces problems in a particular place to the benefit of its occupants.

Hardware, in both the literal and new figurative meanings, is the next level of protective equipment that needs consideration. Locks and bars may not be attractive matters to the designer, but suitable equipment is a necessary defense in many modern situations. New systems of locks that include

---

*Oscar Newman: *Defensible Space*, Macmillan, 1972.

locks controlled by magnetic card "keys" activated by computer controlled central systems are useful devices for control of access, possibly a complex, zoned system. Voice and closed-circuit TV communication can aid in providing supervision of spaces and controlling access. Various types of alarms of varied degrees of sophistication are available and best provided as original equipment rather than as afterthoughts.

Vandalism and problems arising from terrorism and riot are increasing, unfortunate problems of modern life. No total protection is possible but certain situations require at least some level of consideration. Vandalism in public places has become commonplace in modern cities and is increasing outside of cities. Choice of materials and fittings hard to damage and easy to repair is a first line of defense. Elements that would otherwise be desirable aesthetically or for convenience must often be omitted when and where they attract vandals. Supervision is, of course, a major line of protection, but the designer can do no more than to try for layouts that make the available personnel effective to a maximum degree.

When projects are in the planning stage and optimistic expectations dominate, it is often difficult to focus on some of these unpleasant matters, but the designer has an obligation to review such topics with a client. Remember too, that there is a distressing pattern of worsening problems. A situation that may seem trouble-free now, can face problems some years in the future that could have been dealt with best if they had been foreseen.

BARRIER-FREE ACCESS

While not closely related to the topics discussed above, barrier-free access is a special concern that has drawn increasing attention in recent years. Traditionally, most buildings have been planned with an assumption that all users would be fully able physically. Potential users with handicaps, confined to a wheelchair, blind or deaf, often find buildings full of obstacles. The old and rather callous view seems to have been that people with such problems are few, that they should fend for themselves, and that dealing with such problems would, in any case, be too costly and difficult.

Recently, people with handicaps have succeeded in drawing public attention to the problems buildings can present and have succeeded in obtaining legislation that will require many government and other public buildings to be made "barrier-free" according to rather specific regulations. Older buildings have a tremendous number of problems that need correction, but change is often not easy. A post office or other official building can often be entered only by climbing a monumental flight of steps. Elevators have controls that cannot be reached from a wheelchair and cannot be "read" by the blind. Concert halls and auditoriums are without provision for the problems of deafness. Washrooms are built without space to turn a wheelchair. The problems of an existing subway or railroad system can be tremendous. In all of these cases, showing concern for these problems when the facility was being planned could have dealt with these situations, often at little or no cost.

If the increasing regulation on behalf of the handicapped may seem too much trouble on behalf of a small minority, it is appropriate to remember that a very *high* proportion of the population turns out to be handicapped at some time or other, often only temporarily or perhaps in old age. An accident can suddenly mean crutches or a wheelchair for a time, cataracts can mean partial blindness for a period. Provisions for easy and safe access by the handicapped are often beneficial to everyone. A safe facility for blind persons will probably be safer for everyone else.

The specific regulations for barrier-free access are still under development and subject to change, but the general principles and a few specifics are offered here. The general issues are easy to grasp on a "common-sense" basis. Access and circulation inside of a building needs to be free of stairs and open enough to permit easy movement on crutches or in a wheelchair. Avoiding stairs means that level changes must be dealt with through elevators (needed in taller buildings, anyway) and, in the case of small level changes, ramps that can be negotiated in a wheelchair. Anything that must be reached, door handles, light switches, elevator controls, drinking fountains, plumbing devices must be within reach to a wheelchair occupant, and usable by the blind. Situations that might be dangerous to a blind person are to be avoided. Non-visual means of orientation need to be considered. The less specific problems of the elderly relate closely to these considerations and return attention to the issues of safety discussed at the opening of this chapter. Ramps and elevators avoid stair hazards. Non-slip floors, uncluttered layouts, and avoidance of sharp edges and corners and hazardous materials (unprotected glass areas, for example) are advantageous to all users.

Data sheets and handbooks are now widely available offering specific dimensional standards for such critical matters as wheelchair clearances, particularly in congested spaces such as washrooms where access is crucial and clearances are often tight. Some examples of typical dimensional standard charts are illustrated.

Guidelines For Accessibility

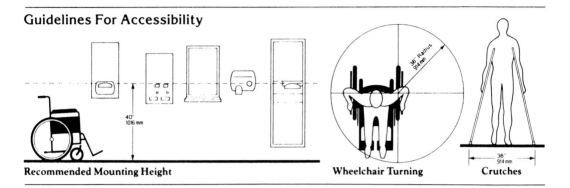

Recommended Mounting Height   Wheelchair Turning   Crutches

As in the issues of safety, it is important to remember that compliance with minimum standards, so often thought of as "all that is necessary" is often shortsighted—particularly when legal requirements are minimal or nonexistent. Planning an office, a house or an apartment to make it barrier-free can involve no more than a small measure of extra thought and care—often at no extra cost. The resulting space may serve some occupants at some future time in a way that would be totally impossible if this extra concern had not been developed. Once problematic situations are built, change can be very difficult or impossible. The planner has special obligations to plan for solutions that go beyond the minimal.

Diagrams charting dimensional standards for barrier-free access. (Courtesy Boberick Washroom Equipment, Inc.)

ENERGY AND ENVIRONMENTAL ISSUES

Other issues that have become centers for design concern relate to the recently recognized limits on the availability of energy and the environmental consequences of energy consumption and uses of certain materials. As with the matters discussed above, these are not new problems, but have taken on important roles as our modern technological civilization has accelerated changes in once stable situations.

Buildings use energy for heat, light, cooling, and various incidental services. Historically, energy consuming devices in buildings have been limited to fireplaces, stoves, and lamps and their fuel consumption and waste products have been so limited as to present no significant problems. Improved heating brought sooty air to the nineteenth century English and American cities. The coming of gas and oil as fuels and electricity as a major energy supply seemed at first to alleviate air quality problems, but with increasing use of energy for improved services and with increasing population concentrations, these problems have resurfaced in new forms. At the same time, reduction in availability of fuels has driven energy costs upward so that the combined pressures for economy and environmental quality have combined to exert pressure toward minimizing a building's energy dependence. Architects and engineers must deal with the major problems of making buildings energy efficient, but interior design must adjust to new situations and can often make a contribution toward energy conservation. The primary concerns are:

Heating is a major energy consumer. Design to minimize heat loss through walls and windows and, where possible to make use of solar heat are prime energy conservation measures. Interior design usually has a secondary role in these matters, but various types of window shades and blinds are available to help collect and control sun heat (see also below for the related impact on cooling.) Where careful solar design is undertaken, special materials may be needed in floors and ceilings to aid in storing and returning collected solar heat. Close cooperation between interior designer, architect, and engineer is vital in such schemes.

Cooling through air contioning in the typical "HVAC" (heating, ventilating and air conditioning) systems in modern buildings is also a major energy consumer. A return toward increased use of natural ventilation systems and choice of materials and layouts that reduce the need for mechanical air conditioning might follow practices used in traditional, vernacular building in hot climates for thousands of years. Modern industrial society has hardly begun to explore these possibilities, but the economic pressure to do so is on the increase. On a more limited level, control of solar heat gain through use of suitable shades and blinds, possibly automatically controlled to respond to the changes in solar heating, can make a significant contribution toward reducing air conditioning loads.

Artificial lighting, of all energy consumers in buildings, is of most concern to the interior designer. Electric lighting also generates heat and places additional loads on air conditioning systems, multiplying the energy costs that artificial lighting entails. Reasonable design can:

1. Try to maximize the use of natural light when and where it is available.

2. Adopt reasonable standards for illumination. The human eye has a wide range of responsiveness and illumination standards developed in the recent years often call for excessive lighting levels.

3. Use new types of illumination that are more energy efficient than older light sources. Incandescent light is particularly *in*efficient and many new types of lamps are available to make its visual qualities more approachable with fluorescent and HID (high intensity discharge) sources. These may be more expensive in initial cost, but they pay their way through energy conservation.

4. Design of lighting installations and fixtures can increase efficiency by delivering light where it is needed with maximum effectiveness. "Task" and "task-ambient" lighting are techniques discussed in more detail in Part VI.

One further environmental issue has arisen from the realization that certain materials used in building and interior contruction can create environmental hazards. The best known case is asbestos, a cheap mineral substance easily available and an excellent insulator. It has been widely used as sprayed-on insulation, in floor and ceiling tiles and in many other commonly used products. The awareness that asbestos fibers wear off and float in the air and are breathed in by building users has only developed recently. A respiratory disease called "asbestosis" and various types of cancer can result from exposure to asbestos. Replacing asbestos in existing buildings can require costly changes to insure safe conditions. Materials using asbestos must now meet strict safety standards, but their use should be a matter for continuing concern.

Other interior materials such as recently introduced synthetics contain chemicals which can give off deadly fumes. Many plastics and plastic foams are suspect—formaldehyde is a chemical ingredient that has been found harmful to air quality.

Finally, it should be noted that HVAC systems that distribute air through ducts can also circulate harmful materials, fumes, bacteria and smoke in a way that has only recently become known. Several outbreaks of disease of a puzzling sort are now thought to have been the result of infectious material "cultured" in the damp humidifying components of air conditioning systems and then distributed throughout the building by the system's fans and ducts.

Obviously, there is no total solution to the control of all the hazards involved in complex, technological, modern life, but every designer has an obligation to be informed and to constantly update awareness of the problems that relate to the profession's areas of concern.

7

SYSTEMS DESIGN

The systems approach to architecture that has emerged during the past decade differentiates it entirely from the traditional structure of architecture of the past. The difference can be detected in a qualitative change of attitude on the part of designers toward architectural problems.

Buildings, with the increasing use of industrialization, tend to be hand-assembled rather than hand-made. It is more evident in the building approach than in exterior appearances. Architects in the past have not thought in terms of systems or industrialization. The level of industrialization seems to run parallel to the acceptance of systems building by the architectural profession.

The idea of systems building is basically contained in the concept of the function of the building, that is, in the way the building operates. A building can function as a place to park automobiles, to teach children, to care for the sick, for religious observance, or for a multitude of other uses.

A system can be defined as an assemblage of parts connected so that they constitute a whole. Its function is the result of the manner in which the respective parts act together due to their specific nature. To explain the functioning of buildings we must understand their parts and how these parts are connected. If the attributes of the parts or their connections change then the function of the system as a whole changes.

A simple illustration is the children's "Lego" toy. A series of a few different kinds of simple blocks, with integral connectors, can be used to make a variety of forms: automobiles, buildings, animals, helicopters. The combinations are limited only by the child's imagination. The interaction of the parts constitutes the whole.

The function of the building is what it does with its parts. To conceive of a building as an aesthetic whole is quite different from examining it as a process. To visualize the building as a function, or a process, is to conceive of it as a succession of events or occurrences and included in this process is interior design. What people do in the interior of a building, how they are affected by it perceptually, how its components act, how the materials weather and wear, and how the spaces interact are all component parts of the building.

An analogy might be made to bodily functions. Blood circulation transports oxygen and withdraws carbon dioxide from the burning of air in the lungs. It provides the cells with nourishment, removes wastes, and assists white blood corpuscles as a passageway to infected areas. These are functions of the blood. It can maintain this process only as long as its parts act together in a certain way. An inability to coagulate or any occurrence that causes blood to react differently affects the functioning of the entire body: it will perform differently, or not at all.

The wholeness of a function resides in the process. When this process exhibits enough uniformity to be isolated and persists, then it is a totality or unity as the design of an interior is a totality within the design of the building. The functional unity does not reside in the blood, but in the circulation of the blood. Function is behavior. To look at anything in functional terms is to observe the way it behaves.

The distinction between a function and a system is the degree of complexity. A system is composed of several functions. The system is part of the whole and is related to other systems that constitute the behavior of the whole.

The notion of systems is a broad concept that has been forced upon designers to permit a more rapid adaption to the changing environment. Conceiving of a problem in its entirety generates a larger concept of the whole.

When we speak of environment in the systems context, we refer to all objects or conditions external to the system whose attributes are influenced by the behavior of the system or which themselves influence the system. Defining the boundaries between a system and its environment is arbitrary and depends on the systems objective. Ideally the environment should include all things that affect or will be affected by the system, but practically the environment is limited to the things that significantly affect the system.

How System Design Works

Basically three steps are involved in systems design. First, a theory is formulated to account for a set of isolated facts or observations of the environment; second, the theory is checked to see if it actually explains the known facts and predicts the known events; and third, the system is separated into its component parts.

The first step, called "establishment of mission requirements" or "problem definition", continues on throughout the study and research as the nature of the problem becomes more clearly defined. This step simply involves continual evaluation of what the problem really is, as well as continual formulation of it so that the various members of the team can understand and accept the definition.

As a second step, all aspects of the system under study are quantified. Experiments and research are performed on those aspects of the system for which no data exist. Designers may state that it is questionable that the human factors in interior design are quantifiable. On the other hand, scientists predict that eventually mathematical models can be devised to simulate human reactions to every kind of environment and that these environments can be constructed so that they will be acceptable to humans.

The third step of the systems method is the separation of the system under study into its component parts, identifiable components, and subsystems. For example, a brick can be considered a component of a brick wall, which is a subsystem of a particular college building. The college building may be itself a subsystem of the university system. It is at this point during the third step that mathematical models are made of the parts of the system and that the mathematical model of the whole system is derived from the model of its parts.

Part of the purpose of the third step is to display the component parts of the system so that the influence of the characteristics of the part and their effect on the overall performance of the system can be quantitatively identified. For example, the brick may be too expensive, increasing the cost of the wall, making the building too costly for the college, and finally causing the taxpayers to refuse the bond issue and not build the university. This of course is a farfetched example; however, it

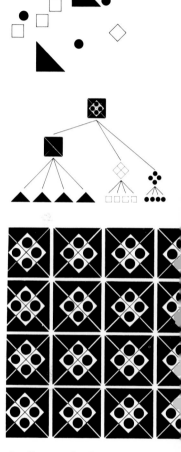

A collection of isolated parts combined into two systems.

The systems approach to architecture described in this section is based on the material presented by A. B. Handler, *Systems Approach to Architecture*, American Elsevier, New York, 1970.

does show how a part (the brick) is examined in relation to the system (the entire university). By varying the characteristics of the subsystems and manipulating the mathematical models, it is possible to affect the total system.

This is also the step in systems analysis in which "trade-offs" between subsystems are performed. This means a sort of bargaining or compromising among subsystems with a view to enhancing the overall system. It is at this point that rough cost estimates are made and alternative solutions considered. For example, the cost of a chair might be compared against the cost of benches or other seating.

Hardware is now designed—"hardware" being the actual functioning elements indicated by the system, as distinguished from "software" which is the information fed into the system. For example, the software might indicate a horizontal surface for working which would hold a telephone, with storage underneath, while the comparable hardware might be a desk, a counter with files underneath, or some other solution.

The hardware is tested theoretically to see if it will function as intended. Finally it is manufactured and operated. This begins the feedback stage of the system, in which actual performance is checked against planned performance. Faults are corrected and fed back into the original system to see how they perform and how these changes affect the other subsystems.

The Computer

The computer is the handmaiden of systems design. Beginning as a humble calculating tool: a logical extension of the abacus, the slide rule, and the adding machine, it has branched out to encompass a range of activities inconceivable only a few years ago. The computer is changing the shape of architectural and interior design practice through its use in systems design as well as every other facet of the interior design profession.

Many interior designers recognized the possibilities inherent in computer application as quickly as their engineerng colleagues. Yet, its applications in engineering practice, highway, structure and air-conditioning systems are further advanced than in all but a very few design offices.

The engineers already possessed technical theories upon which their design methods were based. They were well-defined and widely accepted as the basis of professional practice. No such commonly held theoretical nor analytical base existed in architecture and interior design. Secondly, the problems and responsibilities of the designer are more complex.

Further research and application is needed before the designer can expect the computer to be a major aid in the process of design. In the more clearly defined areas of construction scheduling, estimating, cataloging, and mechanical, electrical, and specification writing it is of tremendous assistance.

As computer applications become more sophisticated on the one hand and more easily operable on the other, the designer will find them increasingly useful. The architect will then most probably use the computer as he designs, to compare, analyze, and synthesize a great number of mutually related factors as existing interrelationships are determined through a comparison of all the building elements as the basis for design decisions.

Programming

Programming is the technique of setting up a specific series of steps by which a digital computer solves problems. There are five functions performed by computers of this type: they are input, memory, arithmetic, control, and output.

Input devices read information into the computer. The information is on punched cards, punched tapes, or magnetic tapes, which are read by the computer input devices into the computer memory. Input is in one of two forms, either instructions that tell the computer what to do, or data for computation. These two types of instructions form the computer's program.

Memory is, as its name implies, a place for storing information, instructions or data. The ideal memory is one that is large enough to contain all the information necessary and from which the information can be retrieved as required. Instructions are stored in the memory. For example, an address or the price of a piece of furniture may be stored in the computer's memory.

The arithmetic part of the computer is that portion which actually does the computations. It can add, subtract, multiply, divide, and make certain logical decisions.

Instructions are interpreted in the control section of the computer. This is a matter of decoding the information in the instructions to make the computer perform the indicated functions.

The output portion of the computer stores information until it is required. It also records the information obtained from computations in any of several forms, including printed sheets or paper magnetic tapes, punched cards or punched paper tapes.

Preparing a Problem for a Computer Program

As previously mentioned input has two integral parts, data and instructions. The data are the raw material—such as facts, figures, pieces of information—and the instructions tell what must be done with the raw material. Two plus two equals four. The twos are the data and addition is the instruction.

Data are comparatively simple, but instructions are a different matter. Computers can perform only a few fundamental operations, as a result, the data analysis procedures must be broken down into thousands, sometimes millions, of single precise instructions. This list of instructions telling the computer what to do with the data is the program.

Even though the designer is not likely to get deeply involved in the programming process, he should be aware of the steps it entails and how, roughly, it is approached. The steps are as follows (note that these are similar to the steps of systems analysis discussed earlier):

1 Problem identification and goal description
2 Mathematical description
3 Block programming
4 Detailed programming
5 Testing the program

Problem identification is the first step in developing a new program and entails a complete description of goals and an outline for a general approach toward attaining these goals. Specifics are not important but it is important to realize what computers can and cannot do.

The mathematical process must be described in steps that involve operations that the computer can do. To prepare this description requires specific knowledge about what the machine capabilities are and an extensive background in mathematics and numerical analysis.

Block programming is the preparation of a flow chart or logic diagram and is possibly the most important step in the programming process. This means breaking down the general method of solution into discrete steps. The steps are then connected by lines to give a diagram similar to the one shown.

Detailing the program is making the problem into something the computer can digest. The computer's basic language

Flow chart to heat water

1 Turn on stove
2 Wait
3 Is water hot ?
4 Pour

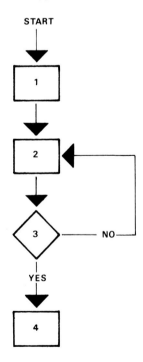

consists of many instructions. The problem-solving procedure must be translated into these terms.

Computer Terms

There are two types of computers, the digital and the analog. The analog computer operates by measuring quantity. It is simpler and more direct than a digital computer, but ordinarily is not a high-precision device. Like a slide rule, it functions at its best within a precision of three or four digits. A digital computer is like an adding machine. It counts rather than measures. It is really an ultra high-speed electronic calculating machine.

Binary A condition in which there are only two choices, the *on* or *off* of an electric circuit. *On* or *off* represents all numbers and symbols.

Bit The single character of a binary number. A unit of information in a storage device.

Compile A machine language produced from a program.

Input Data and instructions introduced into the computer.

Instruction A set of characters defining an operation which causes the computer to perform the operation.

Memory Information stored in a computer system.

Program The complete plan for a problem solution, including the set of machine instructions and routines necessary to do the job.

Time-Sharing Use of the computer for two or more purposes, or by two or more users during the same time interval.

Prefabrication

Fabrication of interior elements away from the building site is not a new event in history. Medieval interiors were absolutely bare. Interior furnishings traveled with the lord of the castle who set them up when he arrived and took them with

House Type	On-Site Work	Off-Site Work
Log Cabin		Fell trees Shape and fit logs Hew planks for roof, floor, furniture, etc.
Early Baloon Frame	Mill lumber Hardware Paint factory—made furniture	Cut and fit lumber for framing, siding, etc. Construct windows, doors, stairs, cabinets, plaster Paint and finish
Conventional Frame	Mill lumber hardware Paint factory—made furniture, cabinetry, windows, doors, stairs, wallboard	Cut and fit lumber for structure and closure Install factory—made components Paint and finish
Package Home	Design and fabricate a set of coordinated building components for structure/closure, plumbing cores, windows and storage units	Assemble prefabricated components
Mobile or Sectional Home	Fabricate complete factory—made house with all finishes and appointments	

him when he left. On the other hand, the building itself was built on the site and fitted into place with very few consistent measurements. With the industrial revolution and the increasing use of factory products in building, more and more elements of the building are produced away from the site. It is now possible to transport buildings as the medieval lord transported his furniture.

Prefabrication and industrialization, which are synonymous terms, were introduced into the building industry to reduce costs. Factory production is less expensive and permits better control of production. The tradesmen use increasingly sophisticated machines powered by motors rather than using tools on the job site powered by their muscles. In the factory, workers are protected from the weather, which is often the cause of on-the-job delays. Factory laborers have traditionally been lower paid than on-site building craftsmen.

The reduction of the cost of building products as a result of decreasing the labor expended upon them is a consistent tendency. Labor is the basic cost element, since materials are given value by human labor. Iron ore in the ground, trees in the woods, gypsum in the rocks have no value for building until labor is used to convert them to useful building products. Economy in building calls for the reduction of the amount of labor by substitution of material or machines for hand labor. The major cost factor in building as well has always been field labor. Industrialization, in its search for economy, moves away from the building site toward factory prefabrication.

The design implications of increasing prefabrication are slowly emerging. The first approach to prefabrication is to take traditional building elements, reduce them to their constituent parts, manufacture the parts in the factory, and reassemble them on the site. As designers become more familiar with industrial techniques the form of the building elements tend to change. All artifacts eventually mirror the technology that brings them into being.

Buildings, since the revolution in modern architecture, have been designed to look like machine manufactured products even though often built by hand. As the actual machining of building products takes place in the factory, the appearance of hand-made parts comes in conflict with the idiosyncratic realities of machine production. Joints change, dimensions are altered, and finishes no longer imitate natural materials but rather assume the unique characteristics of machine production.

A change also occurs in the design process. The designer finds that s/he details less and depends more on the experience of the machinists and factory designers. Working drawings give way to specifications, design drawings become more schematic and less detailed, and more emphasis is placed upon design methodology and less on intuition.

With increasing prefabrication and the accompanying industrialization of building products a change occurs in the professional relationships within the building process. Subcontractors are usually small business men; building product manufacturers, in comparison, are major industries. In the

Traditional Building Conceived as an Entity

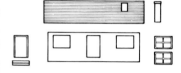

Building Divided into Elements for Prefabricated Manufacture

Building Reassembled of Industrialized Parts

Building Parts Designed for Prefabrication

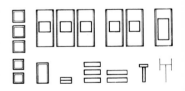

Prefabricated Industrialized Building

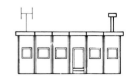

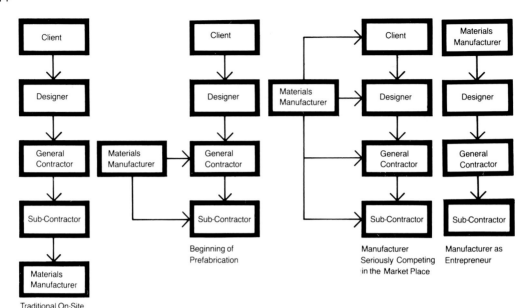

Changing Role of the Building Products Manufacturer in Industrialized Building

traditional building relationship the building product manufacturer is subservient to the sub-contractor since he must convince the sub-contractor to market his products. As more of the building tends to be manufactured a difference in business practice takes place. Building product manufacturers employ marketing analysts, building product representatives, use advertising and aggressively seek to influence the market. Their efforts are not only to fulfill a need for their products, but to create one. In some instances they have even entered the building market as entrepreneurs themselves.

New products originate with the building product manufacturer and the research and development staff, who are usually under the control of the sales division. The building product manufacturer is not adverse to appropriating and incorporating into his product line designs that have proven successful. New designs of manufactured products usually are not the creations of interior designers, but of building product manufacturers. Design copyright laws exert little controlling influence. Building product manufacturers therefore are seldom innovative in their design approach. They have found that design research cannot be protected. The tendency is therefore to restyle traditional products that have been successful in the market place.

Industrialization and prefabrication are ambiguous terms.

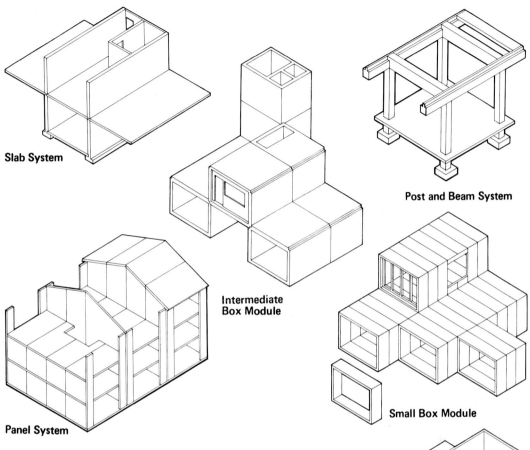

Slab System

**Intermediate
Box Module**

Post and Beam System

Panel System

Small Box Module

They are used here to define building components, sub-systems, and systems manufactured in factories (off the building site) and brought to the building to be assembled or attached.

The process is not new. The pilgrims were manufacturing building components: frames, siding, and shakes, and shipping them to England shortly after they arrived in the New World early in the 17th century. During the American Civil War portable barracks and hospitals were common. These were entire buildings manufactured in a factory and delivered to the site by train or horse and wagon. The settling of the American West and housing for the California and Alaskan gold rush was supplied by prefabricated buildings shipped across the plains in covered wagons or around the horn in sailing ships.

A century ago a midwestern entrepreneur advertised entire factory manufactured prefabricated towns. Individual houses

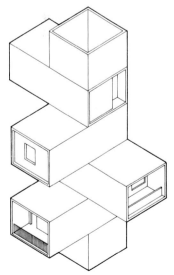

Large Box Module

were sold at $200.00 and City Halls at $1,000.00 with a range of greater or lesser prefabricated buildings priced between.

Today the focus of industrialized building is concentrated on the housing industry. It is in this area that the most pub-licized innovations have taken place. Industrial change has not occurred in the housing field alone: prefabrication has affected the entire building industry. Change has occurred slowly; the building process has become industrialized without anyone realizing that it has taken place.

There is little or no comparison between the functioning of the building industry today and the state of the industry at the end of the Second World War. As an example of the nature of change in building we can look at the history of the plastics and the metal industries in their attempts to capture the housing market. The "Lustron" metal house was designed and delivered as a manufactured product just prior to World War II and Buckminster Fuller began to manufacture and market his Dymaxion house in the late 1940's. The architects Goody and Clancy designed their plastic "Monsanto House" shortly thereafter. Each of these ventures within the space of 15 or 20 years used manufacturing and design techniques ra-tionally in relation to industrial prefabricated elements. Yet each failed to effect significant change due to causes that had no bearing on the worth of the designs themselves, all of which were further advanced than any prefabricated housing offered today. Marketing, building codes, financing, distribution and public acceptance proved stumbling blocks to rational indus-trialized building design.

After the failure of these ventures manufacturers re-evalu-ated their position in the market place and re-entered it on more modest terms. They supplied substitutes for existing materials and found uses within the building process that avoided direct confrontation with codes, and labor practices. They reverted to traditional methods of sales and marketing. The result has been that almost every item found in the build-ings interior has plastic and metal counterparts.

Plastics and metals are used in building today in greater quantity than ever before and their use continues to expand. Slowly and circuitously these products are capturing the market that they failed to gain by frontal assault.

It is now possible to specify and have delivered to the build-ing site an entire steel or aluminum house frame with trusses, studs, and joists designed on the same principles as those of traditional wood construction. Metal cabinets, doors, trim, and windows are increasingly common building elements.

Plastics have also been substituted for almost every conventional material found in building construction. These range from protective plastic coatings valued for their decorative properties, durability, and ease of maintenance, through light-transmitting materials in skylights, windows, and light fixtures. Plastic piping, furniture and fabrics are readily available. The growth of the use of plastics in building continues to increase more rapidly than the growth of the building industry itself.

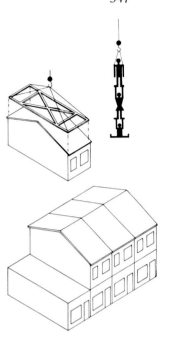

Plastic flooring in the form of vinyls, carpet, sheet materials, and coatings for wood and masonry are widely used. The plastics industry supplies electric and acoustic insulation as well.

Plastics find no legal difficulties in most of their present applications. However, fire resistance and the inherent problems of smoke and flame spread, corrosion, temperature dimensional variation and vermin resistance are still questioned by the building code authorities.

The rolled steel section, a derivation of railroad technology, made high rise buildings possible. However it was the development of new metallurgy for World War II which launched the widespread use of new metal products in building.

Among these new products, sheet aluminum with color added by anodizing, porcelain, and plastic coatings are widely used in panels, furniture and every other application that can compete, as substitutes, against traditional materials.

Steel has found widespread acceptance in household and laundry equipment. Heating and air conditioning units, furniture, hardware and a variety of wall panels. This is particularly true in high rise buildings which make the specification of fireproof steel elements mandatory.

With the introduction of power tools, millwork was one of the first building operations to move from the site to the factory. The on-site cabinetmaker lost much of his work to the millworker and factory assembler. Power tools which were originally set up at the site were first moved to the builder's shop then to the lumber yard and eventually to the factory as tools become more complex, bulky, expensive, and demanded more specialized skill.

The introduction of manufactured woodwork presaged the introduction of generally acceptable woodwork standards, and a national distribution system then developed. Today it is an unusual building design that does not take advantage of standard wood molding, bases, stair treads, handrails, saddles, and door and window trim.

The most significant change in wooden products since the

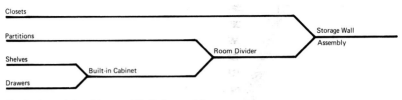

Evolution of the Storage Wall Assembly

Second World War is in factory manufacture, assembly, and finishing of larger and larger elements. The size of preassembled and shop-finished woodwork in an interior is limited only by the size of access openings to the space.

One of the most important features of this development is shop-finishing. Shop-finishing allows more control, better quality, and is saving of on-site labor.

The tendency of industrialization generally is to finish manufactured items in the factory whenever possible, from light gauge metal that is factory-finished before it is formed to architectural woodwork.

In some areas of Interior Design, prefabrication of wooden elements has been commonplace for some time. For example the entire interior of a major department store, including paneling, cases, cabinets, counters and all attendant lighting fixtures are commonly prefabricated, brought to the site and installed in one night.

In the mechanical equipment trades such as plumbing, heating and air conditioning, industrialization is taken for granted. Opposition to prefabrication in these fields occurs in the area of labor. To counteract this the design of mechanical systems has been modified to reduce the hand labor of ductwork installation whenever possible.

The production of bathroom and kitchen units that include the fixtures as one component has steadily increased. Entire kitchen and bathroom cores are available from several manufacturers. The only on-site work required is connecting them to the building.

While the image in most people's minds of prefabrication in building has been patterned after the automotive industry, with buildings moving off an assembly-line like automobiles, in reality, change has been small, but with consistent incremental changes in the techniques of building, construction, and assembly.

Change has been facilitated by the introduction of a variety of small power tools. The hand-held circular saw, power drills, scroll saws, staplers in place of nailing, and nailing guns that

Custom Cabinet

Prefabricated Cabinet
(with filler strips)

shoot fasteners through steel and concrete have greatly facilitated the task of on-site building assembly.

Concrete, formerly a traditional building material for building structures has found increasing use as precast decorative elements. The industrially manufactured panels are stronger and more uniform in workmanship than field-cast concrete as concrete mixes are more carefully controlled in the factory. Aggregates, admixtures and new techniques have brought concrete to the fore as a decorative material, often usurping the place of natural stone in interiors.

Plywood, probably the best known sheet material and the most common, has been in use for some time. Plasterboard, fiber and hardboards, wood chip-board, cement-asbestos boards, plastic laminates and sheet vinyls find increasing use in accelerating the erection of the structure and for special decorative effects.

Sheet materials also reduce the number of pieces in an assembly and reduce on-site labor. They offer increased strength, rigidity, and weather tightness. Panels are shaped and fitted at the site by traditional crafts and do not require manufacture to close tolerances. They can also be specified with a wide variety of finishes and surface treatments.

The designer finds himself designing filler pieces and adapting standard elements as the result of industrialization in building. It is only on the most expensive installations that the designer can measure and have manufactured items pro-

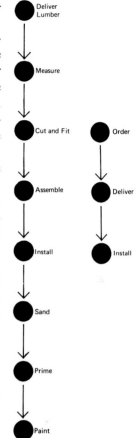

Construction Sequence–Custom Cabinet (Left)

Construction Sequence–Prefabricated Cabinet (Right)

Evolution of the Bathroom Assembly

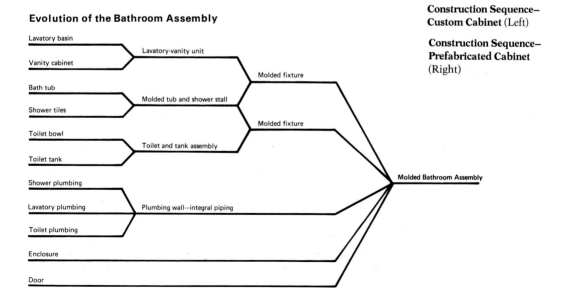

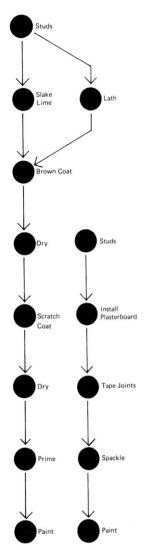

Construction Sequence of Plaster Wall (Left)

Construction Sequence of Plasterboard Wall Finish (Right)

duced to the sizes that he specifies. The situation is somewhat analogous to that of ready-made clothing. A set range of sizes is provided by the clothing industry and these must fit every human form as prefabricated building parts must fit every building condition.*

An exception to the dictatorship of set dimensions may occur in large buildings where a large quantity of material will be manufactured. The designer in this instance may design special dies or moldings. The cost of special equipment is spread over a large quantity of material and does not raise the cost of a single item appreciably.

As the craftsman in building has changed from the fitter of individual pieces with individual dimensions on the job site to the assembler and installer of factory-made elements, designers find that their function consists more and more of specifying prefabricated parts. Individual design flexibility is sacrificed, but larger elements can be produced with more time left for the designer to be concerned with other design problems. Detailing of individual items and the checking of shop drawings gives way to specifying from catalogs, checking invoices, coordinating and supervising job installations.

Industrialized Building Terms

Assembly   A construction of parts with a defined function such as a window, door, cabinet, etc.

Building   The structure resulting from the act of construction. The word system can be used synonymously with the term building. A building is the result of assembling a set of sub-systems that are the result of combining components.

Closed System   Dimensionally related sub-systems and components.

Component   An assembly of materials and parts with a defined function such as a window, door, cabinet, etc.

Element   Interrelated components such as a wall, floor, roof, ceiling, etc.

*For a thorough discussion of prefabrication and its alternatives consult *A Crack in the Rear-View Mirror; A View Of Industrialized Building*, written by Richard Bender and edited by Forrest Wilson. Van Nostrand Reinhold, New York City.

Industrial Building Usually refers to building elements and sub-systems manufactured in factories. Almost all buildings, except log cabins and igloos, make use of industrial products such as lumber and wire nails. The term is arbitrarily applied to the percentage of manufactured components and sub-systems used in the building. A definition of building could be the assembly of parts at the building site and manufacture of the assembly of parts away from the building site. The distance is not important. For example precast concrete elements are manufactured at the building site and lifted with cranes onto the poured-in-place building frame. The distance may be less than 100 feet, but the building frame is not an industrialized building element and the precast panels are.

Material Building products without a definite specified geometric shape such as concrete, asphalt, plaster, insulation, etc.

Module A unit of measure specified for dimensional coordination.

Module (Basic) A unit of measure whose value has been set to coordinate the sizes of prefabricated building components. It is chosen for its flexibility and convenience. The basic module is 4 inches for most American and European countries (10 cm).

Module (Planning) A modular dimension used for the design of buildings. It is a multiple of the basic module.

Modular Grid A grid in which the lines are spaced in multiples of the basic module (multiples of 4 in.).

Prefabrication The assembly-of-building components, sub-systems, or systems away from the building site.

Prefabrication (Site) Construction at the building site of components and sub-systems.

Sections Building materials usually manufactured by a continuous process of

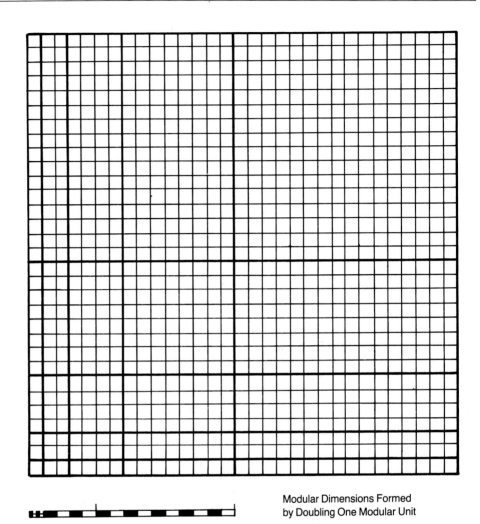

Modular Dimensions Formed
by Doubling One Modular Unit

definite cross-section, such as the section
of a steel beam, planking, wire, cable, or
extruded aluminum shapes.

Stick Building The construction of buildings piece by piece on the site. This usually refers to small dimensional lumber
building such as house framing.

Sub-System An interrelated set of components.

System Dimensionally and physically interrelated sub-systems and components
that form a building. A "Building System" has been defined as the use of selected components to form a structure.

VI

AN INTRODUCTION TO INTERIOR CONSTRUCTION AND MECHANICAL SYSTEMS

The steel frame of a modern office building under construction.
(Photograph by John Pile)

Interior design is an architectural discipline. Like architecture it can be defined as the art of building and, since design is impossible without building, the definition is appropriate. Designs that are not built are ideas, not designs. In the transition from idea to physical reality the design is invariably tempered by its structure. The strength of building materials dictates structure, while structure defines the limits and form of interior space. Thus the limiting physical laws that determine the extent of material strength are design tools.

Design is essentially problem solving; in fact, design cannot exist without problems. A design without problems is a design without solutions, and we might consider construction as among the most fascinating of problems that create design.

Every building has a structural logic. The building owes its physical being to structural laws since these laws cannot be circumvented without the collapse of the building. The difference between a good design and a bad one is the designer's skill in interpreting structural laws. Structural design is in reality a selection of options within the framework of building possibilities. For example, the increased depth of the spanning structural member is the price the designer pays to avoid frequent columns. Reduced soundproofing is the price of partition flexibility and beauty of material is often purchased at the cost of maintenance. The designer unaware of building options is ignorant of design possibilities.

Dramatic new expressions of structure do not change the content of building problems nor do they nullify basic structural principles, nor change the role of the designer. The elementary laws of structure can and must be studied, understood, and applied by the designer to all structures since these laws are universal.

Although building principles remain unchanged, differences in construction techniques can alter the designer's tools. In the case of past historical buildings, the craftsman arrived at the job site with raw material and fabricated it in place. His hand skill was a valuable element of building design. Modern buildings are an assemblage of premanufactured components. Hand skills have been all but eliminated from the job. The tradesman is a specialist, an expert in one facet of building work.

The designer must, as a result of this condition, be highly skilled in all the coordinated facets of the assembled building. He must know how each of the manufactured building elements fits together and the exact functions of the various tradesmen involved in their assembly. If design is to appear in the interior, the interior designer will have to put it there. The better the designer builds, the less the structure is noticed and the better the resulting design appears. This is probably why designers are called designers instead of builders.

This brief introduction to interior construction is not intended to be a comprehensive text on either structure or aesthetics. It is merely an introduction to what must be learned. A study of construction will never tell us what makes a building beautiful, but it will do the next best thing. It will help us understand many other things about it—why it has the form that it has, how it divides spaces within itself and why the spaces are formed the way that they are, where the light comes from, and even why the building sounds the way that it does.

The best way to learn about something is to define what we are talking about. If we define it thoroughly enough we will do two things: first, learn a great deal about what we want and have to know and, second, probably find we know something about it already.

1

THE THREE FORMS
OF STRUCTURE

How is a tree like a fish, a thread spool like a cave, and a lobster like the TWA building at Kennedy Airport? There is one thing they all have in common and that is their structure. The tree and the fish are both structured by skeletons, the lobster and the TWA terminal are both shaped by shells, while the hole in the thread spool and the hole in the mountain are alike because, independent of their external structures, they could be any shape.

There are three structural families made up of the three dimensions just mentioned. All buildings are members, or combinations, of one or another of them. Thus a building species can be recognized by the way it uses the three dimensions. The three families are one dimension (length), the line or skeleton; two dimensions (length and width), the plane; and three dimensions (length and width and depth), the solid.

One Dimension: The Skeleton

When you push or pull hard enough perpendicular to a linear structural member, it will bend in any direction. Most of its strength is along its length. Depending upon the material, it can be pushed or pulled a great deal in one direction. It is therefore a one-directional member. The strength of the skeletal structure shared by man, tree, and fish is in the individual one-directional members working together to create the other two dimensions of width and depth.

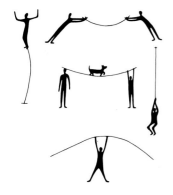

Two Dimensions: The Plane

When you push or pull perpendicular to the surface of a flat plane, it will bend, but if you push against its edge, it has a great deal of strength. It is therefore a two-dimensional member. It has strength in its length like the linear structural member and also strength in its width. The lobster and the TWA are special conditions of the plane called the "shell". Their surfaces are curved to give them strength in the third dimension of depth, which they would not have if they were flat.

Three Dimensions: The Solid

When you push or pull against a solid, it will not bend no matter what direction the force comes from. It is therefore a three-dimensional member, for it has strength in its length. width, and depth.

Keep in mind these three dimensions when you observe a building and you will be able to recognize its structural system. The form that the building structure assumes and, as a result, the shape of its interior space are both determined by the structural family the building belongs to.

The structure of the building must counteract forces that will destroy it. If we think of a building as being in a state of balance—that is, possessing tremendously powerful forces with the possibility of violent motion, but caged and held motionless by the counterforces in its structure—we have in mind the underlying principle of building structure whether that structure be skeleton, plane, or solid.

The major force on a building is the pull of gravity. The earth must push up as hard as the building pushes down against it. When it does not, the building sinks. The earth itself is part of the structure of the building. However, gravity is not the only force to be contended with. Winds try to push the building over and can create vacuums that will cause it to explode from the inside out, or pull it over backward. Buildings are subject to shock waves or the sonic boom of airplanes; they must withstand the movements of the earth and vibrations which can sometimes be extremely dangerous.

All of these contingencies must be considered by the structural designers of buildings. Buildings are not designed to counteract only one structural condition. If they are to stand, they must successfully wage battle against all the forces of destruction brought against them, caging these forces and holding them motionless through the counterforces in their structure.

The Forces by Name

The three destructive forces fighting against a building which its structure must have the muscle to control are called "tension", "compression", and "shear".

Tension is the force tending to pull the material apart. A bucket of sand tied to the end of a rope pulls the rope in tension. *Compression* is the inclination of a material to push together and squash. A nutcracker works by using a levered compression. *Shear* is the term used when two forces push on a body in opposite directions but not on the same line. A pair of scissors shears paper.

Tension is potentially stronger than compression, for tension does not introduce the problem of bending. For instance, a thin iron wire may be strong enough to support the weight of a man in suspension, but the same wire held upright does not have enough strength to support its own weight except for a short distance.

One of the most common stresses exerted on a structural member is bending. This is a combination of compression and tension. If you grasp a sheaf of papers tightly in both hands and bend them, the bottom papers will tear and the top, crumple, thus illustrating the two different stresses in bending: tensile and compressive. There are of course other destructive forces at work in structures. For instance, the beam might shear off against its supports because of its tendency to push down and their tendency to push up. This is called "vertical shear" in contrast to horizontal shear, which was illustrated by the movement of the sheaf of papers across each other horizonally as they changed from compression to tension in the middle of the pile. In linear (one-dimension) members bending is the hardest condition to counteract and is usually given the major consideration in structural design.

The three-dimensional families of building—skeleton, plane, and solid—are born and given shape by the way they handle the three destructive forces—tension, compression, and shear.

Before we go any further we should define some of the terms of building we will use. The following short illustrated glossary will review what we have discussed thus far, define some of the words that we will be using in later discussion, and provide a continuing reference for later studies.

Building Terms

Arch

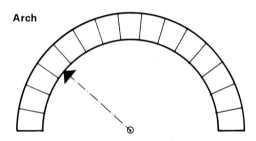

Beam

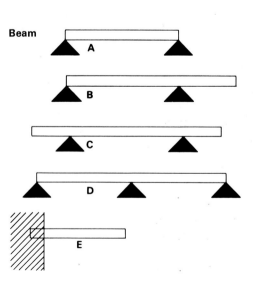

Admixture Material—such as color, water repellent, or a chemical that controls strength or setting time—which is added to plaster or concrete mix in addition to the base mixture of water, binder, and aggregates.

Aggregate A collection of granulated particles of different substances in a compound, or conglomerate, mass. In mixing concrete, the stone or gravel used as part of the mix is commonly called the "coarse aggregate", while the sand is called the "fine aggregate".

Air-Dried A term used to refer to lumber or wood which has been dried or seasoned by exposure to the atmosphere without artificial heat.

Arch A self-supporting structure, usually of brick or stone, carrying a superimposed load. Arches are usually curved although they may be almost flat.

Beam A structural member that supports transverse loads resting on supports. There are in general five kinds of beams, their classification depending upon the position, number of supports, and method of end fastening:

    A   Simple beam

    B   Cantilever beam

    C   Overhanging beam

    D   Continuous beam

    E   Fixed beam

Bending (Beam) A condition in which, when loads are applied, a beam tends to change shape, curving either downward or upward. If the beam is curved downward its lower portion is in tension, tending to pull apart. If the beam is curved upward its lower section is in compression, tending to push together. Bending stresses are a combination of compression and tension.

Brittle Material that is neither malleable nor ductile, like glass.

Cement Portland cement is the cement most commonly used in building construction. Produced to specifications which assure it uniform strength, it is a dependable material for building structures. The name "portland" comes from its resemballance in color to the early Portland stone used in English masonry.

The Romans manufactured cement from a mixture of slaked lime and pozzuolano or volcanic ash, and a natural cement is made from natural cement rock as quarried, but neither of these cements is as strong nor as durable as modern portland cement.

Chase In masonry, a groove or channel cut in the face of a brick wall to allow space for receiving pipes. Also, a trench dug to accommodate a drainpipe, or a recess in a masonry wall to provide space for mechanical equipment.

Column A pillar, usually round in masonry, but a variety of shapes in steel. It is a vertical shaft which receives pressure in the direction of its longitudinal axis. The parts of a column are the base of which the shaft rests, the body or shaft, and the head, known as the capital.

Compression A force which, when acting on a body, has a tendency to shorten it. Such stresses acting within the structural member are called "compressive" stresses.

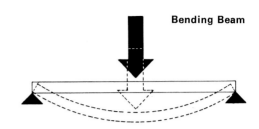

Bending Beam

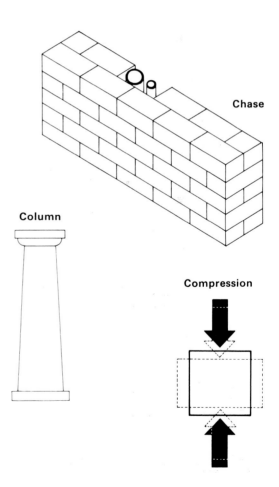

Chase

Column

Compression

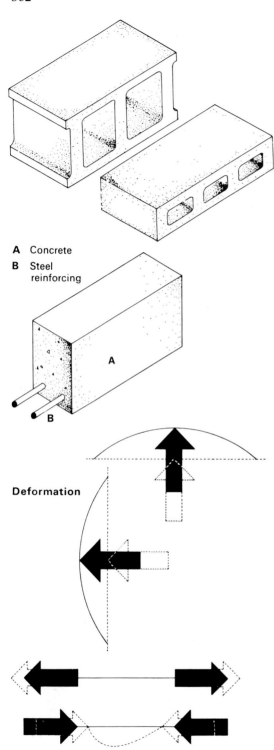

A Concrete
B Steel reinforcing

A

B

Deformation

Concrete In masonry, a mixture of cement, sand, and gravel with water in varying proportions.

Concrete Blocks Hollow or solid blocks of concrete used in the construction of buildings.

Concrete (Reinforced) Concrete containing steel reinforcing to give it tensile strength. The concrete reacts against the compressive stresses and the steel against the tensile. This concrete is made with portland cement.

Curtain Wall Non load-bearing wall. Usually a thin wall between structural members.

Deformation The change in shape or size of a body which occurs whenever a force acts on a body. Regardless of the magnitude of the force, the deformation is always present. It may sometimes be so small that it is difficult to measure with even the most sensitive instruments. *Deflection* is the term used for deformation with bending. *Elongation* is tensile deformation and *shortening* is compressive deformation.

Direct Stress Stresses evenly distributed over the cross-sectional area of a body. Tensile and compressive stresses tend to be direct. Bending stresses are not direct, since they vary over the cross-sectional area of the body.

Ductility That property of a material that permits it to undergo plastic deformation when subjected to a tensile force. A material that may be drawn into wires is a ductile material. A chain made of ductile materials is preferable to a chain in which the material is brittle.

Elasticity That property of a material that enables it to return to its original size and shape when a force to which it has been subjected is removed. The property varies greatly in different materials.

Façade The entire exterior side of a building, especially the front; the face of a structure; the front elevation or exterior face of a building.

Force That which exerts motion, pressure, or tension. In building construction we are concerned only with forces in equilibrium, forces at rest. If a force is at rest it must be held so by some other force or forces.

Foundation Wall That portion of a load-bearing wall below the level of the adjacent grade or below the first floor beams or joists.

Framing The columns, beams, and girders of a building. In wood construction, the studs, sills, plates, joists, and rafters of the building. The framing usually refers to the skeletal structural members that are later covered by curtain walls, siding, or other materials which enclose the building.

Furring A method of finishing the inside of a masonry wall so as to provide an air space for insulation, to prevent transmittance of moisture, and to level up irregularities in the wall surface.

Girder A large supporting horizontal member used to support walls or joists; a beam, either timber or steel, used for supporting a superstructure.

Grounds Nailing strips, usually of wood, placed on masonry walls to which finished woodwork is attached. When furring strips are used to true up a wall they are called "grounds".

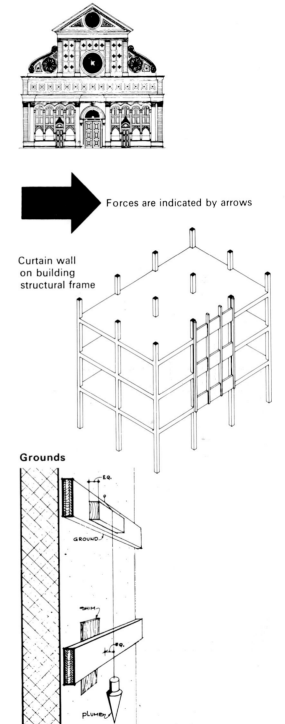

Forces are indicated by arrows

Curtain wall on building structural frame

Grounds

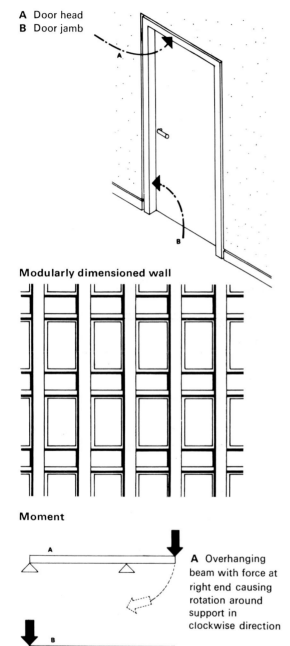

A Door head
B Door jamb

Modularly dimensioned wall

Moment

A Overhanging beam with force at right end causing rotation around support in clockwise direction

B Overhanging beam with force on left end causing counterclockwise rotation

Jamb The side-post or lining of a door-way or other aperture. The jambs of windows outside the frame are called "reveals".

Lintel A piece of wood, stone, or steel placed horizontally across the top of door and window openings to support the walls immediately above the openings.

Malleability The property that permits deformation of a material when subjected to a compressive force. Materials that may be hammered into sheets, for example, are malleable. Ductile materials are generally malleable. A material that is neither malleable nor ductile, such as cast iron, is called "brittle".

Masonry Brick, tile, stone, or other similar building units or combinations thereof, bonded together with mortar.

Mechanics The branch of physics that treats of the phenomena caused by the action of forces on material bodies.

Module A term used in historic architecture in determining the relative proportions of the various parts of a columnar system, the column diameter being taken as a unit of measure. In modern architecture the module is a convenient unit upon which all dimensions of a building and its components are based. This system is particularly important in standardization and prefabrication of building elements.

Moment The tendency of a force to cause rotation about a certain point or axis. (*Axis*. A straight line, real or imaginary, passing through a body that actually or supposedly revolves upon it.) The moment of the force with respect to a given point is the magnitude of the force multiplied by the distance to the point. The distance is called the "lever arm". It is measured by a line drawn perpendicular to the line of action of the force to the point. The point is called the "center of moments". It is important to remember that you can never consider the moment of a force without having in mind the particular point or axis about which it tends to cause rotation.

Mullion An upright division member between windows or doors.

Rafters Roof joists or small beams that are used for roof framing.

Reactions The upward forces acting at the supports which hold in equilibrium the downward forces or loads. A beam resting upon two columns has the columns as the reactions.

Rivets Bolts or pins made of soft metal used to fasten two metal plates or a metal plate and a piece of wood together.

Shear The resistance of a body to being cut by the action of two parallel forces or loads acting in opposite directions. Also a deformation in which parallel planes in a body remain parallel but are relatively displaced in a direction parallel to themselves.

Shrink A term applied to the natural contraction of lumber that has not been properly dried and seasoned.

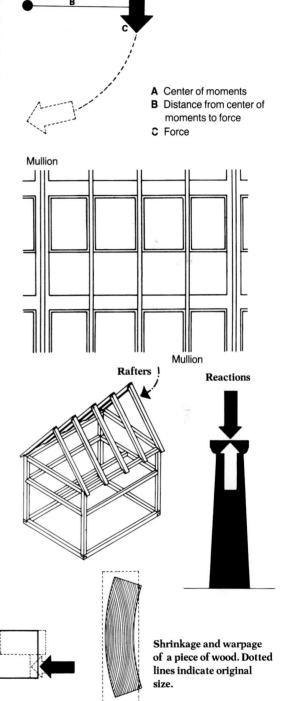

A Center of moments
B Distance from center of moments to force
C Force

Mullion

Mullion

Rafters

Reactions

Rivets

Shear

Shrinkage and warpage of a piece of wood. Dotted lines indicate original size.

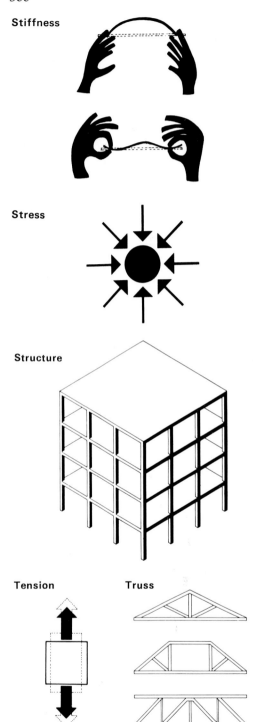

Stiffness

Stress

Structure

Tension   **Truss**

Soffit   The underside of a beam, lintel, or reveal.

Stanchion   An upright bar, prop, or support.

Statics   The branch of mechanics in physics that treats the conditions of equilibrium.

Stiffness   That property of a material that enables it to resist deformation. If, for instance, blocks of steel and wood of equal size are subject to equal compressive loads, the wood block will become shorter than the steel block. The deformation (shortening) of the wood will probably be thirty times that of steel, and we say steel is thirty times stiffer than wood.

Stress   An internal force in a material that resists a change in shape or size caused by external forces.

Structure   Construction in which all the parts are intended to be in equilibrium and at rest relative to each other.

Tension   A force acting on a body in such a manner that the body tends to lengthen or pull apart.

Tolerance   Dimensional allowance made for the inability of men and machines to fabricate a product of exact dimensions. Various materials due to their methods of manufacture and working have various tolerance allowances. For example, one sixteenth of an inch is tolerable with finished woodwork, one quarter of an inch with ornamental iron, one half of an inch with masonry.

Truss   A structural framework composed of a series of straight members so arranged and fastened together that external loads applied to the joints will cause only direct

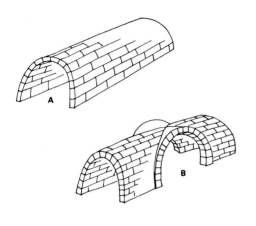
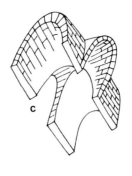
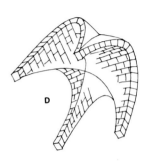

A   Vault
B   Intersecting vaults
C & D Intersecting vaults from below

stress in the members, either compression or tension.

Vault   A continuous arch of brick, stone, or concrete forming a self-supporting structure over a building.

Veneer   A thin covering of building material. Veneers are usually valuable or beautiful material layed over cheaper and coarser building substances. For example, cut stone used to cover the surface of a rough masonry wall is a veneer.

2

BUILDING MATERIALS

We will discuss five building materials: wood, metal, stone, concrete, and manmade masonry. Of course, these are not all of the materials used in construction. There are a great many more—glass, plastics, lead, rubber, etc.—and new ones are being added to the list every day. Obviously we cannot list all of the pertinent facts concerning even one of these five materials nor would the reader be able to store such a list of facts in his head, even if he had a mind to.

The acquisition of such facts by themselves is a difficult and often barely useful activity. On the other hand, learning the principles that generate facts is a stimulating and valuable undertaking because it teaches us how to think about materials. Our objective will be a method of analyzing facts, rather than listing them.

Wood, steel, stone, concrete, and manmade masonry will give us an excellent contrast in building materials. Wood and stone are natural materials, while the other three are manmade. Each is used for its particular attributes. To fit the characteristics of the material to the structural family, gaining the maximum efficiency of each material in the process, is what construction is about.

Materials are not limited to one family of construction. It is how they are used that determines their family grouping. For example, stone in a pyramid is part of solid construction, but in the columns and vault ribs of a Gothic cathedral, it becomes part of the skeleton construction, and as it is used for the in-fill of the vault, it becomes surface or plane construction. Wood in a log cabin is solid; rafters and beams and columns

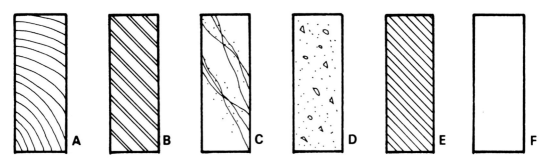

are skeleton; and in plywood sheet, wood is transformed to a member of the surface or plane family.

Buildings before modern architecture were confined to basic natural materials such as stone, wood, and burnt clay or bricks. Today designers are seeking and finding all sorts of things to use for building: inflated balloons, cables, canvas, plastic foams, and anything else they can lay their hands on. However, no matter how new the material, it must withstand the same forces—tension, compression, and shear—and must belong to one of the three families of building.

The selection of wood, steel, concrete, stone, or masonry for any particular structural function in design is dependent upon the designer's knowledge of how these materials react to the given structural condition in the family of building in which they are to be used. The designer must determine the nature of the forces and then decide how to counteract them.

This is nothing more than a choice of options, since any material will work in any system. For example, space may be covered over by a beam, a cable, an arch, a truss, a dome, an

A Wood
B Metal
C Stone
D Concrete
E Masonry
F Plastic

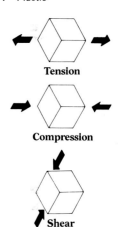

Wood used as skeleton, plane, and solid construction.

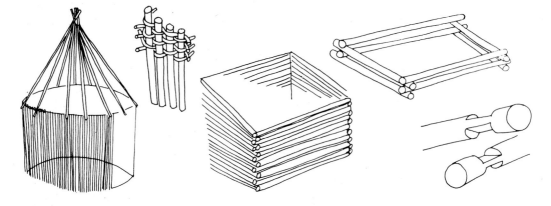

Reinforced concrete structure establishes the character of the new Boston City Hall. Kallman, McKinnell and Knowles, architects.

A pioneering use of cast iron structure to create a unique sense of space and light. Reading room of the Bibliothèque Nationale, Paris; 1858-68.
Henri Labrouste, architect.

Charles Eames House, Venice, California. Eames designed this house in 1948, using standard industrial products to produce a house full of spatial delight. The spirit of the house is carried to the interiors through the use of many beautiful objects and accessories collected by the Eameses.

inflated balloon, foaming plastics, or methods we have not even considered. But how and why? We must ask ourselves which material is the most economical, and we do not mean economy in the narrow sense of the word—that is, in nickel and dime thrift—but in the larger sense of efficiently using the means available, or choosing the correct structural idea to express the design.

Wood

Briefly the essential things that should interest the designer about wood in construction are its growth, manufacture, defects, strengths, and weaknesses.

Essentially there are two kinds of wood used for lumber, the hardwoods and the softwoods. The characteristic by which both kinds are designated has little to do with either actual hardness or softness. Some of the softwoods have strength characteristics superior to the hardwoods. The softwoods are the evergreens, and the hardwoods, the broadleafed trees. Generally speaking, softwoods are used for construction, and hardwoods for furniture and interior trim.

Spring and summer wood

The structure of wood consists of longitudinal bundles of fibers or cells crossed in a radial direction by binding fibers called "medullary" or "pith rays". Fibers vary in size and density in the various species and are to a large extent responsible for the appearance of the wood. A loose comparison between these fibers and a bunch of soda straws tremendously magnified might be made if we thought of the tree cells as hollow tubes sucking up the juices from the earth and distributing them through the trunk of the tree to the branches.

The cells determine wood strength, the direction of expansion and contraction when wood absorbs moisture, how wood can be glued, indeed almost all the important facts we have to know about it.

Knots

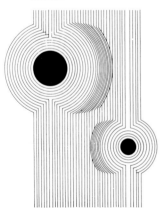

Tree growth takes place twice a year—in the spring and summer—over the old wood under the bark and marked by annual growth rings. Spring wood is generally lighter in color and more porous than summer wood. As time goes on, the central rings become clogged with substance and fall out of use as sap carriers, serving only to strengthen the tree. The result of this action upon the cells is two types of wood from the same tree, heartwood and sapwood. Heartwood is almost always stronger, darker, and more impervious to rot and insect attack than sapwood. The differentiation in annual rings, contrast in color between heart and sapwood, and the shape of the wood cells are the three characteristics which determine the appearance of wood. These characteristics may vary markedly in trees of the same species, however, they remain unique enough to distinguish a particular species from any other.

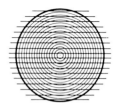

The grain direction has a marked influence upon the strength of wood. It is a primary consideration in the design of wood joints and the planning of wood construction. For example, wood can be easily split in, but must be cut across, the grain direction. It will hold a good deal more compressive weight without crushing in line with the grain than it will perpendicular to it. If wood is used in tension, it must pull in the direction of the grain. Pulled at right angles it will split. Knots and other abrupt changes of grain direction must be studied in relation to the structural stresses to which a piece of wood will be subjected.

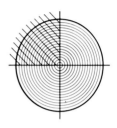

Besides grain direction, the strength of lumber may be altered by the way that it is cut from the log. There are basically two ways of sawing lumber, plain and quarter sawing. Plain sawing consists of a series of horizontal cuts through the log parallel to its diameter, quarter sawing quarters the log, then cuts each quarter parallel to the radius. Plain sawing results in a variety of grain slopes varying from maximum at the outer edges to perpendicular at the log's center. Quarter sawing maintains a more consistent grain direction varying from about forty-five to ninety degrees. It is more expensive because it is more wasteful of lumber and requires more labor. However, because of the consistency of grain direction there is less wood warpage and therefore less waste in construction. It is therefore preferred for floors or applications where wood movement must be minimized and an even-grain appearance is desired.

Lumber will warp in relation to its grain direction. Vertical grain produces uniform shrinkage. Cuts from near the log's perimeter will cup away from the log center.

Another structural factor in lumber manufacture is the method by which it is seasoned. Seasoning adds to the wood's strength and prevents shrinkage in the building, thereby adding to its stability and increasing the resistance of the wood to the attack of insects and fungi. Wood expands when it absorbs moisture and contracts, often checking or cracking, when it loses moisture. It is therefore very important that wood be properly dried after it is cut from the tree.

There are two types of drying used, air drying and kiln drying. Air-dried lumber loses its moisture through air circulation after it has been cut. This is usually a lengthy process lasting several months to a year and is seldom used any more. Kiln drying it more satisfactory and will reduce the moisture content to within working limits in a short space of time. The wood is placed in ovens or kilns, where warm dry air is played across it reducing the moisture. Since the climate varies in various parts of the country, wood may reabsorb or further lose moisture after it has been shipped. It is best to have the wood dried to a moisture content approximating that in which it will be used and then to take the further precaution of allowing wood to adjust to the climate before it is used.

The expansion and contraction of wood members due to moisture is one of the most difficult problems for the interior designer. It is almost impossible to seal a piece of wood to prevent its movement. For this reason, in wood detailing one has to take possible expansion and contraction into careful consideration.

Plywood

Plywood refers to a laminated wood-panel construction used to gain the advantage of stability, strength in both directions, and greater resistance to checking and splitting. Modern plywood panels also make possible the use of thin veneers producing a consistent matched appearance impossible in solid wood. Solid wood will vary greatly in color and grain direction, while thin veneers are consistent in grain and color since they are all cut from the same piece of wood.

The construction of plywood is that of an uneven sandwich, the plys being three, five, seven, nine, etc., in number. They are layed at right angles in grain direction to each other. The altering of grain directions gives strength in both panel directions. Panels are called by their interior construction as either veneer core, as explained above; lumber core, whose center is solid lumber pieces about one-half an inch thick in a three-quarters of an inch panel; mineral core, whose center is made of an inert fire-resistant substance; and chip core, a panel whose center section consists of chips of wood adhered with resins and bonded together with heat and pressure.

Rotary cutting. Log is mounted centrally and turned against the blade. Veneer is unwound from the log like a paper towel from its center.

Veneer

The veneers used for plywood vary in thickness from about one-twentieth of an inch to one-eighth. Veneers are cut three ways: sawing, rotary cutting, and slicing. Sawn veneer is produced in long strips by sawing, as its name implies. These veneers are about one-eighth of an inch thick. This method is seldom used today. Rotary-cut veneer is made by placing the log in a lathe and rotating it against a knife. The wood is unpeeled in one continuous sheet, like the peeling from a huge pencil sharpener. Sliced veneers are produced by moving a log against a heavy knife. The longest slicer presently in use is about sixteen feet long, which is the maximum length for a veneer (however, the average flitch size is usually much shorter). It is also possible by the use of end matching to give the veneers the appearance of greater length.

The sheets of veneer cut from a log are called a "flitch". After veneers are cut they are kept in cutting order so that they can be matched, that is, layed up so that their grain patterns correspond.

There are four methods commonly used to match veneers. Book and slip matching are the most common in premium installations. Random matching is also used and when veneers are not long enough in one piece, they can be end matched. Book matching is using the leaves of the flitch turned over like the leaves of a book. Slip matching joins veneers edge to edge without turning as they come off the pile in sequence. Random matching means the veneers are mixed in sequence and flitch. End-matched veneer matches the end grain of one piece to the corresponding end grain of the next. Special matching of highly figured veneers—such as diamond, reverse diamond, checkerboard, etc.—are sometimes used in special applications.

Figures in veneer depend upon the grain characteristics of the species and the method of cutting. In rotary cutting the knife passes through the annual rings, resulting in varied grain patterns. In slicing, grain patterns may be varied by the position that the log takes against the knife. Flat slicing has the log split lengthwise and sliced parallel to the long axis. A quartered log is sliced perpendicular to the growth rings. In half-round slicing the log is mounted off center on a lathe and cut slightly across the growth rings for a wavy grain between plain sliced and quarter sliced in effect. In general, the same log may produce a variety of grain effects depending upon the method used to slice the veneer.

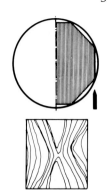

Plain or flat veneer slicing. The half log, or flitch, is mounted with the heart side flat against the guide plate of the slicer and is cut parallel to a line through the log's center.

Quarter slicing. Flitch is mounted on the guide plate so that the growth rings strike the knife at approximately right angles.

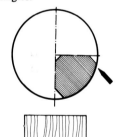

Summary

Wood can be used in any of the three families of structure. As mentioned earlier, lumber for skeleton construction, plywood for plane structures, and logs for solid construction demonstrate the versatility of this material.

Sometimes these methods are combined. In a box beam, the top and bottom members are linear while the sides are stressed as a plane. In each instance the stresses in the wood act differently. For example, a piece of plywood used as a shelf is less efficient than a solid piece of lumber because the cross

grains of the alternate plies running perpendicular to the shelf's length do not help to counteract bending stresses. On the other hand, plywood used as sheathing for a house is five times stronger than ordinary lumber nailed horizontally since it acts as a structural skin giving strength in all directions.

It is important to remember what happens to a piece of wood in regard to its cellular structure. We know that wood splits easily with the grain and therefore must be cut against it; it will hold more with the grain in its direction, and will compress and dent under the same load applied perpendicular to the grain. Its strength is altered by the way it is cut from the log, and it will expand and contract with moisture.

This knowledge is necessary to us in the design of wooden joints. A joint that pulls in the grain direction is liable to shear horizontally; on the other hand, if the joint is compressive, it would use the same grain direction to its advantage. Once the designer envisions the nature of the forces working on a joint and compares them to the strength of the material, the design of the joint itself is easily resolved. Think of the possible structural conditions for the wood joints shown in the glossary that follows. Ask yourself which joints are best for compression, tension, and shear.

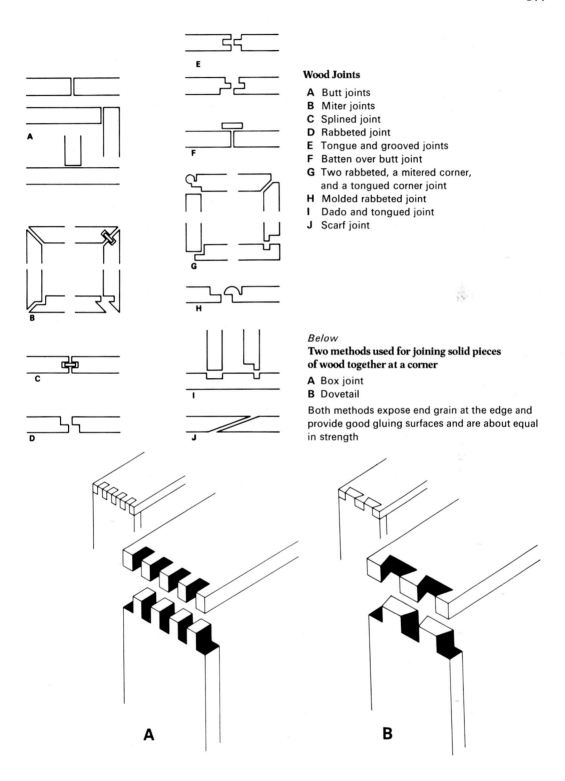

Wood Joints

A Butt joints
B Miter joints
C Splined joint
D Rabbeted joint
E Tongue and grooved joints
F Batten over butt joint
G Two rabbeted, a mitered corner,
   and a tongued corner joint
H Molded rabbeted joint
I Dado and tongued joint
J Scarf joint

Below
**Two methods used for joining solid pieces
of wood together at a corner**

A Box joint
B Dovetail

Both methods expose end grain at the edge and
provide good gluing surfaces and are about equal
in strength

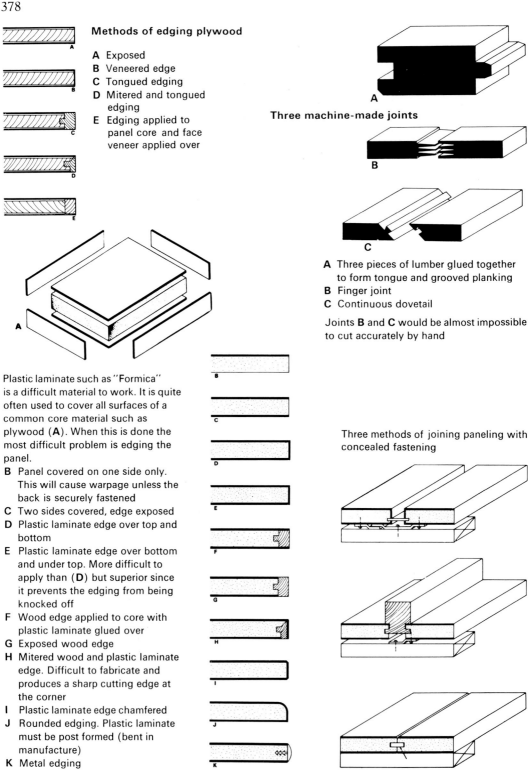

Methods of edging plywood

A Exposed
B Veneered edge
C Tongued edging
D Mitered and tongued edging
E Edging applied to panel core and face veneer applied over

Three machine-made joints

A Three pieces of lumber glued together to form tongue and grooved planking
B Finger joint
C Continuous dovetail

Joints **B** and **C** would be almost impossible to cut accurately by hand

Plastic laminate such as "Formica" is a difficult material to work. It is quite often used to cover all surfaces of a common core material such as plywood (**A**). When this is done the most difficult problem is edging the panel.

B Panel covered on one side only. This will cause warpage unless the back is securely fastened
C Two sides covered, edge exposed
D Plastic laminate edge over top and bottom
E Plastic laminate edge over bottom and under top. More difficult to apply than (**D**) but superior since it prevents the edging from being knocked off
F Wood edge applied to core with plastic laminate glued over
G Exposed wood edge
H Mitered wood and plastic laminate edge. Difficult to fabricate and produces a sharp cutting edge at the corner
I Plastic laminate edge chamfered
J Rounded edging. Plastic laminate must be post formed (bent in manufacture)
K Metal edging

Three methods of joining paneling with concealed fastening

Two joints compared

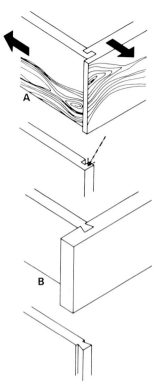

A Dadoed drawer front. The forces are shown by the black arrows. The front is pulled forward against the weighted inertia of the drawer, creating tensile stress. Most of the stress is exerted against the narrow tongue of wood on the side of the drawer at the point indicated by the dotted arrow. The side of the drawer meets the front at right angles. Gluing is end grain to end grain. This is not a very efficiently glued joint; therefore glue would be of little help.

Our conclusion would be that all of the pull is against a very weak section of wood and in the wrong grain direction, with little help from the glue. Not a very good joint for hard use.

B Comparison with slip dovetail joint. If we compare the two joints, assuming the forces acting on both are the same, we find that this is a more efficient solution. The dovetail cut on an angle allows gluing to hold better and provides twice as much cross-sectional wood area against the horizontal shear created by the tensile forces.

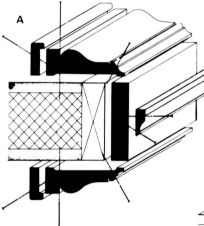

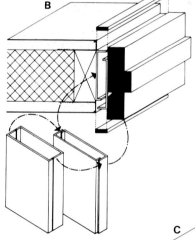

Three methods of fastening door frames

A Traditional use of nailed moldings. All pieces are nailed to the rough door buck
B Use of cut metal tubing to secure door frame without surface fastening
C Glued frame

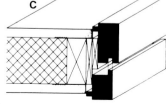

Mortise and tenon

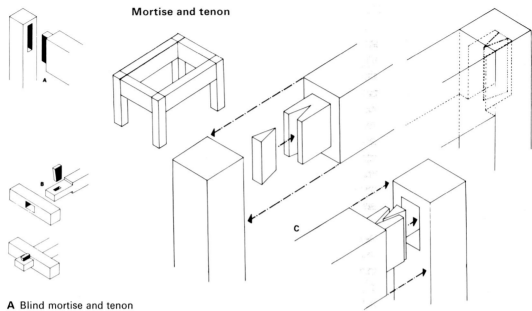

A Blind mortise and tenon
B Through tenon pegged on the other side to lock the joint
C Mortise and tenon with wedge inserted in tenon. When tenon is driven into mortise the wedge forces the sides tightly against the mortise. This joint, when properly glued and fitted, creates a very strong fastening.

Wedged wooden joint for heavy loads

This joint is locked together with wedges. Since the joint is the weakest part of the beam, it is important that it be located where the stress upon it will be minimal. The diagram **A** shows beam bending under loads. The joint has been placed at the point of minimum stress.

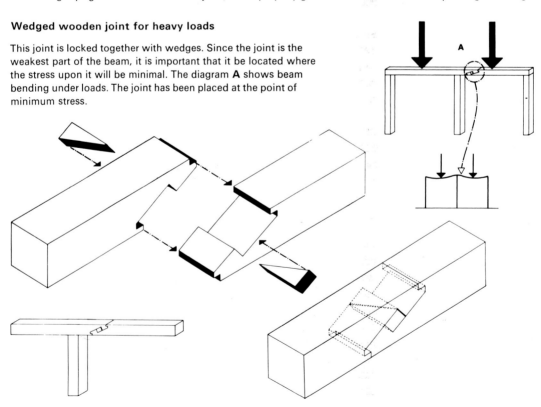

Metal

The architectural ferrous metals are the iron alloys, such as carbon steel, high-strength steel, stainless steel, cast steel, wrought iron, cast iron, and malleable iron. All of these metals contain carbon, which hardens them. Other elements are present in controlled amounts. Pure iron is rarely produced and is used almost exclusively for laboratory experiment.

The architectural nonferrous metals are aluminum, cadmium, chromium, copper, lead, magnesium, nickel, tin, and zinc. Of these only copper, lead, and zinc are sometimes used in relatively pure form for architectural purposes. The nonferrous metals, when combined in controlled proportions, form the nonferrous alloys.

Structural steel is elemental in most building construction in the United States. It is relatively inexpensive to produce and is claimed to be the strongest low-cost material, measured in volume and weight, used in building.

An interior designer is seldom called upon to design a steel structure. This is usually done by structural engineers. But he should know how to read a steel framing plan. It will tell him a great deal about the job conditions in the space he is designing.

The designer will find frequent use for small structural sections in the interior and may have to calculate their capacities himself since the structural engineer is only concerned with the structural steel frame of the building. For this reason he should familiarize himself with the various structural shapes and their structural capacities.

We do not have space here to describe the manufacture of steel or nonferrous metals. However, a listing of the most common structural shapes (called sections) follows. We will then discuss the tools used to work them.

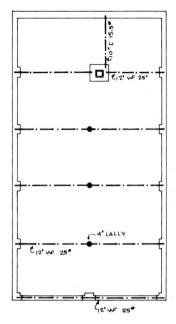

Steel as indicated on the framing plan for a small building. Steel sections are indicated by heavy lines with dots. Size of beam is shown by lettering.

Steel Fabricating and its Tools

The fabricating shop cuts, shapes, drills, and prepares mill steel for erection following the designer's specifications. Mill steel before it is worked (cut to size, milled, punched, etc.) by the fabricator is called "plain material". Plain material may be either hot or cold-rolled when it comes from the mill. "Hot-rolled" is the mill term describing steel that has been passed through the rollers hot. This leaves a thin scale called "mill scale" on the worked material. Cold-rolled steel has been cleaned of mill scale and rolled or run through dies cold. Cold-rolled or cold-finished steel sections, as they are sometimes

A Web
B Flange
C Fillet

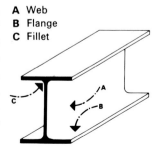

called, are more accurate in size, stronger, and possess a clean surface.

Following is a brief description of some steel working operations and the tools used in them.

Common structural steel sections

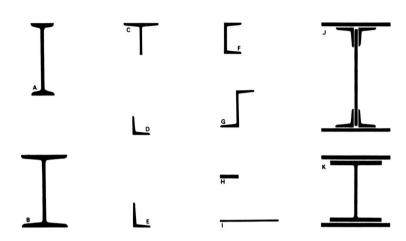

A Standard I beam
B Wide flange beam or column
C Structural T
D Angle
E Unequal leg angle
F Channel
G Z section
H Bar (six inches or less in width, $\frac{31}{64}$″ or over in thickness)
I Plate (over six inches in width, $\frac{1}{4}$″ or over in thickness)
J Plate and angle columns or girders
K Cover plated wide flange column

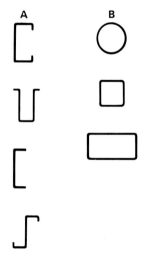

A Light gauge steel shapes are formed from flat rolled steel. They are made from either a single bent or bents welded together. They differ from rolled structural sections in that they are the same thickness throughout, are rounded where bent, and do not have fillets.

Light gauge structural members are used for light framing, sometimes taking the place of standard wood framing such as studs, joists, rafters, etc. They are bolted together or attached with a wide variety of patented fastening devices.

B Seamless tubing may be made from light gauge steel. Tubes are often used for light steel framing.

Bolting Threaded bolts are used to hold the steel together.

Break This is a machine for bending angles or wide sheets or plates.

Drilling This operation is largely confined to material that is too thick for the punches or to steel that is too hard to punch because of its alloy composition.

Flame Cutting For the cutting of material too heavy for machine capacity and the cutting of curved forms.

High Speed Saws These cut beams, channels, and light columns.

Milling Members that must have a very careful fit are milled. A milling machine has one or more rotating heads fitted with teeth or blades and a bed to hold the work securely during the operation. It produces a clean, smooth, exact surface. The milling machine is equivalent to a carpenter's plane.

Punching Punching is the most economical and commonly used method of making rivet and bolt holes in steel. If punching comes within the range of the machine size and the material is not too hard, it will be punched.

Reaming In close work where the holes must be exact they are either punched or drilled smaller than their finished size. Punching and drilling produce holes with burrs and distortions. They are then worked with a reamer, which is a small, rotating finishing tool which smooths out the hole imperfections left by punching and drilling.

Riveting A hot rivet is inserted in previously drilled holes and backed by a plate. A plunger strikes it and forms the rivet heads on both sides of the hole.

Shear   This is a guillotine-type cutter for cutting plates.

Welding   The process of fusing two pieces of metal together. There are two broad categories of welding: the metals are bonded by pressure and heat or they are welded together with heat and added metal. Most welding in building is done by heat and added metal, using either electric (arc welding) or gas (acetylene welding). Welded joints are as strong as the original metal. Welding rods used for the added metal to the welded joint are usually of the same metal as that being welded.

The nonferrous metals and their alloys are much softer than steel and easier to work. They are manufactured in a greater variety of shapes than the ferrous metals and are usually used for ornamental purposes rather than structural—although structural shapes such as I and H beams, channels, and angles can be obtained in the nonferrous metals. Tubing is often used structurally in furniture and occasionally in interiors as stanchions for partitions or mullions.

The aluminum and copper alloys can be easily extruded, which means that their sections can be made more uniform in shape, able to possess sharp corners as contrasted with the rounded edges and fillets of rolled structural steel.

Aluminum is obtained in a great number of alloys which vary slightly in color but greatly in strength. Copper alloys, on the other hand, vary tremendously in color—from red brass to nickel silver—but their strength is about the same. Matching the color of the copper alloys requires investigation and preferably samples from the manufacturer. The metal surface can be finished in graduations from rough to mirrorlike surface. The finish can be protected from discoloration in a variety of ways, none of which is permanent.

Methods of joining nonferrous metals include riveting, bolting, and welding, and a great number of seaming operations as will be shown in the dictionary of metal joints. The three methods most commonly used with steel are riveting, bolting, and welding since the joint formed must withstand great stress. The nonferrous metals are joined in a much greater variety of ways.

When welded, nonferrous metals, unlike steel, tend to lose strength around the welded area from the heat of the welding operation. This requires that the member be heat treated, that is, placed in an oven so that the entire piece along with the weld can be retempered to uniform strength. This requirement limits the size of a member that can be welded to the size of the heating oven.

A recent development in light-gauge ferrous metal finishing is changing methods of metal fastening. Synthetic metal coatings are beginning to appear earlier in the basic process of production. Whereas formerly finished surfaces were applied to manufactured items as the last act of production, they are now increasingly found on roll and sheet metal prior to fabrication.

Conventional welding techniques cannot be used with pre-finished metal surfaces. Fastening methods such as lock seaming, snap fitting, concealed riveting, and adhesive bonding are most commonly employed.

Metals have been glued very successfully to each other and to the surface of other materials. There are a number of adhesives to glue metal and a variety of methods by which gluing can be done. Since this form of fastening is becoming increasingly popular, it is best for the designer to obtain comprehensive technical information before he specifies fastening with adhesives.

Wood and Metal

Wood and metal are somewhat similar, except for the strong grain direction of wood. They are both used linearly as beams and columns, have great strength as planes, and are seldom used in solid construction. They are both worked by similar machinery to cut and form them. The milling machine is like the carpenter's plane; both wood and metals can be sawn; rivets are like nails; and wood gluing is analogous to metal welding. Both materials have a high degree of tensile and compressive strength. However, despite these similarities, the differences are extreme. A cubic foot of steel weighs over ten times a cubic foot of wood, and its tensile and compressive strength is at least twenty times that of lumber. These are of course rough estimates since the species of wood and the type of steel alloy both affect the strength.

The greatest difference, as we mentioned before, is the difference due to grain direction, which of course does not occur in the metals. Metal also does not have the frequent imperfections common to a natural material and is unaffected dimensionally by moisture, although it is highly susceptible to thermal expansion and contraction. Fortunately this is not a major concern of the interior designer.

Fastening with extruded sections

A Flush lap
B Interlocking
C Dovetail
D Spline

Extrusions produce sharp edges and clean profiles, making possible complicated metal joinery.

Welding

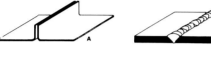

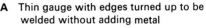

A Thin gauge with edges turned up to be welded without adding metal
B Light-gauge metal where two pieces are butted together and welded, adding metal with welding rod
C Medium thickness where one edge has been beveled and welded with rod
D Heavy metal with two edges beveled and welded from both sides using welding rod

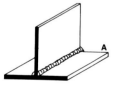

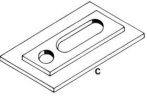

A Butt weld
B Lap weld
C Holes in plate for plug and slot welding

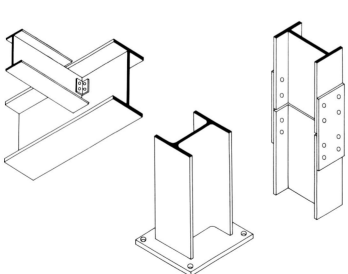

Structural steel is fastened with heavy plates and angles. It is either bolted, welded, or riveted. The base of columns are milled for a close fit against base plates.

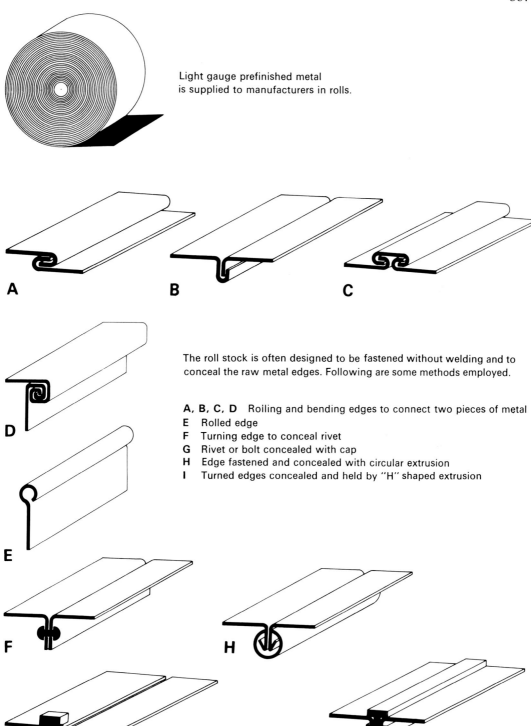

Light gauge prefinished metal
is supplied to manufacturers in rolls.

The roll stock is often designed to be fastened without welding and to
conceal the raw metal edges. Following are some methods employed.

A, B, C, D Rolling and bending edges to connect two pieces of metal
E Rolled edge
F Turning edge to conceal rivet
G Rivet or bolt concealed with cap
H Edge fastened and concealed with circular extrusion
I Turned edges concealed and held by "H" shaped extrusion

A

B

C

D

E

F

H

G

I

Stone

Rocks have been described as the essential building material of which the earth is constructed. They are, for the most part, combinations of minerals, which are in turn compositions of inorganic, chemical substances, although it is possible to find rocks—such as gypsum, pure sandstone, and quartzite—composed of one mineral.

All minerals and rocks have their primary origin in molten rock, which is called "magma". This rock, which is believed to exist in molten pockets within the earth's crust, periodically erupts and begins the cycle of creating rocks as we know them.

The rocks or stones that are used in building construction can be classified into three types. The *igneous* rocks, such as granite, have their origins in the molten rock which flows near the earth's surface and cools slowly, allowing crystals to develop. These rocks are very hard, with an almost imperceptible grain. The *sedimentary* rocks—such as sandstone, limestone, and slate—are formed by the erosion and breakdown of other rocks, which were formed originally by hardening through pressure and chemical action. In some of these rocks, the limestones particularly, are sometimes found the shells of prehistoric shell creatures. *Metamorphic* rocks are the result of a drastic change in either igneous or sedimentary rock. Heat from an invading magma will metamorphose sedimentary rocks; other transforming factors are pressure and the chemical action of liquids or gases. Marble is a metamorphosed limestone.

All rocks that are exposed on the earth's surface are readily altered. The process may be either mechanical, like the action of wind and rain, or chemical, like the releasing of chemicals

in the rock to react upon it; however, change is most often caused by a combination of both conditions. Stones are sometimes cracked by water, which enters their fissures and expands when it freezes. In dry and arid climates the stones may eventually flake away. The action of wind and sand may abrasively wear down stone faces, or cracks may invite the depositing of seeds which, when they sprout and their roots expand, act like wedges to crack huge portions of the stone away.

Throughout the process from original magma to metamorphic rock, stone is in the process of change. Placing it upon the façade of a building does not stop this process. Thus in many instances the stone of Gothic cathedrals has rotted away, while the gases and acids of today's polluted air accelerate the process. The ancients recognized this danger and often covered their stone buildings with coats of stucco to protect the stone.

The various kinds of stone are quarried and fabricated quite differently for use in and on buildings. The result of the quarrying and later cutting process determines their joinery and joints. Fine marbles may be fitted to hairline joints, while hard granites must have larger joints and thicker setting beds.

Stones are sliced and cut by saws and continuous wires with a mixture of water and sand. Their leaves, that is slabs of stone, are numbered in sequence much the same as wood veneers. If the grain is pronounced, it must be matched carefully.

Because of the great variety of stones and the varied ways they come into being, they differ greatly in strength characteristics, as well as in appearance. For example, the grain direction of granite is slight, while grain in sedimentary rocks, formed in layers and compressed into shape by pressure, can be more pronounced than that of wood.

The interior designer is not primarily concerned with the structural properties of stone since it is mostly used in interiors as a veneer. He is more concerned with its decorative potentials. In decoration a stone's soundness only affects the design in relation to its setting. For example, the strength of marbles varies tremendously. The highly decorative foreign marbles are usually the least sound. However, this is of little concern to the designer since stoneworkers are wonderfully skilled in invisibly repairing these natural imperfections.

We have not discussed stone masonry here since the process of setting stone is, in principle, very similar to other forms of masonry. The interior designer is usually more concerned with the lighter manmade masonry units than he is with masonry of rock. Specific points concerning stone joinery are discussed in the following illustrated glossary.

STONE JOINERY

Stone joints are not used for strength. Their purpose is to fit the two pieces of stone together as tightly as possible. In some easily worked stones it is possible to fashion joints as close as 1/16″. In granite, joints are larger. Joints also offer the best possibility of fastening the stone veneer to its backing material.

Plaster of paris or nonstaining cement used between the back of the stone and the back-up wall are called "spots." Spots help hold the stone in place but are not strong enough in themselves. For this reason a system of wires or metal anchors is used to connect the stone to the back wall. These are usually connected at the joints as shown in the drawings. On large pieces of stone they are also used between the joints.

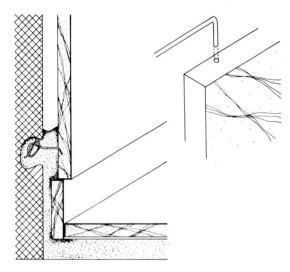

Stone is tied to the backing wall with wire ties. A hole is drilled into the stone and a wire about $\frac{1}{8}″$ in diameter is inserted into the stone. A hole is then cut in the concrete block wall and the end of the wire is set into it. The stone is held to the wall by a setting bed which holds both the marble and the wire in place.

Interior corner details   Exterior corner details

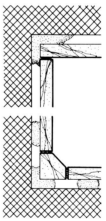

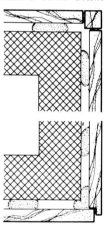

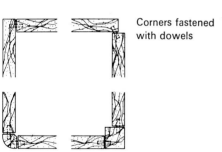

Corners fastened with dowels

Stone Setting Terms

Ashlar Stone masonry having a face of square or rectangular stones.

Grout Concrete with small aggregates and heavy liquid consistency, capable of being poured to fill small interstices, voids, or joints.

Marble A metamorphic, recrystallized limestone composed predominantly of crystalline grains of calcite or dolomite or both, having interlocking or mosaic texture.

Rodding Reinforcement of a structurally unsound marble by cementing reinforcing rods into grooves or channels cut into the back of the slab.

Setting Space A term used to indicate the distance from the finished face

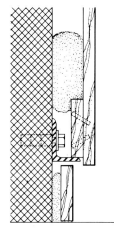

Panels are sometimes supported at the base on structural steel angles fastened to the backing wall. In this instance the panel is resting on a cleat of stone fixed to it with dowels and mastic.

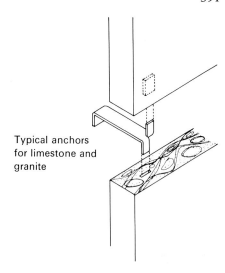

Typical anchors for limestone and granite

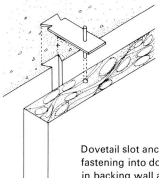

Dovetail slot anchor with dowel fastening into dovetail channel in backing wall and dowel hole into stone.

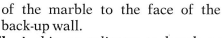

Two-way strap anchor fastening with slots cut into stone joint

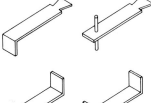

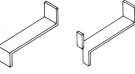

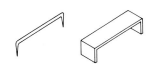

of the marble to the face of the back-up wall.

Spall A chip or splinter; to break or split off in chips or fragments.

Spot or **Spotting** An adhesive contact, usually of plaster of paris. Applied between the back of marble veneer and the face of the back-up wall to plumb or secure standing marble.

Tolerance A dimensional allowance made for the inability of men and machines to fabricate a product of exact dimensions.

Waxing An expression used in the marble-finishing trade to indicate the filling of natural voids with color-blended materials.

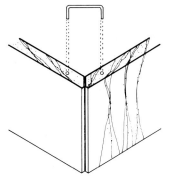

Wire U-shaped fastenings called "cramps" are sometimes used at the corners to hold two pieces of stone together.

Concrete

Concrete has been called a "liquid stone". It is a mixture of materials in which a paste of cement and water binds together sand and rocks into a stonelike mass.

Like stone, concrete is strong in compression and weak in tension. For this reason reinforcing is used to give it tensile strength. Steel rods are placed in the concrete where the stresses tend to pull it apart. Most concrete is reinforced except in very large installation such as dams or huge abutments, where it functions only as a mass of solid material.

Concrete is made stronger by the type of aggregates used and by the water-cement ratio. In lightweight concrete the aggregates may be comparatively weak material, such as blast-furnace cinders, which reduce the weight and the strength of the concrete. Usually the less water used to mix with the cement, the stronger the concrete becomes. Water as it evaporates leaves holes or air bubbles which weaken the finished casting. It usually requires twenty-eight days for concrete to gain its full design strength; however, it is usually strong enough to work on in seven or eight days. Concrete is held in place by wood, metal, or plastic forms until it hardens. These are removed when the mixture has set.

Although concrete appears to be a rough material, it must be mixed and placed with great care if it is to be strong and durable. There are a number of chemicals called "admixtures" that can be added to concrete to cause it to set quicker or to make it more waterproof or more resistant to freezing. Concrete can also be colored in a variety of colors either by using colored stone aggregates, by adding chemical colors, or even by adding dyes after it has set.

There are a variety of cements used in today's construction. White cement is used for its appearance in decorative work. It has the same strength as the ordinary cements used structurally. Special cements are used for building dams and mass concrete, and there are also special cements manufactured for setting under water.

Portland cement, which we mentioned earlier, is the principal cement used in modern building. It is made up of a combination of materials. Essentially this combination is of clayey rocks and limestone. The rocks are mined and crushed. They are then ground, proportioned and mixed, pulverized, and burned to incipient fusion at a temperature exceeding 2700 degrees.

The resulting clinkers are ground to powder. Gypsum and other ingredients are added to produce the powdered cement. The cement is mixed with aggregates and water added to

A Fiberglass form for
   precast concrete
B Reinforcing steel to be
   placed in precast form
C Shoveling concrete
   into form
D Precast elements
   stored in casting yard

form a manmade stone much harder than any of the materials originally mined.

Summary

Concrete combines the virtues of stone, wood, and steel. It is a liquid stone that can be formed into almost any shape, but unlike stone it can encase steel tenons to give it tremendous strength.

Its drawbacks are its great weight and the difficulty in forming. Concrete itself is an economic material, but forming and finishing can make it more expensive than any of the natural building stones. When designing with concrete the designer has to consider the form that holds the concrete in place and its cost, as much as he does the concrete itself.

Concrete is ideal for shells, like the TWA building at Kennedy Airport in New York City. However, the forming of such structures is quite expensive, so designers have been seeking forming methods that are more economic than the ordinary wood forms. Among these are placing concrete over a dirt mound, which is dug out once the concrete has set. Another

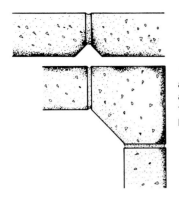

Typical concrete joints are wider than stone, which allows more tolerance for fitting the heavy units into place.

Precast structural double Tee's are used for long spans.

method is spraying concrete under pressure against formed metal lath. Yet another method has been to spray concrete over an inflated balloon, letting the air out of the balloon when the concrete is hard. From these examples it can be seen that concrete is a very versatile material with its use limited only by the designer's imagination.

Concrete poured in place creates a homogenous structure with strong solid joints; however, the control of the finish is not as accurate. For this reason precast concrete has become popular. This consists of concrete elements cast either in a concrete fabricating factory or on the site. They are lifted into place and are either attached to another structural system or are used to form part of the structure. Precast concrete can be more exactly controlled than concrete poured in place, and with the use of such forming material as fiberglass, very fine finishes may be obtained.

The possibilities of concrete design are unlimited. However, it should never be forgotten that, although it seems simple to handle, concrete in reality is a very difficult material to work with. An illustrated glossary of concrete joints follows.

Concrete Terms

Admixtures Prepared formulations added to concrete mixes to alter certain characteristics, for example to speed or slow setting, to increase water repellency, aid workability, add color, etc.

Aggregate Cement paste binds together fine and coarse aggregates. The fine aggregate is sand under ¼ in. Coarse aggregates may be riverbank gravel, crushed rock, or lightweight materials such as blast furnace slag. The size of coarse aggregates varies in relation to the thickness of the concrete section. The strength of the concrete is affected by the kind of aggregate used.

Cast in Place   Concrete cast into forms on the building site.

Concrete   A mixture of sand, gravel, crushed rock, and other aggregates held together by a hardened paste of cement and water.

Concrete Weight   Varies according to the aggregates used. Stone concrete usually weighs 150 lbs. per cubic foot. Lightweight concrete may weigh around 100 lbs.

Cubic Foot   Unit of measure. A sack of portland cement containing 94 lbs. net weight equals 1 cubic foot. Fine and coarse aggregate is measured by loose volume. Water is measured by the gallon.

Grout   Cement mortar used for various purposes such as filling holes, setting tiles, etc.

Forms   Molds into which the concrete is poured. They support the plastic mixture until the concrete has set. They are made of wood, metal, and fiberglass.

Finishes   Concrete finishes can be divided into three categories: finishes made by the concrete forms, finishes applied to the concrete when it is wet, and finishes applied to the hardened concrete surface. Concrete to be covered is usually left as it is. Exposed concrete decorative form finish is as varied as the forms the designer can devise. Wet concrete finish can range from the rough surface created by an ordinary straw broom to a smooth steel troweled surface. Hardened concrete surfaces are sometimes chipped with a "bush" hammer or sandblasted to expose the aggregate underneath.

Inserts   Before the concrete is poured, building hardware, such as slots, hangers, etc., are placed in the

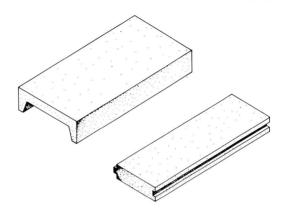

Precast concrete structural elements. Channels and tongue and grooved concrete plank are used for short spans.

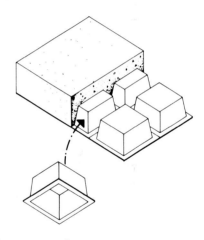

Metal pans are used for concrete slab construction. Concrete is poured over the pans. When the concrete has hardened the pans are removed, creating a "waffle" slab.

Waffle slab

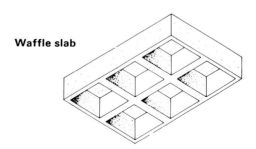

forms for the concrete to be poured around. These allow attachment to the concrete.

Joint-Construction Only a certain amount of concrete can be poured in one day. The method of closing off this pour and preparing the concrete joint for the next pour is called a "construction joint".

Joint-Expansion Materials move with temperature differentials. When they are heated they expand, when cooled they contract. Seasonal changes invariably cause movement. Special joints called "expansion joints" are designed to relieve the pressure and prevent possible damage to the concrete due to such movement.

Water-Cement Ratio The water-cement ratio controls the binding power of the paste which coats and surrounds the aggregates and upon hardening holds the entire mass together. Enough water is needed to make the mass plastic so that it can be placed in the forms, but too much water will weaken the strength of the concrete.

Masonry

The masonry division of building includes all of the work done by bricklayers. Although stonework is masonry, as is tile setting, the term "masonry" usually refers to the various units of man-made masonry. There are two categories: those units that are formed and hardened through chemical action and those that are hardened through the application of heat. Gypsum block, concrete block, and cinder block are examples of chemically hardened material, while brick and terra cotta tile are examples of materials which have been heated to harden. Both types are formed from shapeless masses of material which are refined and reformed into modular units.

Brick is the oldest artificial building material used by builders. It is still in extensive use, using the same techniques employed when it was first invented, probably seven millenniums ago. The first bricks were sun dried and formed of mud with straw for a binder. Later, bricks were made in wooden forms and burned in ovens. Until comparatively recently bricks were placed in beehivelike mounds with fires kindled in their centers to form their own ovens or kilns. These were dismantled after the bricks were baked and the bricks were used for building. Bricks made in this way display a marked variation in color and hardness. The bricks nearest the fire were burned black with a glasslike surface. Those farthest away, near the outside of the kiln, were slightly burned and pink in color. The bricks between these two extremes were the cherry-fired bricks most commonly seen. You may notice this range of brick color in some very old buildings.

Clays from various parts of the country make bricks of different colors, and a variety of means are used to texture, glaze, and color bricks to create unique brick surfaces.

In modern brick-making the kilns burn the bricks evenly, creating a uniform color. However, it is possible to find bricks that are manufactured to resemble those from the old kilns.

Brick sizes have been standardized so that it is possible to buy bricks anywhere in the United States of the same size. There are, however, a variety of styles of bricks other than the standard structural face and back-up brick, and there are also a great variety of finishes and glazes with which the designer should become familiar.

Concrete blocks are used like large bricks. Since they are larger than bricks, a single-block course is usually sufficient for the walls of one- or two-story buildings. The same is true of terra cotta tiles, tile simply being another word for block. Gypsum block is quite large and very soft. It can be cut with carpenter's handsaws and is usually used for interior partitions. Instead of framing a partition and covering it with lath, the mason simply sets a wall of gypsum blocks and the plasterer plasters both sides. Gypsum blocks are almost never left exposed.

Summary

The essential quality of masonry that differs from the other four materials we have briefly discussed is its modular characteristic, that is, each brick is uniform in size and usually has a dimensional relationship between its sides. For example, a common brick is normally twice as long as it is wide. This characteristic is extremely important. Bricks being relatively weak units in themselves have to be bonded into an integral mass. The bonding agent, the mortar, is much weaker in strength than the bricks; therefore the bricks must be layed up in such a fashion as to minimize continuous planes of mortar, as can be seen in the following dictionary of brick joints. Bonding with concrete block, gypsum block, terra cotta tile, stone, and other forms of regular masonry is usually a simplified variation of the brick-bonding technique.

Following is an illustrated glossary of masonry joints.

MASONRY JOINTS

There are three bonding methods commonly used in brick construction.

Common Bond

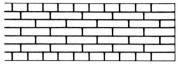

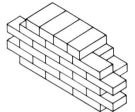

Every sixth course (row) of brick is set with the short end (header) to the face of the wall. This ties the five courses of brick layed with their long dimensions (called stretchers) together.

English bond

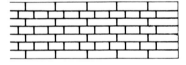

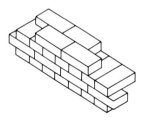

Alternating header and stretcher courses.

Flemish bond

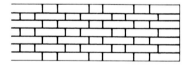

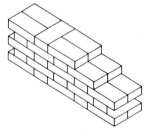

Alternating headers and stretchers in the same course.

Running bond

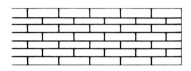

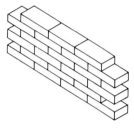

Stretchers without any headers. This is usually found in brick veneers where only one thickn ss of brick is used.

Decorative Bonds

A Stacked bond. Bricks are layed directly over each other horizontally with joints aligned.

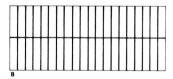

B Soldier courses. Bricks are layed directly over each other vertically with joints aligned.

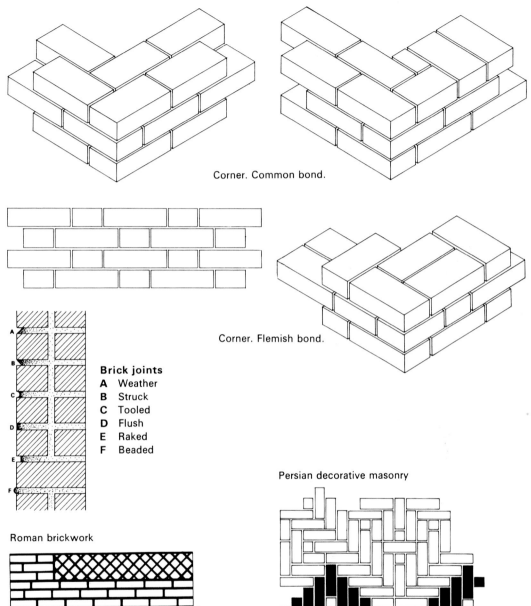

Corner. Common bond.

Corner. Flemish bond.

Brick joints
A Weather
B Struck
C Tooled
D Flush
E Raked
F Beaded

Persian decorative masonry

Roman brickwork

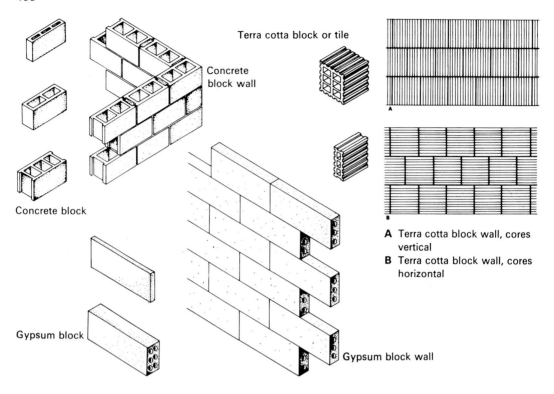

Terra cotta block or tile

Concrete block wall

Concrete block

Gypsum block

Gypsum block wall

A Terra cotta block wall, cores vertical
B Terra cotta block wall, cores horizontal

Masonry Construction Terms

Admixtures Materials added to mortar, such as water-repellent or coloring agents, or chemicals to retard or speed setting.

Anchor A piece or connected pieces of metal used to attach building parts, such as plates or joists to masonry or to masonry materials.

Architectural Terra Cotta Plain or ornamental (machine-extruded or hand-molded) hard-burned clay building units, generally larger in size than brick and most facing tile, and having a glazed or unglazed ceramic finish in an unlimited variety of colors.

Ashlar Masonry Masonry composed of rectangular units of burned clay, shale, or stone—generally larger in size than brick and properly bonded—having sawed, dressed, or square beds and joints laid in mortar.

Back-Up That part of a masonry wall behind the exterior facing.

Bat A piece of broken brick.

Bed Joint The horizontal layer of mortar in which each unit is layed.

Bond Tying the various parts of a masonry wall by lapping one unit over another; also refers to the pattern formed by the exposed faces of the units. The adhesion of the mortar to the units is also referred to as the bond.

Bond Course The course consisting of units which overlap the joints of those below.

Breaking Joints The arrangement of masonry units so as to prevent continuous vertical joints in adjacent courses.

Brick A solid masonry unit of burned clay or shale, formed while plastic into a rectangular prism and burned in a kiln.

Cavity-Wall A wall built of masonry units so arranged as to provide a continuous air space at least two inches wide and not more than three inches wide within the wall. The facing and backing are tied together with rigid metal ties.

Chase A continuous vertical recess built into a wall to receive pipes, ducts, etc.

Common Brick A term referring to the ordinary bricks used for walls and piers.

Corbel A shelf or ledge formed by projecting successive courses of masonry out from the face of the wall.

Course One continuous horizontal layer of masonry.

Drip A projecting piece of material so shaped as to throw off water and prevent its running down the face of the wall or other surface of which it is a part.

Efflorescence A whitish powder, sometimes formed on the surface of masonry by deposition of soluble salts.

Face The exposed surface of a wall or masonry unit.

Face Brick A name denoting a brick especially made or selected for its color, shape, evenness or irregularity of contour, and surface texture, or for other features that will give a desired effect. It is used upon the exposed surfaces of walls and may be backed by common brick.

Fire Brick Bricks having a very high fusing point, due to the material from which they are made. They can be subjected to great heat.

Glazed Brick Bricks having a smooth outer face with a dull satin or high-gloss finish.

Header A masonry unit laid flat and with its greatest dimension perpendicular to the face of the wall. Generally used to tie two thicknesses of masonry together.

Header Course A continuous bonding course of header brick.

Mortar A plastic mixture of cementitious materials, fine aggregate, and water.

Pargeting The process of applying a coat of cement mortar to the back of facing material or to the face of the backing material; sometimes referred to as parging.

Pointing Troweling mortar into a joint after the masonry unit is laid.

Reinforced Brick Masonry Brick masonry in which steel reinforcing bars are embedded in such a manner that the two materials act together in resisting forces.

Salt Glaze A gloss finish obtained by the mechanical reaction of the silicates of the clay body with vapors of salt or chemicals.

Soldier A brick laid on its end so that its greatest dimension is vertical.

Stretcher A masonry unit laid flat with its greatest dimension parallel to the face of the wall.

Struck Joint Any mortar joint that has been finished with the trowel.

Structural Clay Tile A hollow masonry building unit composed of burned clay, shale, fire clay, or mixtures thereof, and having parallel air cells.

Veneered Wall A wall having a masonry facing which is attached to the backing, but not so bonded as to exert common action under load.

Vitrified That characteristic of a clay product resulting when the temperature in the kiln is sufficient to fuse all the grains and close all the pores of the clay, making the mass impervious.

Plastics

The materials we have discussed thus far are the age-old workhorses of building. Honest and dependable, they form the backbone of building construction and despite their age are still the materials of which most of our buildings are constructed.

There are other materials born of our technology which are neither worked directly from nature—as wood and stone—or reconstituted by man from natural substances—as brick, concrete, and steel. These are the plastics, which are born by breaking down and building up molecular structures.

There is a little bit of magic in the process that sets the designer to dreaming of the perfect building material: a handful of powder thrown into a converter that will build any shape or form—lighter than aluminum, clearer than glass, cheaper and more abundant than dirt, and stronger than steel. Such a miracle substance exists, but there is a catch; it is not just one material but can be found in small parts of the elements in each of thirty-nine known plastics and their countless variations.

Since all the virtues of plastics have not yet been combined into one material, each of the plastics by itself—while it contains part of the dream material—also has in its composition, to greater or lesser degree, part of the building material nightmare—flammability, expense, rapid deterioration, structural weakness, and unpredictability.

Plastic development is at present in the replacement stage. Plastics have not yet arrived on the building scene as materials designed for their own specific virtues. For the most part they are marketed as slavish imitations of leather, glass, wood, and countless other substances.

The designer must look beneath the surface of plastics, not dismiss them out of hand as cheap imitations. Their properties are unique. Plastics are here to stay and be developed. In fact, new plastic formulations are being announced every day.

Of all the professionals involved in building at the present time, the interior designer is the most concerned with the use and the development of plastics since they are used almost exclusively in building at present as interior surfacing materials.

Plastics are somewhat magical compared to traditional building materials. They can have high light-transmission qualities, are easily colored, possess infinite textural possibilities, can be easily maintained with a flexibility in the manufacturing processes to fit almost any design problem. Plastics can have high resistance to wear, water, corrosion, and weathering and are lightweight, with high impact resistance. They have low thermal conductivity and can produce excellent adhesion to almost any building material.

On the negative side the cost per pound is high, although plastics are among the exceptional building materials that have been reduced in price over the last ten years. Plastics are not usually as strong as most structural building materials; however, sandwich construction and the inclusion of glass fibers strengthens them considerably. Ultraviolet light will deteriorate some plastics; and most plastics will burn, although many of them are presently available which are self-extinguishing, and research is being concentrated in reducing their flammability.

An elemental division exists in plastics dividing them into two distinct categories. "Thermo" (heat) appears in the names of both types, but they possess exactly opposite reactions to it. One melts on the application of heat and is called "Thermo plastic" (plasticity induced by heat). The other fuses into hardness with the application of heat and is called "Thermo-set" (solidification with heat) plastic.

Plastics and their various abbreviations and combinations of names are extremely confusing even to the experts. The continued development and new combinations of the basic thirty-nine types do not assist the untangling of definitions. As a consequence, it is best for the designer to determine as well as s/he can exactly what the composition and the properties are of any plastic s/he contemplates using.

The following list of the ten most used plastics is given as a beginning aid to help unravel the confusion. Trade names are not much help in identifying plastics; however, the manufacturer or retailer will tell the designer the kind of plastic in his product. The designer can then identify it with the plastic type.

Polyethylene A strong and flexible plastic that can withstand up to 100 degrees Fahrenheit. It cannot be used over fire. It is resistant to chemicals, food stains, and short contact with cleaning fluids. Its typical uses are for flexible ice cube trays, flexible or rigid bottles, tumblers, dishes, toys, packaging, etc.

Vinyls These plastics are recommended for indoor use only. Most are unaffected by contact with water, oil, foods, common chemicals, and cleaning fluids. They can withstand heat up to 130 degrees Fahrenheit. They can perform at food-freezing temperatures and make good insulators for electrical wiring. Their typical uses are for raincoats, garment bags, wire and cable insulation, clear blow-molded packaging containers, electric plugs, floor and wall covering.

Polystyrene This plastic withstands ordinary household use, but not for articles subject to severe impact or flexing. If higher strength is needed, glass-filled types are used. It is not recommended for continuous outdoor use, and cleaning fluids, gasoline, and turpentine will harm it. It is not harmed by continuous use at food-freezing temperatures. Typical uses are for kitchen items, such as refrigerator food containers. It is also used for battery cases, wall tile, and portable radio housings.

Phenolics These plastics are rigid and strong. They can withstand severe knocks and are excellent electrical insulators. They are heat resistant up to 330 degrees Fahrenheit. They are poor heat conductors and are fire resistant. They will withstand oils, greases, acids, and common solvents, but tend to yellow on exposure to light. Their typical uses are for cooking utensil handles, radio and TV cabinets, appliance parts, protective coatings, electrical insulation, etc.

Urea and Melamine These plastics are hard and scratch resistant. They are strong, but not unbreakable. They are unaffected by chemicals, acids, oils, and cleaning fluids. Their performance temperature range is from 70 degrees below Fahrenheit to 170 degrees above for urea, and 210 degrees above for melamine. They should be considered as permanent in indoor use; neither should be used over an open flame; they will not burn, but discoloration or charring may occur. Typical uses are for tableware, tabletop laminated surfaces, and as a plywood adhesive for melamine. Urea is used in appliance housings, electrical devices, and buttons; in resin form it is used for plywood adhesives and in various industrial coatings.

Alkyds These plastics are strong and dimensionally stable under high temperatures. They are resistant to most acids and oils. Typical uses are, in liquid form, in enamels and lacquers; in solid form they are molded into TV tuning devices, light switches, fuses, motor insulation, automobile starters, and similar things.

Polypropylene This plastic has exceptional surface hardness and is abrasion resistant. It is fine for electrical insulation and can be laminated to paper, cloth, or aluminum. Typical uses are for packaging film sheets, safety helmets, pipe fittings, appliance and houseware parts, etc.

Polyesters These plastics have superior surface hardness and rigidity. Their flexibility as laminates and moldings can be varied through reinforcing material. They are highly resistant to most acids, salts, and solvents. Typical uses are in the impregnation of materials in manufacturing reinforced plastics, in translucent roofs and skylights, boats, automobile bodies, luggage, etc. (Reinforced plastics are those that are strengthened by the addition of another plastic. The process in some instances could be compared to the strengthening of concrete with steel.)

Cellulosics These are among the toughest of plastics. They will withstand moderate heat but most should not have continuous outside use. They are good insulators and will withstand below-freezing temperatures. Typical uses are for numerous packaging applications, recording tape, photographic film, fabric coatings, pipe and tubing, and tool handles.

Epoxy A highly weather and corrosion resistant plastic. Most resins have good flexibility. Typical uses are for surface protective coatings, as a bonding agent for wood, metals, glass, ceramics, and rubber, and, in combination with glass fibers, to make many reinforced plastic products.

Plastic Processing Methods*

Blow Molding A method of forming used with thermoplastic materials. It consists of stretching and then hardening a plastic against a mold. One way of doing this is where a glob of molten thermoplastic material is formed into the rough shape of the desired finished prod-

*These descriptions of the working of plastics are from information supplied by The Society of the Plastics Industry, Inc.

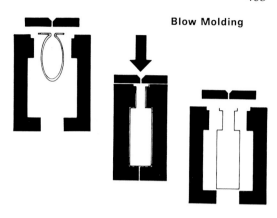

Blow Molding

uct. It is then inserted in a mold and air blown into the plastic as into a balloon, forcing the plastic against the sides of the mold. The formed material is then cooled and removed from the mold.

Calendering This is the method used to process thermoplastics into film and sheeting. *Film* refers to thicknesses up to and including 10 mils, while *sheeting* includes thicknesses over 10 mils.

In this process a plastic compound is passed between a series of three or four large, heated, revolving rollers which squeeze the material between them into a sheet or film. The thickness of the finished material is controlled by the space between the rolls.

Calendering

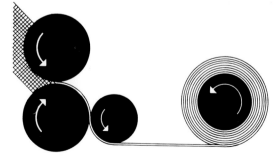

Casting

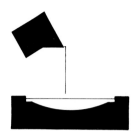

Extrusion

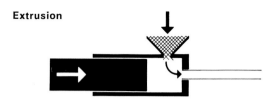

Casting This method is used for both thermoplastic and thermosetting materials in making special shapes, rigid sheets, film and sheeting, rods and tubes.

The essential difference between casting and molding is that no pressure is used in casting, as it is in molding. In casting, the material is heated to a fluid mass, poured into either open or closed molds, cured at varying temperatures depending on the plastic used, and removed from the molds.

Compression Molding This is the most common methd of forming thermosetting materials. It is not generally used for thermoplastics. Compression molding is simply the squeezing of a material into a desired shape by application of heat and pressure to the material in a mold.

Compression Molding

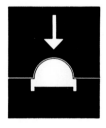

Extrusion Extrusion molding is the method employed to form thermoplastic materials into continuous sheeting, film, tubes, rods, etc. Dry plastic material is loaded into a hopper, then fed into a long heating chamber through which it is moved by the action of a continuously revolving screw. At the end of the heating chamber the molten plastic is forced out through a small opening or die with the shape desired in the finished product. As the plastic extrusion comes from the die, it is fed into a conveyer belt where it is cooled, most frequently by blowers or by immersion in water.

Fabricating Fabricating covers operations on sheet, rod, tube, sheeting, film, and special shapes to make them into finished products. The materials may be thermosetting or thermoplastic.

Fabricating is divided into three broad categories: machining; cutting, sewing, and sealing of film and sheeting; and forming.

Machining. Machining is used on rigid sheets, rods, tubes, and special shapes. The various operations include grinding, tuning on a lathe, sawing, reaming, milling, routing, drilling, and tapping.

Cutting-Sewing-Sealing of Film and Sheeting. In this category of fabricating fall all the operations involved in fashioning plastic film and sheeting into finished articles like inflatable toys, garment bags, aprons, raincoats, and luggage. For all these articles, the film or sheeting must first be cut into patterns. This cutting may be done in a press by a power-driven hand-operated knife or by other methods.

Forming. In working with thermoplastic sheets the first step is usually the cutting or blanking out of sections roughly approximating the dimensions of the finished article. This blank may be beaded for added strength, or creased and folded into final form, such as a box. Rigid sheet may be molded to final form by vacuum forming or molding. Rigid sheet may also be welded.

High-Pressure Laminating High-pressure laminating is done with thermosetting plastics. It is distinguished from the other fabricating processes by high heat and pressure. The plastics are used to hold together the reinforcing materials that comprise the body of the finished product. Reinforcing may be cloth, paper, wood, or fibers of glass. The most common use is in high-pressure decorative laminates such as Formica, Micarta, etc.

The first step in high-pressure laminating is the impregnating of the reinforcing materials with plastics. In producing flat sheets the impregnated material is stacked between two highly polished steel plates and subjected to heat and high pressure in a hydraulic press which cures the plastic and presses the plies of material into a single piece of the desired thickness. If the steel pressing plates are rough or have an embossed surface this will be transferred to the laminate. This is the means used to make the matt finish on Formica and the other decorative high-pressure laminates.

Injection Molding This is the principal method of forming thermoplastic materials. Modifications of the injection process are sometimes used also for thermosetting plastics.

In injection molding, plastic material is put into a hopper which feeds into a heating chamber. A plunger pushes the plastic through this long heating chamber where the material is softened to a fluid state. At the end of this chamber there is a nozzle which abuts firmly against an opening into a cool, closed mold. The fluid plastic is forced at high pressure through this nozzle into the cold mold. As soon as the plastic cools to a solid state, the mold opens and the finished plastic piece is ejected from the press.

High-Pressure Laminating

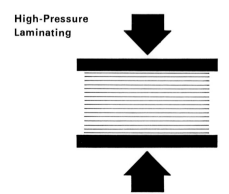

Injection Molding

Thermoforming

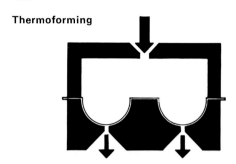

Thermoforming This process consists of heating thermoplastic sheet to a formable plastic state and then applying air and mechanical assistance to shape it to the contours of a mold.

Air pressure may range from almost zero to several hundred psi. Up to atmospheric pressure, the pressure is obtained by evacuating the space between the sheet and the mold in order to utilize this atmospheric pressure. This range is known as *vacuum forming*.

When higher pressures are required, they are obtained by sealing a chamber to the top side of the sheet and building pressure within by compressed air. The system is known as *pressure forming*.

Transfer Molding This method is generally used for thermosetting plastics. It is like compression molding in that the plastic is cured into an infusible state in a mold under heat and pressure. It differs from compression molding in that the plastic is heated to a point of plasticity before it reaches the mold and is forced into a closed mold by means of a hydraulically operated plunger.

3

ARCHITECTURAL DRAWING
THE LANGUAGE OF BUILDING

The language of building is architectural drawing. The term "plans" is loosely used to refer to all the drawings included in a set. Most building drawings are drawn to scale. For example, one-quarter of an inch to equal one foot is the usual scale used for plans, with larger scales—such as one-half of an inch up to three inches—employed for detailing.

Floor plans are drawings such as one would make if s/he were to cut a building through, horizontally, just above the windowsill level, remove the top, and draw what s/he sees looking down. This view of the building shows the arrangement of the rooms and the location of the doorways, halls, stairs, etc., and gives the thickness of the walls and partitions and the size of the various building spaces as measured horizontally. In drawing the floor plan the draftsman uses conventional indications which are fairly well established. These symbols for materials, electrical and mechanical equipment, etc., are usually listed in a legend on the title page (the first drawing in the set) which indicates what each convention is to mean.

Elevations are views of the exterior of the building or, in the case of interiors, front views of walls, etc., such as one would see standing across the room. There is no perspective used in architectural drawing. Perspectives and isometrics may be added, but these do not give building information other than clarification of the plans, elevations, and sections.

Sections show a cut through the building vertically in which the floor thicknesses and construction are noted. In interior design drawings they could be cuts through wall sections, parts of the construction such as door frames, paneling, etc.

Detail drawings are made of the parts of the construction that require additional information beyond that offered by plans and sections. Detail drawings are made at much larger scale than either plans or sections; in some instances they may be drawn full size if the joinery is complex.

The drawings we have just described are called "working drawings". They are the graphic presentation of the information required for constructing the design. They have a legal value as primary contract documents upon which the letting of the building contract will be based. All parties involved—the owner, designer, contractor, and subcontractors—will use the working drawings as their basic source of information.

The draftsman must simultaneously show all the information needed for interpretation of design, instructions for bidding, and directions for construction. Each person involved in these various functions will have somewhat different interests in the drawings and their particular requirements must be met.

The preliminary design is based upon a broad overall conception that is primarily concerned with meeting the requirements of the program given to the designer by the client. The working drawings must comply fully with the preliminary design intentions in all details.

Each detail will also influence the cost of the project. Details must therefore be analyzed and coordinated in relation to the total project. The owner may have to approve many of the decisions worked out on the working drawings which were not shown on the previous design drawings.

The working drawings are usually used to secure bids for the cost of the work. Projects are bid by a number of contractors and the job goes to the lowest bidder. The strength of the contract and the reliability of the bids depends upon the completeness of the working drawings.

Incomplete or poorly conceived working drawings cause the contractor to bid high to protect himself and then haggle over the omitted or conflicting details. This is costly to the client and very time-consuming to the designer.

The specifications that accompany the working drawings deal mainly with the quality of the materials, legal considerations of the job, insurance provisions, and various directives about the quality of the workmanship. The working drawings show the extent of the work and, through the details, the quality of the joinery that is expected. Each is a distinct and separate function. Working drawings should not be used as specifications nor can specifications take the place of drawings.

The success of the building project depends greatly upon the

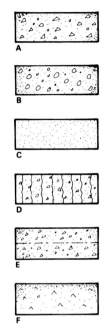

A Concrete
B Cinder concrete
C Concrete in elevation
D Concrete or cinder block
E Concrete plank
F Terazzo in section and plan

Concrete symbols vary depending upon how the concrete is used. If it is poured in place it may have the symbol of cast stone. The symbol may also vary according to the material used for aggregate.

Symbols or conventions are used to indicate the composition of the building material. While generally accepted, they vary in different offices. Therefore it is best always to check the legend (a listing of symbol meanings) on a set of drawings. Symbols for the same material may also be changed in plan and elevation, large or small scale.

It is also commonplace to indicate the material convention only on one part of the drawing, leaving the observer to infer that the entire area is the same material. For example, a masonry wall would be hatched in at the corners and around openings only.

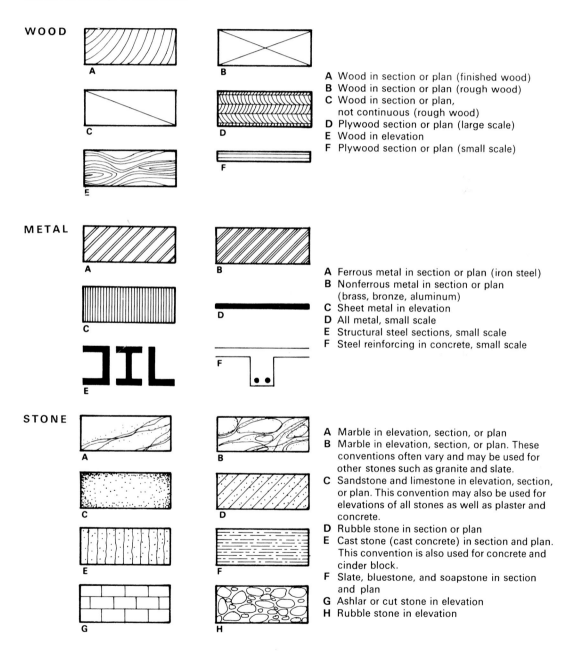

WOOD

A Wood in section or plan (finished wood)
B Wood in section or plan (rough wood)
C Wood in section or plan, not continuous (rough wood)
D Plywood section or plan (large scale)
E Wood in elevation
F Plywood section or plan (small scale)

METAL

A Ferrous metal in section or plan (iron steel)
B Nonferrous metal in section or plan (brass, bronze, aluminum)
C Sheet metal in elevation
D All metal, small scale
E Structural steel sections, small scale
F Steel reinforcing in concrete, small scale

STONE

A Marble in elevation, section, or plan
B Marble in elevation, section, or plan. These conventions often vary and may be used for other stones such as granite and slate.
C Sandstone and limestone in elevation, section, or plan. This convention may also be used for elevations of all stones as well as plaster and concrete.
D Rubble stone in section or plan
E Cast stone (cast concrete) in section and plan. This convention is also used for concrete and cinder block.
F Slate, bluestone, and soapstone in section and plan
G Ashlar or cut stone in elevation
H Rubble stone in elevation

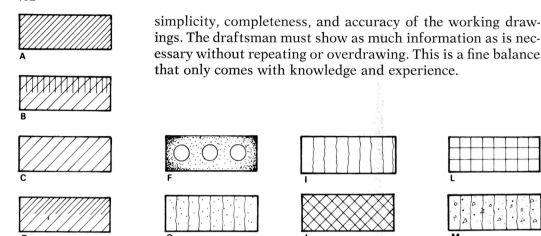

simplicity, completeness, and accuracy of the working drawings. The draftsman must show as much information as is necessary without repeating or overdrawing. This is a fine balance that only comes with knowledge and experience.

MASONRY

Because of the wide variety of materials used in masonry construction, ranging from natural stone to manmade brick and cast units, there are a great number of conventions employed. Conventions overlap—that is, the same convention may be used to indicate several materials. They are also combined—as when a wall is built of two or more masonry materials. For example, the face of the wall might be face brick or architectural terra cotta with a backing of common brick, structural clay tile, or concrete block. This composite wall construction might be shown combined in one convention.

A   Face brick in section and plan
B   Fire brick on common brick in section and plan
C   Common brick
D   Face brick on common brick
E   Brick elevation

F   Gypsum, or plaster block, in section and plan
G   Architectural terra cotta in section and plan. "Architectural terra cotta' 'is the term used for the finished or decorative terra cotta blocks and specially modeled terra cotta masonry units.
H   Architectural terra cotta on brick
I   Structural clay tile in section and plan. Structural clay tile and terra cotta tile are the same thing. This convention is also used for ceramic tile.
J   Structural clay tile in section and plan. This convention and the one used at (I) signal the same material. Sometimes (J) is used in large scale and (I) in small
K   Structural clay tile in elevation
L   Ceramic tile in elevation
M   Concrete block in section and plan
N   Face brick on concrete block in section and plan

Illustrated on following pages:
Drawings for a Maine summer home by architect Earl Flansburgh. Foundations are of poured-in-place concrete. The house is wood frame with cantilevers beyond the foundations of laminated wood girders. The exterior is finished with vertical rough sawn pine.

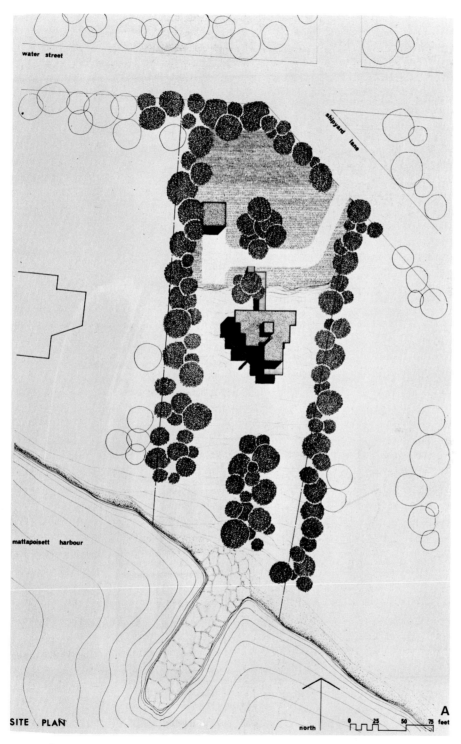

water street

shipyard lane

mattapoisett harbour

SITE PLAN

north

0 25 50 75 feet

A

A Site Plan

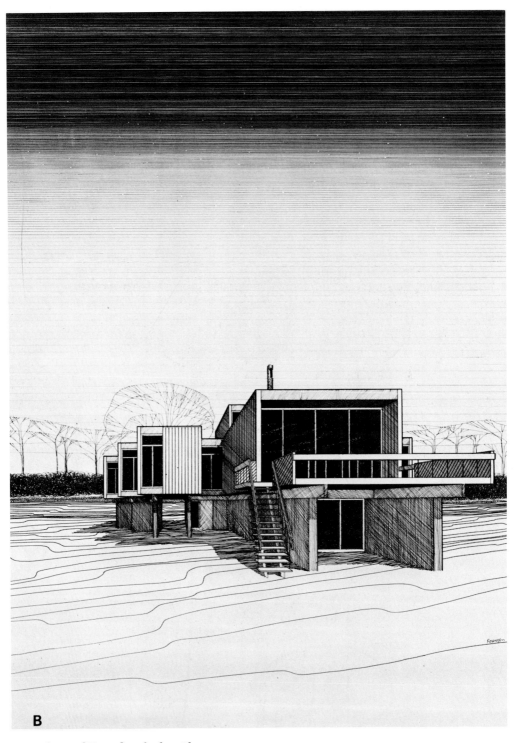

B   Rendering of House from harbor side

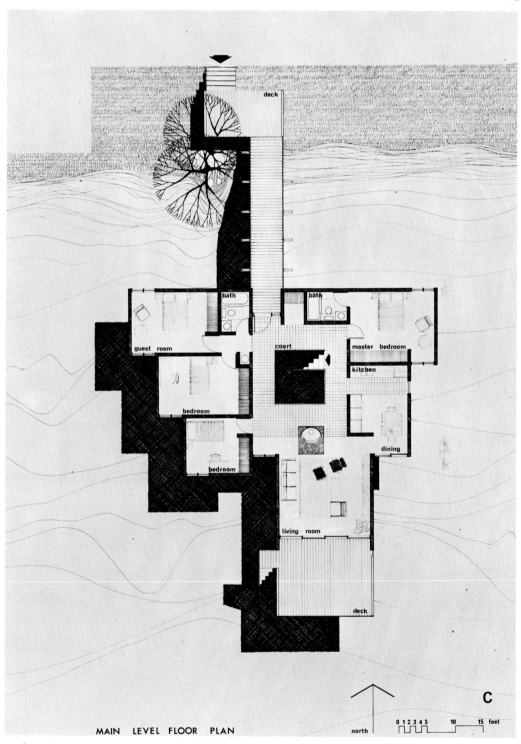

deck

bath bath

guest room

court

master bedroom

kitchen

bedroom

bedroom

dining

living room

deck

MAIN LEVEL FLOOR PLAN

north

0 1 2 3 4 5   10   15 feet

C

C Floor Plan

416

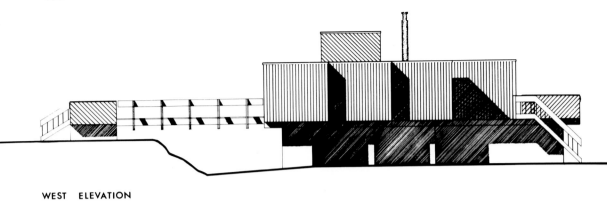

WEST ELEVATION

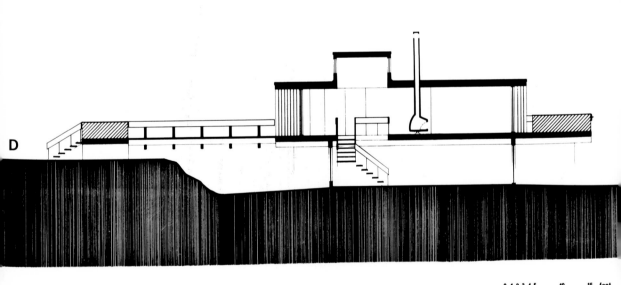

D

SECTION

0 1 2 3 4 5   10   15 feet

D Elevation and Section

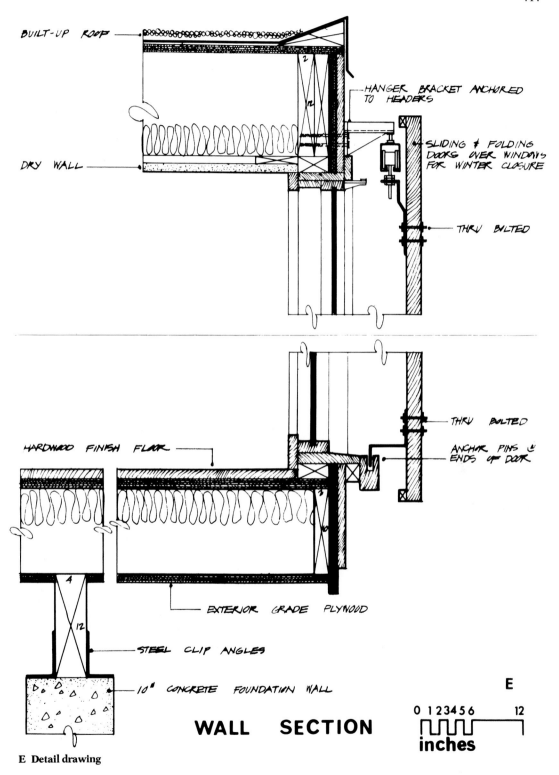

BUILT-UP ROOF

HANGER BRACKET ANCHORED TO HEADERS

DRY WALL

SLIDING & FOLDING DOORS OVER WINDOWS FOR WINTER CLOSURE

THRU BOLTED

THRU BOLTED

HARDWOOD FINISH FLOOR

ANCHOR PINS @ ENDS OF DOOR

EXTERIOR GRADE PLYWOOD

STEEL CLIP ANGLES

10" CONCRETE FOUNDATION WALL

E

WALL SECTION

0 1 2 3 4 5 6   12

inches

E Detail drawing

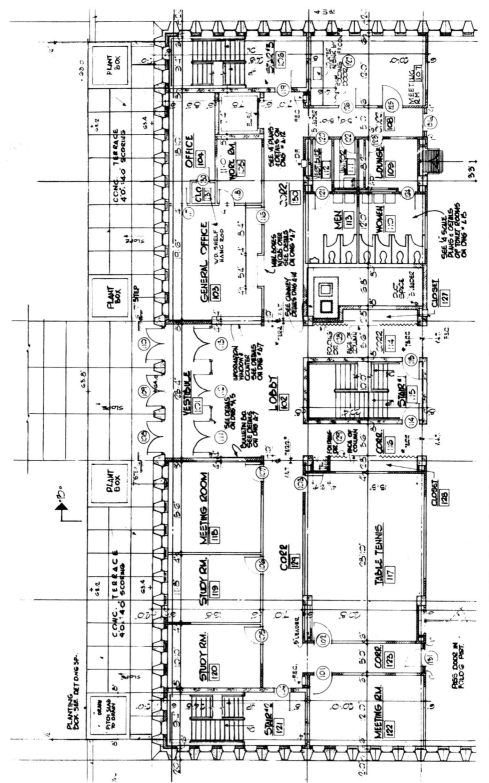

Working drawings for Rutgers Building by Frank Grad and Sons. Excellent examples of working drawings by a major architectural firm. Note how clearly all dimensions are shown, and how finely the details are drawn.

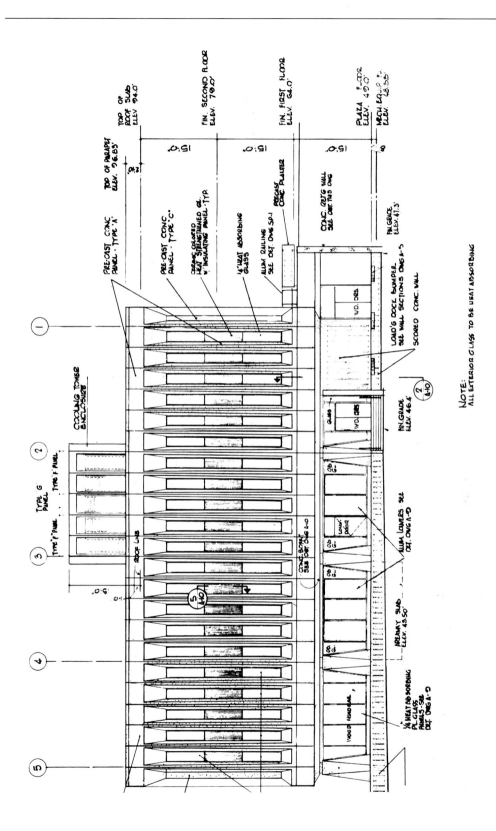

NORTH ELEVATION

NOTE:
ALL EXTERIOR GLASS TO BE HEAT ABSORBING

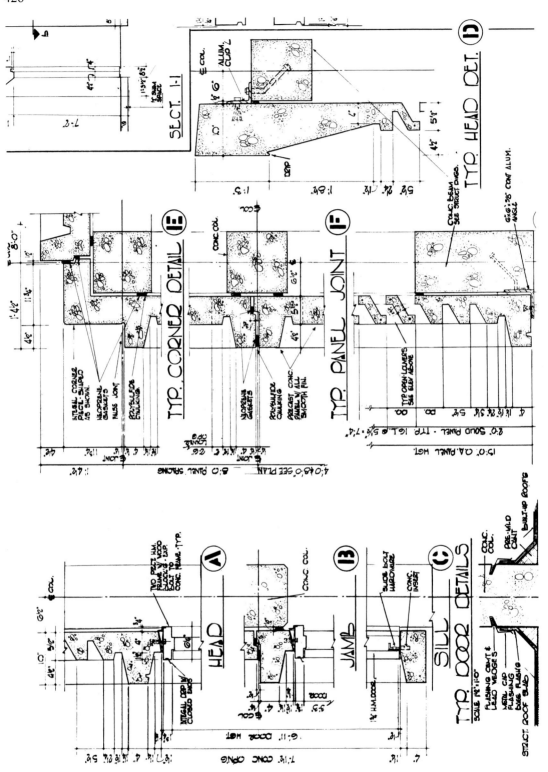

SECT. 1-1

TYP. HEAD DET. D

TYP. CORNER DETAIL E

TYP. PANEL JOINT F

HEAD A

JAMB B

SILL C

TYP. DOOR DETAILS
SCALE 1½"=1'-0"

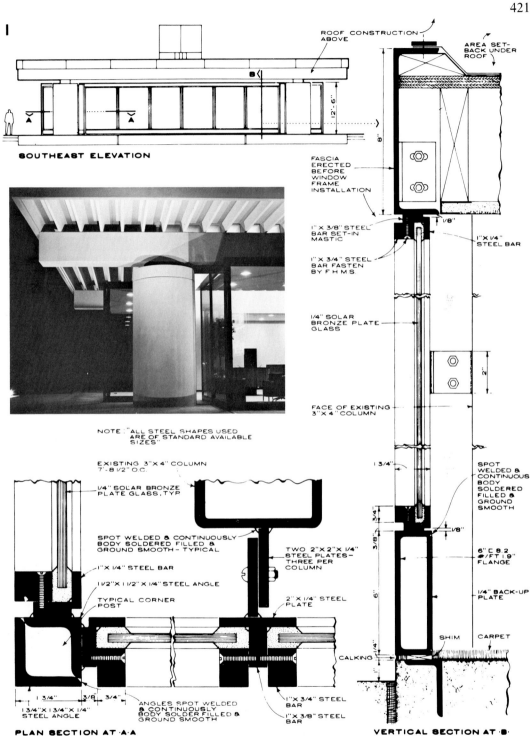

SOUTHEAST ELEVATION

ROOF CONSTRUCTION
ABOVE

AREA SET-
BACK UNDER
ROOF

12'-6"

8"

FASCIA
ERECTED
BEFORE
WINDOW
FRAME
INSTALLATION

I" X 3/8" STEEL
BAR SET-IN
MASTIC

I" X 3/4" STEEL
BAR FASTEN
BY F H M S.

1/4" SOLAR
BRONZE PLATE
GLASS

FACE OF EXISTING
3" X 4" COLUMN

1/8"

1" X 1/4"
STEEL BAR

2"

1 3/4"

SPOT
WELDED &
CONTINUOUS
BODY
SOLDERED
FILLED &
GROUND
SMOOTH

3/4"

3/8"

6"

1/4"

1/8"

6" C 8.2
#/FT 19"
FLANGE

1/4" BACK-UP
PLATE

SHIM   CARPET

CALKING

VERTICAL SECTION AT ·B·

NOTE : "ALL STEEL SHAPES USED
ARE OF STANDARD AVAILABLE
SIZES"

EXISTING 3" X 4" COLUMN
7'-8 1/2" O.C.

1/4" SOLAR BRONZE
PLATE GLASS, TYP.

SPOT WELDED & CONTINUOUSLY
BODY SOLDERED FILLED &
GROUND SMOOTH- TYPICAL

I" X 1/4" STEEL BAR

I 1/2"X I I/2" X 1/4" STEEL ANGLE

TYPICAL CORNER
POST

TWO 2"X 2"X 1/4"
STEEL PLATES-
THREE PER
COLUMN

2" X 1/4" STEEL
PLATE

1 3/4"   3/8"   3/4"

1 3/4"X I 3/4"X 1/4"
STEEL ANGLE

ANGLES SPOT WELDED
& CONTINUOUSLY
BODY SOLDER FILLED &
GROUND SMOOTH

I" X 3/4" STEEL
BAR

I" X 3/8" STEEL
BAR

PLAN SECTION AT ·A·A

Detail Drawings. Three examples of detail drawings done by a very fine architectural detailer,
Nicholas R. Loscalzo, Chief Draftsman for Progressive Architecture.

I Detail of steel curtain wall composed of standard steel sections designed by architect
Don Hisaka for a small bank building.

J

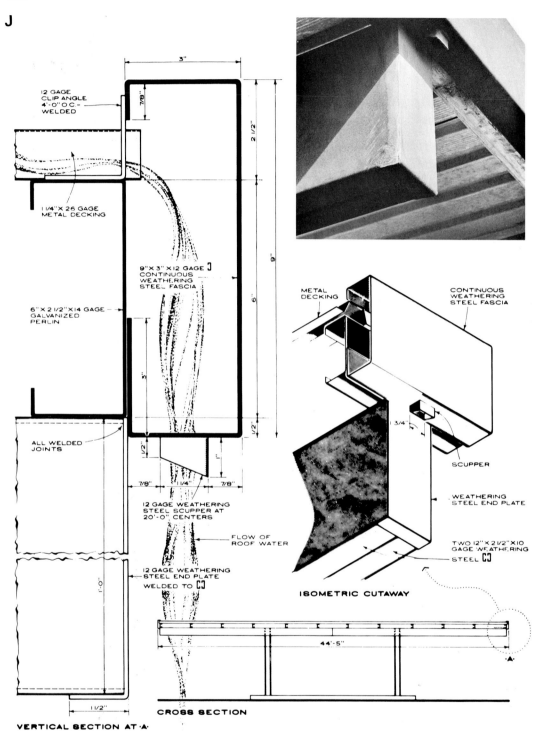

12 GAGE
CLIP ANGLE
4'-0" O C -
WELDED

3"

7/8"

2 1/2"

1 1/4" X 26 GAGE
METAL DECKING

9'

9" X 3" X 12 GAGE ⅃
CONTINUOUS
WEATHERING
STEEL FASCIA

6"

6" X 2 1/2" X 14 GAGE
GALVANIZED
PERLIN

3"

ALL WELDED
JOINTS

1/2"

1/2"

1"

7/8"   1 1/4"   7/8"

12 GAGE WEATHERING
STEEL SCUPPER AT
20'-0" CENTERS

FLOW OF
ROOF WATER

12 GAGE WEATHERING
STEEL END PLATE
WELDED TO ⅃⅃

1'-0"

1 1/2"

VERTICAL SECTION AT ·A·

METAL
DECKING

CONTINUOUS
WEATHERING
STEEL FASCIA

1 3/4"

SCUPPER

WEATHERING
STEEL END PLATE

TWO 12" X 2 1/2" X 10
GAGE WEATHERING
STEEL ⅃⅃

ISOMETRIC CUTAWAY

44'-5"

·A·

CROSS SECTION

J Detail of drain through the facia of a parking structure of weathering steel by Todd, Tackett, and Lacey, architects.

K

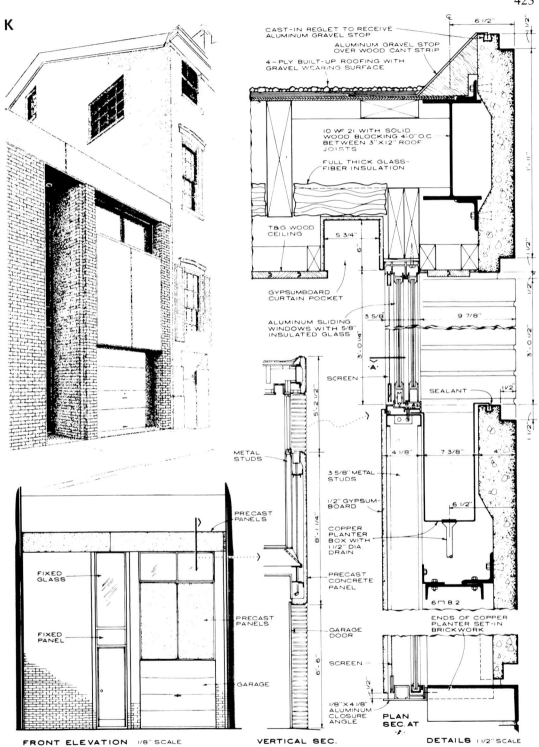

CAST-IN REGLET TO RECEIVE
ALUMINUM GRAVEL STOP

ALUMINUM GRAVEL STOP
OVER WOOD CANT STRIP

4 - PLY BUILT-UP ROOFING WITH
GRAVEL WEARING SURFACE

6 1/2"

IO WF 21 WITH SOLID
WOOD BLOCKING 4'-0" O.C.
BETWEEN 3"X12" ROOF
JOISTS

FULL THICK GLASS-
FIBER INSULATION

1'-11"

T&G WOOD
CEILING

5 3/4"

6"

1/2"

GYPSUMBOARD
CURTAIN POCKET

ALUMINUM SLIDING
WINDOWS WITH 5/8"
INSULATED GLASS

3 5/8"

9 7/8"

3'-0 1/4"

3'-0 1/2"

·A·

SCREEN

SEALANT

1 1/2"

1 1/2"

METAL
STUDS

4 1/8"

7 3/8"

4"

3 5/8" METAL
STUDS

1/2" GYPSUM-
BOARD

6 1/2"

COPPER
PLANTER
BOX WITH
1 1/2" DIA
DRAIN

5'-2 1/2"

8'-11/4"

PRECAST
PANELS

PRECAST
CONCRETE
PANEL

6 ⊓ 8.2

FIXED
GLASS

PRECAST
PANELS

FIXED
PANEL

PRECAST
PANELS

GARAGE
DOOR

ENDS OF COPPER
PLANTER SET-IN
BRICKWORK

GARAGE

6'-6"

SCREEN

1/2"

1/8"X 4 1/8"
ALUMINUM
CLOSURE
ANGLE

PLAN
SEC. AT
·A·

FRONT ELEVATION 1/8" SCALE

VERTICAL SEC.

DETAILS 1 1/2" SCALE

K Detail of precast concrete facia and window for a New York City residence designed by Helmut Jacoby.

4

INTERIOR ENVIRONMENT THE MECHANICAL SYSTEM OF BUILDING

The mechanical system is the engine of the building. It is quite distinct from the architecture of the building and is often in conflict with it. Part of the reason for this is that the tradition of building has been with us since the dawn of time, while we have only been putting mechanical equipment in buildings, to any large extent, for less than half a century. As a consequence the plumbing, heating and ventilating, and electrical wiring that comprise the engine of the building have to fit into a framework that in most instances has not changed since man depended on fireplaces for heat, drew water from wells, and read by candlelight. It is the coordinating of the structural system and the mechanical system of the building which causes the interior designer the most difficulty in realizing the construction of his design.

The cost of architectural and mechanical components of the modern building are about equal. This has not always been the case. Beginning at a fraction of building cost at the turn of the century, mechanical systems have rapidly assumed more and more importance in buildings until today, in some building types, they outweigh architectural costs and are continuing to increase in expense and sophistication.

In most instances the interior designer reaps the harvest of confusion sown by uncoordinated architectural and mechanical design. He is also often faced with the difficulty of adapting mechanical systems to existing buildings built long before such systems were even dreamed of. Our skylines with water towers, exhaust ducts snaking up the sides of buildings, and intake grills perforating classic façades are adequate testimony to the dominance of mechanical systems over architectural form.

Following is a brief introduction and description of the basic elements of mechanical systems for buildings.

Mechanical drawings differ from architectural ones in that they are drawn schematically, that is, one line indicating a pipe and a symbol illustrating the placement of units of mechanical equipment rather than scale-drawn pictures of the actual objects themselves. The interior designer has to check these drawings against the architectural drawings to see that the mechanical system does not conflict with the design.

Mechanical equipment travels either vertically or horizontally through a building. Vertical travel is usually provided by pipe chases and duct shafts, while horizontal openings are provided by piping and conduit placed in the floor, or hung beneath and concealed by hung ceilings.

Flooring systems must be considered carefully for their ability to house conduit for electrical and telephone systems, and the fixture branches of small piping to and from the plumbing fixtures. They are usually inadequate for concealing

Symbols used in plumbing drawings
The piping sizes vary. Sizes are usually marked on the drawing next to the line indicating the piping.

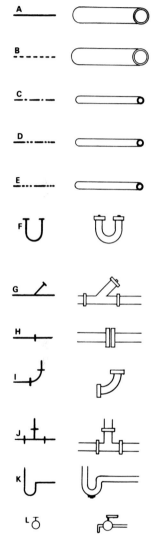

Plumbing fixtures in plan

These have been taken from a manufacturer's template.

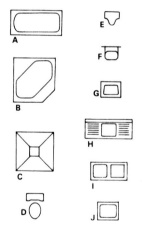

A	Bathtub
B	Corner bathtub
C	Shower
D	Toilet
E	Urinal
F	Drinking fountain
G	Wash basin
H	Sink and drainboard
I	Double sink
J	Janitor's sink

Plumbing fixture symbols in elevation

These are geometric representations of fixtures selected by the draftsman. They should be identified on the drawing or in the legend.

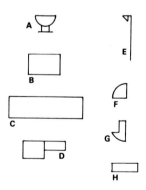

A	Toilet
B	Bathtub (short dimension)
C	Bathtub (long dimension)
D	Basin and laundry sink
E	Shower
F	Drinking fountain
G	Urinal
H	Wash basin

A	Drainage	**G**	Clean out
B	Vent		
C	Cold water	**H**	Joint
D	Hot water	**I**	Elbow
E	Hot water return	**J**	Tee
F	Trap	**K**	Trap
		L	Valve

The function of the water supply system is to get fresh water into the building and the function of the drainage system is to convey the waterborne wastes out of the building.

The water supply system operates from pressure, either the pressure in the street main or gravity pressure from tanks on the roof or pumps. The drainage system depends upon gravity.

Essentials of a water system supplying a residence from the water pressure in the street (upfeed system)

A   Water main
B   Curb box (valve for turning off water outside the house)
C   Water meter
D   Main
E   Riser
F   Valve
G   Fixture

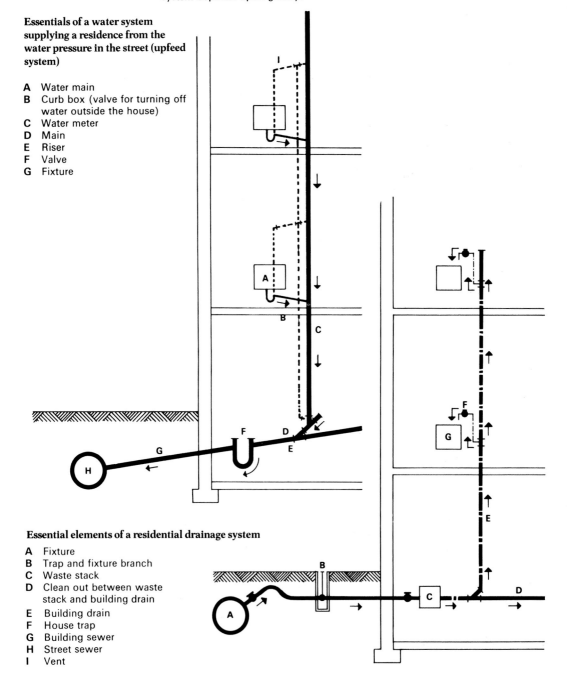

Essential elements of a residential drainage system

A   Fixture
B   Trap and fixture branch
C   Waste stack
D   Clean out between waste stack and building drain
E   Building drain
F   House trap
G   Building sewer
H   Street sewer
I   Vent

air conditioning ducts unless the floor is specially designed, with duct spaces provided for in its thickness.

Walls are sometimes used to conceal mechanical supply lines. They are almost always used to house electrical and telephone conduit since these are small, but double or specially designed walls are required to accommodate the large piping and duct work required of plumbing and air conditioning.

An essential consideration for the interior designer in the design of his interior is access to those parts of the mechanical system that have to be adjusted or repaired. For this purpose access doors must be provided in ceilings, through closets, or by whatever other means the designer's ingenuity can devise.

Water Systems

Water provided for buildings can be divided into two uses; that for human use—drinking, bathing, cooking, washing, etc. —and that for mechanical systems and fire protection of the building.

The architect and engineer provide in the design of the building for the correct quantities of water for the building. The

A Street main
B Curb box
C Water meter (valves before and after meter permit meter servicing)
D Main
E Risers (hot and cold water and hot water return)
F Valves (valves at the bottom of water lines are called "drips" and are used for draining the line)
G Fixtures
H Water conditioning. Valves permit by-passing conditioner.
I Hot water heater
J Hot water storage tank. Note that the hot water is a return two-pipe system.

Complete water supply system for a residence, including hot water system

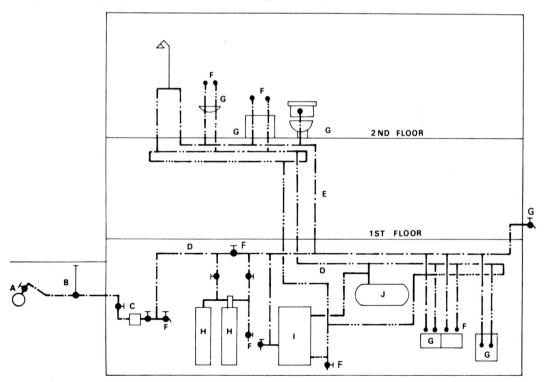

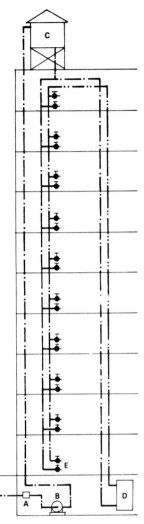

interior designer is concerned when he specifies fixtures or systems other than those already specified for the water system. He must then confirm the amount of water they will use and the connecting piping.

It is usually assumed, except for special areas such as the basement and mechanical rooms or for special conditions, that the piping will be concealed. The quality and kind of piping and controls will be specified by the building designer. The interior designer's responsibility is coordination of the fixtures he selects with the existing system.

A good system utilizes many valves, clean-outs, and other equipment that must have access for maintenance. These positions are specified by the engineer and the interior designer must coordinate his work to provide for them.

Water is received from city mains at street level at about fifty pounds pressure. Pressure diminishes at upper stories. The various fixtures require certain pressures for operation ranging from five to twenty-five pounds.

When pressures are insufficient to maintain adequate individual fixture service, water is pumped to wooden or steel elevated tanks for gravity downfeed. The lower part of the tank is often used as a reserve system for fire use.

Hot Water

Water expands and becomes lighter when heated. Hot water supply systems therefore usually consist of a heater with storage tank, piping to carry the heated water to the farthest fixture, and a continuation of this piping to return the unused

Simplified water supply system for a ten-story building (downfeed system). Water comes from the street main, passes through meter **A**, goes to pump **B**, is pumped to tank on roof **C**, drops down from roof tank to heater in basement **D**, or to cold-water system **E**. Water is heated and rises to fill hot-water line.

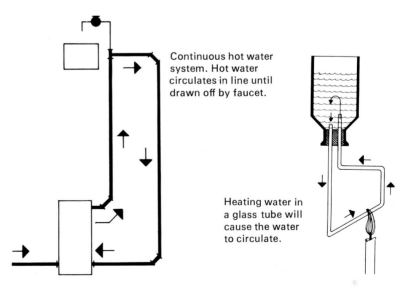

Continuous hot water system. Hot water circulates in line until drawn off by faucet.

Heating water in a glass tube will cause the water to circulate.

water back to the heater. A constant circulation is thereby maintained; and hot water may be drawn at once from a fixture without first draining off, through the faucet, the cooled water which may be standing in the supply pipe.

The parts of a water supply system can best be understood by looking at a drawing. These systems may be more or less complicated. The drawing on the preceding page shows the various parts of a typical residential system combining water supply and hot water systems.

Sanitary Drainage

Building occupancy results in the accumulation of fluid waste and organic matter liable to rapid decomposition. It is the function of the plumbing system to dispose of these wastes as quickly as possible.

Piping conducts the wastes from the plumbing fixture to the sewer. Gases of decomposition are generated in these pipes or may penetrate into them from the public sewer. It is necessary to form a seal against the passage of gases into the fixtures and through them into the living spaces. To accomplish this, a trap is connected close to the fixture and leading into the drain

A House sewer
B House drain
C House trap
D Fresh air inlet. This admits fresh air to the drainage system to provide free air circulation and to eliminate air compression.
E Soil stack. Soil stacks carry human waste. Waste stacks do not.
F Fixture branches
G Traps. These hold water to form a seal against the entry into the living quarters of offensive sewer gases. Traps must always be vented to prevent their being emptied by siphoning.
H Vents
I Leaders. These drain water from roof. They are connected directly to the house drain.
J Drains
K Clean outs

Complete house drainage system

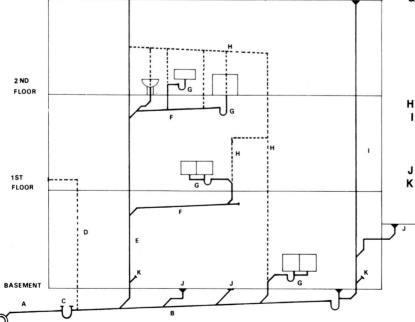

pipe. This trap catches and holds water from each discharge, forming a water seal through which the gases cannot pass.

Fixtures are connected in fixture branches horizontally and feed into the waste and soil stacks, then pass into the house drain in the basement, from there into the house sewer, and on into the public sewer.

The entire system must be vented for a variety of reasons. Traps are vented to break the suction which would empty them of water; and the stacks and house drain are vented to relieve pressures, to prevent suction, and to circulate air within the system in order to reduce corrosion within the pipes.

The essential parts of a sanitary drainage system are shown in the accompanying drawing.

Hot water passed through coils set in floors or ceilings, warming them through radiation. This is termed "radiant panel heating." The temperature of the water is lower than that used in radiators since more heat would crack the plaster. Electric power is also used for this type of heating. Steam is not, since it is too hot.

The system consists of a heating unit and coils. In most installations a series of coils is used which are serviced by supply and return headers (piping which brings the hot water from the heater to the coils and returns it to be reheated).

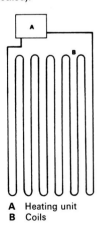

A Heating unit
B Coils

Heating

Heating systems may be classified in a number of ways: by fuel, by heat-producing equipment, or by various heating media. The choice of a particular heating system depends upon the climate, the available fuel and desired comfort level, and, of course, the cost.

The first step in the design of a heating system is to determine the heat losses the building will sustain from its construction and external conditions. The heating system must replace these losses and maintain an even, comfortable temperature within the heated spaces.

The function of the heating system is to heat the medium used—water, air, steam—and transport it to the heating element or the space in which it is to be used. For example, hot water is heated; travels through pipes to the rooms where it gives off its heat in the radiator; then after it has cooled, returns to the boiler to be reheated. Steam acts in the same way. The water is heated until it changes into steam, travels through pipes to the radiator, gives off its heat, turns back into water, and flows back to repeat the cycle. Hot air systems heat the air, which is ducted to the various rooms, gives off its heat, and returns either through gravity (hot air rises, cold air falls) or through ducts to be reheated and reused.

There are other methods of heating—for example, electricity and combinations of methods, such as heating coils with hot water and blowing air over them with a fan. However, the theory remains the same: there must be a heating source and a way of transporting the heat to the area where it is desired. The heat must replace the heat losses of the building and maintain a constant comfortable temperature. Various heating systems have specialized equipment. The designer makes his choice in relation to the needs with the assistance, usually, of a heating engineer.

The following drawings illustrate the various essentials of several heating systems.

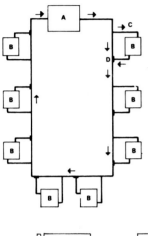

Hot-water heating system using one pipe and special fitting. Hot water is heated at **A** and travels through a main circuit of piping. It goes from the main piping to the fixture at **C** through the fixture **B** and back into the main piping at **D**. A specially designed "T" fitting allows the hot water to be carried in the main line and diverted to the fixtures.

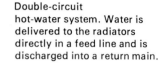
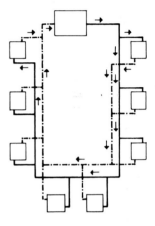

Double-circuit hot-water system. Water is delivered to the radiators directly in a feed line and is discharged into a return main.

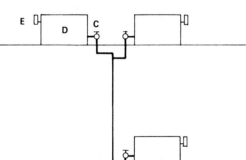

One-pipe steam heating system

A Furnace and boiler where water is heated until it changes to steam.

B Riser and return pipe. Steam rises to radiator, gives off its heat and changes back to water. The steam rises up the pipe while the water drops down in the same pipe.

C Valve at radiator

D Radiator

E Vent to let air out of the radiator. Orifice in vent is too small to allow the steam to escape.

F Water returning from radiators flows by gravity back into the boiler.

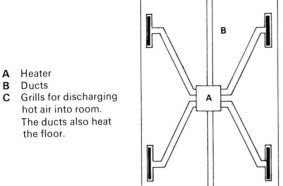

A   Heater
B   Ducts
C   Grills for discharging
    hot air into room.
    The ducts also heat
    the floor.

Plans for hot air heating through concrete slab floor

Section detail of duct
in concrete slab at grill

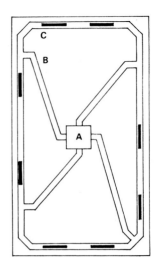

Furnace for hot air heating.

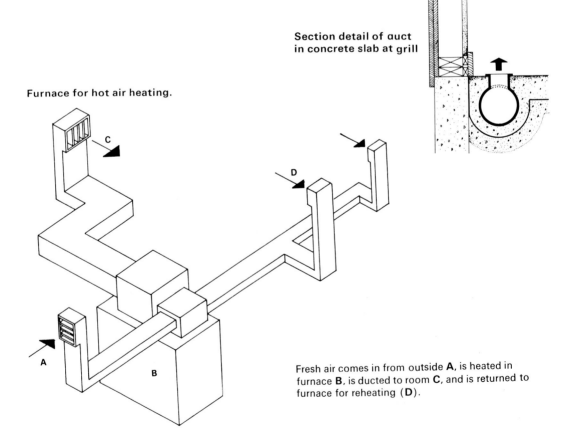

Fresh air comes in from outside **A**, is heated in
furnace **B**, is ducted to room **C**, and is returned to
furnace for reheating (**D**).

Air-Conditioning

Air conditioning or environmental conditioning is usually an integral part of modern architecture. It promotes human health and comfort, and is essential for some manufacturing processes. Modern buildings with fixed sash are uninhabitable without interior environmental control.

Air conditioning in its full meaning is a system of complete all-year climate control. It is not just summer cooling. It performs the function of heating and cooling, humidifying and dehumidifying, cleaning and circulation of air. There is a proportion between air temperature, relative humidity, and air motion most favorable to human comfort. Therefore the regulation of the following items may be regarded as essential: temperature of the air surrounding the occupant of the room space, temperature of the surrounding surfaces, relative humidity of the air, air motion, and the cleansing of the air from dirt and odors.

There are a number of methods of conditioning air. Some only blow the air around or bring in fresh outside air and therefore merely employ ventilating devices. Others are only for summer use to cool and dehumidify the air. More elaborate systems fully condition the air for year-round comfort.

Small air conditioning units are for summer cooling only, although the fans in them may be used to circulate air at any time. They are installed in window or wall openings and are

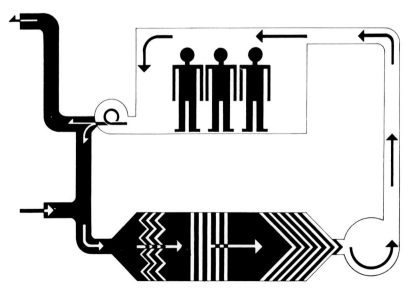

A total air-conditioning central system brings air in from the outside; cleans, heats, or cools; adds or removes humidity; and delivers the air to the building. Used air is partially exhausted to the outside and partially reused. It is returned to the conditioning system to be combined with outside air to repeat the cycle.

usually of less than one-ton capacity. They take up no floor space and no plumbing connections are necessary. These units may be easily moved from room to room and are the cheapest way to air condition. The units give an uneven drafty cooling effect and are often noisy.

Free-standing air-conditioning units are made in capacities of one to five tons, usually in complete package cabinets. They are easily installed but require water and drainage connections as well as adequate electrical connections. Ducts are sometimes used with this type of installation to better serve a small complete building or specific areas within a building.

Central systems are used for large projects. The conditioned air is distributed throughout the building to individual areas. If properly designed and properly constructed, this is the most efficient system providing positive air distribution and individual room control. In the most expensive systems the air is distributed at high velocity through pipes, mixed, and discharged into the room. Large ducts are required for a complete system with complicated air-moving equipment.

Ductwork symbols

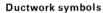

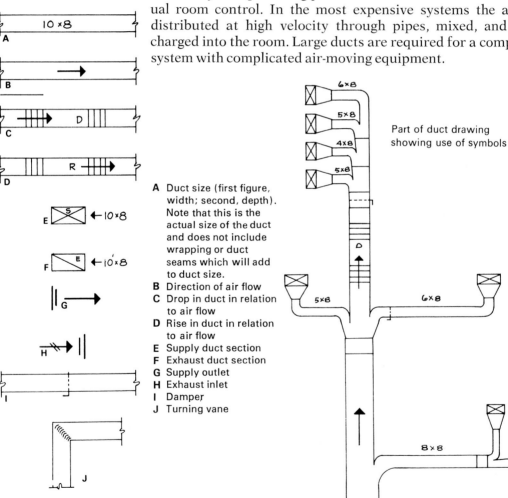

Part of duct drawing showing use of symbols

A Duct size (first figure, width; second, depth). Note that this is the actual size of the duct and does not include wrapping or duct seams which will add to duct size.
B Direction of air flow
C Drop in duct in relation to air flow
D Rise in duct in relation to air flow
E Supply duct section
F Exhaust duct section
G Supply outlet
H Exhaust inlet
I Damper
J Turning vane

Air Conditioning and Heating Terms

Air, Ambient The air surrounding an object.

Air Changes A method of expressing the amount of air moving into or out of a building or room in terms of the amount of air in the space volumes exchanged.

Air Circulation Air movement.

Air Cleaner A device for the purpose of removing airborne impurities, such as dusts, gases, vapors, fumes, and smokes. This is accomplished by washing, filtering, or electrostatic precipitators.

Air Conditioner, Room A unit designed for independent installation in a space without ducts. It may be mounted in a window or through a wall.

Air Conditioner, Unitary One or more factory-made assemblies which include cooling and may also include a heating function; the separate assemblies are designed to be used together.

Air Conditioning The process of treating air so as to control simultaneously its temperature, humidity, cleanliness, and distribution.

Air Cooling Reduction in air temperature due to the abstraction of heat.

Air Diffuser An air-distribution outlet to discharge air-conditioned air.

Air Washer Device for cleaning, humidifying, or dehumidifying the air.

Blow (throw) A term used to describe the distance an airstream travels from an outlet.

British Thermal Unit (BTU) Approximately, the heat required to raise the temperature of a pound of water from 59 degrees F to 60 degrees F.

Calorie Heat required to raise the temperature of one gram of water one degree C.

Ceiling Outlet An air diffuser located in the ceiling.

Centigrade A thermometric scale in which the freezing point of water is called 0 degrees and its boiling point 100 degrees at normal atmospheric pressure. Indicated with a C (see *Calorie*).

Change of Air Introduction of new, recirculated or cleansed, air to conditioned space.

Coil A cooling or heating element made of pipe or tubing.

Comfort Zone The range of effective temperatures over which the majority of adults feel comfortable.

Condensate The liquid formed by condensation of a vapor. In steam heating, water condensed from steam; in air conditioning, water extracted from air, as a condensation on the outside of a cold beer glass on a hot day.

Conductance Transfer of heat through a material.

Control Any device for regulation of air-conditioning equipment.

Convection Transfer of heat by movement of fluid or air.

Convector An agency of convection; a surface designed to transfer heat through air or liquid movement.

Damper A device used to vary the volume of air passing through an air outlet, inlet, or duct.

Dehumidify To reduce by any process the quantity of water vapor within a given space.

Duct A passageway made of sheet metal or other suitable material, used for conveying air.

Dust Air suspension of solid particles as differentiated from smoke.

Evaporation Change of state from liquid to vapor.

Exhaust Opening Any opening through which air is removed from a space being heated or cooled, humidified, dehumidified, or ventilated.

Exhauster A fan used to withdraw air under suction.

Fahrenheit A thermometric scale in which 32 degrees denotes freezing and 212 degrees, the boiling point of water under normal pressure at sea level. Usually indicated by F.

Filter A device to remove solid material from air or fluid.

Flammability A material's ability to burn.

Fumes Vaporous exhalation, usually odorous.

Grille A louvred or perforated covering for an air-passage opening.

Heat The form of energy that is transferred by virtue of a temperature difference.

Humidifier A device to add moisture to the air.

Infiltration Air flowing inward as through a wall, crack, etc.

Insulation, Sound Accoustical treatment of parts of the mechanical system and equipment to isolate vibration or reduce transmission of noise.

Insulation, Thermal A material having a high resistance to heat flow; used to retard the flow of heat.

Pneumatic Operated by air pressure.

Plenum Chamber An air compartment connected to one or more distributing ducts.

Preheating In air conditioning the heating of the air in advance of other processes.

Radiation The transmission of heat by direct waves.

Refrigerant A substance which produces a refrigerating effect.

Register A combination grille and damper assembly covering an air opening.

Resistance The reciprocal of thermal conductance.

Steam Water in the vapor phase.

Temperature The tendency to communicate heat. If no heat flows upon contact of two materials there is no difference of temperature between them.

Thermometer An instrument for measuring temperature.

Thermostat An instrument that responds to changes in temperature and controls temperature.

Ton, Unit of Refrigeration A ton of refrigeration is the cooling effect obtained when one ton of ice at 32 degrees F melts to water at 32 degrees F in 24 hours. The cooling effect or rate of one ton of refrigeration (2000 lbs.) is taken as 288,000 BTU per day of 24 hours or 12,000 BTUH (BTUH is BTU per hour). The required capacity of a refrigerating machine in tons may therefore be found by dividing the total heat gain in a building in BTUH by 12,000.

Ventilation The process of supplying or removing air by natural or mechanical means, to or from any space.

Water Cooling Tower An enclosure for evaporating cooling water by contact with air.

Electricity

Electrical energy furnishes power, heat, and light and ope-rates a multitude of appliances and services in the building interior. In order to accomplish this, a current of electricity must flow around an electric circuit. The exact nature of electricity is not known, but the flow of it through an elec-trical circuit is analogous to the flow of water through a system of pipes. The flow of water can be measured in gallons. The flow of electricity is measured in amperes. Amperage indi-cates the quantity of electricity flowing through an electrical appliance.

When a current of water flows from one point to another in a pipe it is because it is pushed by a hydraulic pressure. Similarly, when a current of electricity flows from one point to another in an electric circuit it is because there is an elec-tric pressure present which causes it to flow. This pressure is measured in volts. The pressure that causes one-half ampere current to flow though an incandescent lamp is usually 115 volts.

The electric company installs wires to a building and then maintains an electric pressure of 115 volts between them just as the water company maintains a pressure in the water pipes. This electric pressure tends to force electricity from one wire to the other across the space between the two. The rubber wire insulation prevents this flow. But when one terminal of a lamp is connected to one wire and the other terminal to the other wire, the electric pressure sends a current through the lamp and causes it to glow.

The wire bringing the current to the lamp is marked with a + and the wire taking the current away is marked with a −. No current can flow unless a path is afforded between the two wires. An open switch interrupts the flow of current.

The power required to keep a current of electricity flowing is the product of the current in amperes multiplied by the pressure in volts, with the result given in watts. The term "watt" is merely a unit of power, and denotes the power used when one volt causes one ampere of current to flow. The watts consumed when any given current flows under any pressure can always be found by multiplying the current in amperes by the pressure in volts. Thus if an incandescent lamp takes one-half an ampere when burning in a 110-volt line, the power consumed equals one-half times 110, or 55 watts.

Incandescent lamps are rated as to the voltage of the line on which they can run and also as to the amount of power it takes to keep them glowing.

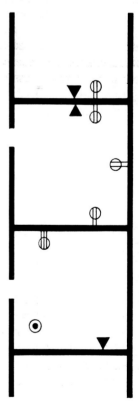

Plan showing electrical and telephone outlets

Electricity is sold on the basis of the amount of power consumed and the amount of time it is used. It is usually measured in kilowatt (1000 watt) hours.

Electric current always heats the material through which it passes. You have probably experienced this with a hot electric light bulb. It is necessary in a major installation that is air conditioned to take this heat into consideration and provide cooling to counteract it in the summer. Some systems have been using the heat from lighting to augment the required heat load of the building during the cold seasons.

The amount of current a wire will safely carry depends upon the gauge or size. The wire that comes into the building is of much heavier gauge than the wire that runs from the panel box to the individual circuits. In large buildings, large pieces of copper called "busducts" measuring one-quarter of an inch thick and one inch wide or larger—are used instead of wires.

Fuses and circuit breakers are used to disconnect the line when it becomes too hot due to too much current. This prevents the wires from igniting flammable parts of the building.

The decisions as to wire sizes and amount of current that will come into the building are determined by the architect and electrical engineers. However, the interior designer must estimate the amount of power he will need and coordinate it with the existing facilities.

Fixtures must be placed in circuits. A safe circuit capacity on a 110-120 volt line is usually about 1200 watts. Stoves, machines, and appliances that use larger amounts of power are usually circuited separately.

Sophisticated electrical equipment, such as dimmers and more complicated wiring arrangements, need the assistance of an electrical engineer.

Wiring

The electrical service may be either a simple two-wire service or a three-wire one. The three-wire system is preferred since it provides the regular voltage for lighting and also provides double voltage for power requirements such as machinery.

Metallic tubing or conduit is commonly used in higher quality work and in all commercial buildings. It is like rigid pipe but is lightweight and easy to bend and cut. The ends are not threated but fastened with clamplike couplings. Wires are pulled through this conduit. Flexible cable is permitted to be used from junction boxes to fixtures.

Wiring diagram

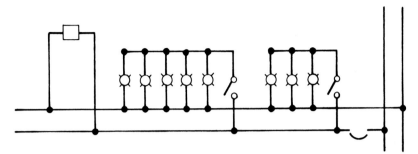

Electrical wiring comes from the outside, either from overhead or underground. It is attached first to the meter and main switch, which feeds to the distribution panel. From the distribution panel the various circuits are led out into the building to service fixtures and appliances, machines and convenience outlets. There are fuses or circuit breakers attached to the circuits and main fuses for the entire line.

The bulk of electric energy used in buildings is AC. DC generators furnish energy in a few important building applications, however, including passenger elevators, intercommunication telephone systems, control or signal systems, clock systems, and special business machines; they are used also for recharging storage batteries used for emergency hallway and exit lighting should the power system fail. (See the following list of terms for difference between AC and DC current.)

Symbols used on electrical drawings

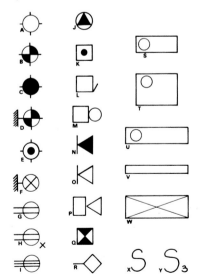

A Ceiling outlet
B Ceiling outlet (gas and electricity)
C Pull switch
D Wall bracket (gas and electricity)
E Floor outlet
F Exit light
G Duplex convenience outlet (single outlet indicated by one line through circle)
H Convenience outlet other than duplex (small letter indicates type)
I Range outlet
J Special-purpose outlet (described in legend or specifications)
K Push button
L Buzzer

M Bell
N Public telephone
O Interconnecting telephone
P Telephone switchboard
Q City fire-alarm station
R Annunciator
S One foot by two foot fluorescent fixture and outlet box
T Two foot by two foot fixture and outlet box
U One foot by four foot fluorescent fixture with outlet box
V Fluorescent lighting channel, single tube
W Special fluorescent fixture, such as recessed, etc.
X S for switch
Y S with small letter indicates special switching condition

Electrical and Telephone Terms

Alternating Current   A flow of current that periodically varies in time rate and direction.

Appliance   Current-consuming equipment, either fixed or portable, such as toasters, electric fans, etc.

Busways (Busbar, Busduct)   Large conductors normally constructed of solid copper or aluminum. They are assembled with other bar conductors in a metal housing and called "busducts" or "busways".

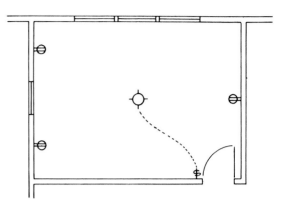

Wiring diagram of room

Branch Circuit   A circuit that supplies a number of outlets for lighting and appliances.

Cabinet   An enclosure designed either for surface or flush mounting and provided with a frame in which swinging doors are hung to protect the connecting devices inside.

Circuit Breakers   This device performs the same protective function as a fuse and in addition acts as a switch. Heat resulting from excess resistance causes it to disconnect the line.

Cellular Metal Floor Raceways   A structural floor composed of hollow metal cells utilized for running utility services in the floor and feeding the spaces above and below the floor.

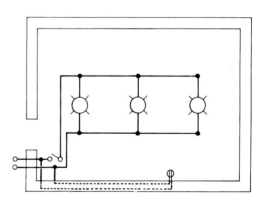

Electrical plan showing switch

Conductors   Wiring or other means by which current is conducted through the electrical system.

Current Carrying Capacity   Wire capacity is determined by its maximum safe operating temperature. For any given current being carried by a wire its operating temperature depends upon the insulation capabilities of the material that encloses it.

Conduit   A pipe for protecting wires

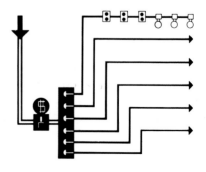

Typical wiring symbols

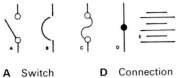

A Switch   D Connection
B Circuit breaker   E Battery
C Fuse

from mechanical and chemical injury.

Conduit (Metal Flexible) Spiral-wound interlocking tubing that is flexible.

Direct Current A flow of current that takes place at a constant time rate, practically unvarying, and in the same direction around the circuit.

Electrical Closet Electrical equipment grouped in a small room.

Fuse A simple device consisting of an alloy link or wire of relatively low melting temperature, which melts and breaks the connection when the heat in the circuit rises beyond a certain level.

Grounded A term meaning connected to earth or some conducting body which serves in place of an earth connection.

Insulation A material used to cover conductors in order to prevent the metallic conductor from contact-

ing other conductors or the grounded raceway.

Meter A device for measuring the amount of current consumed.

Outlet Box A box that connects the conduit to the electrical outlet or fixture.

Panelboard An insulating panel on which are mounted various fuses, switches, and circuit breakers.

Parallel Circuit A circuit in which more than one branch is connected between the same two points; the electricity can flow in two or more paths.

Raceway Any channel for holding wires, cables, or busbars that is designed expressly for and used only for this purpose.

Series Circuit A complete conducting path carrying current from a source of electricity to and from some electrical device and back to the source. All separate parts of the circuit carry the same current and the current can travel in only one path.

Switch A device intended for on-off control of circuits and for electrical isolation of equipment.

Transformer A device which changes alternating current of one voltage to alternative current of another voltage.

Telephone Installation

The telephone company will furnish, install, and maintain a complete system, but will not provide for facilities that become part of the permanent structure of the building, such as conduit to house wires, cabinets, risers, etc.

The telephone company cables require facilities that will extend them throughout the entire building. These usually consist of a service entrance, a main cable terminal cabinet, or an entire room on a larger installation. They must have riser shafts or vertical riser conduit, and then a splicing cabinet or splicing closet on each floor. Floor conduit between the riser-shaft splicing cabinet and distribution-terminal cabinets must also be provided. From the distribution-terminal cabinet the wires are run to the instruments. The above facilities are built into the building, and since they must be provided by the owner of the building, they are the responsibility of the architect or interior designer.

Since provision for telephone equipment frequently changes, it is best to design for maximum needs, allowing adequate space in cabinets and conduit for additional wiring.

There are a number of sophisticated combinations of telephone hookups and specialized equipment that require consultation with the telephone company engineers to ascertain their requirements.

Lighting

Electric light has become increasingly important in interiors. Natural light is a secondary source. Even though the shortage of energy may change our present design ideas about artificial light, it presently remains the major source of interior illumination.

The selection of equipment in lighting design presents a continuing and increasingly important challenge. The task is considerably more complex than the basic need to provide a quantity of light. Bare light sources will supply this requirement. The subtle aspects of comfort and aesthetics to promote perceptual well-being are almost as important as seeing itself. The designer must control and modify light sources to establish a suitable visual environment.

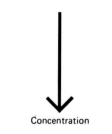

Concentration

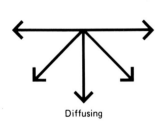

Diffusing

By the design and placement of lighting elements the designer decides upon the combination of surfaces to be illuminated or left in shadow. The selection of lighting equipment requires a design appraisal of the relationship between light, space and vision to define the design objectives, and insure appropriate distribution and direction of light. Rather than a mere adjunct to daylight, the control of electric light is a creative medium in its own right.

The usual appearance of interiors is strongly influenced by the quality and character of the lighting system. Lamps and lighting systems are the actual working tools of the designer and it is only through knowledgeable use of these tools that the desired luminous environment can be achieved.

An object or surface that reflects or transmits light becomes a secondary light source. There is a fundamental and inseparable relationship between the distribution of light from the luminaire and the action of architectural surfaces in redirecting the light.

The relative area of these surfaces and the inherent intensity of light reflected from them determines their visual significance in the design composition. Light reflected from room, ceiling and floor surfaces is generally diffuse or multidirectional causing inter-reflection between surfaces and objects. Interreflection tends to fill in shadows, reduce contrast and produce a more uniform brightness. Surface finishes are therefore important elements in lighting design.

Lighting techniques involve creative selection of luminaires, surfaces and colors and thus assume design implications far beyond the normal connotations of illumination engineering. For this reason there are no universally applicable rules of practice governing the use of lighting techniques.

Minimum light conditions may be sufficient for seeing tasks involving large objects and strong contrasts. When demanding seeing tasks are involved, light must be carefully considered. Although designers may instinctively recognize adequate lighting levels, a scientific evaluation is necessary to establish exactly how much light is necessary for a particular activity. Research involving the ability to see has established exactly how much light is needed for a particular activity. It is therefore possible to measure the effect of light on visibility.

Scientific study and research indicates that illumination properly controlled makes it easier and more enjoyable to perform visual tasks. Charts are available that recommend lighting levels for various activities. The designer may use these as a resource adjusting them to the various requirements of his/her design.

Downward
Concentrating

Upward Diffusing

Downward Diffusing

Multi-Directional
Concentrating

Upward Concentrating

Multi-Directional
Diffusing

Types of Luminaires

Design of a General Lighting System

Lighting design to supply a quantity of uniform light in a given space is a comparatively easy task. The task may be reduced to a few simple mathematical calculations. Complex factors such as the effects on the design of different room sizes, the value of light falling on various reflective surfaces, the reduction of illumination due to fixture aging and accumulated dirt and the unique lighting characteristics of the fixture have been simplified in tables supplied by lighting product manufacturers.

General interior lighting calculations are used to determine how many luminaires are required to provide an average

specified illumination level. One method of doing this is the "Zonal Cavity Method" recommended by the General Electric Company. This method, which is reviewed here, indicates how the luminaires should be arranged to provide uniform illumination throughout.

Conversely, if the quantity and type of equipment is known for a given space, the illumination level may be calculated by transposing the simple formula.

Calculations are based on the fact that

$$\text{Illumination (footcandles)} = \frac{\text{lumens}}{\text{sq. ft. of space}}.$$

There are however other factors to be considered such as the absorption of light of wall, ceiling and floor surfaces, the interreflection of light, and the efficiency or distribution capability of the luminaires. The formula does not consider the shape of the room or where illumination is measured. The factoring of one quantity, the Coefficient of Utilization (CU), which embodies all of these considerations just mentioned solves the problem.

The formula then becomes

$$\text{Footcandles} = \frac{\text{lumens} \times \text{CU}}{\text{area}}.$$

The method proposed by General Electric is a systematic way of determining the accurate Coefficient of Utilization and involves a simple method of combining all the related conditions into one coefficient.

To allow for the depreciation of illumination over time due to dirt accumulation on luminaire surfaces and aging of the light source, two other factors are usually added to the equation. These are termed Lamp Lumen Depreciation (LLD) and Luminaire Dirt Depreciation (LDD)

The equation with these factors added is now complete.

$$\text{Footcandles} = \frac{\text{lumens} \times \text{CU} \times \text{LLD} \times \text{LDD}}{\text{square foot area}}.$$

It represents the average maintained illumination resulting from the use of a given luminaire in a given room.

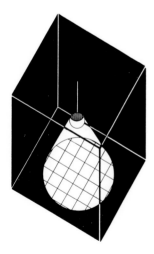

The Zonal Cavity Method derives its name from the procedure of dividing the room into zones or "cavities" for the purpose of deriving the Coefficient of Utilization.

A room with suspended luminaires and a work place above the floor has three cavities: ceiling cavity (from the center of the luminaire to the ceiling), room cavity (from the center of the luminaire to the top of the work surface), and floor cavity

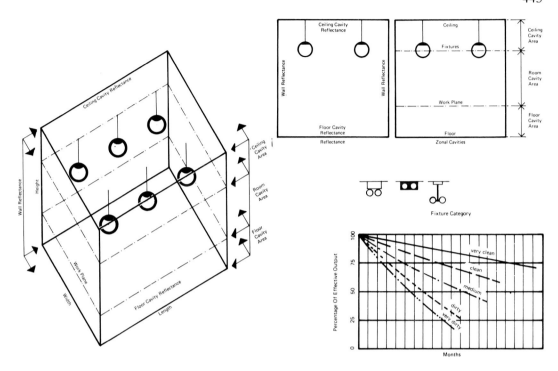

(from the work surface to the floor). These distances are taken as the height of the cavity, which when combined with the length and width provide the cubic footage of the three cavities. If luminaires are surface mounted on the ceiling or ceiling recessed and the work area is the floor, then there is only one cavity, the room cavity.

Luminaire Dirt Depreciation Factor (LDD)

The step-by-step method of solving the problem by deriving the factors of the equation follows.

1. A lamp and luminaire is selected.
2. The average maintained illumination for the space is decided. This is usually selected from illumination recommendation charts for various seeing tasks.
3. Calculate the area (length × width of the work plane area).
4. Calculate the Coefficient of Utilization:
    (a) Determine the cavity ratio;
    (b) Determine the effective reflectances;
    (c) Find the CU on the tables using the information derived from steps (a) and (b).
5. Consult the manufacturers catalog to find the lumens per lamp.
6. Find the LDD and LLD. The LLD (lamp lumen depreciation) will be listed by the manufacturer with lamp

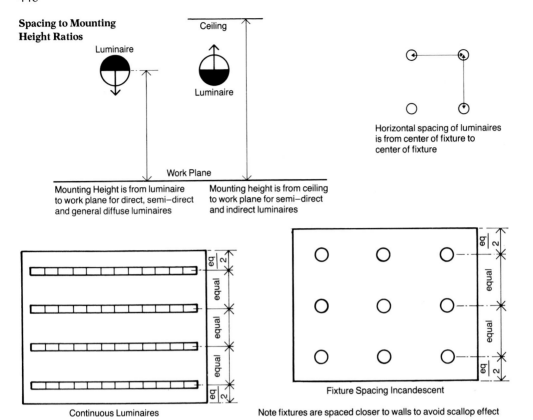

Spacing to Mounting Height Ratios

Luminaire

Ceiling

Luminaire

Work Plane

Mounting Height is from luminaire to work plane for direct, semi–direct and general diffuse luminaires

Mounting height is from ceiling to work plane for semi–direct and indirect luminaires

Horizontal spacing of luminaires is from center of fixture to center of fixture

Continuous Luminaires

Fixture Spacing Incandescent

Note fixtures are spaced closer to walls to avoid scallop effect

descriptions. The LDD (luminaire dirt depreciation) should appear as a maintenance number with the lamp description. The various luminaire categories and their characteristics are listed in graph form which shows the LDD percentage over time.

The manufacturers catalog also lists the typical distribution curve of light lumens which varies with the various fixture configurations both as to direction and light trapped in the fixture. It also lists the ratio of maximum spacing between luminaires. Max S/MC = ratio.

Cavity Ratios are listed in manufacturers charts. Once a ratio has been established by finding the correct room cavity ratio, percent ceiling cavity reflectance, floor cavity reflectance, and wall reflectance, the coefficient of utilization is easily found.

If catalogs or other particular information is not available the designer may make assumptions concerning the figures in the formula. If lamp lumen output is not known, the following approximation will result in fairly accurate calculations.

Lamp type	Lumens per watt output
Incandescent	20
Mercury	50
Fluorescent	80
Multi-Vapor	85
Lucalox	100

If the reflectances of the surfaces are unknown a light meter could be used or the quantity approximated from previous experience.

If a table for Cavity Area Ratios is not available, the formula

$$CR = \frac{5 \times height \times (length + width)}{length \times width}$$

will give the figure.

As the designer gains experience his estimates will become more accurate.

If surfaces are light, the room is large without obstructions, and the fixture has no louvers the CU can be assumed to be high (7 or 8). If the opposite conditions prevail then the CU would be appropriately reduced.

It is recommended that the designer consult the various manufacturers catalogs which are usually available without cost. Most lighting manufacturers maintain sales staffs and product representatives who will be of valuable assistance in comprehending the basic lighting principles. They should be consulted.

Task and Task-Ambient Lighting

In the design of offices, where dependence on natural light is hardly practical (people work late, in the evening and on dark days and building shape creates inner space far from windows) it has become customary to provide ceiling lighting sufficient to light the entire office area at desk top level with enough light to make even demanding work quite possible. In recent years, this often meant levels as high as 150–200 footcandles. The cost of this much light in a large installation has become so high that it has stimulated a search for more economical techniques.

Task lighting recognizes the fact that strong light is needed only in a small work area, usually the central portion of each desk top. Providing the same level of illumination to aisles and passageways, to file cabinets and the tops of workers' heads is totally unnecessary and very wasteful. Besides, a given wattage fixture will produce a higher level of illumination when it is brought

Adjustable task light unit with double swinging arm support. (Photograph courtesy Herman Miller, Inc.)

down closer to the task. Task lighting has, in a sense, reintroduced the old desk lamp, placing a light source at each station, close to the work surface where minimum wattage will be most effective.

Leaving the balance of office space in near darkness might be inconvenient and would also lead to too much contrast between task and background, another source of seeing problems. It is therefore necessary to add some overall or "ambient" lighting. 'Task-ambient' lighting permits the task lights to also direct some light up toward the ceiling with a resultant "spill" of general light all through the space. Problems can occur if the uplights are not shielded to prevent standing persons from looking directly down into the source and, if furniture layout is irregular, "pools" of brightness on the ceiling can generate excessive brightness contrast. Special floor-standing indirect ambient lighting "kiosks" can be used to fill dark areas. Ceiling lighting is *not* provided in such task-ambient installations.

An alternative approach, believed by many lighting consultants to reach a best compromise, includes conventional ceiling lighting, but only enough to provide a very low level of general light–perhaps 15 or 20 footcandles. Task lights are then used at the individual work station to raise the level to 60 to 75 footcandles. Task lighting units are usually incorporated into "office systems" products under shelves or storage units or as attachments on panels. The actual light unit must be carefully designed to avoid glare and reflections that often result when a fluorescent task light is placed in its most obvious position, directly in front of the user. A special lens which directs light to the side and blocks rays that would generate glare and reflections is the usual remedy in good quality task lighting units.

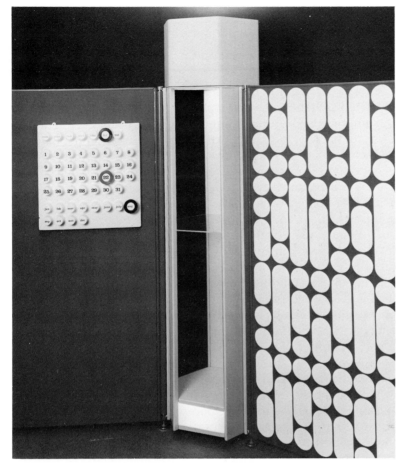

Lighting "kiosk" directing illumination up to ceiling to provide ambient lighting. (Photograph courtesy E.F. Hauserman Co.)

Energy Economy Issues

The rising cost of electrical energy has led to a restudy of lighting design practice. It is customary to discuss the efficiency of a lighting installation in terms of "watts per foot," that is, the installed wattage demand of the lighting divided by the square footage of the space in question. If 5000 watts are used to light a 1000 square foot space, an efficiency of $^{5000}/_{1000}$ or 5 watts per foot results, unsatisfactory at today's prices. Levels of 3, 2, and even 1.5 watts per foot can be obtained in highly efficient installations designed with serious concern for efficiency. Building codes are now specifying maximum permissible watts per foot figures for various building types making it mandatory, in many cases, to design lighting with this issue in mind even if economy is not of primary concern. In designing lighting, it must always be remembered that wattage used for lighting is converted to heat; the higher the wattage, the more heat is introduced into the space.

This factor may reduce energy costs for winter heating a bit, but has a far greater impact in increasing summer air conditioning costs. Any evaluation of the usefulness of an energy-saving lighting installation must include a study of the impact of the planned system on both heating and air conditioning costs.

Energy efficiency in lighting may involve other issues as well–localized switching, for example, means that lights are not left burning needlessly during lunch hours or when occupants are away for the day. Individual switching may, on the other hand, be an inconvenience to cleaning and maintenance staff that require general light to do their jobs, most often at night. Double switching (both local and a central master on-off) can be an alternative but involves extra wiring costs that can be excessive.

Efficient light sources are often expensive in terms of initial cost. A study of the overall cost of a lighting installation becomes a complex problem in relation to first cost of fixtures, lamps ("bulbs"), switching and wiring; operating costs and costs of maintenance, including relamping and cleaning, and impact on heat and air conditioning costs over the life of the system. Since only estimates can be made of the cost of future consumed basic energy, such calculations can not lead to precise findings, but are a help in comparing alternatives and often will rule out obviously uneconomic plans quite easily.

In small projects and, particularly in residential design, energy costs for lighting are not often primary issues–the cost of home lighting is usually small compared to that of other electrical devices such as ranges, refrigerators, water and space heaters and air conditioning machines. It is still advantageous to notice that doing an equal or better job with less energy has both immediate economic and long-range advantages to the community by reducing the overall problems of energy supply in the modern world.

Lighting Definitions

Absorption All materials affected by lighting design absorb some light. The absorption factor is the ratio of light absorbed by a material to the incident light.

Black Light Lamps A popular term used to describe ultra-violet energy. This invisible energy causes some materials and chemicals to glow.

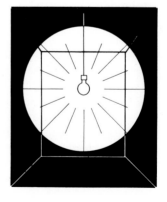

Candle Power The unit of light intensity. One candle power is the light given off by a standard candle whose composition, size and burning rate have been specified. The modern method of measuring the candle power of light is to compare its brightness with that of an electric light of fixed candle power, rather than with that of a standard candle. A 40 watt electric lamp is rated at about 32 candle power.

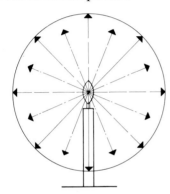

Diffusion When parallel rays of light strike a smooth surface they are reflected uniformly or parallel, but when they strike a rough surface they are reflected in all directions. The reflected light is diffused. This results in a soft light. Light reflected by smooth surfaces often results in uncomfortable glare.

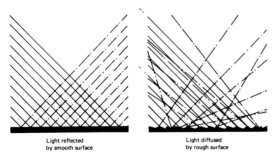

Light reflected by smooth surface

Light diffused by rough surface

Efficiency The efficiency of a luminaire is measured by the ratio of output of luminous flux to luminous flux generated by the lamp. The efficiency of an electric lamp is the ratio of output in luminous flux expressed in lumens to the power input in watts expressed in lumens per watt.

ESI Equivalent sphere illumination. A newly developed technique in which a laboratory measurement is made to calculate the level of light coming from a spherical surrounding that gives equal seeing ease to a lighting device under test. The aim is to provide a measure for comparison of effectiveness of lighting devices taking into account their performance in controlling glare and "veiling reflections".

ESI Footcandle Unit of measure in which the results of ESI tests are expressed. Compared with "raw footcandles" as measured with a light meter, the ESI footcandle gives a better measure of performance. When comparing two lighting devices, the one offering a higher ESI footcandle output should be superior, even if the raw footcandle comparison suggests otherwise.

Fluorescent Lamp A complex electrical device in which light is produced by an electronic action that consists of a flow of electrons emitted by the cathodes that excite mercury atoms within the glass bulb and cause them to give off radiation. The phosphorus coating on the

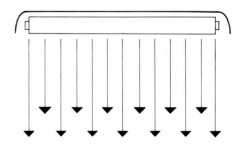

glass bulb converts this energy into visible light.

Flux The rate of flow of energy across a surface.

Footcandle The illumination of a surface produced by spreading one lumen uniformly over an area of one square foot.

Footlambert The unit of brightness of an evenly diffused surface emitting or reflecting light at the rate of one lumen per square foot. Footcandles and footlamberts are both expressions for lumens per square foot. Lumens measured at the surface gives footcandles. Lumens measured coming from the surface are footlamberts.

Glare Excessive brightness within a viewer's field of vision that handicaps seeing even if sufficient light is present. Glare from a sun low in the sky or from a too bright window are familiar problems. Ceiling lights without proper lenses or louvers can be a source of glare as can "veiling reflections" (q.v.) coming from glossy surfaces. Lighting fixtures can be properly designed to avoid this.

Globe An enclosing device of clear or diffusing material that protects the lamp, diffuses or redirects its radiant energy or modifies its color.

HID Lighting Lighting using one of a number of gaseous discharge lamps as a source. The term stands for "high intensity discharge" since such sources generally have a high lumen output from a relatively compact "bulb". HID lighting combines the globe-like form usually found in incandescent lamps with the high efficiency of fluorescent lighting. HID lamps are now available with varying color characteristics useful in differing situations. HID units re-

quire a warm-up time on starting and can not be restarted at once if turned off.

Illumination The density of luminous flow of energy on a surface.

Incandescent Lamp A simplified description would be a hot wire in a bottle. The tungsten coil is heated by incandescence by passing an electric current through it. The bottle is the sealed glass bulb.

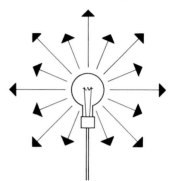

Incidence/Reflection When a ray of light strikes a reflective surface at right angles it is reflected back to its source. If the ray strikes at an angle it is reflected at an angle. The angle between the perpendicular and the ray as it strikes the surface (incident) and the angle between the perpendicular and the reflected ray are equal. The angle as the ray strikes the surface is the angle of incidence and the angle as the ray bounces back is the angle of reflectance. The angle of incidence is equal to the angle of reflection.

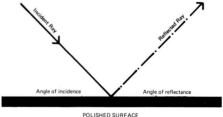

POLISHED SURFACE

Intensity Light travels in a straight line. As it moves away from its source it spreads out. The greater the distance from the source, the less intense the fall of light on the surface. It can be shown that light from a point source varies inversely as the square of the distance from the source (see *Point Source*).

Lamp Manmade lighting source. An incandescent filament lamp is often referred to as a "bulb" and a fluorescent lamp is sometimes called a "tube".

Light Visually measured radiant energy. Light as energy exists in pure form. Since there is no artificial energy there can be no artificial light. Light in building is produced by electricity and is therefore called electric light.

Linear Sources Light output from sources of relatively large dimension such as fluorescent lamps cannot be measured by the inverse square law. Data is supplied by the manufacturer of the equipment to determine lighting intensities.

Lumen The unit of luminous flux which is equal to the luminous flow of energy on a surface all points of which are of uniform distance from a source of one candle. The measurement is made on one square foot of surface at a distance of one foot.

Luminaire A complete lighting unit consisting of the lamp or lamps, elements that distribute the light, and connect the lamp or lamps to the power supply. The luminaire is sometimes termed a "fixture".

Mercury Lamp The mercury lamp combines the filament lamp attribute of a concentrated source with the higher efficiency and longer life of the arc source. The light produced is predominantly blue and green resulting in poor color quality. The inherent long life and adaptability to beam projection make mercury lamps particularly useful for remote and inaccessible equipment installations.

Point Source A lighting source is considered as a point when its maximum dimension is less than one-fifth the distance from source to plane of measurement. Most incandescent lamps can be considered as a point source. The fundamental relationship for determining illumination in foot candles for a point source is the inverse square law in which E (illumination in foot candles at a point on a plane normal to the light ray) equals l (the candlepower directed at the point) divided by d (the distance in feet from source to point) or $E = l/d^2$.

Reflector A device for redirecting the radiant energy of a lamp by reflection in a desired direction.

Characteristics of Reflectors

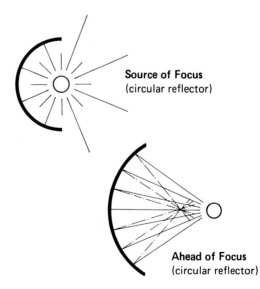

Source of Focus
(circular reflector)

Ahead of Focus
(circular reflector)

Refraction Refraction is caused by the bending of light rays as they pass from one transparent medium such as water to another medium of different density such as air. Although light travels in a straight line it travels more slowly in some media than in others depending upon the density of the medium involved. As a result the rays alter their direction when they reach the surface that separates the two mediums.

Source of Focus
(parabolic reflector)

Behind Focus
(circular reflector)

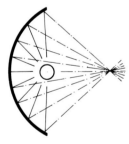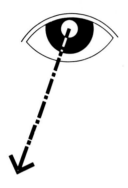

Seeing Three different actions are possible when a ray of light falls on an object. The light may be allowed to pass through, transmitted; or it may be caught and transformed into heat energy, absorbed; or it may be bounced back, reflected. The sun, stars, and incandescent filaments are visible because of the light they generate. These are called luminous bodies. The vast majority of objects around us are visible because they reflect light to the eye from outside luminous body.

Veiling Reflection Reflection from a glossy surface making it difficult to see print or other patterns. These seem to be hidden by a "veil" of light. Ink on paper and pencil lines have enough gloss to be obscured by veiling reflections even on dull paper. Veiling reflection can be tested by placing a mirror in the position where a task will be viewed–if an image of the light source is seen, reflections will occur. Proper design of fixtures (with suitable lenses and louvers) and proper placement of fixtures can control the problem.

Visibility When the eye focuses upon an object three important characteristics are visible: size, contrast, and brightness. Time is required to be aware of the object. The eye must focus upon it and transmit the stimulus to the brain. The common denominator of these four factors is brightness. A poor contrast of the object with its background can be improved by increasing the brightness of the background. The speed of seeing can be increased or decreased by varying the brightness. Decisions as to the amounts of light, distribution, brightness, and reflection factors are affected by the fundamental influence of light on external vision. Some of these decisions have already been made in part, in the preparation of footcandle tables or the specification of brightness limits and ratios in charts available to the designer

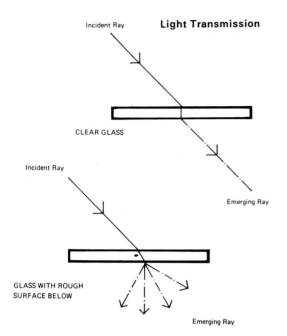

furnished by the manufacturer. Brightness is one of the most controllable factors in the design of good visual conditions and a pleasant environment. The direction of light and its amount can improve the visibility of the task. An object of given size and contrast with its background will be seen faster under increasing levels of illumination. A small object can be made equal in visibility to a larger one by increasing its brightness. The small object at a higher brightness can transmit as much energy to the retina as a larger object at lower brightness and thus become as easy to see.

Sound

The interior designer considering the problem of acoustics must be concerned with both sound and noise. Nearly all activities in a building result in the production of sound. The designer must design so that wanted sounds are heard and unwanted noise eliminated.

Sound is a wave motion that acts upon our ears through the fluctuations of pressure in the adjacent air. Sound waves are propagated by compressional waves and are caused by or can give rise to vibrations in solid bodies.

The major problem of the designer is noise control. Ensuring adequate quiet in the various parts of a building is essentially a matter of good planning. Construction details and the choice of materials are important, but these cannot compensate for errors in the plan. It is essential that quiet areas be placed as remotely as possible from sources of noise and that the noise be prevented at its source.

Sound cannot be considered with reference to isolated walls and floors, but must be thought of traveling from one part of the building to another by vibrations or from the outside to the inside by clear air paths. Cracks, open doors, and windows can be sound paths, for the sound comes through them without obstruction. Sound will travel along pipes, through air-conditioning systems, and along parts of the structure. Noise or sound control must therefore be considered in terms of the entire planning and construction.

It is difficult to provide a high degree of sound insulation in a structure. It is therefore imperative that the amount of objectionable noise be minimized at its source. Silence in running should be considered in the selection of mechanical equipment, sanitary appliances, office equipment, and plumbing.

Continuous air paths can be stopped with weatherstripping placed around doors and windows. The more massive the structure the less will be the intensity of vibrations imparted by a compressive air wave. However, massive structural components are too expensive for the interior designer to use except in extreme cases where components such as lead-lined doors or panels might be considered for special installations. A break in the continuity of structure will help isolate sound vibration, such as staggered studs that do not contact each other (shown in the drawing).

Once all action has been taken to eliminate noise, the next step is the absorption of excess sound. This is done by the use of sound-absorbing materials.

When a speaker or musician appears before an audience, the sounds he creates proceed outward in spherical waves until they strike the boundaries of the room. Here they are deflected, transmitted, and absorbed in varying amounts depending on the wall configuration. Sound travels at about the speed of a rifle bullet, about 1100 feet per second at ordinary temperatures, so that by successive reflections it quickly fills the room. Depending upon the size and shape of the room, about one-tenth of a second after the sound has been made the volume of the room has been filled with sound waves going in every direction, which means that everyone in the room hears the sound with the same average loudness.

While the reflection of sound has the advantage of increasing the loudness, it also is responsible for most of the acoustical defects in a room, such as echoes, resonance, and reverberation. It is of practical advantage to reduce reflected sound with absorbent materials.

Echo occurs when the interval between the direct and reflected sounds is about one-fifteenth of a second or more, which corresponds to a difference in paths of these two sounds of about seventy-five feet. Concave walls focus the sound and a convex wall fractures it. Walls set off parallel to each other deflect the sound and reduce reverberation.

Reverberation (the prolongation of sound) and resonance (the sounding back of sound) are caused when sound strikes plaster or other hard surfaces with only about 3 percent of the energy absorbed and the remaining 97 percent reflected. At the next reflection, the same action follows so that as many as three or four hundred reflections may take place in a room before the sound energy is used up. To correct this, material must be installed that absorbs sound energy on each reflection.

It is possible for acoustical engineers to calculate the acoustical requirements of a room, and the designer will usually follow their specifications if the sound control is very important. Eventually the designer acquires enough knowledge through experience and consultation with experts to design the acoustical properties himself. Materials have their acoustical properties rated in relation to sound-absorption characteristics. The designer need merely to choose from among these to fit the acoustical engineer's recommendations or to fulfill his own calculations.

Killing sound with an area is comparatively easy, but controlling the sound that is borne through the structure is an uncertain and difficult task usually outside the province of the interior designer.

In offices, particularly where open planning is used, a problem of "acoustical privacy" may arise; people may hear one another's conversations with enough clarity to form a distraction. This can bother people who are speaking by feeling that private conversations are being overheard and can also bother those who overhear them and find it difficult to concentrate as a result. Offices now use various sound absorbing materials (carpet, ceiling tile, acoustical screen or partitions) as acoustical treatments but, as the space becomes more quiet, acoustical privacy prob-

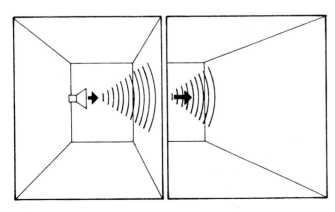

Sound travels through a medium because it sets up vibrations in the medium. Almost all building materials are sufficiently elastic to transmit sound.

When a body is set to vibrating by sound waves, then the body itself becomes a sound source. A wall panel separating two rooms is an example of this type of reaction. Sound from a source in one of the rooms sets wall vibrating, and the wall transmits the vibrations to the air in the adjoining room.

lems may increase. A nearby conversation that would be lost in a noisy office (or restaurant) may be all too audible in a quiet space.

The realization that the hum of activity in a busy place, even the slight hiss or rustle of air conditioning can help with problems of acoustical privacy, has led to another approach known as a "background" or "masking" sound system. This involves installation of hidden speakers above the ceiling connected to an artificial electronic sound generating device to produce a carefully designed mix of sound frequencies in random pattern–sounds similar to a breeze or distant sea waves. This sound, constant and at a very low level, is not noticeable, but masks the frequencies of speech that aid intelligibility. As a result, when masking sound is in use, problems of acoustical privacy can usually be solved quite easily. The suspicion that background sound might be an annoyance, often voiced by those who have not experienced it, is not supported through experience. Visitors and office users do not detect a masking system but do notice that privacy problems are solved. Masking sound will be noticed if it is turned on or off while the space is occupied (something to avoid) and may be noticed if it is spottily distributed through an office. Various manufacturers who make the equipment will plan masking sound systems, but it is usually best to retain an acoustical consultant with experience in this field to design a system and supervise its installation and adjustment.

Acoustical Terms

Absorbents Materials that absorb sound readily; usually building materials designed specifically for the purpose of absorbing acoustic energy.

Absorption, Sound Conversion of acoustic energy to heat or another form of energy within the structure of sound-absorbing materials.

Acoustic Used in conjunction with a basic property of sound.

Acoustical Used in conjunction with apparatus or sound control.

Acoustical Tile Acoustical absorbents produced in the form of sheets or units resembling tiles.

Acoustical Treatment Use of acoustical absorbents to correct acoustical faults or improve the acoustical environment.

Acoustics The science of sound, including its production, transmission, and effects.

Airborne Sound The sound transmitted through air as a medium rather than through solids or the structure of a building.

Background Level The normal sound level present in a space, above which speech, music, or similar specific wanted sound must be presented.

Decibel A division of a uniform scale

based upon 10 times the log 10 of the relative intensity of sound levels being compared.

Diffusion Dispersion of sound within a space so that there is uniform energy density throughout the space.

Dispersion The scattering or distribution of sound in a space.

Distortion Any change in the transmitted sound that alters the character of the energy-frequency distribution so that the sound being received is not a faithful replica of the source sound.

Distribution The pattern of sound-intensity levels within a space.

Echo Any reflected sound that is loud enough and received late enough to be heard as distinct from the source.

Fidelity The faithful reproduction of the source sound.

Flutter A rapid reflection or echo pattern between parallel walls, with sufficient time between each reflection to cause a listener to be aware of separate, discrete signals.

Focusing Concentration of acoustic energy within a limited location in a room as the result of reflections from concave surfaces.

Frequency The number of complete cycles per second of vibration.

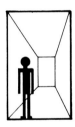
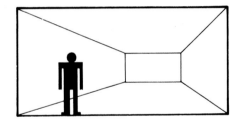
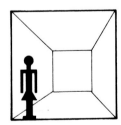
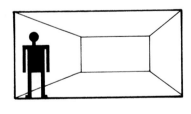
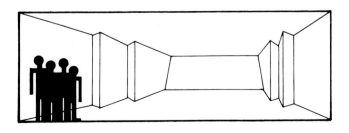

Room shape is an important factor in acoustical design. Parallel surfaces cause excessive reverberation and concave surfaces tend to focus sound. Long narrow rooms should be avoided; high ceilinged corridors and rooms which are cubical in dimension are also not desirable. Large unbroken surfaces should also be avoided. Splayed room surfaces will diffuse reflections.

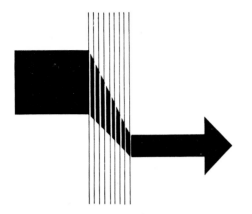

It is seldom necessary to provide a partition capable of preventing transmission of all the sound in a room. It is only necessary to reduce the sound below the normal background level in the quieter room.

If a wall material has the capability of reducing the sound below the level of the adjoining room it is judged to be adequate. The decible reduction level of wall construction is listed in various charts. The designer selects the wall construction necessary to reduce the noise level.

Intensity The rate of sound energy transmitted in a specified direction through a unit area.

Isolation, Sound. The use of materials of construction that resist the passage of sound through them.

Leaks, Sound Any opening that permits airborne sound transmission.

Level, Sound A measure of sound pressure level as determined by electrical equipment.

Loudness The effect on the hearing apparatus of varying sound pressures and intensities.

Masking The increase in threshold of audibility of a sound necessary to permit its being heard in the presence of another sound.

Noise Any unwanted sound.

Pitch The physical response to frequency.

Reflecting Surfaces Room surfaces from which significant sound reflections occur.

Resonance The natural vibration of a volume of air or a panel of material at a particular frequency as the result of excitation by a sound of that particular frequency.

Reverberation The time in seconds required for a sound to decay to inaudibility after the source ceases.

Sabin A measure of sound absorption of a surface, equivalent to one square foot of a perfectly absorptive surface.

Sound A vibration in a medium; usually in the frequency range capable of producing the sensation of hearing.

Structure-borne Sound Sound energy transmitted through the solid media of the building structure.

Transmission The propagation of a vibration through various media.

Transmission Loss The decrease in power during transmission from one point to another.

Velocity The time rate of change of position of a reference point moving in a straight line.

Vibration An alternation in pressure or direction of motion.

Wave, Sound A disturbance that is propagated in a medium in such a manner that at any point in the medium the displacement is a function of the time.

Conclusion

The foregoing introduction to the elements of structural knowledge and mechanical systems that the interior designer must possess to practice his profession is, as we said in the beginning, only the briefest outline. It is, however, sufficient for a beginning because the designer's knowledge increases as he designs, facts change, new techniques come into being, and design itself alters its objectives.

If the designer has learned from this introduction to reduce problems to their essentials, he can decide among the options presented him by structure and materials. Design is problem solving, and problems whose elements and options are known to us are no longer problems. When we know what we can do, solving the problem is merely a matter of choosing the best solution.

VII

PROFESSIONAL PRACTICE

We have covered much ground discussing design in broad terms and describing much of interior design in detail. In some professions, such as medicine, the professional activities are public knowledge and do not need any elaboration at all. In the field of interior design, though, the practice is quite varied and a discussion devoted to the general types of interior design activities seems well worthwhile. It is in fact a considerable attraction for knowledgeable beginners that so many varieties of professional opportunities exist. The vast differences of practices also account for the fact that there are many designers involved as professionals in the field of interior design, without realizing that some of their colleagues practice the same thing in quite different ways.

Modern practice ranges from work done by individual designers without staff, to work done in very large design or architectural offices. Each office, in fact each individual, uses somewhat differing procedures and approaches to the performance of design services. It will be necessary therefore to make certain generalizations and to recognize that no description of one type of design office will be an accurate report on the existing conditions or procedures in all offices. Perhaps it would be wise to emphasize once again that we are concerned with nothing but serious design in this book. We realize that there still exist a number of decorators who "operate" out of their dinettes, and who "design" apartments over their kitchen telephones by simply placing furniture orders with so-called wholesale merchants. This is not serious interior design, nor is it decoration. There are also a good many respectable furniture dealers, particularly in the field of office furnishings, who offer some kind of design or "layout" service as part of their sales operation. This is not serious interior design either. However, some very good design firms have emerged from these office furnishings dealers and have managed to form independent design groups after getting their start in business. It is still true that in many of our smaller cities the demand for design services is minimal, and for that reason the only design services available to the public in those cities are through firms who sell furniture for either homes or offices. There are also a number of very competent and ethical designers who practice interior design based in some kind of store. Then there are the department stores and large furniture stores who maintain a design service or "decorating studio" as part of their merchandizing program. The better stores have separated the designers' activity from sales, and again there are some good professionals in those situations.

A relatively new opportunity for interior designers is in direct employment by large corporations such as major manufacturing enterprises, banks, or other large businesses. Some of the country's major corporations maintain fairly large design offices to plan their constant changes and new facilities development. Some of these offices are headed by very experienced designers or architects who employ several staff members. Often their job is to develop programs together with independent design or architectural firms or to work with these outside firms in representing the interest of their parent corporation. Obviously there are many highly specialized activities or jobs, ranging from the designer working as educational facilities coordinator for a university to the staff de-

signer employed by an hotel. More and more designers find employment in public agencies on the local, state or federal level. Design services in the public sector are needed for community health care facilities, institutions such as schools, hospitals and facilities for the elderly, and frequently these needs are met through planning agencies on municipal or county levels. There are, however, a number of rather specialized agencies dealing exclusively with the design of hospitals or mental institutions whose primary concerns include the physical environment. Government agencies responsible for the planning of new buildings and the design of governmental offices are increasingly aware of the needs for design, and a good many "in house" design departments deal with those needs. Our concern is not to present a complete list of employment and career opportunities in the field, but rather to present the role of the designer in professional practice in its most typical aspects.

1

INDIVIDUAL DESIGNERS
AND SMALL OFFICES

Each job begins with the client, who may be either one person or a large corporation. Since the client is the beginning of any job, in both large or small offices, the relationship to the client is of great importance to the designer. Interior design is always concerned with the solution of a problem, even if the problem posed to the designer by the client is presented in aesthetic terms only. This is a very important fact to remember. The designer who considers each job as an opportunity to exercise his creative imagination, without bothering to find out the needs of the client, is not going to perform a valid design service. Contrary to some amusing films or television programs, it is not necessary for the client to be analyzed by his interior designer; however, the needs expressed by clients are indeed frequently imagined rather than real. The first step in a job is therefore to find out through interviews and research precisely what the real needs are, what the budget is, and whatever aesthetic preferences there are on the client's part which the designer can incorporate into a successful scheme. Many clients come to interior designers with prejudices, or with ideas picked up from popular decorating magazines or from misguided friends, and often a designer must spend a good deal of time in reorienting and educating his client. When this does not succeed and the requests made by the client are in conflict with the designer's convictions, the serious professional will usually decline the job rather than compromise his convictions.

Individual designers and small offices can rarely handle jobs of large scale; much of their work is therefore in residences, small offices, stores, restaurants and, in general, spaces of limited scope. An individual practitioner performs all the services that will be described in more detail in the following pages devoted to the larger offices; however, usually the number of drawings for a job, the extent of specifications, and the number of contractors involved, are smaller and are in proportion to the smaller jobs that he normally handles. Some of the best interior designers prefer to work alone or with a very small staff because they like the total involvement and control of each job, which is not possible in a larger organization. Often they enjoy the great variety of work—ranging from interviewing clients to the specification of furnishings, from the beginning sketches to the finished working drawing, and from the supervision of contractors to the selection of the last ashtray. The larger an office, the more specialization within it. The owner or chief designer in a larger office is often forced to become a kind of business executive, and there are quite a few excellent designers who have for that reason given up successful design firms in favor of smaller scale individual work.

No two jobs and no two designers are ever quite alike. For the purpose of clarification of design procedures, we shall briefly describe the steps that would be the norm for an individual designer engaged to design offices for a physician. During the interview, or interviews, the designer will determine the general and specific needs, including special equipment such as X-ray equipment. He will, in many cases, advise the client on the space under consideration whether it is a new building or an old one. (The designer will have arrived at a contract or letter of agreement with his client by that time.) He will make sure that mechanical equipment needed for a physician's office can be provided, including special plumbing facilities, lead-lined walls for X-ray room, etc. Depending on the number of spaces required (examination room, office, nurses, etc.) the designer will proceed with preliminary plans to make sure that the space under consideration can accommodate all of his client's needs.

If the building is an old one, the chances are that the designer will have to measure existing conditions in order to draw up plans. In a new building the plans will be provided by the architect or builder. Once a satisfactory scheme has been arrived at and has been approved by the client, the designer will produce the working drawings and details required to get bids from contractors. As a rule, even on small jobs, the designer will recommend to his client that two or three contractors bid on the job, based on the designer's drawings and specifications. The general contractor who has been awarded the job will employ a number of subcontractors for electrical, air-conditioning, and plumbing work, for example. The subcontractors, although responsible to the general contractor, must still be supervised by the designer. While the job is under construction, or possibly before construction has started, the designer will have prepared furniture plans, made selections of all materials, floor, and wall coverings, colors, special lighting, furniture, and in some cases will have designed special features such as a nurse's desk, bookcases, or seating for the reception area. The client must approve all these choices in terms of his personal preferences and in terms of the budget. If the designer is competent, all considerations for maintenance and wearability will have been thoroughly studied and considered.

After approval has been given by the client, the designer will have to place all the orders, making sure to coordinate delivery schedules such as delivery of upholstery fabrics from the textile firm to the furniture manufacturer's plant, ensuring proper identification for whatever pieces of furniture the fabrics were specified. The designer must also make sure that the floor coverings are installed prior to the delivery of furniture, and that the luminaries arrive while the electrical contractor is on the job. On a small job, such as the imaginary one described above, the responsibility of timing, schedules, and even partial supervision is often shared with the client. In the past, the standard procedure on smaller jobs was for the designer to place all orders for furnishings, pay the bills, and invoice the client. Many designers charged a fee or percentage for these services. Now more and more of the truly professional designers prefer to charge a straight fee for all their services. They will have to place the purchase orders, since most of the suppliers will not deal with individual clients, but designers who wish to work on a strict fee basis will turn over the manufacturers' invoices to their clients for payment, after having checked and approved them for payment. The chances are that by the time most of the physician's offices were completed, he will have developed a healthy respect for his designer's ability and judgment, and he will expect help in the selection and purchase of paintings, in the arrangement of his various medical diplomas, and in the selection of ashtrays and other accessories. Few jobs will be completed without some small problems. A strike by one of the trades can mean a long delay; a delayed delivery of furniture may be a serious difficulty if the office is to be opened in time; and at times the client may be unhappy about the results of certain aspects of the job. But in spite of minor difficulties, it is probable that by the completion of the job, the client and the designer will have become well acquainted and, often, friends. Indeed the client is a very important member of the "team" responsible for any job. In case of a one-man operation, the team may simply be client-designer, and will frequently be a very successful and well-attuned working combination.

2

THE LARGE DESIGN OFFICE

Large design offices are usually divided into a number of departments: these include a design department headed by the chief designer or principal of the firm; a production department that is responsible for the production of working drawings and all drafting; a number of specialized functions such as accounting, purchasing, or color work, which are sometimes staffed by just one person; and a supporting office staff responsible for the administration and function of the organization.

The titles and division of functions can vary greatly. Some offices have decorating departments or color departments, where all furniture, fabric, and color selections are made. Some offices have a special business or purchasing department responsible for the ordering of all materials and furnishings. In recent years, more and more of the large design offices have tried to stay away from the actual purchasing of furnishing, merely specifying all orders for execution by the client's purchasing department; if the client does not have a purchasing department, the design office may place all orders and submit invoices to the client for direct payment to the suppliers.

The key person in each design office is the chief designer. The success and reputation of a larger firm is often due to the chief designer's ability. If the firm grows to more than a score of staff members, it is physically impossible for one person to be responsible for all design and detail decisions. Most firms handle a good many jobs at one time and employ a number of "project directors", each one responsible for a number of jobs under the general guidance of the firm's head.

Some offices call this position "coordinator"; some others use a term borrowed from the world of advertising, "account executive". Those designers in charge of a job as a rule carry all responsibility from client contact to field supervision. Most offices supply supporting staff members, from assistants to specialists for field supervision, or from draftsmen to specialists in rendering.

On larger jobs, preliminary drawings are developed after a thorough study of job requirements has been made. These drawings will be approved by the client and will probably be sent to contractors for preliminary budget costs. After a number of revisions are made, the drawings will be turned over to the production department, where working drawings and details are developed under the supervision of a chief draftsman. These drawings and details, along with schedules and specifications, become the contract drawings, which are the basic element in building any job. During the process of detailing design changes may be necessary, in which case the designer clarifies his intent and accepts alternatives. It is almost impossible to foresee all of the small details necessary to build a job. The problems of hardware, of mechanical equipment, of costs, and of available materials often force design changes. The construction department usually compiles budget estimates so that a designer will know how much a job may cost while he is designing. After the contract drawings have been issued, bids are submitted by the various contractors. The design office will examine these bids and will make recommendations to the client as to which contractor should be awarded the job. The specifications that accompany construction drawings are legal documents containing precise instructions to the contractor pertaining to materials and methods of construction. They are usually prepared by the construction department. Furnishings specifications are handled by the design or decorating department if the office is large enough to support such specialized functions.

Wherever special conditions occur, the general contractor or his subcontractors are expected to submit shop drawings to clarify his intent to the design office's satisfaction. These drawings—whether from the sheetmetal shop showing air-conditioning ducts, or from the woodworker showing cabinet details—must be carefully checked by the designer or the production department.

All steps involved in the design of any small space by an individual designer are involved and magnified in larger commissions. When, as mentioned earlier, a thorough study of job requirements must be undertaken, this can involve many months or even years of work for large projects. The design of new corporate headquarters for a large firm might involve a survey of all existing conditions and furnishings; and analysis of procedures and equipment might fill up several sets of booklike documents. The scheduling of deliveries towards the completion of a job may have to be coordinated with the moving of existing equipment. If a firm occupies many floors of a large building, the logistics involved are highly complex and require careful planning.

The client is as important in a large job as he is in a small job. If the client is represented by a group or committee, the designer or project director may have to be a diplomat as well as a patient saint. In order to avoid problems caused by personal prejudices of top executives (or their spouses), most design firms attempt to clarify the lines of authority very clearly through the initial contract. Many large design offices go to great length in their initial presentation of design schemes to the client or to the client's committee. Sometimes rather theatrical presentations, carefully rehearsed, are staged in an attempt to impress the client and obtain opproval for a thorough scheme without changes.

It must be pointed out again that the procedures described in the foregoing paragraphs vary widely. Some design firms consciously avoid growing too large in the realization that the creative process must suffer if the organization becomes too complex and if the design firm becomes a large business enterprise in its own right. A number of medium-sized design firms do much of their work in collaboration with architectural offices and do not have to employ a large production department if the working drawings are being produced by the architectural firm.

The precise definition and separation of design services in a variety of firms becomes increasingly blurred with the trend towards offices offering environmental design in a broad sense. Some large industrial design firms maintain interior-design departments; so do some engineering firms who combine their services with management consulting. There are many architectural firms and constantly increasing numbers of these firms who have in the past years established departments of interior design. A few words about these firms will clarify the role of the interior designer in such offices.

3

INTERIOR DESIGN
DEPARTMENTS
IN ARCHITECTURAL OFFICES

The ideal result of interior design done in architectural offices is the kind of job in which one cannot tell where architectural work stopped and interior design began. The complexity of large jobs necessitates departmentalization in most of the larger offices and, as a rule, the interior design work is done separately or as an addition to the basic building design. In some offices the interior department is small and is confined to the specification and selection of materials, colors, and furnishings—with resulting mediocrity of the finished job. The best work results from situations in which the interiors are planned together with the initial conceptual design of the structure and in which the interior schemes are determinant factors in the planning and shape of the building. In many cases interiors are treated as separate contracts, and, when the building is in its initial design, there is no assurance to the architectural firm that they will be awarded the design contract for the interiors. In some building types such as theaters, museums, or other public buildings, it is almost impossible to divorce the two aspects of design. The best architectural firms insist on total control over their jobs and will, therefore, take responsibility for all aspects of design, including landscaping, lighting, interiors, and building graphics. Often the attitude of the principal or partner in charge makes the difference between an indifferent or a superb interior design job. In some offices the partner in charge will go to the client meetings together with his interior staff members in order to emphasize the importance attached to that phase of the job. In some offices, the architectural design scheme is so strong that there are few decisions left to any designer but the architect in charge. A building like Eero Saarinen's TWA terminal (see pp. 52, 53) is an example of a strong design statement that left no piece of furniture or no material as an entity or component to be considered apart from the architecture. Frequently the interior-design department begins its involvement on a new project through programming and development of clients' needs. The programming of a new building involves space planning and analysis. In order to arrive at a budget figure for a new structure, the interior designers often must submit estimates of all interior furnishings and materials even before the project goes into the working-drawing stage. The choice of materials is a matter of aesthetics as well as cost, and there is never a very clear line between the architect's and the designer's sphere of influence. Some architectural offices consider all architectural materials, which form integral parts of the building, the responsibility of the architectural design and assign the choice of surfacing materials to the interior designer. In the better offices no such clear distinction is drawn, and the decisions are arrived at jointly. The same divisions of labor apply at times between built-in architectural features and free-standing furniture. More and more architectural offices depend on the special skills of the interior designer to design and detail special features such as architectural woodwork, and a certain amount of overlap between the production department and interior draftsmen may exist.

The bulk of the interior-design work in architectural offices does not differ measurably from similar work done in the large interior firms. There might, however, be more involvement with the design and specifications of mechanical equipment and subsequent supervision, and often there may be involvement with decisions affecting the landscaping. Certainly the lighting is designed as a team effort between the architect and interior designer, together with lighting designers or illuminating engineers as special consultants. Architectural offices depend on their interior staff members for research into new materials and for a familiarity with all products available for interior finishes. Those aspects of a job that deal with furniture and all the interior furnishings are exclusively handled by the interior departments, and require the steps and procedures normally followed by interior designers in small or large offices alike.

A good many small architectural offices consisting of no more than a handful of people are engaged in work which is in effect interior design. Many of these architects, often younger members of the profession, form partnerships with interior designers and work hand-in-hand with their colleagues on all aspects of a job. Interior designers employed in small architectural offices often perform a number of tasks that are handled by draftsmen and architects in the larger offices and spend much of their time in architectural drafting and design.

Regardless of the organizational structure in large or small architectural offices, the key to the successful total job is the teamwork and cooperation between all the designers, who must perform together very much like members of a symphony orchestra. Each one must be a competent artist in his own right; but as a group they must perform with proper ensemble under the direction of a leader, whether he is the partner in charge, the chief designer, or the project director.

4

SPACE PLANNING OFFICE

There is no precise borderline between the large design offices, the offices known as "contract designers", or the firms called "space planners". The reference is usually to design concerned with large corporations or governmental agencies, occupying or planning occupancy of many thousands of square feet of office space. The term "space planner" has become the most accepted term for people concerned with the analysis of spatial requirements, the programming of needs for clients, the preliminary space layouts, and ultimately the final planning. The uses of space studies, especially in their preliminary stages, are often for prearchitectural planning or for lease negotiations. Space planning requires competence and much specialized knowledge about the workings and needs of large firms; it does not, as a rule, encompass many aesthetic considerations. There are, in fact, some large design offices that have within their organizational setup departments of space planning, together with design, production, and the usual subdivisions. Considering the enormous cost of office space (in large cities rentals for prime office space may range to $10.00 per square foot per year and more) the careful analysis of needs is a vital service for those businesses contemplating buildings, moves, or renovations. A number of space-planning firms have developed thorough procedures for analysis and programming as an independent service. That means that frequently a space-planning firm will be retained for the development of a program, but will not necessarily be awarded the job of designing the space, even if the same firm offers design services. Specialists in space planning usually have design

Armstrong Cork Company, Lancaster, Pennsylvania. Skidmore, Owings, and
Merrill, designers. An example of a large office space carefully designed for
audio-visual privacy in spite of the large number of work stations in the space.
Contrast this with the examples of Office Landscape designed more recently
and discussed in the chapter on that topic.

training and often architectural training. They must have
learned to understand the vast complexities of corporate business and the office equipment from large IBM systems to the
latest filing cabinets on the market; they must also be adept
at grasping the particular operational needs of each firm in
order to help their clients arrive at better working procedures.
There is a similarity in these services to management-consult-
ing services, and indeed there are a number of firms who
combine management consulting with space planning and

program development. The concept of "office landscaping" described briefly in another section grew out of the work of space planners working with management consultants. It is also one of the early uses of computer technology for the solution of design problems. It stands to reason that future years will find many space planners (as well as other design offices) using computers as valuable tools for design.

There are relatively few design offices restricting their activities to space planning and related activities. Most firms offer a series of related services in the field of design. The aims of space planning are mostly functional and do not as a rule lead to spectacular design solutions. It is, however, one of the many special activities in interior design that requires thorough training, talent, and much experience.

5

DESIGN PRESENTATION

The term "presentation" is an odd one, suggesting as it does the formal giving of a gift. It has entered into the jargon of the profession, probably coming from the advertising business, where it means a showing of proposed work. There are two kinds of presentations made by designers: one is an effort to persuade a prospective client to select a particular designer while the other is a presentation of design work in order to get approval from a client. In the first situation, the prospective client has no business obligation to the designer. Some designers will prepare promotional sketches "on speculation", that is, without any contract or fee in an effort to obtain a commission. Since this is really giving free design service (a kind of "free sample"), most serious designers regard doing this as unprofessional or even unethical. Other serious professions (medicine or law, for example) will never offer free advice in this fashion.

Almost any designer, even the most carefully ethical, will show a prospective client examples of his previous work and discuss how he would approach a new project. Showing ones ability in this way is quite ethical and can be done very informally or through a more organized presentation according to what seems most appropriate in a given situation. Students find that they face a similar problem when they look for a first job and must organize their work into a "portfolio" or some other presentation format so that prospective employers can evaluate their work.

This chapter is primarily concerned with the second type of design presentation, the type that forms an integral part of

An interior perspective drawn by Steve Oles showing his own design for a house to be built in Wellfleet, Mass.

a project already under way with a client who has selected a designer and authorized him to develop his ideas and plans in enough detail to be ready for the client to review. Design presentations of this type are a tool; they are a means to an end. They are the designers language of communication. A superb design presentation can only be meaningful if the content is good; if the design presented is poor, the presentation is just

Color Rendering by Ettore Sottsaas, Jr. (shown here in black and white) of an experimental house to be built in Grand Rapids, Michigan, Nelson and Chadwick, architects.

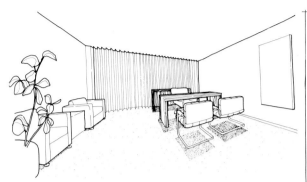

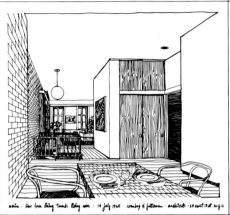

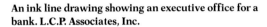

An ink line drawing showing an executive office for a
bank. L.C.P. Associates, Inc.

Line drawing by Eugene
Futterman of Rosenberg
and Futterman.
Living-dining area in a
city house renovation.

that much fancy wrapping for a package of questionable content. Student designers and some design firms, unfortunately,
spend a large percentage of their time or fees on impressive
presentations, with resulting mediocrity of design solutions.

Before a presentation reaches the client it serves a number
of purposes:

(a) Each plan, elevation, section or perspective sketch in its
rough form is part of the process needed by the designer
to visualize ideas.
(b) Since most large projects involve teams of designers,
these drawings are also a means of communication among
fellow designers, employers, and employees.
(c) Rough studies or finished presentations also serve as a
means of communication with contractors, engineers,
and various trades (in addition to working drawings).

Clients need presentations in order to visualize and compre-
hend the proposed design solutions. Often the participation of
the clients in real solutions to problems is essential, and only
through complete understanding of what is proposed can such
intelligent participation be obtained. It need not, however, be
an elaborate and costly presentation in order to communicate
the design intent, especially if the job is simple and of moderate
scope. A major design commission presented to a board of
directors or to a committee, may require considerably more
effort than a design solution presented to a single client. A
presentation to a board or a group might be the one and only
opportunity given the designer for the presentation of his

Photograph of a model for an experimental house to be built in Grand Rapids, Michigan. Nelson and Chadwick, architects.

Sketch with superimposed color tones illustrating a public service lobby for an insurance corporation. Drawing by John Pile for Sandgren and Murtha, Inc.

ideas; it might be impossible to get the group together again for supplementary submissions. Larger jobs also provide more adequate budgets to cover the expenses of thorough presentations. Design firms use judgment and experience as a guide to the kind of presentation deemed necessary. A small residential job may need no perspective drawings at all. The design of major corporate offices for a group of bankers or lawyers might need elaborate staging. It is possible that carefully staged presentations of elaborate drawings are essentially "sales jobs", but even the most excellent solution needs that kind of approach at times, in order to obtain final approval for proposed schemes.

Design presentations vary considerably from firm to firm. Some design firms have special presentation rooms with sophisticated audio-visual equipment for the expressed purpose of staging impressive presentations for clients. Other design firms prefer simple and plain sets of drawings. Full color perspective renderings may be done within the design firms by staff members, or may be given to professional renderers. The latter often command impressive prices for their work. It is for that reason that many designers prefer simple techniques, and perhaps use line drawings supplemented with boards showing the actual colors, materials, and photographs of furnishings. At times these presentations are done in form of booklets, or at times in the more conventional manner of large presentation boards. Complex architectural spaces are difficult to show in the form of drawings. Architects always prefer scale models of their buildings (also expensive to build), and a good many interior design firms use models rather extensively for presentation purposes. Spaces containing many pieces of furniture are usually shown without every single piece of furniture, and sometimes a combination of a space model, with furniture drawn into the model in plan form only, are effective means of explaining schemes.

Until the early part of the twentieth century, architects and designers tended to spend considerable time on presentation, and this attitude was reflected in carefully drawn and elaborately inked and rendered drawings done in schools. In recent years it has become more accepted to use simple presentations and quick-sketching techniques. It is impossible to state firm rules about design presentations, and it is conceivable that the "fashion" will change again in due time. With the exception of very special needs such as full-size mock ups for certain types (hotel rooms, dormitory spaces) the following criteria are generally accepted:

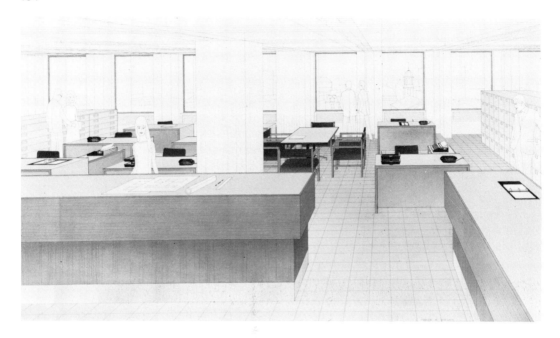

Perspective drawing using both line and color tones. A space in the new Boston City Hall. I.S.D. Inc., interior designers.

Plans of single spaces are the absolute minimum presentations for any kind of job. Elevations, sections, design details, sketches, renderings and models may all be part of a presentation; color charts, material samples, product photographs and budgets might also be required. The format of all sheets or boards should be uniform in size, and the color and texture of paper or board should be coordinated. Lettering and titles should be kept small, but neat and uniform throughout a particular presentation. Presentations should be organized in logical and chronological ways, for clarity as well as appearance. Overlays, acetate wrappings and any overly artsy displays or different media should be avoided. Drafting aids such as press type letters or textures, or repeat forms such as chairs, tables, desks or trees, are acceptable, and are being used rather frequently.

Each single sheet or board is a two-dimensional composition and should be carefully planned that way. Boards should not be crowded, nor should there be just one small plan, or one small elevation on an otherwise empty 20 in. $\times$ 30 in. board. Overly designed presentations can detract from the basic design information to be conveyed, and might indeed be suspect in the eyes of a client. Mats and fancy borders should be avoided for the same reason. Materials and samples should be

neatly arranged and composed to read well, rather than to form a collage-like painting. Full color renderings or rough sketches should be fairly realistic, since exaggerated perspectives can easily lead to disappointed clients upon actual completion of the job. Realism in color and texture on renderings are a matter of judgment. The more sophisticated a client, the easier he or she will understand a schematic or rough sketch; a rough sketch supplemented with actual materials and color samples might convey more information than a careful rendering without supporting material.

There are no set rules about media. A pencil in the hand of a competent delineator is a medium that will do anything that ink can do—cheaper and faster. The elaborately drawn and rendered presentations of a generation ago have given way to magic markers more often than not. But individual preferences and skills have always determined the designer's media.

Sketch perspective showing a portion of a residential interior. Drawing and design by Norman Diekman.

A carefully drafted plan
showing floor coverings
and furniture placement.
The numbers refer to an
informational key.
Showroom for
Georg Jensen, New York;
Warren Platner, architect
and interior architect.

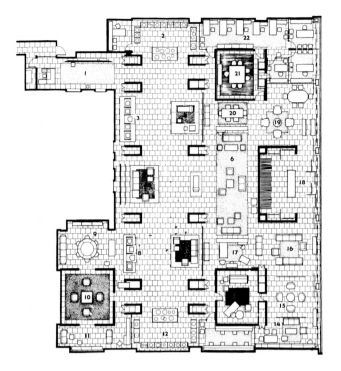

Plan of an apartment
showing proposed
furniture layout. Drawing
and design by
Norman Diekman.

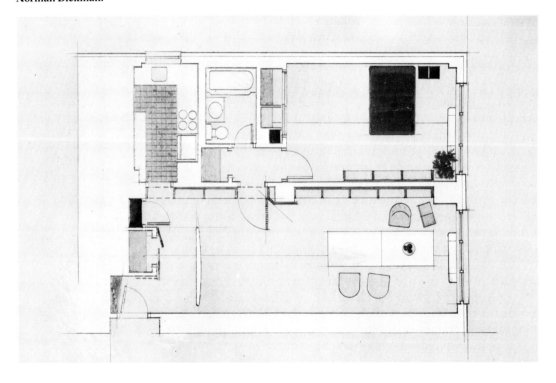

A rough sketch in ink by
Florence Knoll Bassett.
An executive office in the
C.B.S. Building, New
York.

Some great designers were masters of delineation as well, and
some of Frank Lloyd Wright's drawings and renderings are
works of art in themselves.

Design presentations are distinctly different from working
drawings and contract documents. The latter may include sets
of written specifications and many technical details. Since the
presentation stage often includes negotiations for budgets, cost
analysis, charts, and product selections are sometimes included in this stage. It is extremely important to clearly
organize such information, if indeed it is part of a presentation, since nothing is quite as deadly as confused and confusing sets of charts and figures. As important as the visual
presentation, the verbal explanation accompanying such presentations is an equally significant component. High-pressure
sales talk can be damaging to the designer, but many designers
must consciously learn to give clear and forceful explanations
to put their points of view across.

In recent years photography has become an increasingly
important tool for use in making presentations and many
students are exploring the possibilities of some of these techniques. Good color film and processing and inexpensive cameras capable of close-up work (single lens reflex 35 mm
cameras are a favorite type) make it possible to produce color
slides easily, reliably and fairly inexpensively. Using slides has
some disadvantages—there must be a darkened room with a
screen, they cannot be kept conveniently visible for various

A highly realistic pencil drawing by Frank Lloyd Wright showing the living room of the Coonley house, Riverside, Ill.

people to consult as easily as drawings, and the formality of a slide show sometimes hampers informal discussion. On the other hand they are ideal for showing to larger groups and are easy to transport and store. Even when drawings or models are used in a first presentation, it is desirable to have a photographic record for future showings when, perhaps the original material has been lost, damaged or is simply not conveniently at hand. There also seems to be a certain fascination in sitting in a darkened room looking at large clear pictures that holds most people spellbound and often helps the designer to hold his client's attention and obtain his understanding and approval.

Slides can simply illustrate drawings and charts of the more conventional sort, but it is also possible to photograph individual details of drawings, make title slides and organize in a sequence that leads the viewer to a better understanding of the proposals being presented. Sketches and renderings seem much more realistic and impressive when they are projected on a big screen and even rough sketches can take on great authority this way.

Perhaps the most important use of photography is in the showing of models. It is hard to keep a model in perfect condition for long, and transporting a complex model is often a very difficult problem. It is also hard to view a model in a

Photographs of two scale
model interiors built to
show furniture in varied
spaces. George Nelson
and Co., Inc., designers. Models
by Phoebe Murray Chorley.

way that gives a realistic impression—especially a model
interior. Most often the ceiling is removed and viewers look
down from above. Even when a model is placed for eye-level
viewing and arranged so that there are openings to look
through, the effect is more that of a doll's house than of reality.
We go inside real interiors to look at them in a way that is not
physically possible with models. The camera, however can
"go inside", the ceiling can be in place and realistic lighting
can be arranged. Slides taken in this way with many views
arranged in order can give an amazing impression of an actual
visit to a real space. With finely made models, it is sometimes
impossible to tell the model from reality.

Proposed renovation of a First National City Bank branch, New York. Design and model by John Pile for Sandgren and Murtha, Inc.

Model bank branch with ceiling removed. United Mutual Savings Bank, New York. L.C.P. Associates, Inc., interior designers.

Model bank branch (see figure on page 490) **photographed at normal eye level.
United Mutual Savings Bank, New York. L.C.P. Associations, Inc.,
Interior designers.**

Some designers have even experimented with moving pictures and taped TV as a means of giving an illusion of a "walk through" a real space. Such techniques can become very costly and difficult, but can sometimes be justified in relation to large projects where there can be a great deal at stake in the making of design decisions.

In summary it is important to keep in mind that presentations are but a means to an end. Overly elaborate and gimmicky presentations might obscure their basic purpose, which is, or should be, to present a design concept, not to be primarily a sales device. When sales presentations begin to blur the designer's vision, there will be the danger that the designer will sell a presentation, rather than a design solution.

6

COMPUTER AIDED DESIGN
AND DRAFTING

In 1950, in *The Human Use of Human Beings*, Dr. Norbert Wiener suggested that, under the designation "cybernetics", computers and related machines were about to introduce a sweeping change in every aspect of modern life. Now, thirty years later, we can consider how his prediction, like most futurism, turns out to have both overestimated and underestimated actual events. The dream and hope that computers would offer help with the most complex and subtle of human problems seems to have gone largely unrealized, but the extent of their penetration into everyday life has been surprisingly great even if this fact is easy to ignore. Computers seem to have turned out to be most useful for the dullest, most boring, and most repetitive of activities and in these roles they work largely unnoticed.

We hardly give a moment's thought to the ways in which our airline and car rental reservations are dealt with so efficiently. We take for granted the arrival of prompt and painfully accurate utility bills, enjoy depositing computer drawn checks and worry about what may be happening to our tax returns at an IRS computer center. In all of these situations, computers are dealing with vast amounts of data of a quite routine sort, doing it with lightning speed and great accuracy with a minimum of human help. If these situations all involve a slightly indirect involvement of computer use (we do not operate the reservation terminal ourselves, but watch the counter attendant do so, for example), more and more direct uses are surfacing in ways that bring the average man in touch with the machine almost without awareness. The bank's cash machine is a good example–almost everyone has talked to the little green screen by push-button and been gratified to receive the asked-for dollars. Work activities such as the "word processing" that is replacing stenographic and some secretarial chores are rapidly putting more and more people "on line" with esoteric machinery that does its routine work tirelessly and expertly.

The design community has stayed a bit aloof from the computer world with a tendency toward love-hate relationships that include great hopes and promises expressed by a small number of enthusiasts balanced by fear and suspicion, less openly expressed but more often acted upon. Designers are trained to deal with difficult problems requiring the resolution of conflicting values and are also trained to believe that qualities of "talent", "artistic skill", and even genius are needed to do well with such problems. In addition, the training of architects and designers includes a large measure of direct manual skill in the ability to draw well. Good design training makes a person into a good draftsman and the ability to do this chore well is often the trained designer's most visible and salable skill. The client can, or may believe he can, come up with ideas for a house, office, or factory, but he remains utterly dependent on a skilled professional for the production of the "blue-prints", the contract documents needed to make an idea into a reality. It is not easy to believe that an electronic gadget box can help with design creativity and it seems to be unwelcome to admit that it most certainly can help with the chore work of design: drafting.

Whatever the intellectual or emotional reasons for resisting computer aid, it has been easy for designers to hide behind the reality that computer equipment is expensive and, (to a diminishing extent) demanding of such inconvenient circumstances as air conditioned rooms with raised floors. Several forces are at work to bring to an end the era of designers' isolation from the computerized world. These forces are:

1. Computer gear constantly becomes smaller, cheaper, simpler and less demanding environmentally.
2. Communication networks, tied to phone lines make access to remote, expensive, and complex equipment simple and easy.
3. Manufacturers of products that designers specify are beginning to offer computer aids to their customers.

The first of these influences is leading some larger design offices to take the plunge involved in buying equipment and training users to put it to work. It takes a big firm (as design and architectural offices go) to finance this step and justify it with a sufficient volume of work to keep the machinery and people busy and productive. An example of this development would be the adoption of a system designated CAD (for computer aided draft-

Drawing by keyboard command with results held in computer memory at Caudill, Rowlett, and Scott's Houston office.

ing) at Caudill Rowlett Scott, a large architectural office in Houston. Designers produce sketches, marked up plans and details, and notes according to their usual routines containing enough information for the drafting of production drawings. Instead of these being processed by draftsmen working with the conventional tools of T-square, triangle, pencil and paper, they go to the computer drafting operators who feed the information into the computer's memory using keyboard instructions and, occasionally a tracing tool (cursor) to order up the web of lines, symbols, dimensions and lettering that make up construction drawings. A plotter can then produce an actual drawing on paper at a frantic speed with superb mechanical precision. What are the advantages? Repeated elements (symbols, details, lettered blocks) can be kept in memory and called up instantly instead of having to be laboriously redrawn. Related drawings can be precisely coordinated, corrected and updated and remain stored in computer memory more compactly and conveniently than conventional paper (or mylar) can ever be. The same drawing can be consulted at various remote terminals at the same time and can be delivered electronically (at least in theory) anywhere that a plotter is available. A sheet of details that would take 40 hours of manual drafting can be produced in 20 minutes with a level of finish and accuracy beyond what the best human draftsman can manage. Extensions of the system can take off quantities and produce cost estimates. At present, CAD is in use for architec-

A computer driven pen plotter draws at speeds up to 20 inches per second. (Photographs courtesy Caudill, Rowlett and Scott, architects)

tural, engineering, and interior design drafting. It does not design, it does not "think", but it is a masterful draftsman.

A survey of a major furniture manufacturer's* computer graphics involvement leads to the second and third issues. The furniture industry, at least its larger units, have been using general business computers for years in the familiar roles of inventory control, production management, and accounting. It is not surprising that, with both experience and hardware at hand, furniture makers should be led to consider what this machinery can do to make the designers' work easier and/or better. In practice, the hardware preexisting, the typical business general computer turns out not to be very useful, but the new generation of smaller and smaller computers makes it possible to consider a "dedicated" (special purpose) unit to take on design-related assignments.

At its corporate headquarters, this firm is heavily committed to the use of computer aided drafting equipment for in-house use in turning out engineering drawings, much like that described at CRS. Here, the subject matter is the parts drawings and assembly drawings that are the basis for furniture production. An existing drawing can be "traced" into computer memory, a new drawing created by keyed-in instructions that order up lines, curves, symbols, dimensions and lettering. The drawing is built

*Herman Miller, Inc. of Zeeland, Michigan

up as an image (or succession of images) on the TV screen-like CRT tube which can look at a small part of a complete drawing or zoom in to magnify a tiny detail. The actual complete drawing is being built up in the computer's magnetic memory and only comes to exist on paper when it is ordered printed out on a copying machine (for small drawings and details) or drafted by pen on a large plotter. Designers and engineers work in their accustomed ways but turn over the necessary sketches and notes to the specialists in computer drafting for conversion into the highly standardized and mechanically perfect final computer drawings.

Two input centers feed the computer and operators can keep the equipment busy in shifts, 24 hours a day when necessary. The typical operator is an engineer with conventional drafting experience who has had a two-week briefing on the operation of the equipment provided by its manufacturer. Skill in the technique then develops with experience reaching its full potential after months of work on the actual drawings needed for the particular work involved. A skilled operator becomes something of a virtuoso producing perfect results at lightning speed and development of special details and functions held in memory making work gradually improve in efficiency. It is possible, for example, to produce a pair of drawings, one in foot and inch and one in metric dimensions with total precision on simple command. Items of hardware and connectors already in use are in memory and can be instantly drawn upon in appropriate places in new product development. It is estimated that efficiency of drawing production is at least doubled in terms of man-hours involved and there are obvious gains in convenience and precision which are harder to evaluate. Although of no direct usefulness to the design world outside, experience with this system has encouraged involvement with a next step, closer in reach to every designer.

For some time several manufacturers have offered computer aided studies to help the office planner and the office furniture dealer who plan or work with planners. These people deal mainly with non-graphic data, lists of office users and their equipment requirements, studies of communication interactions and the financial impact of investment in new equipment. The input is survey lists of names and numbers, the output, other lists and occasional charts of the sort dear to the hearts of open or "landscape" planners. Input can be mailed in, results mailed back and at the computer center, data entry is by keyboard and output is typed out as in most familiar computer applications using typewriter-type terminals. Equipment is now in place and software is available to offer a direct link, over phone lines and

Space planning in three dimensions with the designer able to "walk through" the space as it is developed. (Photograph courtesy Herman Miller, Inc.)

related communication networks into any office, dealer showroom or other centers where suitable terminals are available.

A user, designer, architect, planner or dealer who subscribes to the service dials in to contact a central facility, places the phone handset in the recess of the remote terminal, and is connected to the computer with access to its programs as if the computer was in the building. If the terminal in use is only a keyboard and print-out unit, communication is of the sort found familiarly at airline ticket counters—data is typed in, responses are typed back. This is useful for expediting the processing of the word and number studies discussed above, but graphic communication requires a somewhat more specialized terminal such as the Tektronix unit with a large TV-like screen on which visual material can be displayed. The remote subscriber, once dialed in is now time-sharing use of the central system and can proceed, on the basis of rather quickly learned routines, to generate plans and elevations of furniture system layouts. Proposed grouping are instantly displayed, can be revised until satisfactory and then carried forward into further steps of identifying catalog numbers, selecting finishes, and totaling up costs. Adding a small plotter to the equipment array makes it possible to produce an almost instantaneous drawing of the configuration developed on the screen.

Held in computer memory are all the physical and numerical data that relate to the real furniture components—instead of poring over complex data in price lists, appropriate information appears on demand and decisions, tentative or final can be accumulated along with related totals of workstations, components, and costs. Elevation drawings, rarely made by most planners because of the time and trouble involved, can be generated at lightning speed making it easier to communicate with clients and with final installers as to what an actual office work stations will be like and how it is to be assembled. Data about an installation can be held in memory to be called up again when changes are to take place so that the intricacies of replanning and accounting for what components are excess, which are to be newly ordered, are vastly simplified.

In theory, a planning firm could enter the entire roster of products expected to be used on any project and plan at the keyboard with full freedom to select from any desired sources. Costs to a user are based on time in actual communication, the extent of the computer effort demanded, the amount of on-line data storage (information "parked" in computer memory), and the cost of print-outs by the page. In addition, the user must provide the terminal equipment at his end, either by purchase or lease. Minimum equipment leasing would cost very little but a full array of terminal equipment could cost much more, with terminals that can access other computer services by phone, and that can work as input and output devices for any micro- or mini-computer units a user might want to acquire (purchase or lease) to do other chores, graphic, word or numerical.

It is common experience that first steps toward computer involvement are taken with trepidation and uncertainty. As actual experience develops, enthusiasm rises and the inclination to acquire more equipment and extend uses expands. Perhaps larger dealers will be inclined to set up terminal centers where planners and designers in smaller firms can gain first-hand experience with the techniques. For really small design firms (one-person up to ten, perhaps) access to such service on an occasional basis may be all that is needed. For larger firms, increasing use of more extensive computer systems seems inevitable and is well under way as the notes on CRS above suggest.

One more step into computer graphics is not fully into use as yet and still a future possibility as far as access for the outside user is concerned. This involves the highly sophisticated visual display and related input devices tied into "mainframe" computer equipment with sizeable capacity. Ownership can run to $375,000 and the hardware is on a scale that demands a room of some size and suggests some fairly specialized personel to exploit the possibilities offered. This is the kind of system that can display moving images of highways or airport runways simulating reality in startling illusion—in full color if the necessary gear and software is present. In space planning, it is possible to enter into memory the full three-dimensional reality of a space so that it becomes available for display from any point of view or from a moving point of view. Also held in memory can be the forms of a roster of objects, pieces of furniture or other components ready to be placed within the space shell at any location. Objects appear where wanted on demand and can be moved about as if they were models within a model space—then one can seem to "walk through" the furnished space, moving up or down, forward or backward as desired. Connection to the simpler system described above makes it possible to move from a plan layout designed in realistic perspective to plans, elevations, lists and specifications printed, finally on paper as desired.

In this system, the operator uses a stylus to "draw" on an electronic "slate", placing lines in tentative postions and moving them about until they are "fixed" by pressing down the stylus tip. A keyboard and small CRT display control entering and calling up images from memory. Conceptually, the special ability of this system is to hold in memory not merely a fixed drawing of an object, but a full "visual description"—almost seemingly the object itself, so that it can be rotated into any position, looked at from all sides, entered into and generally treated as if it were a reality. Thus, there is the possibility of placing a complete multi-story building shell in memory, viewing it externally, moving into the space of any floor and placing walls, lighting, and furniture in desired locations. Placements can be experimental until they are decided upon and then fixed so that quantity counts and costing can follow. It is impossible to watch demonstrations without sensing the potentialities for a total new way to approach design and planning.

Other possible uses include the making of graphic charts of acoustical conditions so that study of speech privacy, for example, becomes a matter of manipulating elements in response to visual signal rather than a struggle with confusing numerical data.

At the moment there is no easy way to make this kind of function easily available at remote locations—the terminal involved is large and costly and, when in use, makes heavy demands on the capacities of a fairly large computer. The necessary "software" to exploit all of the possibilities discussed above is also complex and under constant development. Possibilities that can be displayed on a demonstration basis are not always easy to put into use on a real project. Certain seemingly minor issues can be hard for the computer to deal with—for example, drawings of objects show up as "skeleton" or "X-ray" perspectives just as they do when a draftsman constructs a line perspective drawing. A draftsman

An existing drawing is "traced" into a computer memory with a movable "cursor". (Photograph courtesy Herman Miller, Inc.)

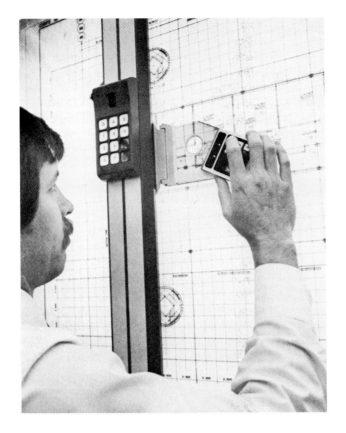

omits or erases hidden lines routinely because his intelligence tells him on a "common-sense" basis what lines to show, which will be hidden. The computer lacks "common-sense" and programs to instruct it on how to decide what lines to treat as hidden are difficult to develop. For the moment it is easier for the operator to "erase" hidden lines on the basis of his own judgment, rather than computer intelligence.

Obstacles to wider use of computer graphic techniques still exist. Cost of equipment is an obvious one, particularly for the most advanced, and therefore most exciting of functions. The small terminal with access to remote computer capacity is already commonplace in larger firms and will probably soon be available to small offices and dealerships as well. Computer drafting is a reality for large firms and will filter to smaller ones as equipment becomes more compact and less expensive. Design work at a fully interactive terminal with possibilities to move from rough sketch to finished drawings and specifications remains something of a future dream—technically possible but still so demanding of expensive equipment and programming as to keep it out of reach of all but large industry users.

Still, the greatest obstacle to acceptance probably remains the uneasiness felt by the typical designer who is the potential user. Lawrence Lerner of Saphier Lerner Schindler (SLS Environetics), a firm with considerable experience in actual use of computer graphics for large office planning projects, such as the Sears Tower in Chicago, recently stated the opinion that "it is easier to train a computer operator to work as a designer then it is to teach a designer to work with a computer." A more optimistic view of this resistance is that it is mostly a matter of inexperience. Once actually "hands on" at a terminal with lines and images moving about with magic ease, even the most resistant will yield to a feeling of excitement and pleasure in what has become so easy.

One other issue still seems to invite further study. At the moment, larger manufacturers are beginning to offer access to their hardware primarily as an aid in specifying their products. A complete design job involves many product lines, many *types* of products (ceilings, partitions, lighting, furniture, floor coverings, and so on) from many different sources. The full potential of computer design activity will not reach its peak until there is a coordinated data management system in which most manufacturers can enter into a network of communication so that a remote design firm can draw on any number of sources as one can now draw on only a few in unrelated ways. To sit at a terminal choosing products from many suppliers, watching the visual result emerge on a screen, observing a budget automatically assembled and with the knowledge that orders and inventory records can all be executed with total accuracy on demand is still a dream. Its realization depends on development of standardized formats for data storage, communication and display. As long as each manufacturer, each design firm, each consultant enters the computer world on a basis of every man for himself, progress will occur, but it will be at a modest rate and with only a small fraction of the possibilities turning into everyday realities. It has taken almost a century to move from telephones that were curious novelties, only able to communicate with the few other instruments subscribing to the same phone company, to the near universal system that we now take for granted in which any phone can access any other anywhere in the world (almost) virtually instantaneously and with extreme ease. A similarly universal network for communicating the visual, verbal and numerical data that are the essence of design work could be put together almost at once with techniques now available. We can hope for actuality in less than a hundred years.

7

EDUCATION
FOR INTERIOR DESIGN

A profession that is quite new obviously does not have a strongly established educational tradition leading to its ranks. Until the late 1940's there was little formal education offered in the field and the only courses available were basically concerned with interior decoration.

The years following World War II saw a sudden demand for well-trained designers and a number of leading schools started serious curriculum revisions towards a strongly professional training in interior design. A number of faculty members had come from Europe just a few years earlier, and several designers or architects who had studied at the famous Bauhaus School in Germany became instrumental in establishing a new educational direction in design. The profession is still young enough to have among its members many practitioners whose educational background was in architecture or other related fields. By today, the objectives of the profession are clear and demanding, and all educational institutions that have not done so yet are in the process of planning new curricula.

A study conducted by the Interior Design Educators Council in 1968 revealed that programs leading to a baccalaureate degree with a major in interior design existed at seventy schools. The report also revealed that many semiprofessional schools exist and that a number of universities offer some interior-design courses without a complete professional education. Many of the seventy schools and a few additional professional schools of art were in the process of changing their course offerings, and at this time it is likely that the picture has changed again. During 1967 a study on architectural education was conducted at Princeton University. That report was published under the title, "A Study of Education for Environmental Design". Significantly the term "architecture" was not used in spite of the fact that the project had been commissioned by the American Institute of Architects. That study and the one conducted by IDEC point to a direction of ever-changing and developing curricula for design education. Interior design is only one area of many other special areas in the field of environmental design, and no single architect or designer can master all the knowledge required today. Schools of architecture and schools of design will continue to teach the basic knowledge and skills that are the foundation of design and architecture. Professional specialization will continue to become more specific, but based on a thorough educational foundation and combined with general knowledge, this trend should be of great benefit to the environmental-design professions.

Most professional programs are of four-year duration, terminating with a bachelor's degree. There are several schools whose programs last five years (which is the average duration for architectural courses), and it is apparent that more and more universities will change their interior-design courses to five-year programs. The average design and professional course-load in major courses consists of 60 percent of the total required credit, with the rest being devoted to academic courses and specialized art and architectural history course work. Many students enter professional courses with previous college work or a junior college background, and indeed there is no doubt about the desirability of devoting more than the minimum four-year time period to professional education. There is an increasing trend towards the requirement of graduate degrees in almost all academic disciplines and interior design is no exception. A few years ago a master's degree in design or art was rare for anybody, but a university teacher. Today there exists a steadily growing number of graduate programs in all fields of art and design, as well as in architecture. The needs and demands of our society have been changing rapidly.

Until two or three decades ago, university education leading to degrees was hardly available in interior design, nor was it universal in architecture. Many of the great designers or artists of the early part of the century had no formal training. The increasing trend towards college training in all fields of learning makes it almost essential for any serious designer to seek a formal education. The name of a school or its department of administration is not the key to the quality of its program. The IDEC study of 1968 found that a number of schools, departments, and administrative units offer satisfactory programs in interior design, as a rule within a specific department of interior design.

The IDEC curriculum study contained a strong recommendation for a program of accreditation of schools, as well as an accrediting procedure for individuals who wish to join one of the major professional societies. A Foundation for Interior Design Education Research (FIDER) was formed by the professional societies together with IDEC in 1971 for the purpose of establishing and administering a voluntary plan for the special accreditation of interior design education offered at institutions of higher learning located throughout the United States, its possessions and Canada. According to the guidelines established by the National Commission on Accrediting, formal recognition to an accrediting agency can be granted after several years of provisional accrediting visits. FIDER has in a short period become a forceful body setting standards for various levels of interior design education, and accrediting those programs that seek such recognition.

In 1974 a National Council for Interior Design Qualifications was formed by major design societies, including representation from the Industrial Design Society. Examinations prepared by NCIDQ with the help of the Professional Testing Services are now given twice yearly in several national testing centers for those candidates who apply for membership into one of the professional societies. It is apparent that within a span of half a dozen years great strides were made by the design professions and by design educators to establish clearer standards in the field, and above all to make sure that designers are well-educated, and qualified to practice.

In spite of the demands for formal education and degrees, it is important to remember that interior design is above all a creative field. All forms of design are creative endeavors, but differ considerably from the fine arts. Design is a teleological activity; it is concerned with the solution to problems in aesthetic terms. Art in its many forms is a personal and emotive expression of the artist. No matter what precise definition is given to design, the fact that it is a creative activity makes it impossible to establish rigid rules for its practice and education.

Most of our cultural and artistic tradition emanates from Europe. It is interesting to note that there are still several European nations where architecture is considered a "free profession" without the rigid governmental controls for licensing that we have in the United States. Interior architecture in

Le Corbusier's drawing (ink line) of a projected house interior.

Europe is known and recognized more clearly than in America, yet there are no uniform educational requirements or governmental controls for training of interior designers. The exception is England, where a government-appointed commission has carried out accreditation visits to all schools of art and design. The resulting reorganization of these schools has been extremely beneficial to design education in England. As the newly constituted programs have only been in existence since the early 1960's one cannot yet judge the ultimate results. It is apparent, however, that the general state of design in England has seen a remarkable upsurge in recent years and that there is a very obvious cause and effect relationship to the educational institutions training young British designers.

Writing about education in definitive terms is an almost futile effort; curricula in superior schools, especially in a creative field, are constantly undergoing changes. Both recent curricula studies, the Princeton report and the IDEC report, recognize this need for change. Neither study has spelled out one single "correct" program. The Princeton report proposes a national framework for environmental design education based on a series of two-year "modules", which would, by combining these modules in varying ways, give students and schools much flexibility in choice. Interior design is one of the many "modules" implied in this very broad approach to design education. In the much needed attempt to strengthen the existing offerings in interior design education, the IDEC study contains a basic outline for interior design education, followed by a listing of recommended curriculum content. In it, subject matters are listed under the headings of Creative Work, Technical Work and Communications Skills, Professional Procedures, and Academic Studies-Liberal Arts. Under each of these basic categories specific courses are recommended. They range from drawing and three-dimensional design to furniture design; and from drafting and presentation to the planning and design of public buildings. The IDEC recommendations and now the standards and goals established by FIDER recognize the differing emphases of various schools and therefore present specific subject matters under the four subheadings in such a way that each school can vary its curriculum sequence and emphasis of courses within the framework of the suggested 60 to 80 percent creative and professional work, and 20 to 40 percent in liberal arts.

The mastery of design is always a goal, a goal which can never be reached completely. For a serious and committed designer, reaching for this goal will be a lifelong endeavor. It will be an exciting endeavor that each day will bring new knowledge and growth. The fact that the ultimate goal is elusive is the challenge that makes design a rewarding and satisfying profession.

8

THE PROFESSION

In a period of approximately 25 years, interior design has developed from a field dominated by dilletantes into a serious profession recognized as such by society. This does not mean that every aspect of the field is perfect; nor does it mean that everybody who is called an interior designer is qualified to do so. To strengthen the profession and to ascertain that the public is served competently, is one of the goals of the professional societies. The largest society is the American Society of Interior Designers (ASID); it is also the oldest (AID and NSID merged into this one strong organization in 1975) and most respected in the country. Institute of Business Designers (IBD) is another major society consisting of serious professionals. Both groups, together with several other groups (including the Canadian Society) have formed the National Council for Interior Design Qualifications, mentioned in the previous chapter. NCIDQ performs a vital role in the ongoing attempt to improve and strengthen the profession of Interior Design. At this time every professional society whose members are interior designers makes it mandatory for new members to pass the national examination given by NCIDQ. In most cases candidates are required to have completed a four year interior design program or its equivalent, and have two years of professional experience in the field.

The examination consists of two parts given on two consecutive days. The academic part consists of questions designed to test the candidate's knowledge of history, modern design, technical information, professional practice and ethics.

The second part is an all day design problem testing the candidate's ability to arrive at a conceptual solution of a realistic design problem involving space planning, furniture arrangement and selection, lighting and electrical plans, finish selection, schedules, elevations, details and a perspective sketch.

The academic section of the examination is machine graded while each design section is graded by three highly qualified interior design professionals and educators. Similar to other professional qualification examinations the NCIDQ tests are rather difficult, and the rate of failure at first attempt is high. Candidates who have graduated from good programs tend to do well; but many candidates who do not pass the first time are given the opportunity to take the examination over.

When NCIDQ was chartered it was given the mandate to develop and administer examinations; it was also asked to consider the question of licensing interior designers, and to develop guidelines. Licensing a profession such as interior design is a goal which not everybody agrees upon. There is the question about the validity of any form of licensing–whether it is meaningful and whether it might constrain creativity, and in this age of consumerism–whether licensing in general is not a form of unwarranted elitism. Detractors from the idea of licensing have advanced the argument that many service professionals such as electricians and beauticians are licensed, whereas interior design is a "free profession" or a form of art. The chances are that at this point in time it would indeed be useful for interior designers (and for the public they serve) to be recognized officially and legally through some form of licensing–most likely a form called a "title act". That term does not exclude any person from the practice of his or her profession, but it prevents unqualified practitioners from using the title. Since the title "interior designers" is widely misused, a title act would seem a good idea; it appears likely that this or a similar form of licensing will come about within the next few years. It is interesting to note that in related fields official licensing is not a uniform standard. Architecture has been a licensed profession for over sixty years. Yet there are a number of countries where this is not the case, including some European countries. Landscape Architecture is now a licensed profession in most of the United States, yet this trend was only started some two decades ago.

The fact that architecture is a licensed profession is predicated on the need to protect life and safety. It is not based on the quality of good design. Actually, in spite of licensing, there are a large number of buildings that are ugly–a fact which is of course equally true in the field of interior design, and will continue to be true, even with a title act or some form of licensing. What is being debated then are titles rather than competencies. The NCIDQ examination is designed to establish minimal professional competencies, not to select the nation's greatest interior designers. By the same token, the architectural licensing examination does not guarantee masterpieces of architecture, and indeed the shape of our environment bears witness to that.

With professional recognition and with licensing possibly to come soon, interior designers face new responsibilities, many of them of a legal nature. Even without official licenses, interior designers are liable for their work and like other professionals can be sued for malpractice. Legal responsibilities include proper specification of materials, appropriate design and specification of lighting, and countless rules and regulations ranging from barrier-free design and accessibility, to local bulding codes. In recent years a plethora of rules and regulations governing flammability of materials, fire codes, means of egress, and health/safety regulations have impacted upon interior design. It has therefore become important for educational institutions to include a knowledge of these regulations in their curricula, and it has become incumbent upon professionals to update their awareness of these requirements. In certain states flammability rules have severely restricted the kind of fabrics and floor coverings that designers can work with in public spaces; regulations governing the amount of wattage per square foot permissible in new interiors are another example of the kind of competence required of today's design professionals.

Many of the new developments discussed in previous chapters such as computer related design, new materials and technologies, and energy efficient approaches to design together with the above mentioned issues are aspects of the new professionalism in interior design. No profession is ever static, but design, perhaps more than many other fields tends to require a continuous awareness of new developments. The professional societies, as well as individual designers, structure programs and participate in programs of continuing education, seminars, symposia and meetings. Perhaps this aspect of professionalism more than anything else will determine the continuing and future success of the interior design profession. As long as practicing professionals realize the need to keep current with new developments, the profession will prosper and keep the respect of the public. The certainty that there will always be new ideas and new things to learn is one more aspect of interior design which makes it exciting and challenging.

BIBLIOGRAPHY

The literature of architecture and design is very extensive and includes innumerable books worthy of reading and study. The following list has been compiled as a guide to those books that the authors believe will prove most useful to readers who want fuller information about the various topics that are surveyed in this book.

It may occasion some surprise that so few books are listed under the topic "interior design". This is a reflection of the fact that many of the available books on this topic are outdated, of poor quality, or so blatantly commercial as to have little value to the serious reader. Fortunately, there is a vast selection of good books on architecture and related fields which, taken together, cover all aspects of interior design very thoroughly. These are the books that make up this list. Some notes are included to help describe books where the title is not fully self-explanatory; and an asterisk (*) has been used to identify a few books that are particularly recommended either because of their unusual interest, or because they deserve attention first among the titles of their group.

Basic Design

These are books about the general principles that underlie all of the visual arts. They are all difficult books best left for study after becoming acquainted with more practical material.

Art and Visual Perception, by Rudolph Arnheim (University of California Press, 1954). A basic book on the psychology of perception.

Language of Vision, by Gyorgy Kepes (Theobald, 1944). A difficult book about the basics of the visual arts. Well illustrated.

Vision in Motion, by L. Moholy-Nagy (Theobald, 1947).

Design and Expression in the Visual Arts, by J. F. A. Taylor (Dover, 1964).

Aspects of Form, edited by Lancelot Law Whyte (Lund Humphries, American Elsevier, 1968). A collection of stimulating, but often difficult, papers on widely ranging topics.

Introductions to Modern Design, by Edgar Kaufmann, Jr. (Museum of Modern Art, 1950–1953; Arno reprint, 1969).

Design: Purpose, Form and Meaning, by John Pile (University of Massachusetts Press, 1979; W. W. Norton, 1979).

History

There is no really excellent history of interior design, as such, but the excellent architectural histories deal with related interior design quite fully.

Art Nouveau, by Mario Amaya (Dutton Vista, 1960).

William Morris, Selected Writings and Designs, by Asa Briggs (Pelican, 1962).

An Historical Outline of Architectural Science, by Henry J. Cowan (Elsevier, 1966).

*****American Building,** by James Marston Fitch (Houghton Mifflin, 1946; Riverside Press, 1966).

A History of Architecture on the Comparative Method, by Banister Fletcher (Batsford [Scribners], 1896; and later editions). A large reference work not suitable for continuous reading, but invaluable for its innumerable illustrations.

Theory and Design in the First Machine Age, by Reyner Banham (Praeger, 1960).

Architecture and Interior Design Volume I. Basic History through the 17th Century and Volume II. Europe and America from the Colonial Era to Today, by Victoria Kloss Ball (John Wiley and Sons, 1980).

Architecture Through the Ages, by Talbot Hamlin (Putnam, 1940). The most readable of serious architectural histories.

Architecture of the 19th and 20th Centuries, by Henry-Russell Hitchcock (Penguin/Pelican), 1958.

De Stijl, by Hans L. C. Jaffé (Abrams, 1967).

*****Made in America,** by John A. Kouwenhoven (Doubleday, 1949; reprinted as **The Arts in Modern American Civilization,** Norton, 1967, paperback). An interesting book dealing with engineering, architecture, and design in historical context.

Art Nouveau, by S. Tschudi Madsen (McGraw-Hill, 1967).

Sticks and Stones, by Lewis Mumford (Boni and Liveright, 1924; Dover, 1955).

The Bauhaus, by Gillian Naylor (Studio Vista/Dutton, 1968).

*****An Outline of European Architecture,** by Nikolaus Pevsner (Penguin, 1943; and later editions). An excellent compact and inexpensive introduction to architectural history.

Crafts of the Weimar Bauhaus, by Walter Scheidig (Reinhold, 1967).

The Ten Books of Architecture, by Vitruvius, translated by Morris Hickey Morgan (Dover, 1960, paperback). A classic work on ancient Roman architecture written in the first century B.C. Of both historical and theoretical interest.

Modern Architecture

Bauhaus 1919–1928, edited by Herbert Bayer (Museum of Modern Art, 1938).

Conversations with Architects, by Cook and Klotz (Praeger, 1973).

*****Towards a New Architecture,** by Le Corbusier, translated by F. Etchells (Architectural Press, 1927). An early manifesto in which Le Corbusier set forth the ideas that are basic to his role as a pioneer and leader. Indispensable.

*****Space, Time and Architecture,** by Sigfried Giedion (Harvard University Press, 1941; and later editions). A long and difficult book, but worthy of careful reading. Excellent illustrations.

Scope of Total Architecture, by Walter Gropius (Harper & Brothers, 1943; Crowell Collier and Macmillan, Inc., 1962, paperback).

Pioneers of Modern Design, by Nikolaus Pevsner (Pelican, 1960).

The Sources of Modern Architecture and Design, by Nikolaus Pevsner (Praeger, 1968).

*****Experiencing Architecture,** by Steen Eiler Rasmussen (M.I.T. Press, 1959). A highly readable introduction to architecture in laymen's terms.

*****Modern Architecture (An Introduction to),** by J. M. Richards (Pelican/Penguin, 1940; and later editions). Compact and inexpensive, but one of the best available books on modern architecture.

Architects on Architecture, by Paul Heyer (Walker and Co., 1966).

Individual Modern Architects

The books listed give very full information about men and works mentioned in this book. Hundreds of other fine books dealing with individual architects are not referred to here.

*(1) **Le Corbusier,** (2) **Mies van der Rohe,** (3) **F. L. Wright,** by Peter Blake (Penguin, 1964). A series of three excellent paperbacks that really form a single work on these three leaders.

Alvar Aalto, by Frederick Gutheim (Braziller, 1960).

Alvar Aalto (Verlag für Architektur, 1963 [Girsberger]).

Marcel Breuer, by Peter Blake (Museum of Modern Art, 1949).

Creation is a Patient Search, by Le Corbusier (Praeger, 1965). Le Corbusier's own text comments, with pictures of his work. Somewhat irascible, but offering interesting insights.

Le Corbusier—Œuvres Complètes, 7 vols. (Girsberger, 1937–67). A vast and superb documentation of this master's complete life work.

Walter Gropius, by James Marston Fitch (Braziller, 1960).

Walter Gropius, by Siegfried Giedion (Reinhold, 1954).

Philip Johnson, by John M. Jacobus, Jr. (Braziller, 1962).

Louis I. Kahn, by Vincent Scully Jr. (Braziller, 1962).

Mies van der Rohe, by Arthur Drexler (Braziller, 1960).

Mies van der Rohe, by Philip C. Johnson (Museum of Modern Art, 1947).

Richard Neutra, by Esther McCoy (Braziller, 1960).

Oscar Niemeyer, by Stamo Papadaki (Braziller, 1960).

Eero Saarinen, by Allen Temko (Braziller, 1962).

Architecture of Skidmore, Owings and Merrill 1950–62, by E. Danz (Praeger, 1963).

Louis Sullivan, by Albert Bush-Brown (Braziller, 1960).

Louis Sullivan, Prophet of Modern Architecture, by Hugh Morrison (Norton, 1935).

Kenzo Tange, by Robin Boyd (Braziller, 1962).

In the Nature of Materials; The Works of Frank Lloyd Wright, by Henry-Russell Hitchcock (Duell, Sloan and Pearce, 1942). A fine and complete (to its date of publication) documentation of Wright's work.

*Frank Lloyd Wright, Writings and Buildings,** by Kaufmann and Raeburn (Meridian, 1960). A compact and excellent paperback.

Interior Design

The Personal House, by Alswang and Hiken (Whitney, 1961). A picture book of highly distinctive residential interiors, mostly the work of artist-owner occupants.

Inside Today's Home, by Ray and Sarah Faulkner (Holt, Rinehart and Winston, 1975 edition).

English Style in Interior Decoration, by Mary Gilliatt and Michael Boys (Viking Press, 1967).

Design for Modern Living, by G. and U. Hatje (Abrams, 1962).

New Interiors, edited by J. P. Morris (Bruno Altieri, 1965).

Living Spaces, edited by George Nelson (Whitney, 1952).

Interior Design, by Diana Rowntree (Penguin, 1964). A brief but interesting introduction to the subject in British terms, in a compact paperback.

Elements of Interior Design and Decoration, by Sherrill Whiton (Lippincott, 1963).

High Tech, by Joan Kron and Suzanne Slesin (Clarson N. Potter, 1978).

Italy: The New Domestic Landscape, by Emilio Ambasz (Museum of Modern Art, 1972).

Special Types of Interiors

Interiors Book of Restaurants, by Atkin and Adler (Whitney, 1960).

Interiors Book of Hotels, by Henry End (Whitney, 1963).

Shops and Stores, by Morris Ketchum (Reinhold, 1957).

Interiors Second Book of Offices, by John Pile (Whitney, 1969).

Office Planning and Design, by Michael Saphier (McGraw-Hill, 1968).

Interiors Third Book of Offices, by John Pile (Whitney Library of Design, 1976).

Furniture

No attempt has been made to include a listing of books dealing with historical furniture since most of these are written from the point of view of the antique dealer or collector.

Modern Furniture, by Mario Dal Fabbro (Reinhold, 1949). Detail drawings of a vast range of modern furniture, including many famous designs.

English Furniture Styles, by Ralph Fastnedge (Pelican, 1955). A paperback on the great historic period furniture of England.

New Furniture, edited by Hatje (Verlag Hatje, volume I, 1952; annual thereafter).

Nomadic Furniture, by Hennessey and Papanek (Random House, 1973).

Furniture from Machines, by Gordon Logie (Allen and Unwin, 1947). One of the few books that makes the technology of furniture-making meaningful to nontechnical readers.

Chairs, edited by George Nelson (Whitney, 1953).

Storage, edited by George Nelson, (Whitney, 1954).

The Art of Furniture, by Ole Wanscher (Wittenborn, 1967). Almost entirely devoted to historic furniture shown with fine drawings and illustrations.

Catalogs: Georg Jensen, Knoll Associates, Herman Miller, Inc., Stendig. Catalogs from these (and various other) modern furniture manufacturers can form a useful reference on contemporary furniture design.

Modern Furniture, by John Pile (Wiley Interscience, 1979).

Twentieth Century Furniture, by Philippe Garner (Van Nostrand Reinhold, 1980).

A Century of Chair Design, by F. Russell, P. Garner and J. Read (Rizzoli, 1980).

The Modern Chair, by Clement Meadmore (Van Nostrand Reinhold, 1979).

Textiles

*On Weaving, by Anni Albers (Wesleyan University Press, 1965). A fine introduction to an understanding of textiles.

Textiles, by N. Hollen and J. Saddler (Macmillan, 1973).

Elements of Weaving, by A. S. Thorpe & J. L. Larsen (Doubleday, 1967). Although addressed to the beginning weaver, a good general book on textiles.

Color

Interaction of Color, by Josef Albers (Yale University Press, revised edition 1975).

Creative Color, by Faber Birren (Reinhold, 1965).

Color for Interiors, Historic and Modern, by Faber Birren (Whitney, 1963).

The Use of Color in Interiors, by A. O. Halse (McGraw-Hill, 1968).

Art of Color, by Johannes Itten (Reinhold, 1961).

Lighting

Illuminating Engineering Society Lighting Handbook (Illuminating Engineering Society, 1959; and later editions).

Lighting and Its Design, by Leslie Larson (Whitney, 1964).

Lighting in Architectural Design, by Derek Phillips (Holt, Rinehart and Winston, 1968).

Drawing

Perspective: A New System, by J. Doblin (Whitney, 1956).

Architectural Drafting, by William Hornung (Prentice Hall, 4th edition, 1966).

Design Drawing and **Design Drawing Experiences,** by William Kirby Lockard (Pepper, 1973 and 1974).

Drawings of Architectural Interiors, edited and text by John Pile (Whitney, 1967).

Construction

Building Structures Primer, by James E. Ambrose (Wiley, 1967). A compact and readily understandable introduction to structural concepts.

Architectural Construction, by Theodore Crane (Wiley, 1947).

Contemporary Structure in Architecture, by Leonard Michaels (Reinhold, 1950).

Building Construction, by Whitney C. Huntington, 3rd edition (Wiley, 1963).

Mechanical and Electrical Equipment for Buildings, by William J. McGuinness, 4th edition (Wiley, 1964).

Simplified Engineering for Architects and Builders, by Harry Parker (Wiley, 1961). A technical handbook covering the most needed structural computation. Not for casual reading.

Materials and Methods of Architectural Construction, by Parker, Gay & MacGuire, 3rd edition (Wiley, 1966).

*Structure in Architecture, by Salvadori and Heller (Prentice Hall, 1963). A particularly good introduction to structural concepts, in terms understandable to any reader. Well illustrated.

Structure and Form in Modern Architecture, by Curt Siegel (Reinhold, 1962).

The Turning Point of Building, by Konrad Wachsman (Reinhold, 1961).

Architecture: A Book of Projects for Young Adults, by Forrest Wilson (Reinhold, 1968). Architectural structure through "do it yourself" work projects requiring only simple tools and ordinary materials, with amply illustrated instructions.

What It Feels Like to Be a Building, by Forrest Wilson (Doubleday, 1969).

Concepts of Structure, by William Zuk (Reinhold, 1963).

Office Landscape

Neue Technik der Mobiliarordnung im Büroraum, by Kurd Alsleben (Schnelle Quickborn, 1966). A basic manual of "office landscape" practice available only in German.

Office Landscaping, by Frank Duffy (Anbar, 1966). The only work on the subject in English, unfortunately not very comprehensive.

Open Office Planning, by John Pile (Whitney Library of Design, 1978).

Environmental Behavior

Ecological Psychology: Concepts and Methods for Studying the Environment of Human Behavior, by Roger R. Barker (Stanford University Press, 1968).

Architecture for Human Behavior, by Charles Burnett (A.I.A. Philadelphia Chapter, 1971).

People and Buildings, by Robert Gutman (Basic Books, 1972).

The Hidden Dimension, by E. T. Hall (Doubleday, 1966). A somewhat controversial work on human behavior traits which influence design decisions.

The Death and Life of Great American Cities, by Jane Jacobs (Random House, 1961).

Designing for Human Behavior, by Lang, Burnette, Moleski and Vachon (Dowden, Hutchinson and Ross, 1974).

What Time Is This Place, by Kevin Lynch (M.I.T. Press, 1972).

The Image of the City, by Kevin Lynch (M.I.T. Press, 1960).

Defensible Space, by Oscar Newman (Macmillan, 1972).

With Man in Mind, by Constance Perin (M.I.T. Press, 1970).

Environmental Psychology, by Proshansky, Ittleson and Rivlin (Holt, Rinehart and Winston, 1970).

Techniques of Evaluation for Designers, by Henry Sanoff (North Carolina State University, 1968).

Design Awareness, by Robert Sommer (Reinhold, 1972).

Behavioral Research for Architectural Planning and Design, by Lawrence Wheeler (Ewing Miller Associates, 1967).

Environmental Design Evaluation, by Friedmann, Zimring and Zube (Plenum Press, 1978).

Designing for Human Behavior, by Lund, Burnette, Moleski and Vachon (Dowden, Hutchinson and Ross, 1974).

Psychology and the Environment, by Terence Lee (Methuen, 1976).

With Man in Mind, by Constance Perin (MIT Press, 1970).

Spaces for People, by Corwin Bennett (Prentice-Hall, 1977).

Reference

The Measure of Man, by Henry Dreyfuss (Whitney, 1967). A very full set of dimensional charts and diagrams on basic human body construction and mechanics.

A Critical Study of Interior Design Education, by Arnold Friedmann (Interior Design Educators Council, 1968). The only serious study of the status of interior design training in the United States.

Anatomy for Interior Designers, by Julius Panero, 3rd edition (Whitney, 1962). Basic dimensional data presented in graphic form.

Dictionary of Interior Design, by Martin Pegler (Crown, 1966).

Architectural Graphic Standards, by Ramsey and Sleeper (Wiley, 1963; and later editions). A very complete set of charts covering dimensional standards and typical construction details. An indispensable reference work.

A Guide to Business Principles and Practices for Interior Designers, by Harry Siegel (Whitney, 1968).

Humanscale 1/2/3, by Diffrient, Tilley and Bargadji (MIT Press, 1974).

Human Dimension and Interior Space, by Julius Panero and Martin Zelnick (Whitney Library of Design, 1979).

Miscellaneous and General

These are books with titles and subjects not closely related to interior design, but which have proved to be of great interest to designers.

The Territorial Imperative, by Robert Ardrey (Atheneum Vintage Pyramid, 1966).

Design of Cities, by Edmund N. Bacon (Studio Viking, 1967).

Townscape, by Gordon Cullen (Reinhold, 1962). A lively approach to the visual aspects of town planning.

Man Adapting, by René Dubos (Yale University Press, 1965).

The Exploding Metropolis, by editors of Fortune (Doubleday Anchor, 1957).

Mechanization Takes Command, by Sigfried Giedion (Oxford University Press, 1948). The design implications of modern industrialization. A long and serious book with many fascinating illustrations.

The Tastemakers, by Russell Lynes (Harper & Brothers, 1949). Written for general readers, but meaningful and entertaining to designers also.

Design with Nature, by Ian McHarg (Doubleday, 1971).

The Culture of Cities, by Lewis Mumford (Harcourt Brace, 1938).

Technics and Civilization, by Lewis Mumford (Harcourt Brace, 1934).

Survival Through Design, by Richard Neutra (Oxford University Press, 1934).

Design for the Real World, by Victor Papanek (Pantheon Books, 1971).

Art and Industry, by Herbert Read (Faber & Faber, 1934). One of the few good books about industrial design, still rewarding in spite of its somewhat dated illustrations.

The Fitness of Man's Environment, Smithsonian Annual II (Smithsonian Institute Press, 1967).

Town and Square, by Paul Zucker (Columbia University Press, 1959).

Periodicals

Magazines are one of the most important sources of information about current design practice. The files of back-date magazines available in libraries include a vast store of reference material on almost every design topic.

Abitare, published by Editrice Abitare, Milan, Italy.

Architectural Forum, published by Urban America Inc., New York City; (successor to monthly published by Time, Inc.). This publication, now discontinued, concentrated on urban problems.

Architectural Record, published by McGraw-Hill, New York City; monthly. This magazine, which concentrates on individual buildings and individual architects, now includes an interiors section.

*Architectural Review,** published in London; monthly. One of the finest magazines published anywhere on any subject. Often difficult, but always interesting and beautiful.

Contract, published by Gralia Publications, New York City; monthly. A trade magazine directed to the contract interior field.

The Designer, published by HDC Publications, New York. Primarily a trade journal, but with frequent serious articles.

Domus, published by Editoriale Domus, Milan; monthly. Italian with limited English translation. A magazine rich in excellent illustrations with particular emphasis on the most advanced and unusual contemporary work. A limited English translation of text is included.

Furniture Forum, published by Furniture Forum, Inc., annual. At one time a magazine, this publication, now discontinued, was essentially a catalog of the products of some of the key manufacturers of modern furniture in the United States.

Industrial Design, published by Whitney Publications, New York City; monthly.

Interior Design, published by Whitney Communication Corporation, New York City; monthly.

Interior Design (British), published in London; monthly.

*Interiors,** published by Whitney Publications, New York City; monthly.

Mobilia, published by Snekkersten, Denmark; monthly with full English translation. A lively review of Danish and other European furniture and interior design developments.

Progressive Architecture, published by Reinhold Publishing Corporation, New York City; monthly. A magazine dealing with the work of individual architects and subjects of broad interest to the design professions, which also features a regular interiors section.

INDEX